THE GENTLEMAN'S GUIDE TO

Passages South

BRUCE VAN SANT

Sailing directions for easier windward passage making
in the islands from Florida to Venezuela
and a handbook of Caribbean cruising

Distributed in the U.S. by:

CRUISING GUIDE PUBLICATIONS

P.O. Box 1017
Dunedin, FL 34697-1017
PHONE: (813) 733-5322 • FAX: (813) 734-8179

IMPORTANT NOTICE...

The chartlets in this guide are intended to assist the reader in following the sailing tactics described, not for taking meaningful measurements for navigation. The prudent mariner will avail himself of official charts and publications, some of which are recommended in this guide, as well as any navigational methods and tools required to ensure the safety of the vessel and the accuracy of navigation. There are no warranties, either express or implied, as to the usability of the information contained herein for any purpose whatever.

Cover Photo by Dougal Thornton

PUBLISHED BY:
Bruce Van Sant & Cruising Guide Publications, Inc.
P.O. Box 1017, Dunedin, FL 34697-1017

FOURTH EDITION

ISBN 0-944428-19-3

Library of Congress: 90-102996

Printed in the U.S.A.

The author, an American refugee from an international career as a systems engineer, lives aboard in the Caribbean. He has cruised many years in the Baltic, the North Sea, the English Channel and the Mediterranean, with stints in Asia and Central America. He has been cruising the Florida and the Caribbean islands more or less continuously for the past dozen years. In addition to 30 years of continuous sailing experience, he had formal training in Sweden and has his American master's certificate.

Over years of shuttling between Florida and the Bahamas and his home ports in the Caribbean, Van Sant has accumulated over 32,000 miles of evidence of what works and what is risky while slogging to windward among the islands. Out of this experience has come a set of windward strategies to avoid mishap on what had heretofore been called the "Thorny Path." He has used these common-sense techniques while bucking the equatorial currents and the trade winds on dozens of windward passages. This recurrent cruising experience on the route to the southern islands is documented in *The Gentleman's Guide to Passages South.* With its detailed chartlets and sailing directions, this guide is an indispensable companion to incident-free cruising.

Jalan Jalan, a Malayu idiom for "aimlessly wandering" or *walkabout*, is a 41-foot, 15-ton displacement ketch. She has surveyed every recommended anchorage, and sounded each one with her long-keeled, 6 ½-foot draft. She has only 37-shaft horsepower with which to jam the 1200 windward miles to South America, and normally sails single-handed. Her deep draft and low power mean that her experiences are especially relevant to today's small boat cruiser who wants to elude harm's way without missing the islands with which the Thorny Path is strewn. Both at sea and at anchor, *Jalan Jalan* has accumulated hard acquaintance on the road south, and found the *thornless* way.

PREFACE

Dear Reader,

It was many trips south before I dared give the least advice to anyone. Invited to cockpit gams and beach seminars with cruisers headed south, I often felt I learned more than I contributed. Steadily, the compendium of notes and sketches increased. Evidence grew that my notes were saving cruisers from repeating my own, and others', misadventures. Now this book. Even after more than 30,000 miles gunk-holing the path described in this book, I still quail at giving unhedged counsel. But I bit the bullet and wrote down unequivocal sailing directions, spurning all but the most durable land-based tips. I've assumed the subject is a small boat jamming 1200 miles to windward with sexagenarians at the helm. That's what I usually see down here. These folks are sufficiently in harm's way without a guide that gives ten ways to do everything. I show only the safe, comfortable way. I hope you don't think it opinionated or dogmatic, but I've pruned the hedges and peeled back the quibbles for my mythical couple, and the result is a book of plain-spoken, straightforward skinny.

Why a *Gentleman's* Guide?

When yachting began in England in the mid-1800s, the young ladies and gentlemen of the privileged classes would take the train down to the south coast where paid crews had delivered their yachts, often made-over workboats. They lounged on the white, canvas-covered decks in their white duck trousers and their white linen dresses. They rolled home under a billow of running white sail. Deck stewards served gin and tonic to the gents and cooled Advocaat to the ladies. "*A gentleman never sails to windward*," they said.

This guide, for ladies as well as gentlemen, gives the lie to that oldest of yachting's traditional sayings. *The Gentleman's Guide to Passages South* connects the major cruising grounds with 17 windward passages between Florida and Venezuela. Each passage is divided into an average of four safe and easy sails for a total of nearly 80 anchorages en route. You may dawdle in each cruising area until your heart is content, but you must return to these tried and true passages when you are prepared to go on to the next. If you want to avoid a shellacking on your windward cruise, you need to have this guide aboard, and you need to have read it cover to cover before setting out.

Baysailing and Daysailing to Venezuela

The windward way south through the islands is referred to as the "Thorny Path" to the Caribbean for good reason. Since I am a retired single-hander living aboard a sailboat in the Caribbean, I have always sought to take the thorns out of my travels by taking the most comfortable and safest passages. I have researched a *thornless path* south since sailing into these waters from Europe in 1979. It is the alternative to beating one's brains out in the ocean, or bypassing all the island cruising grounds that should be enjoyed.

In the tropics, each season brings its own surprises in the weather. No year is just like another. No day is like another. My *thornless strategies* count on and use this constant variation in wind and wave. With a 6 ½- foot draft, long-keeled ketch, I have hoofed up and down my Thornless Path and found that it works in any season.

I have divided this path into short, easy passages between waystations where you can wait for weather. Each passage is divided into short and easy day-sails and bay-sails. Each small step has the objective of being in a snug harbor in time to fish up dinner and relax with a sundowner. *Jalan Jalan* and I have learned the hard way not to skip a single small step of the path (especially on the south coast of Puerto Rico).

You will find a lot of geography in these pages, with systematic details for plotting and making each passage and each short leg, but don't be misled. *Thornless* cruising against the trades is more about *how* and *when* to go than it is about *where* to go.

The Audience

The Gentleman's Guide to Passages South is aimed at the live-aboard, long-term cruiser who can take the time necessary to have a safe and leisurely cruise south. Cruisers like Mom and Pop on their dream retirement cruise, the neophyte cruiser who just bought his first boat, the single-hander who must reduce risk, and the sailors like me, who don't want to get their boats (or themselves) broken, who seek comfort above challenge, and who, like me, are sensibly scared of the sea.

If you are not among the above, you probably don't want this guide. Its purpose is to deliver these cruisers to their various paradises with themselves, their boats and their relationships still intact and healthy. I illustrate each passage with real examples. Either I was there when it happened, or it happened to me directly. I also have tried to keep the cruising mates in mind, debunking some of the bar-story bugbears that can intimidate, while involving them in what should, and can be, the cruise of a lifetime.

This guide is for your passage making between major cruising grounds. You will need other guides to properly do each. It assumes you already have aboard appropriate charts and navigation equipment, that you have read this entire guide, and that, for details of each cruising area, you have a suitable guide from this list:

Field's *Yachtsman's Guide to the **Bahamas***

Nancy & Simon Scott's *Cruising Guide to the **Virgin Islands***

Doyle's *Cruising Guide to the **Leeward Islands***

Doyle's *Sailor's Guide to the **Windward Islands***

Doyle's *Sailor's Guide to a **Venezuela** Cruise*

Doyle's *Cruising Guide to **Trinidad, Tobago and Venezuela***
(Available January, 1994)

— Bruce Van Sant
Luperón

PASSAGE TO VENEZUELA 142

POINTERS ON THE PATH 148

A THORNLESS PATH TO THE CARIBBEAN

With appropriate strategies and the proven sailing directions available in this guide, these short, safe passages provide even the novice blue water cruiser with safe and happy voyages. Delivery skippers and the "*Let's Go For It!*" type of sailor shall have to look for another guide.

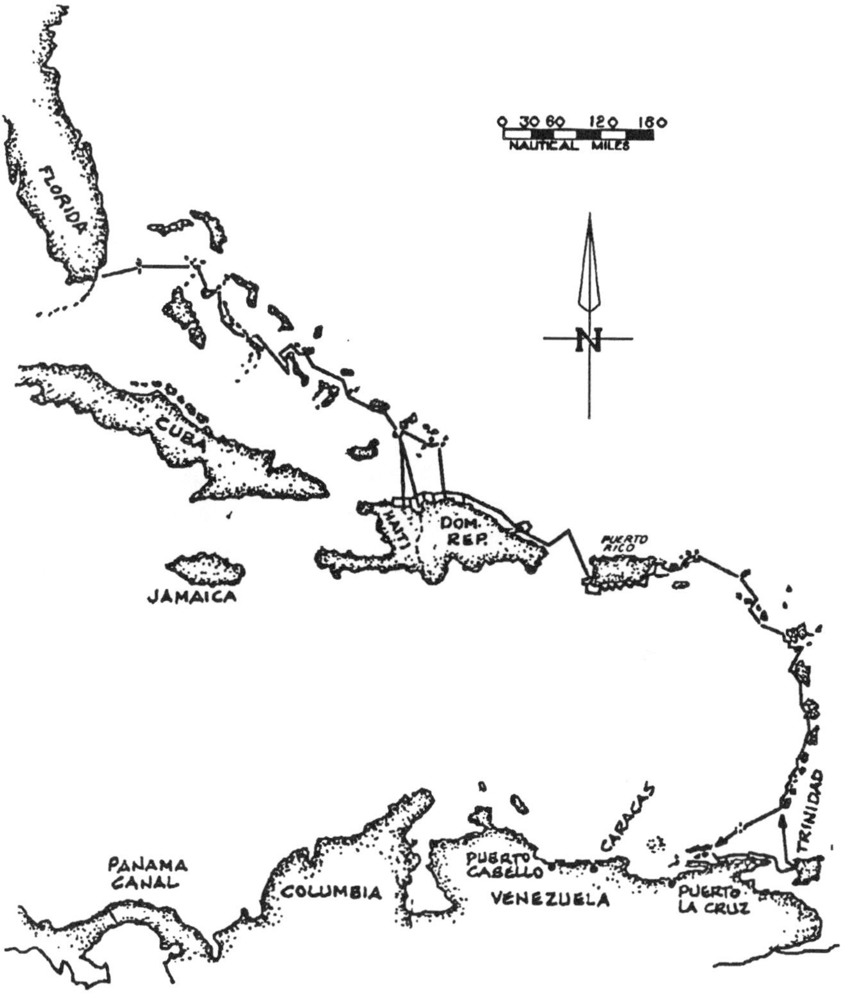

All **bold face** phrases appear in the Index in the back of this guide. Most bold face phrases that are not geographical names are defined in the Glossary.

All degree readings on chartlets have T or M indicators for True or Magnetic. True degrees are used when the intention is to assist the reader with chart work and course plotting. Magnetic degrees are used when the intention is to provide a hand bearing for transits, etc.

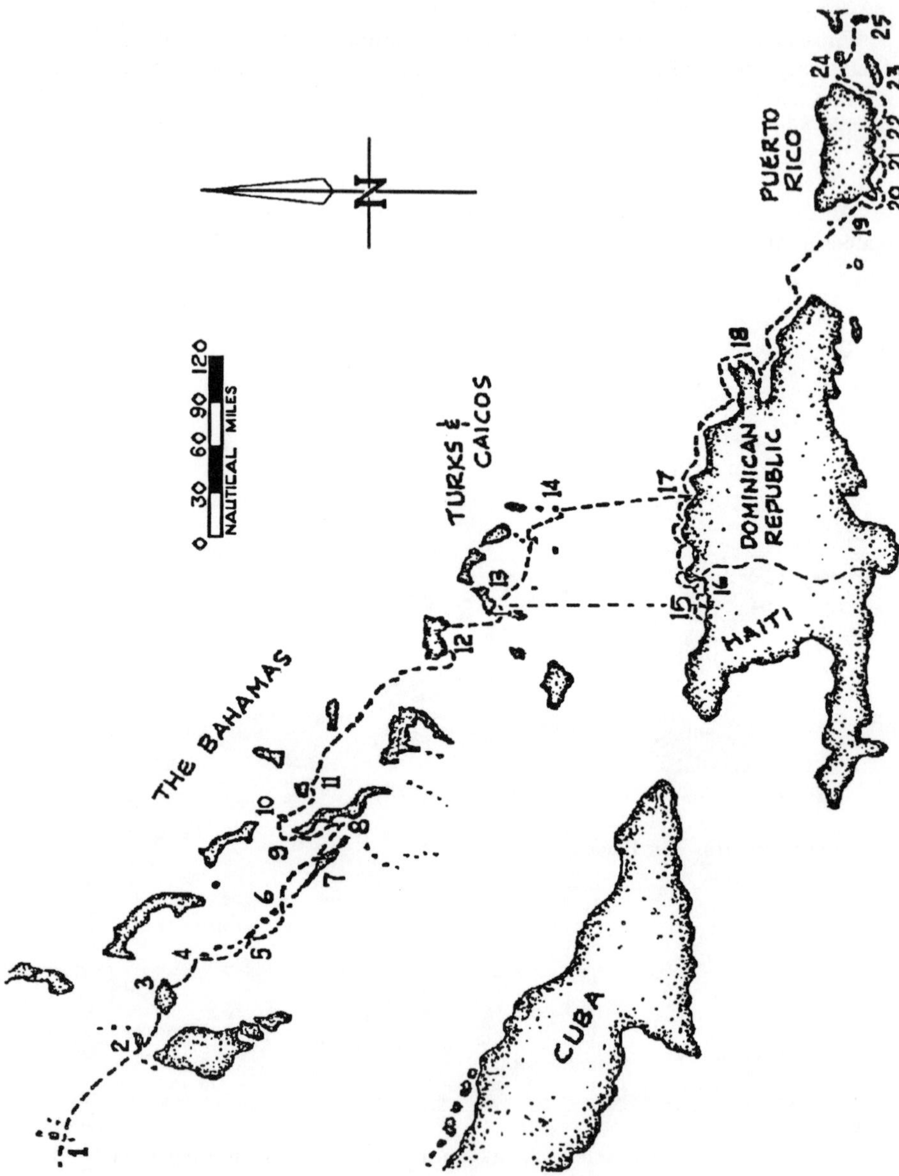

Florida to the Virgin Islands: The Basic Path

Here are some typical stations on the Thornless Path from Florida to the Virgin Islands. These are the key anchorages between which the Leisure Sailor can make Leisure Sails in short legs and at which boat and crew will be snug in a safe haven during the next **Wait for Weather**.

Some stops, such as **Ambergris**, **Sosua** or **Escondido**, are not on the following list because they are not long-term anchorages. Yet, without a west wind, those stops are dead necessary for a displacement sailboat or single screw trawler laboring to windward in search of a Thornless Passage. Conversely, not every station shown is necessary, depending on conditions and the cruiser's inclination.

For instance, **Georgetown** to **Conception Island** can be a fun 7-hour sail in a good southeaster, missing Long Island entirely, although missing Long Island is a shame and 7 hours of sailing is twice too much when you don't have to. Finally, other stations are possible (e.g., **San Salvador**) which are slightly off the path but useful in the right conditions. (See the section Keep North to Go South.) Haiti and the western half of the north coast of the Dominican Republic are included as an alternate path for the cruiser who wants to tour Hispaniola properly. For older cruisers and single-handers I recommend **West Caicos** to **Manzanillo** (13-16) as an easier route with smaller, less windward steps. Haiti may be toured by land while the boat stays at Manzanillo.

Key Anchorages for the Leisure Sailor

1. Gun Cay
2. Chubb Cay
3. Nassau [2,3]
4. Allen's Cay
5. Sampson Cay [2]
6. Cave Cay
7. Georgetown [1,2,3]
8. Salt Pond
9. Calabash Bay
10. Conception Island
11. Rum Cay
12. Mayaguana
13. Sapodilla Bay [2,3]
14. Big Sand Cay
15. (alternate) Cap Haïtien [3] or Fort Liberté [1]
16. (alternate) Manzanillo [1]
17. Luperón [1,3] or Puerto Plata [3]
18. Samaná [1,2]
19. Boquerón [1,2,3]
20. Guánica [1]
21. Ponce [2,3]
22. Salinas [1,2,3]
23. Palmas del Mar [1,2,3]
24. Culebra [1]
25. St. Thomas [2,3]

[1] Stops at which you can safely leave or store the boat in the hurricane season.

[2] Although fuel can be pumped from barrels almost everywhere, these stops are recommended because they have a dockside fuel pump accommodating a draft of up to 7 feet.

[3] Convenient access to airline connections for the embarking and receiving of guests.

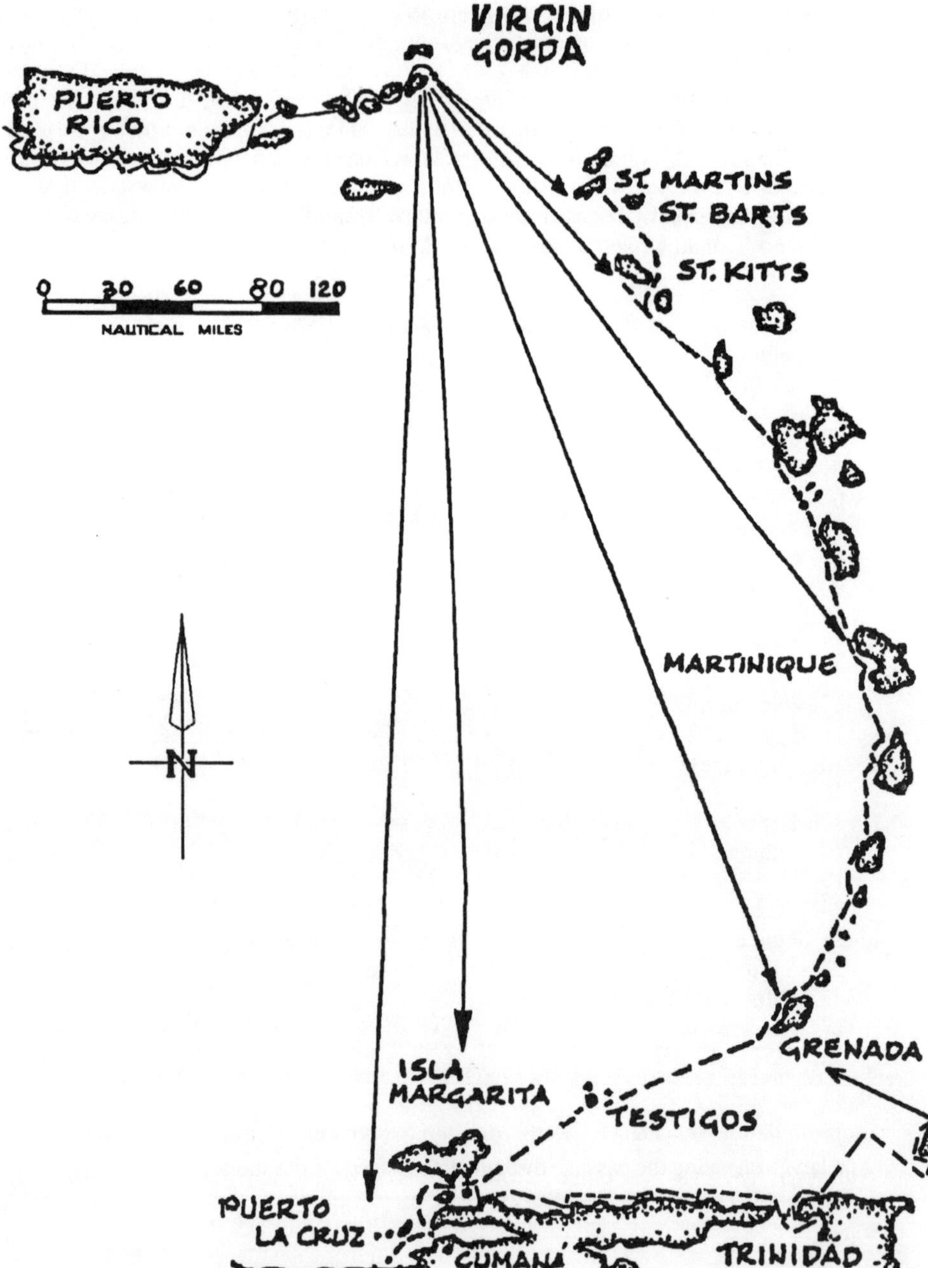

Virgins to Venezuela: Different Beginnings, Trinidad Return

The Gentleman's Guide to Passages South routes you in some detail as far as the Virgin Islands. The trials of windward passage making along rugged coasts are behind you by the time you have reached **Culebra**, the island group between Puerto Rico and the Virgins.

Excellent guides are available to the charter fleets which populate the archipelagos from the Virgins to Venezuela:

- Nancy and Simon Scott's *Cruising Guide to the Virgin Islands*;
- Chris Doyle's *Cruising Guide to the Leeward Islands*;
- Chris Doyle's *Sailor's Guide to the Windward Islands*;

Some cruisers proceed from **Puerto La Cruz** to the Dutch Islands via **Los Roques** and **Las Aves**, thence to Cartagena, Colombia and Central America. For the first year, most cruisers prefer to thoroughly do the Venezuelan offshore islands before wintering in Trinidad. After Carnival in Trinidad one can return home via the northern Antilles, if not cruising further afield. For the Venezuela and **Trinidad** cruises, use:

- Chris Doyle's *Sailor's Guide to a Venezuela Cruise*, and
- Chris Doyle's *Cruising Guide to Trinidad, Tobago and Venezuela (Available January, 1994)*

It is only a few hours of lee sailing from one **Virgin Island** to another. The conditions you will meet on the Leewards portion of the route are much friendlier than what you have had so far. Even though you will still be beating to windward until you get to **Martinique**, the passages are in long, open-ocean swells instead of the Caribbean's chop and coastal hazards.

The farther north one makes landfall in the **Leewards**, or the **Windwards**, the better. **St. Martin** is usually a motor, but well worth the trip for its own sake, as well as for additional islands that route lets you visit with your windward advantage there. The best route, even during hurricane season, is via **St. Martin**. From there south it's island hopping again with each new high island appearing over the horizon just as the last one sinks behind. The best jump-off point for St. Martin is **Bitter End** in **Virgin Gorda**, British Virgin Islands.

If my windward objective is **St. Kitts, Martinique**, or farther off to **Grenada**, from where one clears out for Venezuela, then my jump-off point is always **Round Rock Passage**, just below **The Baths** on Virgin Gorda. **Spanish Town** on Virgin Gorda has a Barclay's Bank, a good spot to bankroll with little or no fees before going, and the marina is an easy and friendly checkout and refueling spot. You don't have all of these elsewhere.

The easting from the **Mona Passage** to Round Rock Passage is so easy (if you follow this guide) that there is no reason to jump off into the Caribbean any earlier than Round Rock Passage. I often meet cruisers in Puerto Rico who, having what they think is the devilish part of the trip behind them, are hell-bent to make South America on a beat across the sea to **Margarita**. They usually fetch **Puerto Cabello** instead. Take a few more days to get further east and you will have a much more comfortable trip south.

Particulars of these passages are given in the following chapters insofar as cruising and passage-making information is needed to supplement the available guides for charter boats. A key to enjoying the passage through these islands is the strategy of ***staging***, which is explained in the following section.

Whether headed north or south, whether you are flying your Q flag and just anchoring through, or whether you stay weeks at each island, when you are ready to shove on, always *stage* yourself the night before at the last safe anchorage next to the ocean pass. Next morning you will have a swift, safe sail and be in before the squalls.

Along the Windwards and Leewards, the Thornless Path strategies still dictate an **SG&T** on each island landfall along the way south, whether going ashore or just sailing onward the next morning.

STRATEGIES FOR PASSAGE MAKING

The intention of this book is to help cruisers plan *windward passages* on the way south, *not* to give the cruiser a precise road map and timetable for the cruise. Its guidance on passage routing gives the cruiser safe and comfortable passages between cruising grounds, seeing as many of the islands as desired in between, and loitering as long as desired along the way.

Descriptions of the islands, and the anchorages themselves, are provided to support the sailing directions when required. There is no intention, however, to rehash information adequately covered in the guides and charts from which local cruising plans can be made (e.g., Field's *Yachtsman's Guide to the Bahamas*).

When you have tired of cruising one area and are ready to move on to the next, you must have a specific *strategy* in mind while planning the passage: a strategy to move you to windward from point A to point B with safety and comfort: a *thornless* passage.

This section of the guide provides cruisers with the planning strategies essential to creating their own Thornless Path between their own chosen landfalls. These are the rules of the Leisure Sailor which, when inflexibly adhered to, create a delightful cruise. Though seemingly elementary rules of seamanship, which we all should know, all the disasters I have met while going south have generated from the failure to obey just *one* of these rules.

Each passage-planning strategy is explained in detail in the following chapters:

1. Wait for Weather
2. Stage Your Departure
    a. Let Landfall Determine Departure
    b. Never Miss a Sundowner
    c. If In Doubt, Stay Out
3. Keep to the North to Go South
4. Think Two Moves Ahead
5. Don't Be Afraid of Open Anchorages
6. Don't Be Afraid of the Dark
7. Think Beaufort
8. Grim and Gray is Great Going
9. Hug the Shore Coasting to Windward
10. Watch Your Back

WAIT FOR WEATHER

I am always amazed at retired cruisers, who, with nothing but time, and having piddled around in harbor for weeks, even months, suddenly break into hives if they can't go right now! Others, equally amazing, insist on going "next Tuesday," or "on the 22nd." Year upon year, like the Tortoise and the Hare, I find myself passing cruisers who are all holed-up with repairs and breathing hard. These are the folks whom I earlier see go stir-crazy, give up their wait at harbor and go because "it's rolly here," or "best to take your bad medicine all at once," or "we've got a strong boat," or "we've seen worse."

Like a tortoise, I change to a less rolly anchorage ("but we were with a group"); I don't like any bad medicine at all, and, although I've got a strong boat, there's a weak me. And he remembers "worse" all too well.

At the edge of the trade wind belt, the weather is cyclic and regular. There are periods of low, or altered, activity in the trades, which are windows of escape from the normally strong windward weather that can be used by the "thornless" cruiser. **Weather Windows** are the conjuncture of favorableness in the cyclic wanderings of four different parameters:

- Wind strength;
- Wind direction;
- Height of wave and swell; and
- Direction of swell.

The basic problem is how to cruise to windward without beating your brains out or performing marathon stunts against any of these conditions while they are adverse.

Depart only when favorable conditions prevail and look like they'll be sustained for 36 to 72 hours.

This will be when the winds back or veer to permit reaching or running, or, if you must beat, when the easterly trades have moderated to less than 15 knots with seas under 6 feet.

When a Weather Window comes by, take the leading edge of it and *don't delay*. If you really want to attend one more beach bonfire, or one more dance at the Peace and Plenty, or you have already invited the folks from the boat next door for cocktails, then enjoy yourself and wait for the next window so you can sail in leisure. Don't drink up half the Weather Window in harbor and bank on the second half holding up for you. Take a new window rather than risk getting the current one slammed shut on your tail.

A **Wait for Weather** means taking advantage of the periodic switching of the prevailing easterlies between northeast and southeast due to the wandering of the trade winds, and, in winter, by the passage of **fronts**, or, in summer, the passage of **tropical waves**.

The **Leisure Sailor** has time and will always wait for the opening of an appropriate Weather Window before casting self and boat onto the mercies of wind and wave. If you feel you haven't got time to wait for an appropriate Weather Window, if you feel pressed to make your next cruising ground as soon as you can, closely examine your motivation and play it off against your reasons for cruising, and more importantly, the safety of your vessel and crew.

If you press on in 20-knot trades and 5- to 8-foot seas in a 35- to 40-foot boat with a small auxiliary engine, you are pleading for disaster to overtake you. When it doesn't, you haven't cheated it—it will only be that much more of a disaster next time.

Some waits may last longer than a week, but that would be rare. It may seem that a window will never open. 1991, for example, was a year in which the **Christmas Winds** came as they should, but they stayed around right through hurricane season. Even in that tougher than usual year, cycles of moderation appeared regularly, if less frequently, than usual. The **Offshore Forecast** (the only one you should be listening to) showed 2-3 day windows of 15-20 knots, 4-7 foot seas at least twice monthly. It is more usual to have windows of 10-15 knots, 3-5 foot seas, every 7 to 10 days in the summer months (10-20 knots, 4-6 foot seas, in the winter months).

The weather you wait for may not always look that good to you at first glance. See the section Grim and Gray is Great Going on page 20. Good sailing days are like good lovers, as my mother used to say: "They're like buses. There's another one right around the corner if you're looking for it." And if you're not looking for it, you'll spend your life getting neither.

How to Get the Weather

While waiting, use the **National Weather Service Offshore Reports** for the **Southwest North Atlantic** until preparing for the **Mona Passage**. Thereafter use the **Eastern Caribbean** reports. Do *not* use the High Seas reports. You may think that's where you are, but that's not where the detail for your zone is given. Refer to the *Radio Frequency List* in the Appendix and the chapter on "Making Sense of the NWS Offshore Report". Do not be fooled into using any other report than the Offshore Forecast of the NWS.

All the advice in this guide is predicated on the wind strengths and sea conditions as given by this report. More importantly, I have listened to this report, *in situ*, every day for a decade, and I can certify its accuracy for the route and the harbors covered by this guide.

One "professional" captain I know insists on listening to the Northwest Caribbean forecasts. He, and anyone who listens to him, makes his decisions to leave Georgetown based on conditions prevailing in *Jamaica*. His nickname is Captain Nogo. He stays and waits because the weather never matches his expectations. No wonder.

Offshore Reports for the **Caribbean and the Southwest North Atlantic** are also repeated on standard AM broadcast out of **Cap Haïtien**, **St. Thomas** and **Bonaire** with additional local details. **Radio Antilles** in **Montserrat** had a 5-zone forecast which is excellent. The station, "The Big R.A.," went off the air after hurricane Hugo in 1989, but should resume its forecasts in 1993.

Use the NWS's **Offshore Forecast's Southwest North Atlantic** reports to Puerto Rico, and their **Eastern Caribbean** reports to **St. Martin** and on down the **Lesser Antilles**. In the Mona Passage itself, listen to both reports and stitch them together with attention to land effects on both sides. From **St. Martin** onward, use Radio Antilles, if it's broadcasting. It is the most complete for its area. *In no case* use NOAA VHF WX-Channel reports except in **Fajardo**, Puerto Rico, and between the U.S. and British Virgins.

Official weather reports such as the NWS's Offshore Forecast have the benefit of using a fixed official lingo which permits you to take shorthand notes of the same forecast each day and compare forecasts. It is the *changes* in the forecasts which interest you, not the particulars of the forecasts themselves. For instance, if you have a forecast of an approaching cold front with a thunderstorm radius of 300 miles, moving at 20 knots, and with 20 knots of northwest wind behind it, you had better batten down for the passage of a reasonably sized front. If, on the other hand, the previous report of this same front gave only a 100-mile radius and a forward speed of 15 knots with only 15 knots of wind behind it, you now know you're in for a granddaddy of a blow and you must make adequate preparations—that thing's growing like The Front That Ate Tokyo! It is the *changes* that count.

Getting Hard Copy

I use the 3M Company's Post-It slips that can be stuck up on the bulkhead over the radio. Because the forecasts are repeated in the identical format every day, my shorthand notes fill the slips in the same way and they can be rapidly scanned, showing a weather picture developing, or disintegrating, just like those still pictures you flicked through with your thumb when you were a kid made the lady take her clothes off.

If your childhood wasn't that colorful, you may wish to employ another method, such as recording the broadcast. However, tape quality is usually poor, and people who do this tend to not have it written down and can't find it when they need it. Then they play you the whole rotten rigamarole from Georges Bank to Texas, while they mutter about which day's recording that is. You can't flip from cassette tape to cassette tape to get the change picture. For that you must have notes.

So, if you record, write while you listen anyway, then replay immediately to correct your shorthand. And erase the blasted tapes.

Don't Listen to Your "Buddy"

Another benefit of knowing the formats and lingo of the reports is that you can separate the wheat from the chaff (nicely said) that's put out by some fellow yachtsmen—especially the talky ones on the **SSB** or **VHF**. For example, if Captain Hornblower gets on the horn and knowingly intones the Offshore Report for the Eastern Caribbean as east 15 knots with swells 3 to 4 feet and waves 1 to 2 feet, you know he's full of it! The **Eastern Caribbean Report** does not give swells and waves—it gives sea conditions in overall heights with notable exceptions. What was repeated was probably the coastal report of the airport Met Office in **St. Thomas** or **San Juan**, about as useful to the passage-making sailor as the beach report from Miami!

One cruiser I know left to cross the **Mona Passage** on this advice, hearing that waves were only one to two feet, forget the swells. When they returned to port they adamantly insisted it was the report that was wrong and Hornblower was an accurate source. On the path south your worst enemy may be your best friend.

Learn To Be Your Own Weatherman

Read carefully the chapter on Making Sense of the NWS Offshore Report. Whatever you do, know your reports, the lingo and the area covered. And always listen to the same reports every day at the same time, so as not to louse up your sense of progression. Get hard copy of the NWS Offshore Report every day at 0600. Get it right; get it from the NWS. In a few months you'll wonder what the mystery was. You'll *smell* the weather windows around the corner.

STAGE YOUR DEPARTURE

The greatest underestimation we cruisers make is upon the stamina of the crew. We often make judgments based on our younger selves. There is hardly a leg on the way south that can't be shortened by 10-30 percent in time, and double that in adrenaline, by one simple rule:

Go to a departure anchorage the night before.

Get away from the crowd. Get near the sea. Get your dinghy up. Go to one shallow hook. Clean up all your rodes. Make sea-ready on deck and below. Take in a reef while at anchor. It will be easier to shake out than to tie in later. Take a swim and a snorkel. Eat a candlelit dinner, listen to music, read a book. Turn in early.

Turn out an hour before anchors-up. Watch the dawn, or listen to the night. Hoist a cup of coffee or two. Then hoist sail, hoist that shallow single rode, fall back on the wind, and slide out. It sure beats doing all that work just before leaving with muddy decks and sweaty crew. You shall be up on the first leg by an hour or more, sometimes much more. And you have an added bonus of a shortened first leg.

In Georgetown, you are two miles ahead of the game (four, if you use the Fowl Cay exit). By going to the Martín Pinzón anchorage in Luperón, you save a mile and perhaps several hours, or a whole day if the *comandante*'s people have wandered off while you cursed the muck on your anchor. Stationing yourself on the harbor nearest the pass you want to cross in the Lesser Antilles will get you a better sail. It will also get you in before the lunchtime squalls. Clean up and **Wait for Weather** in Trinidad's **Scotland Bay** to get many miles behind you.

The examples are legion. If you haven't started staging your departures already, spend a few years *cruising*, not *sitting*, in the Caribbean, and you will do it every step of the path, no matter how insignificant.

LET LANDFALL DETERMINE DEPARTURE

Every delay in departure creates a risk upon arrival.

Plan your departure in time to make landfall in a favorable light, arriving with several hours of daylight left. The way south is full of windward shore anchorages (i.e., entered to the east) where you will need the sun high and over your shoulder for the first time you enter. A 3 p.m. landfall may dictate a 4 a.m. start. If you've been accustomed to waking at 7 a.m. and having your Wheaties before addressing the world, and are reluctant to break that habit, then sell the boat and move ashore. Almost every leg of the Thornless Path requires an early start in order to benefit from land effects that reduce headwinds

Have a variety of departure plans ready for different breaks in the weather and for different landfalls. Be prepared to cancel all your commitments and haul anchor at the first opening of a Weather Window meeting one of your plans. Similarly, never plan a last minute chore, as did one friend who wanted to buy cold milk when the store opened at 8 a.m. That bottle of milk caused him to miss an earlier departure when the situation changed. He tried to use the change in the weather despite a later start and got pinned down in Long Island. He was still there when I reached Mayaguana.

Two weeks later, while I was dining in Puerto Plata, he had a window slam on his tail and suffered some delamination problems from all the pounding he took. He returned to Georgetown. The lengths of the windows and the lengths of the legs just didn't go together for him. The morals are:

- Plot several routes contingent on breaking weather.
- Depart at the earliest time called for by your contingent routes so that you can make changes underway in response to changes in the weather.

For example, if you're in **Calabash** waiting for the wind to go north of east in order to lay **Rum Cay** and it instead goes to the southeast, go anyway! But go to **Conception Island** and depart earlier. Why? You won't be lee-bowing the currents and you will have to take an extra tack or two. So you say you're a motor sailor and you'll motor it? Well, even if you don't have to tack sailing tacks, you'll still do small motor-sailing tacks and you will certainly make slower progress while pinching the wind than you would have if bound for Conception. Another moral you won't appreciate the value of until you've done all the trips I have:

Always reckon on 20% less speed to windward than you are accustomed to. If you get more, great!

Never Miss a Sundowner

A leisurely gin and tonic at sundown, with the boat all squared away and ready to move again, should end every landfall. This is no frivolous rule. To *never* miss a Sundowner G&T, you've got to plan your navigation with lots of margin for engine stops, adverse currents and so on. In order to make your landfall in time to get down secure anchors, square away yourselves and the ship, and make yourselves comfortable with a drink by sundown, you must make your anchorage several hours before. The **SG&T** (some of my friends leave out the gin) is a reward for good planning. Never miss it.

If In Doubt, Stay Out

A $2-million, 92-foot ketch lay on the rocks outside Puerto Plata for three months. It stranded there only one month after launching in Ft. Lauderdale. They went aground early on a clear night at the foot of the lighthouse at the *fortaleza* San Felipe. Maybe you'll bid on the wreck while in Puerto Plata.

Even after you have scrupulously followed all the rules, Murphy's Law eventually will catch up with you. If you can't make the tidy daylight landfalls suggested here, or you are just too uncomfortable with an entrance under certain conditions, stand way out to sea, set the boat to an easy jog in open water or heave to and go below in watches. A properly hove-to boat is snug as a baby's cradle. Of course, your SG&T at sea should be coffee.

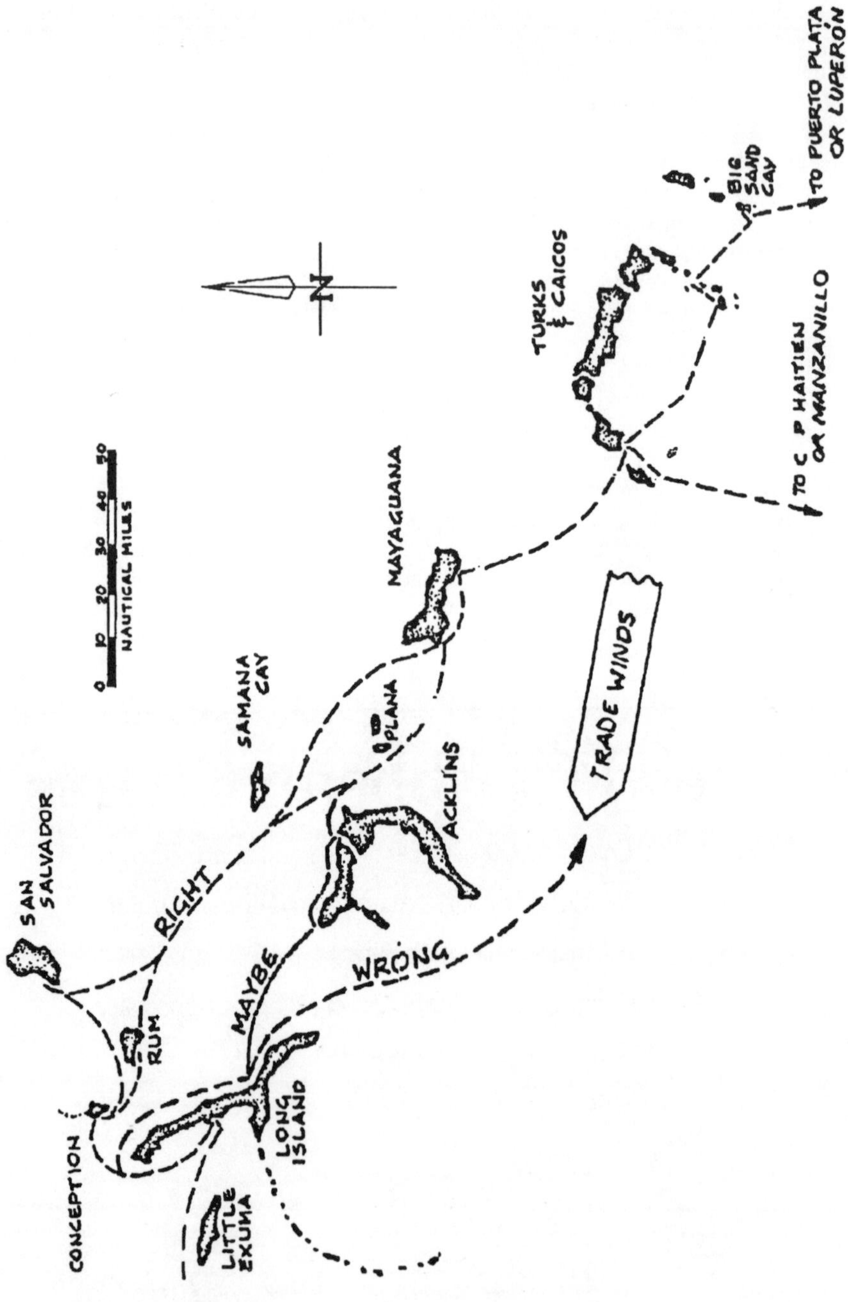

Keeping North to Go South

Given a choice of routes, the navigator should give weight to the *northernmost* to preserve any windward advantage. Since you are heading "south to the Caribbean," this might not be readily apparent. Consider that the "collective eye" of the prevailing winds is east to east-southeast. In order to maximize your possible **Weather Windows** you have to widen your angle on the wind. Either you must get *over* the eye of the wind to sail south-southeast, or you must sail *under* it to sail north-northeast. To do the latter requires fitting wheels on your boat to cross Hispaniola, an expensive procedure. I recommend sailing in the islands to the north, gaining easting by using the prevailing southeasterly flow, then spending the windward advantage accumulated by sailing south-southeast.

Remember, you're playing the slight switches in the wind. If you are in **Great Inagua** and your windward rhumb line is east-southeast, the wind will *never* switch enough for you to lay it. So, when you choose your routes each day, have uppermost in your mind that you won't give up northing, just as you wouldn't dream of giving up easting.

There are always the masochists that take the **Great Inagua** route, lured by the easy 65 south-southeast miles of **Long Island** early on the trip. I have sat in Georgetown and seen a 120-foot charter schooner, with English crew, leave for that route. A contingent of yachties followed. After all, didn't those professionals know best?

The answer is, "No!" They'd never done this before. It's a one-off route they're on. But, anyway, the cruising couple in their 60s with a 35-footer and a 25-hp. engine, let alone the 50-foot ketch with the 120-hp. diesel and bow-thrusters, cannot compare to a passle of temporary hires behind 1200 horses, dragging the bottomless purse of some foundation. They invariably find themselves slogging directly into the eye of the trades, more prevalent the farther south they go, but they also must buck into the mainstream of the **Equatorial Current**, which is three-quarters of a knot NNW in the **Crooked Island Passage** and up to one and a half knots WNW along Hispaniola (but not always). And in their wake are the broken flotsam of retired cruisers and the jetsam of their broken marriages and relationships.

Think I'm kidding? When you get as far as the Dominican Republic, start interviewing yachties who took this mistaken route. You will hear their stout denials that "It wasn't at all a rough trip, it was a good trip, really—glad they came that way, because Rum Cay was too rolly . . . ", etc., as I've heard them for years.

Why didn't they wait it out in Flamingo Bay on the northwest corner of Rum? "Well, we were with a group and . . . well . . ."

When you're in Luperón, notice how the Great Inagua group preoccupy themselves with what are quite major repairs, compared to your "to-do" list. See Great Inagua on the road back, along with **Hog Sty Reef**. To "go south," unless you are going to Jamaica, *keep north.*

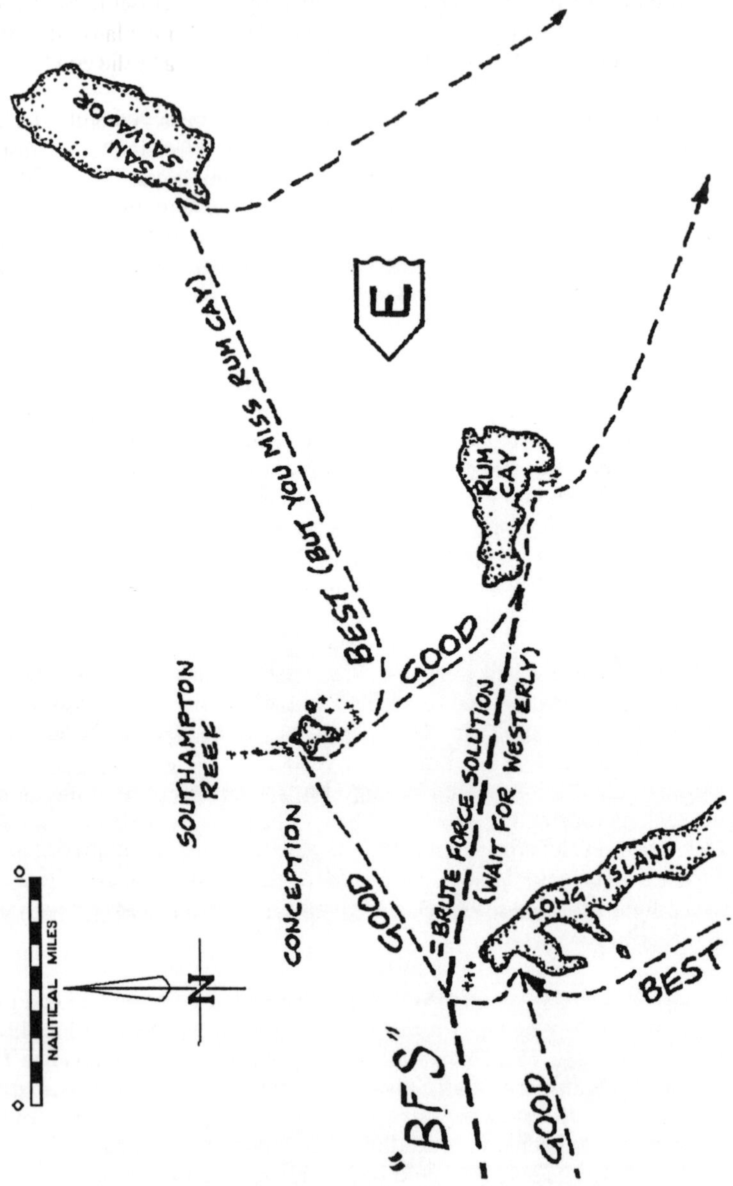

Alternate routes may be longer in distance, but either shorter in time or easier on boat and crew.

This rule, and the next three rules, deal with the strategy for choosing anchorages while wending the Thornless Path under continuously changing conditions. The bottom principle to this rule is to avoid the *idée fixée*, or what the French call, being foolishly stubborn.

One acquaintance left the sanctuary of **Salinas** just before Hurricane Dean to sit in its path at **Fajardo**. His logic, as such, was that Fajardo was "closer to St. Thomas" which, *in his mind*, was some sort of terminus, or cusp, in his cruising plans. St.Thomas became the "be all" as well as the "end all" for him. His idée fixée nearly did end it all for him right there at Fajardo.

Dean didn't turn toward Puerto Rico. He was lucky. I guess. A month later he was nailed in **Culebra** by Hurricane Hugo. As before, he made his "decision" at the last minute, and was practically the last boat to shelter at the overflowing hole.

When planning your next leg, consider not only your staging anchorage and multiple possible landfalls, but ensure that you know what conditions will prevail where you are going, and what possible steps you might have to take when you get there. Like moves in chess, your maneuverability at your next position (and your next...) should be thoroughly considered.

Example 1: Sailing to **Clarence Town** from **Rum Cay** might end your frustration of waiting day after day for the wind to change from dead east, but it will guarantee you two days of motoring against wind, wave and current, while slogging from Clarence Town to **Landrail** to **Attwood Harbor**. Take two more days of the world's finest snorkeling in good companionship at Rum in exchange for those two days of the wham-bangs spent in mutual disgust.

But remember, when it's rolly at Rum, jibsail down the bay and round the corner to anchor in flat calm with good WindBugger breezes on the white sand beaches of the western shore. **Flamingo Bay** on the northeast corner of **Rum** isn't so shabby in a prolonged southeaster—you can freshen your wardrobe from the Salvation Army wreck there.

Example 2: If the wind goes light to 12 knots but doesn't change to the direction you want, you may leave harbor anyway, exercising an alternate plan to go off on the other tack to a different anchorage, at a more stately, close-hauled pace than you had wanted. Or you could motor flat-out to your original goal. Either choice will alter your original plan. Landfall or arrival times have changed. Therefore other contingent conditions have changed: your ability to clear in or out, the angle of light for reading the water, the distance to comfortable harbor when your **Weather Window** closes.

Example 3: If you wanted to visit **Clarence Town** and you had gambled on a front to ride you out of it and lost the gamble, accept your loss like ladies and gentlemen do. **Wait for Weather** a couple of weeks in **Clarence Town**, or sail back to **Rum**, or to **San Salvador** to start another, shorter wait there. In other words: be flexible with your landfall, even while en route. And never, of course, *ever* set a schedule or a deadline. Don't hang up on a particular destination as though you had a pot of gold under only one particular rainbow.

DON'T BE AFRAID OF OPEN ANCHORAGES

There are various criteria to choosing anchorages while you are passage making. If your **Weather Window** starts to close on you earlier than you thought it would, you may get stuck in your anchorage for a considerable time doing another **Wait for Weather**. One wants a good bar, for instance, like Ted Bains' and Kay's in **Rum Cay**. Ditto, the fine fishing and diving found there.

Another consideration is comfort. A rolly anchorage can be miserable if suffered for more than a day out of necessity. And then, there is safety. A land-locked anchorage would be best, according to conventional wisdom.

But wait a minute! You're tucking into an anchorage while en route—you're not setting up winter camp! Conventional wisdom may not always serve you on the Thornless Path. Weather-shore open anchorages may be the best in trade wind conditions where the wind direction is rock steady, or in sub-trade conditions where it at least seems so. Many folks endure the balance of the hurricane season at Bonaire, anchored with their bows over a narrow, sand-over-coral shelf, and their sterns staring at Mexico, while hanging over a bottomless cliff. Except for potential backwinding around the month of October, this is a fine arrangement.

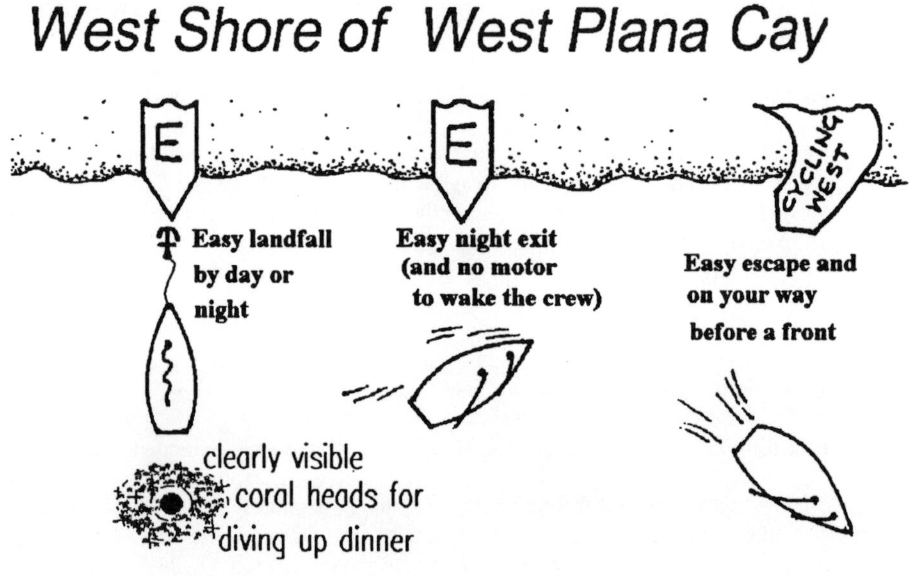

Benefits of an Open Anchorage

Ideally, a weather shore anchorage should be deep sand with lots of productive coral heads or rocks under keel depth. The skipper can anchor to windward of a good fishing spot and let out rode until the stern sits over his dinner. Plans for an arrival during favorable light conditions should of course consider that favorable light is needed underwater to skindive up your dinner from the bathing ladder. This is usually before four o'clock. The dinghy can stay in the davits. Filling this bill are such anchorages as **Santa Maria** (Long Island), **Conception Island**, **Pittstown Landing** (Crooked Island), **West Plana Cay**, **Betsy Bay** and **Start Bay** (in Mayaguana). Those roll-free anchorages so often sought out by the mate may be deathtraps. The landlocked harbors of **Attwood Harbor** (Acklins) is a deathtrap in a northerly, for instance, as can be **Calabash Bay** (Long Island) in anything but east. Besides, who can sleep without some rocking?

DON'T BE AFRAID OF THE DARK

You may find you don't wish to leave your anchorage at night. Wending your way out of some anchorages needs high sun and eats up the daylight hours you should spare for your landfall. If that's the case, have an alternate anchorage you can make in the dark. **Pittstown Landing**, for instance, can be made by starlight, as can **West Plana**. Creep due east until the bright white sand beach is under your bow.

Certain night passages often become mandatory: coasting to windward along the Dominican Republic, Puerto Rico, or along the **Paria** peninsula in Venezuela.

If the requirements of a well-timed landfall means leaving at night, or early in the morning, practice good *staging* by moving your anchorage the day before to an easy night, or dawn, departure site nearby. I've seen countless cases of fear of night sails leading a cruising couple into problems.

Here are some examples of when positioning for a night, or early morning departure is important to a good margin of safety on the coming leg:

Example 1: First light departures from **Georgetown**: don't party all night under the monument or in the hole at **Stocking Island**. Move down to the **Fowl Cay** anchorage for a dawn departure around Fowl Cay. Leaving from Fowl Cay you usually have a better angle on the wind and always a better angle on the sun, as it rises, than you have at **Conch Cay Cut**. Spend your last afternoon there fishing the Fowl Cay heads, and retire early after a relaxing evening.

Example 2: After several days in **Calabash** with strong easterlies, get ready for when it lightens and goes to the south a bit by moving over to the beach just south of **Cape Santa Maria**. You can leave there even before sunup without negotiating reefs by going west one mile, then north two miles to where you will be clear to the east.

Example 3: Leave **Start Bay** or **Abraham Bay** in **Mayaguana** at noon for a late night or, depending on boatspeed, early morning departure from **Southeast Point**. You must do the **Sandbore Channel** before the wind starts next a.m.

Example 4: Move over to **West Caicos** from **Sapodilla Bay** in the afternoon to leave for **Haiti** or **Manzanillo** at daybreak or before, depending on boatspeed and available wind.

Example 5: When headed north from **Puerto Plata**, leave the dock in the early morning calm to wait for a night departure from anchor. Don't try to disencumber your lines and anchors in the dark, not to mention attacking the cleanup job while half asleep.

Example 6: Many cruisers try to make the **Mona Passage** in two days and one night because they "don't like night sailing." Crossing the Mona in two days and a night instead of one day and two nights compromises your landfall to late in the second day. Just one pause to replace a blown raw water pump impeller, or slowing down to coddle an overheating engine, puts you precisely where you didn't want to be in the first place: close to land in the dark. One guy turned back exhausted after 48 hours jilling around in the Mona precisely because he departed Samaná in the morning rather than the evening.

Sailing at night has many other benefits. You make earlier landfalls, leaving more time to enjoy your anchorage. You avoid sunburn and glare. Watches are quieter and radio reception is better. More important, visibility is better at night, when lights stand out, than in daytime when everything's a vague blur on the horizon. Far from being a scary enemy, the dark is more often than not a friend of the Leisure Sailor.

THINK BEAUFORT

F_B	Wind In Knots	Descriptive Term	Sea Criteria	Waves In Feet
0	0	Calm	Sea like a mirror	0
1	1- 3	Light air	Ripples, but no foam crests	¼
2	4- 6	Light breeze	Small wavelets with glassy crests	1
3	7-10	Gentle breeze	Crests begin to break, glassy foam	2-3
4	11-16	Moderate breeze	Fairly frequent white horses	4-5
5	17-21	Fresh breeze	Long waves, many white horses	6-8
6	22-27	Strong breeze	Extensive foam crests, some spray	9-13
7	28-33	Near gale	Sea heaps up, foam blown in streaks	13-19
8	34-40	Gale	Spindrift forms, clear foam streaks	18-25
9	41-47	Strong gale	Tumbling crests, dense foam streaks, spray may affect visibility	23-32
10	48-55	Storm	Long, overhanging crests; great patches of dense foam streaks; sea surface appears white; tumbling of sea is heavy and shocklike.	29-41
11	56-63	Violent storm	Sea completely covered with long, white patches of foam; everywhere the edges of the wave crests are blown into froth; bad visibility.	37-52
12	64+	Hurricane	Air filled with foam and spray. sea completely white with driving spray. Visibility very seriously affected.	45+

The Force Beaufort Wind Scale

Work in **Force Beaufort**. It accustoms you to consider overall sea conditions including recent or pending changes.

The **Beaufort Wind Scale** encompasses both wind and wave. For instance, a nice 10-15 knot breeze in the morning after three days of 25-30 knots is <u>not</u> Beaufort Force Four. The waves will be 3 to 5 feet over residual swells of 8 to 10 feet! The Beaufort ratings assume relatively stable conditions.

In the winter months the prevailing easterlies run between northeast and east-southeast at Force 5 to 6. In the summer, May through October, they run east-northeast to southeast at Force 4 to 5.

The route south is littered with swells from the 3000-mile fetch of the Atlantic Ocean, superimposed with swells from distant storms and, of course, waves from local wind and chop from currents. These all slow windward progress and make for uncomfortable sailing when compared with similar wind strengths at home. Cutters and spoon-bowed sloops may carve through these conditions better than clipper or schooner bows. The going can be extremely rough. Cutters may have their expected way cut by 20 percent, clippers by half.

Here's a good Beaufort rule of thumb for all hull configurations in these waters, assuming settled conditions and a 36-48 hour forecast. Starting with a rhumb line dead to windward, add one Force Beaufort for each compass point, working aft from the bow until reaching Force Six. For example, if 48 hours of light airs are forecast with a few ripples on the sea, you may motor to windward. If it will blow 17-21 knots aft of your beam, with a few white horses, you'll have a good sail.

Force 5 forward of the beam is for the jocks in their yellow slickers eating cold beans from cans. The Leisure Sailor sails in a swimsuit and eats paté from china (Corningware unbreakable?) plates.

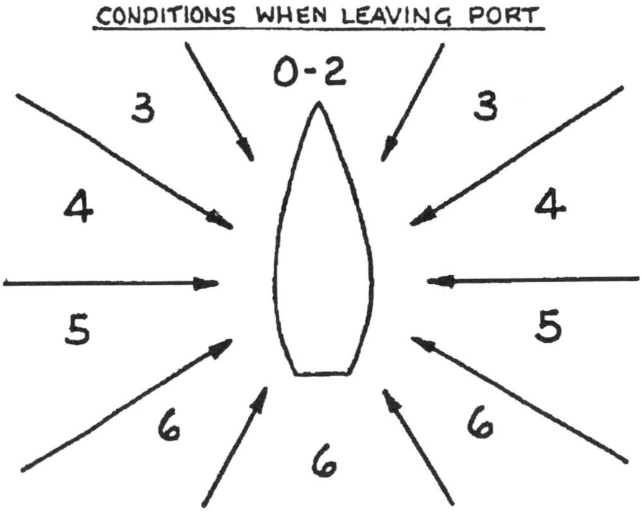

Force Beaufort off the Bow When Leaving Port: The Maximum Tolerated To Still Be on a Thornless Path.

Expressed in degrees (**D**) of the wind off the bow, the **Force Beaufort** (**F_B**) you want is equal to or less than:

$2 + D/30$, max. $6F_B$, or, for the purist . . . **$\frac{1}{2} D^{1/2}$, max. $6F_B$.**

Never start out for any distance in a Force 6-7, but if one develops on the quarter, ride it all you can and don't shelter. It probably won't grow stronger. Finally, if you need a slicker and can't sail in a bathing suit, you should never have left harbor in the first place.

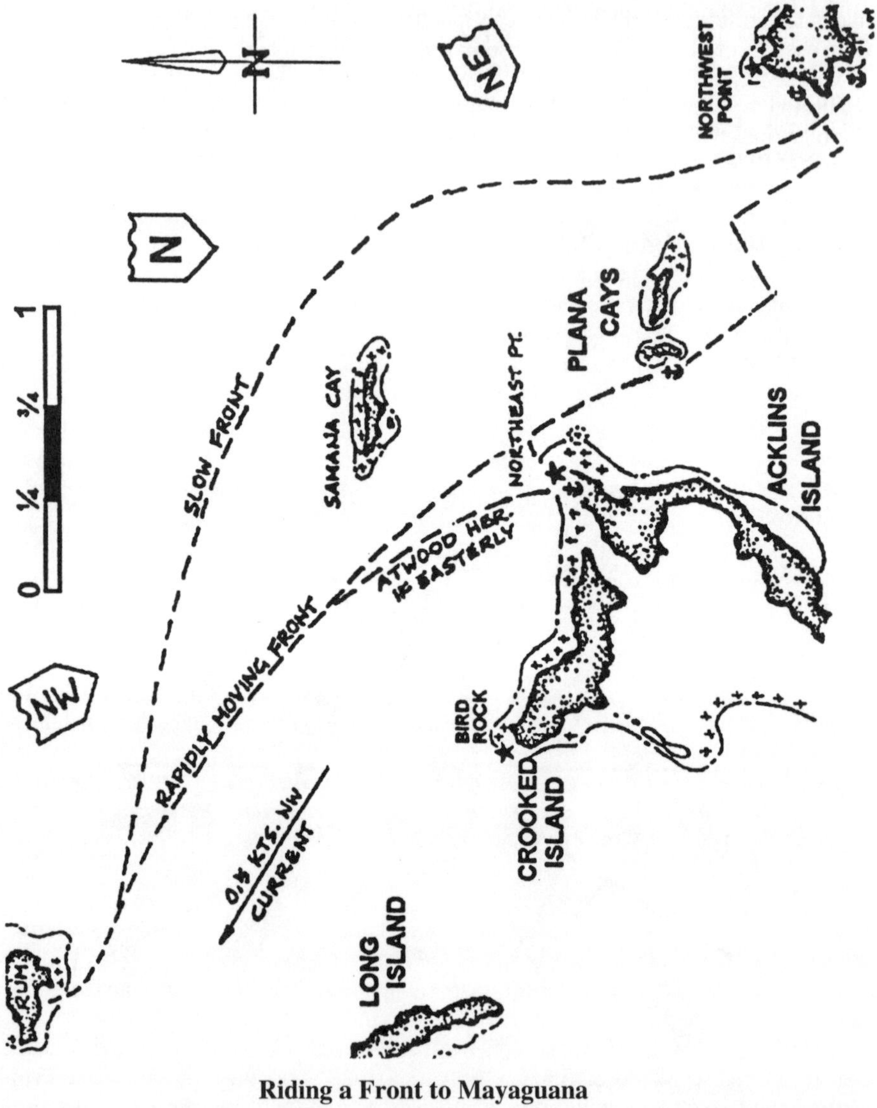

Riding a Front to Mayaguana

In the winter months it is possible to ride the **fronts** down to the Caribbean. In early winter there's a new front every week. By April you'll be lucky to get two good ones. They not only get less frequent but they get slower and weaker late in the season. If you're lucky they'll slow and stall as they sweep down on your little boat, giving you days of pleasant, if somewhat gray, reaching and running. Even luckier if the stalled front backs up as a warm front giving you two rides for your money.

Winter Cold Fronts

Many northern yachtsmen arrive in these waters still applying the term **Norther** to a **cold front**. A cold front in the southeastern extremity of the continental weather pattern is nothing like blue northers up north. Perhaps continued use of the term Norther inhibits the navigator from seeing cold fronts as the very useful friends they really are.

Unlike western European and north American waters, the building grayness of wind and sea during the passage of a front in the lower southwest north Atlantic and the northeastern Caribbean never build to **storm** conditions (Force 10 Beaufort), and they rarely build to a **gale** (Force 8). Don't always run for shelter. Get out your dividers and plot your progress south. The rain is warm and you can still sail with or without your bathing suit, although you may need a sweater when the front passes and it blows clear and cold. Never a slicker!

A front typically veers the wind from southeast through south, all the way around to northeast. When the northeast wind has blown itself out it will soften and dip a bit below east, a very useful fact to remember. As long as the front goes through, the progression through this circle is usually more rapid as the season wears on.

When leaving **Georgetown** I often take a full clock of the wind over to Salt Pond in Long Island, then I stage myself up to **Calabash** via **Simms** and **Joe's Pond** while it blows northeast. When it begins to dither below east, I sail to **Conception**. That strategy sure beats holing out in **Stocking Island**, then beating out into it after its gone. Late in the season you can trim for a broad reach and leave her there all the way from **Rum Cay** to **Mayaguana**, and even as far as **Puerto Rico**, scribing a long arc down islands with the wind's veer.

Early in the season the northeast winds may persist for several days after passage of a strong front. Once you get beyond Rum Cay, a front can be used to take you as far as you want to go. See Kline's *Yachtsman's Guide to the Bahamas* for another discussion of winter winds.

If you want to make it south to the Caribbean and you want to go only in sunny weather, take a plane. Clear weather in the winter usually means 20 knots on the nose and hobby-horsing into 6-8 foot short seas. By including fronts in your winter strategy, you can cut weeks off your trip south and at the same time insure yourself a good 3 days to a week of leisurely fishing while doing a **Wait for Weather**.

Rum Cay is an excellent spot to await a front. If the winds are too south of east you may experience a little roll. In that case, you need to have anchored further in to gain protection of the point. See the section on Rum Cay for details.

Summer Tropical Systems

In the summer months one watches the east for a variety of **Tropical Systems**, the nomenclature of which may sound randomly chosen to the first-time listener. Don't be abused, however: the nomenclature used follows a simple progression of severity, and therefore, it is of interest to the cruiser, especially if he or she is uninsured.

First on the scene are **Troughs** and **Tropical Waves**, which come across the Atlantic and may spawn **Tropical Disturbances**. One of these may begin to whirl to become a **Tropical Depression**, which can become a **Tropical Storm**, which often becomes the dreaded **Hurricane**. So it goes. Rather than continue to confuse these terms, refer now to the Glossary for the definition of each. Learn what these weather features are now and know how they can be used, rather than confuse and dread them all.

One season I left **Salt Pond** to take advantage of the weak circulation around a north-bound tropical depression well to the east of us. The words *Tropical Depression* had alarmed some of the other boats into staying put. Upon the depression's passage, strong winds had returned and stayed for a while. After my usual leisurely sail to Puerto Plata, I heard on the ham net that one couple had got discouraged with their Wait for Weather and had turned back, and that two more had given up waiting and had terrible beats to Rum Cay, where they were still cornered by the full southeast trades which had come up to their northern limit for an extended visit. One of these was Captain Nogo, the fellow who had everyone listening to the Northwest Caribbean reports instead of the Southwest North Atlantic Offshore Forecasts. His idea of a good Weather Window was a breezy, sunshiny sailing day, like in the beer ads. To him, ugly looking days were for staying at anchor regardless of wind strength and direction.

HUG THE SHORE COASTING TO WINDWARD

STRENGTH and DIRECTION of WIND and CURRENT as a function of the DISTANCE OFFSHORE

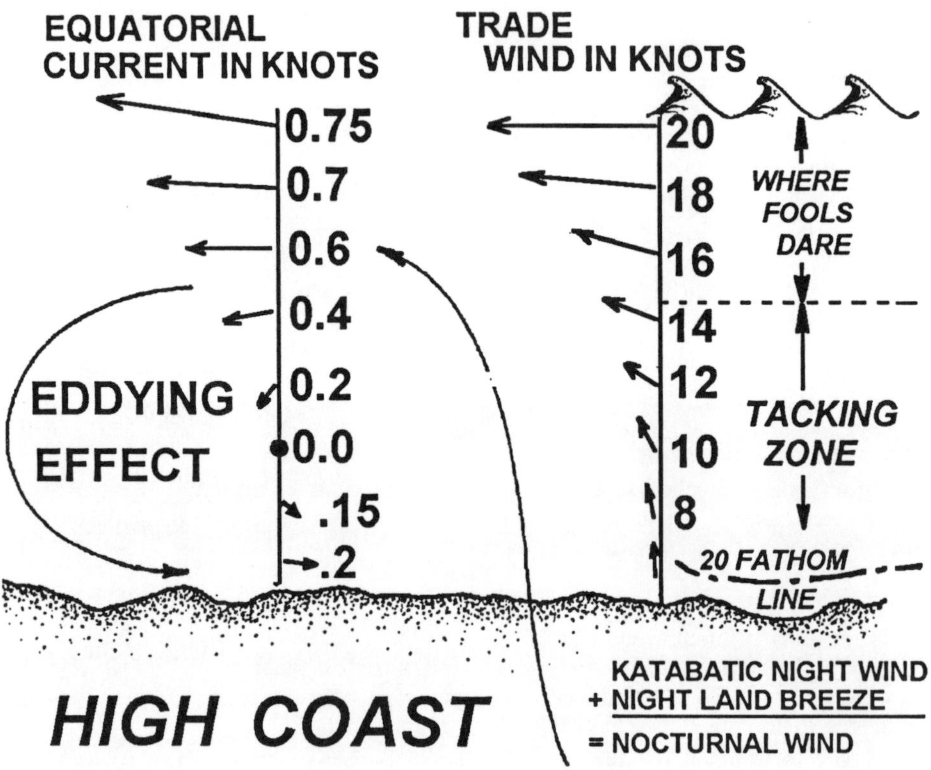

Coasting by Hugging the Shore

The wise navigator, like Columbus, takes advantage of nighttime lees on the high windward coasts. Modern sailing yachts sail well to windward under these light conditions and in calms they can proceed under auxiliary power instead of behind a rowed longboat as Columbus had to do.

My standard rules for coasting are to *tack out until well off soundings*, or until whitecaps are found, then *tack back in until*:

- between 10 and 20 fathoms by day (or eyeball), or
- between 20 and 30 fathoms by night.

This can make for short tacks on a steep coast, but if coasting to take advantage of the lee of the land, the strip of relatively calm water is narrow anyway, from 1 to 3 miles. The north coast of the **Dominican Republic** is a case in point.

Normally I steer a good watch on an inshore tack and go below to read or catnap on the offshore tack, relying on the rougher water to shake me out of the bunk so I can head her back inshore again. One year I was reading below on an outward tack, while comfortably coasting between **Cabo Macoris** and **Cabo Frances** on the north coast of the D.R. An incident occurred which, unfortunately, is common among cruisers headed south.

I was surprised by a barely intelligible call on the VHF. It was from friends supposedly following my advice to hug the coast with me. I marked my book place, heaved the cat off my lap and ambled back over the upright deck to the navstation.

My friend's voice over the radio reminded me of an old Charles Laughton movie where the helmsman is lashed to the wheel during a survival storm. Backdropped by mountainous seas, the terrified man is whipped by buckets of sea water and foam flying horizontally on the screaming wind while the ship groans onto her beam with every wave.

At any rate, that seemed to be the condition of his vessel and crew, judging by the sound effects coming over the VHF and the strain with which he spoke.

"Where the heck *are* you?" I asked.

"A-About six ... miiiiles ... ooout!" he intoned stoically from the heart of the gale.

"Why not come inshore?" I asked after rescuing my peanut butter sandwich from the cat, who almost dumped my coffee cup in her backward scurry.

"We ... We've ... seeeen ... worrrse!" crackled the speaker.

Earlier, this same friend had insisted on punching on through the day, rather than waiting for evening behind the Cabo Macoris headland at **Sosua** because "people were saying we couldn't anchor there." I had anchored off Sosua as usual and, after a refreshing 4-hour nap and a hot supper, continued on. Despite his earlier start I overtook him that night, motor sailing inshore of him. And even though I spent most of the next night anchored at **Escondido**, he made port at **Samaná** only a few hours earlier than I.

He was so zonked out he didn't clear customs until the next day, while I cleared in immediately and went out to lunch to renew old friendships in Samaná. Later, when I asked again why he had punched on in the daytime and why he didn't sail further inshore, he told me that his wife was afraid to sail at night—which they had to do anyway—and he was wary of the rocks along the shore, which his chart told him didn't exist.

Cruising is neither an Outward Bound course nor an endurance contest for retired couples. Sailing this coast requires good sense and planning, *not* a high tolerance for pain. I always find the passage along the D.R. a good trip and I rarely see a white cap. But if you round the capes in midday and fail to coast close inshore, you will indeed have an evil trip—and shame on you.

Double shame if you venture out into more than 15 knots of forecast wind, or wind which is north of east, or into large swells leftover from storms in the north and east.

WATCH YOUR BACK

In the summer and fall months, it is paramount that the skipper always have a storm anchorage less than 12 hours *downwind*. Preferably these should be three to five hours sailing time *downwind*. Warning time can be extremely short due to the patent insufficiency of the U.S. Government's abilities to forecast weather arriving from the east. They are pretty good on cold fronts, however, having had to watch each of them sweep slowly across the continent for five long days before they move off the coast.

For several reasons, among them the frequent loss of satellites, **Hurricanes** and **Tropical Storms** are less obvious to them. They get better at it as the season wears on. You can try writing your congressman, but for now, keep a good **Hurricane Hole** close at your back.

Hurricane Holes

Hurricane Holes are those anchorages which are *closed to dangerous wind directions*, if not all directions, and provide good holding and soft shores to wash up on if need be. September through November one should actually use these holes if possible. For instance, in **Culebra**, Puerto Rico, you can stay close to the single bright light boasted by downtown **Dewey** in order to enjoy whatever Saturday night hoopla it affords, but the wise skipper will stake out a claim across the bay near one of the holes to windward, and dinghy back and forth the ¾ mile to town.

The **Virgin Islands** are not the best place to be. Best is **Venezuela**, where there are virtually no hurricanes. Second best is **Salinas**, on the south coast of **Puerto Rico**, where just about every anchorage is an excellent hole, or **Luperón**, an impenetrable mangrove bay on the north shore of the Dominican Republic, where there is a small village and good communications.

The V.I. has few hurricane holes and there are hundreds of boats plugging them up during a threat, most of which are charter boats or boats with absentee owners that have no skippers aboard. The result is that the holes that do exist in the VI are extremely dangerous from the crunch of boats around. The **Leeward Islands** and the **Windward Islands** have a few good holes, most of which are rather hard-sided, **Tyrell Bay** being a notable exception, and the best in both chains of islands. **Salinas**, in Puerto Rico, is a super place to hang out, and it also has extensive hurricane holes, much larger than Culebra. Most of the other P.R. holes are not at town anchorages but only minutes away from a town, and there are no great fleets of boats around as there are in the Virgins.

Excellent Hurricane Holes are at:

- Manzanilla, D.R.
- Luperón, D.R.
- Salinas, P.R.

Good Hurricane Holes are at:

- Fort Liberté, Haiti
- Samaná, D.R.
- Bahía de la Jina, Samaná
- Bahía de Lorenzo, Samaná
- Culebra, P.R.
- Tyrell Bay, Carriacou

Okay Hurricane Holes are at:

- Boquerón, P.R.
- La Parguera, P.R.
- Guánica, P.R.
- Palmas del Mar, P.R.
- Hurricane Hole, U.S.V.I.
- Simson's Lagoon, St. Martin
- Cul de Sac, Martinique
- Rodney Bay, St. Lucia

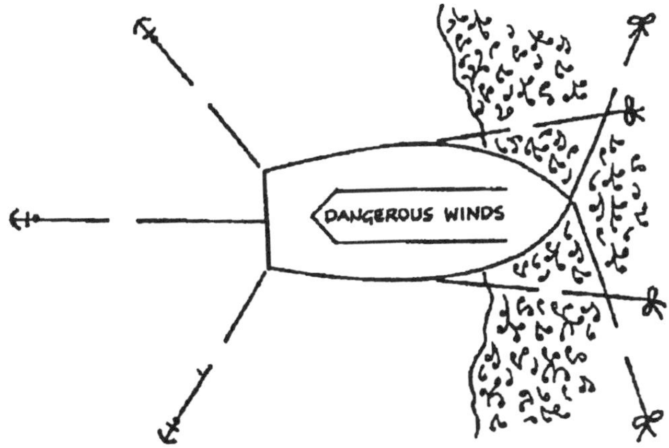

Ideal Mooring, Tied to the Mangroves in a Hurricane Hole

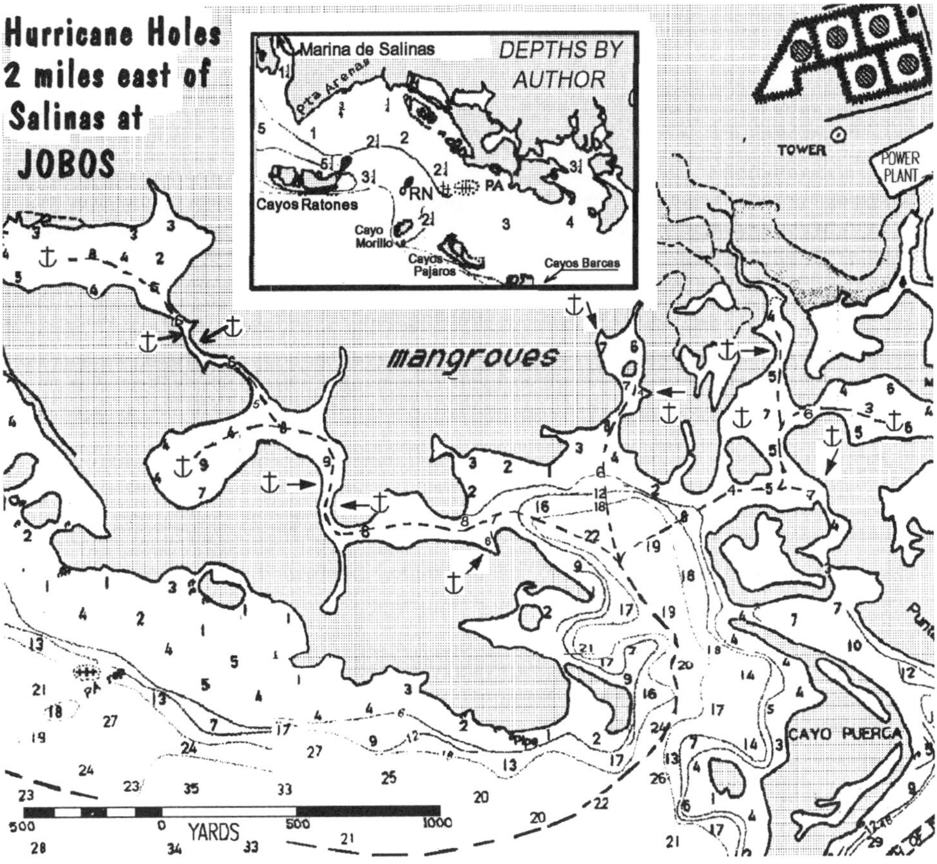

Hurricane Holes at Jobos, by Salinas, Puerto Rico's South Coast

THE DANGEROUS SEMICIRCLE

The dangerous semicircle of a **Tropical Storm** is the half of the rotating system which has its winds moving in the same direction as its forward speed. Typically, the winds in the dangerous semicircle can be 50-percent higher than the winds in the other half of the storm.

If encountering the storm at sea and you are caught in the dangerous half, the directions of the winds tend to sweep you into its path rather than knock you aside. For example: If you fell into the path of one of those street cleaning machines which has rotating brooms, to which side of its rotation would you rather fall? The side which will squinch you forward and into its maw, or the side which will only maul you and spit you back out?

Although you may watch the formation of the 'canes in the Atlantic and plot their probable paths two to three days ahead, they still can be erratic. The **National Weather Service** has had difficulties monitoring the Atlantic in the past, due to lost satellites if not strayed policies. Don't bank on more than 12 hours' preparation time after a warning of a near hit and no more than six for a direct hit. If it is clear that a storm heading west will pass your anchorage to the south, then you don't care if the anchorage is open to the west, and you can put your nose in the mangroves of the eastern shore. If a 'cane is passing north of you and headed west, almost any good anchorage may do.

The permutations are, of course, endless, and should be chosen for the holes you have available. All of these "What If" **Hurricane Games**, like war games, must be played well in advance of a crisis. You must act instinctively when it's apparent a hurricane is on its final approach and may not veer. You won't have time to dither.

Samaná has a great hole across the bay, but Samaná has never had a hurricane problem anyway. A careful look at the geography will show why: Surrounding land masses and mountains defeat the winds, even with a direct hit. There appears to be no way for the dangerous semicircle to penetrate the bay undiminished. The same is true for **Luperón**. For more information on storms, see "When You Can't Listen to the Weather." But not to worry too much, since the odds of a 'cane landing on your little area of the world are slim.

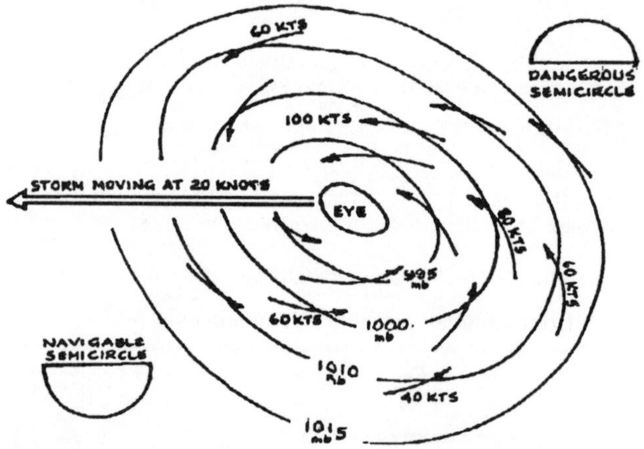

A Hurricane's Dangerous Semicircle: Possible approaches of the high winds should be anticipated when selecting a mooring.

I divide the way south into short, easy passages. The following pages provide advice for plotting and making each passage. When details on anchorages can be found in the guides mentioned in the Preface, those details are not repeated here. However, when it is felt that the cruising sailor needs particular information to make the cruise truly *thornless*, then those for anchorage chartlets are included.

Bahamian beacons and lights are notoriously unreliable. They may be damaged or decrepit, but, wholly visible or not, these are the marks of record you must use.

How To Read The Chartlets In This Section

Latitude/Longitude Interpretation

All GPS coordinates in this guide are given to the nearest tenth of a mile. This should satisfy either WGS-84 (NAD83) and WGS-72 datum. The format used is always **DDMM** (Degrees, Minutes), eliminating the folderol and fritter of ° and ' signs, and **N** and **W** designations for Latitude and Longitude. For example, **2845** instead of **28° 45' N**. Since the area covered by this book is 15-26°N latitude and 60-80°W longitude, there shouldn't be any confusion with this simpler notation. However, if you do get it twisted up, you will no doubt recover your error since 28°45'W is the longitude of Faial, in the Azores, and you probably don't want that right now. In any case, there shall surely be the normal complement of cruisers in Georgetown to rail against the notation. They're usually the ones who don't read the book fore-to-aft, and therefore they miss the keys to its interpretations.

EXAMPLE:

Georgetown is at [2330 / 7545]. Mistake that coordinate for [7545 / 2330], and you wind up in the eastern skœrgaard of Kalaallit Nunaat, which is Greenland.

With the full availability of GPS cruisers have taken to giving each other precise coordinates of reef entrances and channel markers. Use these at your peril. All such arrival way points in this book are adjusted to give you:

1. safe offing distance with which to proceed *visually*, and
2. safe approach from sea at all possible arrival angles.

Passage Elapse Times

To estimate the time required to make a specific passage while using the strategies in this book, you must add *time underway* to *time waiting for weather.* When planning a cruise, you must consider the time of year since winds will vary depending upon season. You must consider your mode of passage making. Are you a purist sailor? Do you motor, or motorsail, at the slightest contretemps? Touring, repairing or partying must never be overlapped with a **Wait for Weather**. Here is some background to these factors in order for you to adjust them for yourself, your crew and your yacht, and make your own estimate of passage times.

I have had to whiz through these passages to make business schedules associated with my yacht, *Jalan Jalan*. I was chartering in the north, building a house in Puerto Plata, and refitting each year in Venezuela. Sometimes legs were taken several times a season to reprovision or work on the house, for instance, between charters. My yacht was uninsured and I was single-handed. I therefore traveled as fast as was feasible without negatively affecting the well-being of either the yacht or myself.

Many trips I've made were for pleasure, or just aimlessly wandering, which is *Jalan Jalan*'s English meaning. *Jalan* is a 15-ton displacement, long-keeled, 41-foot ketch. She has a Perkins 4-108 engine which develops only 37 shaft hp. of the 51 rated. She sails well in ideal conditions, but she has a clipper bow and hobby-horses in steep, choppy seas.

Everyone I meet says they beat 35° to the real wind. C. A. Marchaj (*Sailing Theory and Practice*, ISBN 0-229-64253-5) says 37.5° is the theoretical minimum. *Jalan* persists in giving me 50° on the passages described in this guide. I consider that a 35-foot sloop with a 30-hp. auxiliary and a retired couple aboard will do about as well as we. With 50° tacks at 5 knots, you will put 14.4 miles under the keel for each 10 miles on a windward rhumb line. With the usual minimum of half-knot equatorial current against you, it will be 16.6 miles. To make 5 knots you've got to have a Force 4-5 with seas 4-7 feet. You will lose way with the seas. Your leeway may be more than *Jalan*'s (one degree for each Force Beaufort). A factor of 1.75 keel miles to each rhumb line mile while tacking should not be unexpected for a small boat with a cruising configuration. Don't bet on less!

Jalan and I tack directly to windward only in a Force 4, accept a 3.5 knot average. and don't lie about it. For reaching, running and motoring, reckon as you normally would. Despite all this data many cruisers have asked that I tell them exactly how long a particular leg will take *their boat* (with *them* at the helm, making *their* course and tacking decisions). Well here it is:

> **Calculate the speed you make under full motor and sail, against 20 knots and short 8-foot seas. Divide this into the number of miles your keel shall travel. Add 30 percent for leeway and optimism. You then have the total hours to wherever you want to go.**

If you find yourself actually trying to make these times more often than not, although I wish you well in your cruising, you should closely examine your reasons for cruising.

Cruising takes time. Each stop you make will require rest and recuperation, perhaps some touring or local cruising, and get-togethers with other cruisers. For example, I often do the 60 or so miles to **Rum Cay** from **Georgetown** by following the clocking winds of a medium front to **Long Island**. When the northeast winds blow themselves out and flag briefly south of east, I go to **Conception** for diving on **Southampton Reef**. I take the leg to **Rum** at the end of the **Weather Window**, where I sit during the next **Wait for Weather**.

Novice cruisers try to make Rum from Georgetown. More experienced crews shoot for Conception. Here's how I do those 60 miles (refer to chartlet in the East From Georgetown chapter).

DAY	LOCATION OF FRONT	WIND DIR. AND SPEED	ANCHORED THAT NIGHT	ACTIVITY
1	NO. FLORIDA	E-SE 15-20	REDSHANKS	PARTYING
2	CEN. FLORIDA	E-SE 15	FOWL CAY	STAGING
3	SO. FLORIDA	S-W 10-15	SALT POND	CRUISING
4	NASSAU	NW-N 20-25	SALT POND	WAITING
5	OUT ISLANDS	NE 20-25	SIMMS	CRUISING
6	HISPANIOLA	E-NE 20	JOE'S SOUND	CRUISING
7	PUERTO RICO	E 15-20	CALABASH BAY	CRUISING
8	DISSIPATING	E-SE 10-15	CONCEPTION	DIVING
9	DISSIPATED	E-SE 15	RUM (PT. NELSON)	PARTYING
10	NO. FLORIDA	E-SE 15-20	RUM (FLAMINGO BAY)	SNORKELING
11	CEN. FLORIDA	E 15-20	RUM (WEST COAST)	FISHING
12	SO. FLORIDA	E-SE 15	RUM (PT. NELSON)	STAGING

That's *five miles a day*, folks! And every mile a pleasure!

Remember, if you aren't partied out by the time a good **Weather Window** opens up, or your favorite serious son is flying down to visit his wastrel parents fiddling their lives (and his inheritance) away in the Caribbean, or whatever reason you have for not taking the leading edge of the first window available, then add more time on your total cruise. Take a new window and don't try to make up time by going when you shouldn't.

In all, the trip from Georgetown to Venezuela can take as little as from two to four months depending solely on luck of the draw during each **Wait for Weather**. That does not, of course, include time to satisfy your desire to pause and smell the roses, nor does it account for rest and recuperation which, in my case can be months.

More guesstimates from my experience, which *do not include* touring, fishing or R&R:

1. **Georgetown** to **Puerto Plata**; ten days to three weeks in any season.
2. If you visit **Haiti**; add one to two weeks;
3. **Manzanillo**, but not Haiti; add a week.
4. **Puerto Plata** to **Boquerón**; one to two weeks.
5. Boquerő n to the **Virgin Islands**; one to two weeks.
6. The Virgin Islands to **Venezuela**; four weeks, unless you sail straight across in three to four days from **Virgin Gorda**.

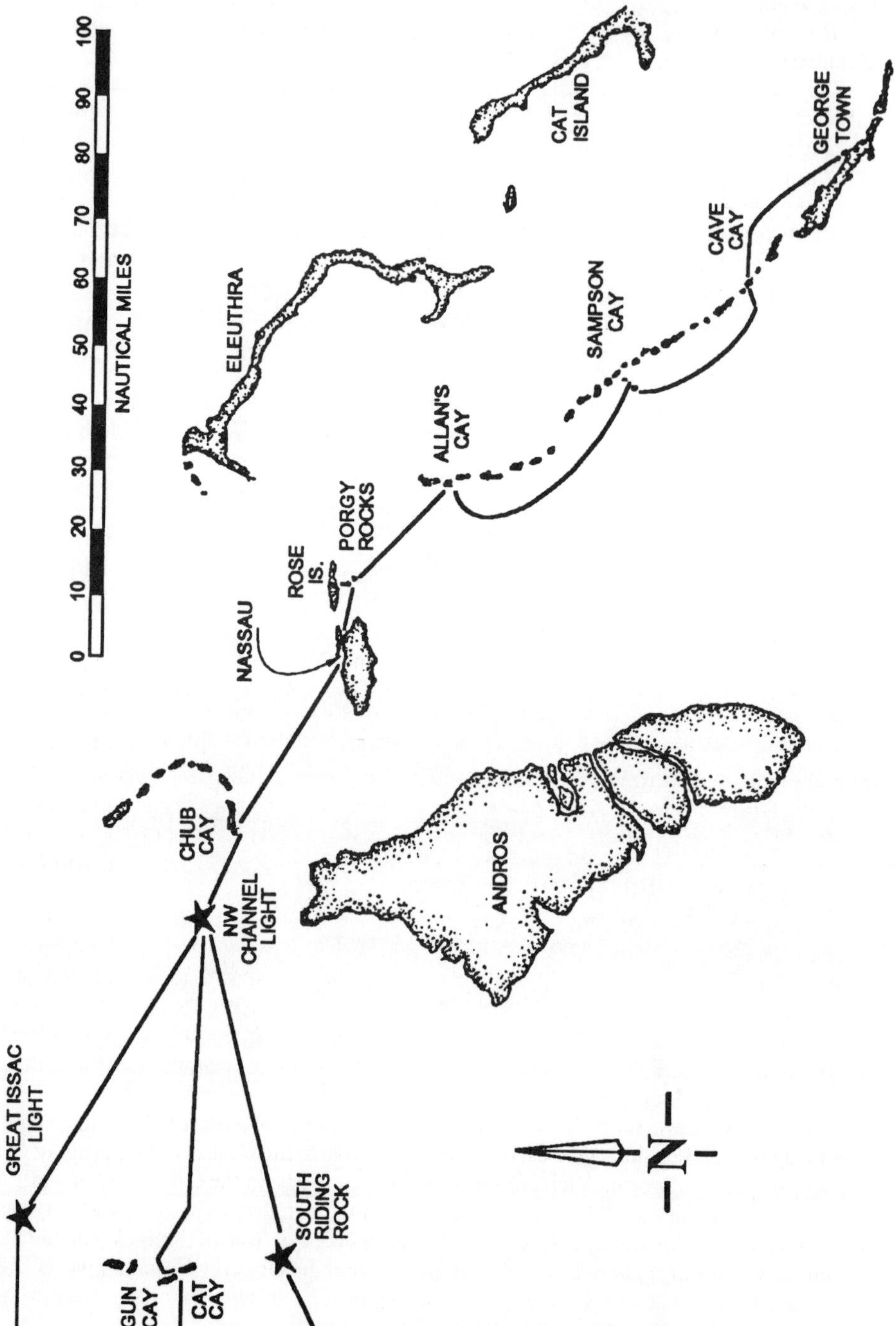

Florida to Georgetown, the critical path.

The route from Florida to Georgetown is more than sufficiently covered by Kline's *Yachtsman's Guide to the Bahamas,* which I strongly recommend. Kline's anchorage chartlets are numerous and accurate for all the upper Bahamas. In addition, you should have the *Bahamas Chart Kit*, published by Better Boating Association and available in most chandleriers.

The Gentleman's Guide to Passages South is meant to provide information not otherwise available in the guides listed in the Preface. Its main contribution is to passage-making and other concerns of the hard-core cruiser. Local information is abundant in the other guides. This guide concentrates on information on sailing directions and arriving/departing the anchorages which are key to the thornless strategies.

Charts for islands from Georgetown to Hispaniola and that great island itself, are less complete in all the guides and therefore more information on these areas is included in *The Gentleman's Guide to Passages South.*

From Florida to Georgetown the cruiser has such vast choices of wholly separate cruising grounds that cruisers could, and should, occupy themselves there for many months. However long, and wherever you choose to cruise the upper Bahamas, your best plan would be to make Georgetown, Exumas, by early March at the latest. Cruising the Exumas and the near out-islands can easily exhaust the months of November until March.

The Gulf Stream

Wait for Weather in any safe hole south of Palm Beach, e.g., **Marathon**, **Plantation Key**, **No Name Harbor** or **Hurricane Harbor** in **Key Biscayne**, or **Lake Sylvia** in **Ft. Lauderdale**. Where you start makes little difference except in heading and departure time, but wait *close* to the ocean. For example, waiting at **Dinner Key** Marina may put several hours on your trip compared with waiting at the marina inside **Government Cut**. Review the strategy on *staging.*

Wait until the **Offshore Forecast** is for southeast winds of 15 knots or less and leave at night from the **Miami** or Ft. Lauderdale area, or before lunch, from Marathon. Never cross the **Gulf Stream** when the wind is against the current or is blowing northwest through northeast. And never cross in conditions over Force 4. An average set of 1½ knots at 10° true from anchor to anchor works fine. Plot a course for an 8 a.m. arrival at **Gun Cay** or **Riding Rock**.

You can take **South Riding Rock** onto the **Great Bahama Bank** if you plan to clear in at **Chub Cay** or **Nassau**. I've found it all around less hassle to do it at **Cat Cay** while waiting for weather. Then you can go anywhere in the Bahamas without worrying about customs. However, the marinas at Cat and Chub Cays sporadically levy a tie-up fee for the mandatory customs boarding. The fuel docks at Nassau do not normally charge for clearing in if you fill up with fuel. For more on the vagaries of Bahamian clearance, see the appendix on Customs and Clearances.

If you ride over the **Gulf Stream** on the precursor winds of a front, be sure to be behind **Gun Cay** before the winds go west of south, then move to the west of Gun Cay again when the winds go east of north. A leisure sailor will in no case be in the **Gulf Stream** while the wind is northerly and over the current. While at Gun Cay, motor over to the **Cat Cay** basin and check in with Customs and Immigration at their office in front of the dock. Anchor back at Gun Cay or off the channel behind Cat Cay, north of the club. If you anchor west of Gun Cay, check out the ledges on the shore for lobster. The weekenders there from Miami assume it's already picked clean and don't bother to look.

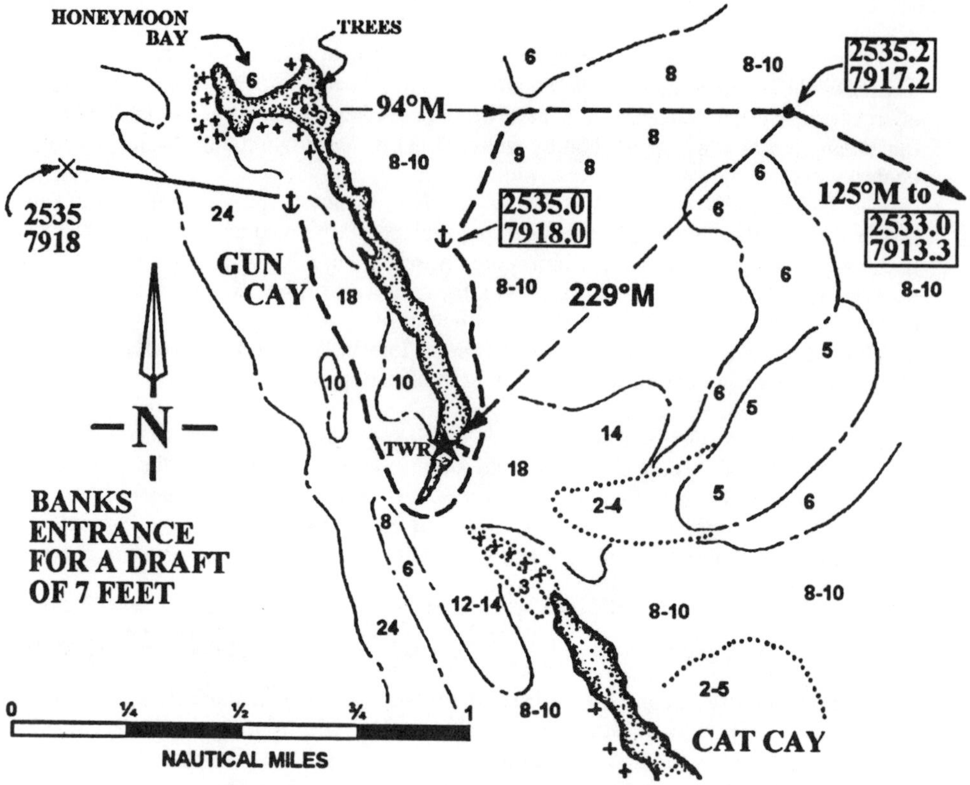

Onto the Banks: to gain an hour on the run across, anchor east of Gun Cay the day before and leave at first light next morning, motoring full out.

To take seven feet onto the **Great Bahama Banks,** proceed north from the **Gun Cay** entrance until the clump of trees on the north end of the Cay is abeam. Then turn east to a point one mile east of the trees and northeast of the Gun Cay light. Now proceed on a course of 125° magnetic for 4 miles. You are back on the rhumb line to **Russel Beacon**.

The Great Bahamas Bank

Try to get to the anchorage south of **Northwest Channel Light** before dark by leaving from the east side of **Gun Cay** just before dawn in good southerlies or westerlies. Otherwise, wait for a calm day and motorsail lickety-damn (see the section on Motorsailing in the Pointers chapter). *Staging* yourself to the east side of Gun Cay the previous afternoon will save an hour, thus shortening the trip by 5 miles.

If forced to anchor in the middle of the banks, do so a good two miles south of the lane you are traveling. Set out a bright light, a long anchor snubber, and hope you don't have visitors.

If you are worried about your draft, you can take the northern route around **Isaac Light** in the ocean, or across the top of the banks from north of **Bimini** to Northwest Channel Light, passing a few miles north of the **Mackie Shoal** beacon which may not be there. This is a good, clear route with never less than 10 feet of water. My 6½ foot draft takes the route from Gun Cay to **Russel Beacon** with minimum 2 feet still under the keel. To navigate the shoal area east of Gun Cay with a 7-foot keel, leave on a rising half tide and follow the sketch above.

Anchor off the beach in front of the marina if you are going to check in there. Better anchorages are available at **Bird Cay** or **Whale Cay**, where you also will have a better angle on the wind when sailing to **Nassau**. All of these anchorages are open for easy night exits. Get used to setting out two anchors (not a Bahamian Moor *per se*) for security from strong westerlies in squalls or thunderstorms year round.

Leave around 3 a.m. to get to Nassau next morning with plenty of time to fuss around getting a secure anchorage or to go shopping and tour the town.

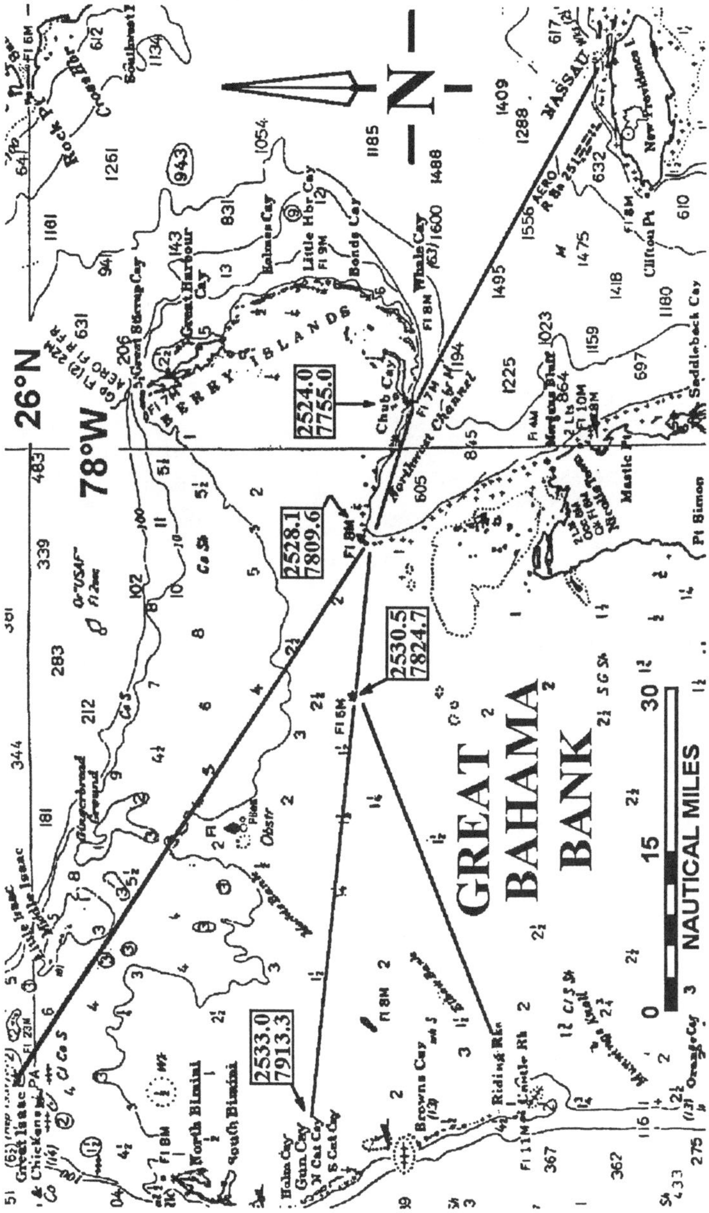

The Great Bahamas Banks to Nassau

Some love it, some hate it, but you have to do it at least once. If you arrive at a large port early in the day, you will have lots of time to fool around changing anchorages as may become necessary, and you will generally get a better handle on the town, than if you arrive late in the day. (See *Dinghy Security*). Whatever time you spend in port thereafter is made much more productive by arriving before lunch the first day.

Anchor west of Club Med at the Yoga center. Set anchors fore and aft against the east flood and the west-going ebb. The anchorage off Nassau Shipyards is fine but often crowded and more available to swimmers from shore. You can land your dinghy at the BASRA dock which is convenient to all of Bay Street. See the section on *Dinghy Security* in *Pointers*.

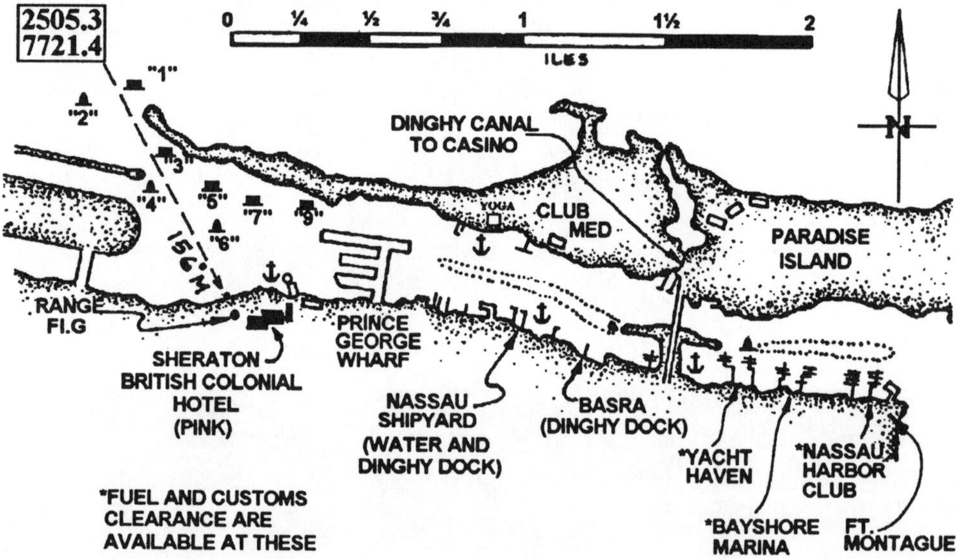

Transient Anchoring in Nassau

Leave **Nassau** for the **Exumas** shortly after daybreak on a day when the wind is easterly and less than 15 knots. Take the direct deep-water route to either **Allan's Cays** or **Highbourne Cay** from a point 2 miles east-southeast of **Porgee Rocks**. This route passes between **Middle Ground** and **Yellow Bank**. The water is deeper than charted and the heads are few and distinctive in the high light of late morning to midday, which is what it will be if you left Nassau early.

To get a leg up on the passage, or to **Wait for Weather**, as the winds may not be from the direction you wish, anchor in **Bottom Harbor** on **Rose Island**. To leave Bottom Harbour, motor west at sunup, close to shore, to the entrance to the salt pans, then head true south 0.8 miles until **East Porgee Rock** bears west, whence you turn onto 145° true for 1.6 miles to the departure point east-southeast of Porgee Rocks. See chartlet (next page).

You should cruise the Exumas slowly and enjoy every anchorage available. There is no better cruising in all the Bahamas, although the **Far Out Islands** offer better diving. These notes, as in the entire *Gentleman's Guide to Passages South,* are for those who have already done their touring and gunk-holing and want to make a rapid and easy passage.

The fastest, safest and simplest passage is to take the **Exuma Banks** all the way down to **Cave Cay**, one of the easiest and deepest cuts and the last cut going south for vessels of any draft. For a rapid passage, do not stop at **Staniel Cay** unless going outside in **Exuma Sound** from there on. There is no reason for a draft under 8 feet to take the outside route. The banks will give you 10 feet or more most of the way, with convenient cays at which to turn upwind and anchor for the night.

Drafts over 7 feet are better off exiting the banks at **Conch Cut**, just above Staniel. Even so, playing the tides and paying close attention to charts of the banks, deeper drafts can go further. Although Staniel Cay and **Pipe Creek** are worthy stops for the cruiser, they are essentially terminals and not convenient waypoints in a banks passage.

The passage down the banks behind the Exumas is one of the best sails you'll ever have, close-hauled on 20 knots of wind without a ripple on the water. Beating was never like this. And never will be again. The water here is 10-15 feet deep, unobstructed with coral heads, and clear as a swimming pool's. *Even with a deep draft, don't be shy of taking the Banks route behind the Exumas.*

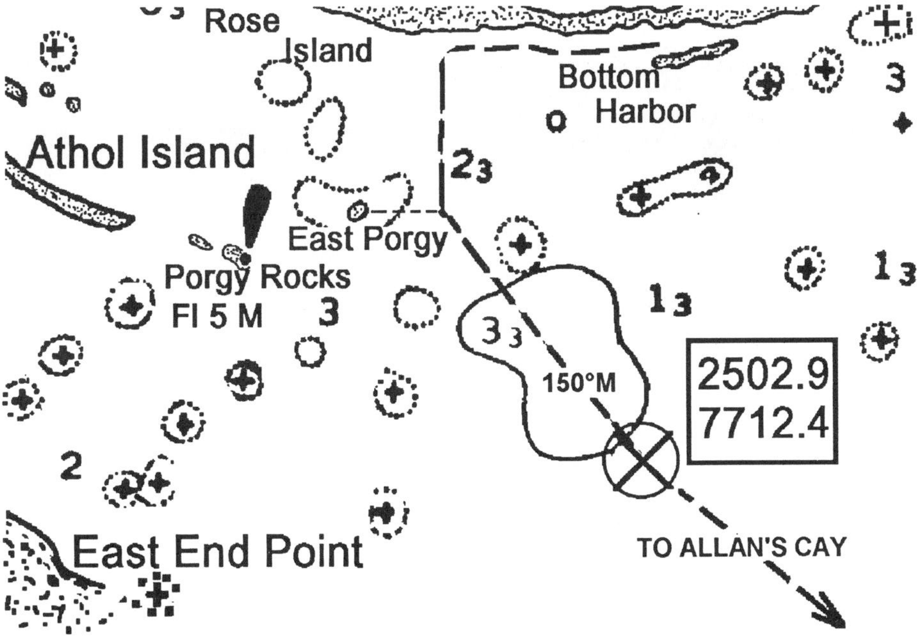

Stage **yourself from Nassau to Bottom Harbour, then jump off from Porgee Rocks.**

	WAYPOINT	LAT	LONG
1	Porgy Rocks Jump-off	2502.9	7712.4
2	Entrance to Allan's Cay	2444.8	7650.4
3	Clear the shoal SW of Allan's	2444.0	7651.5
4	Clear Norman's Spit	2435.7	7651.7
5	Round Elbow Cay Light	2431.0	7649.2
6	Clear Cistern Cay Spit	2425.5	7646.5
7	Clear Fowl Cay Spit	2415.8	7635.3
8	Round Twin Cays	2412.5	7630.5
9	Round Harvey Cay Light	2409.0	7629.3
10	Entrance to Channel from banks to Galliiot Cay	2355.3	7619.3

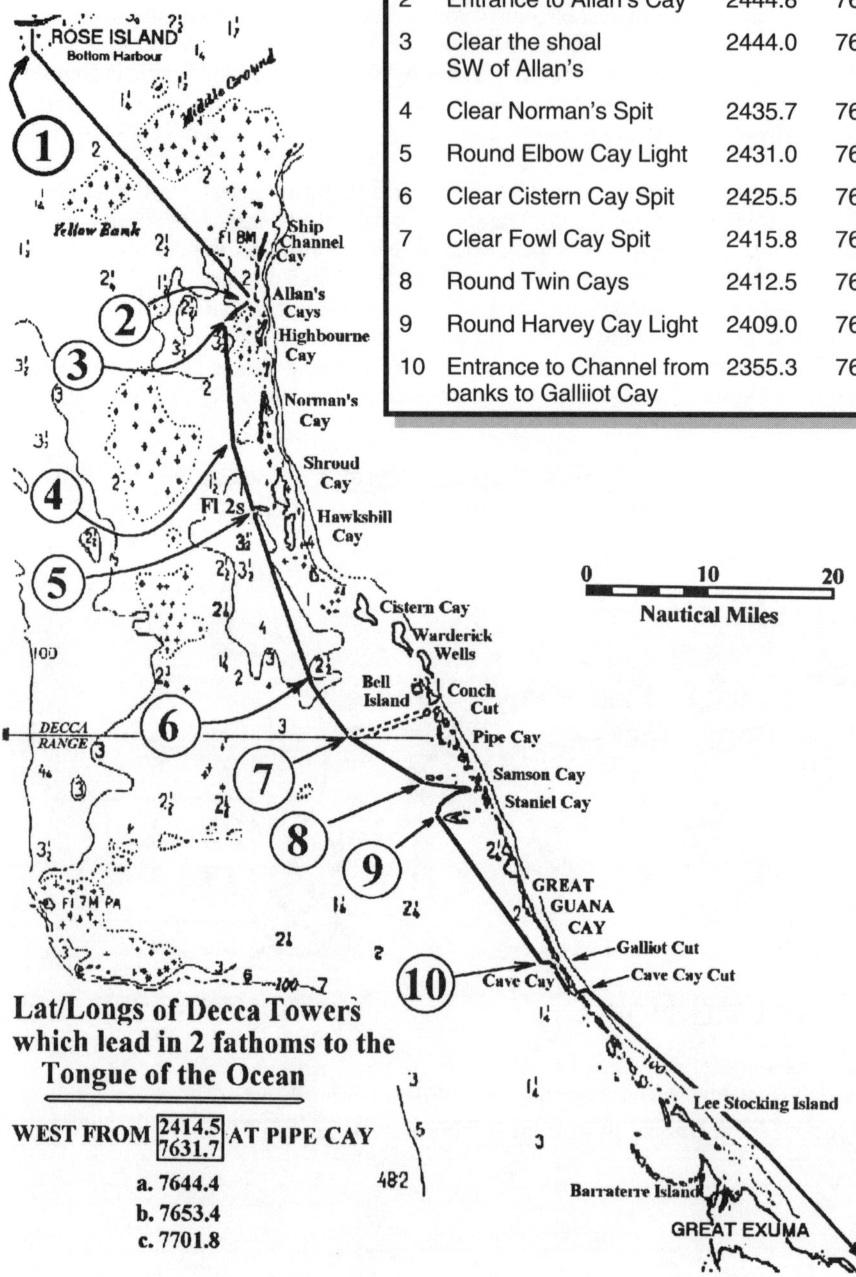

Lat/Longs of Decca Towers which lead in 2 fathoms to the Tongue of the Ocean

WEST FROM 2414.5 / 7631.7 AT PIPE CAY

a. 7644.4
b. 7653.4
c. 7701.8

Fast Path Down the Exumas: Take It Slow.

Allan's Cay Or Highbourne Cay

The anchorage at **Allan's Cay** is great for staying a day or two. The anchorage off the beach at the middle of **Highbourne Cay** is a good, calm waypoint if you want to make better time.

Sampson Cay

This is a good spot to get fuel and water, as well as being central to an abundance of little anchorages which are suitable for easy starts to **Cave Cay**.

Cave Cay

The entrance from the banks is 70° magnetic on the northwest tip of Little Galliot Cay, or 80° magnetic on the northwest tip of **Galliot Cay** for a draft of 7 feet during mid-tide neaps. When in deep water west of Galliot Cay, turn southeast to anchor behind Cave Cay. As almost always in the Bahamas, anchor in shallow water over deep sand with 2 anchors out, in this case, one toward weather threat and outgoing current, the west, and the other toward the incoming current, southeast. Set an anchor light. The mail boats have been known to take this pass at night.

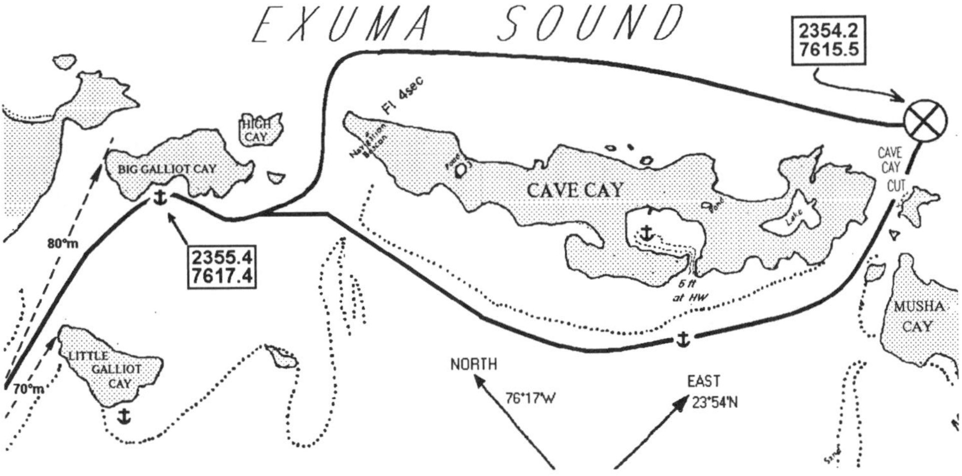

Exuma Banks to Exuma Sound via Galliot or Cave Cay Cuts

In the morning, charge out the deep **Cave Cay Cut**, favoring the north side, and sail off to **Georgetown** in a north of east wind of 15 knots. If you haven't got it, wait for it. Better yet, wait for a westerly and reach down to Georgetown in calm water.

Stay and fish awhile if it has been blowing hard east or northeast for several days. You don't want to enter the Georgetown cuts in what they call a **Rage**, where a combination of wave over swell can catch you wrong and broach you onto the reef inside the cut when you try to make the turn. Check out the underside of the fallen rocks on the south shore of **Little Galliot Cay** for yellowtail snapper, or try further south behind Musha Cay. The rocks on the south side of Cave Cay Cut (out of the current) also can be productive.

February through May, Georgetown is the terminus for the apprehensive who are going back home and for the adventurous who are striking out for the southern islands. Mid-March is the Georgetown **Cruising Regatta** started by then Georgetown dentist Joel Fine in 1981. This is an event put on by the cruisers themselves to raise funds for the **Family Island Regatta** in mid-April. It draws nearly 400 yachts, most of them at the end of their Bahamas cruise and at their southernmost harbor.

The Family Island Regatta is the America's Cup of all the races of classic Bahamian sloops, and is one of the few remaining old-time "Camptown Races" type of expositions in North America. **Salt Pond** has a similar, though smaller and, some think better, event, 6 weeks after Easter, the **Salt Pond Regatta**. Between all these events you have access to the miniature cruising ground of **Elizabeth Harbor** itself. You can sail over to **Conception Island** or **Rum Cay** or **Long Island** for a week's getaway from the partying at Georgetown.

You may, like myself, settle into a habit of Georgetown in the spring and Venezuela for the worst of the hurricane months. It is a wholly satisfying cruising life with lots of safe, short, *thornless* passages to keep crew and boat in condition, and with good provisioning at both ends (Dominican Republic and Puerto Rico being the northern end).

Georgetown earns the moniker of "Chicken Harbor" every season. Cruisers gab about stopping off at Conception on the way to Puerto Rico, or sailing to Rum Cay in one shot, as though they were just stopping by the convenience market before ramping up onto the interstate. Their biological clocks are still set on high from the hassle of getting the boat ready, from the bustle of provisioning, even from the social whirl among the yachts at Georgetown. One after another finds an excuse to return to Florida and "go south next year": a water-maker filter goes bad, an autopilot is on the fritz. The road south looms long and treacherous.

Most of those who do take the plunge and head out have their clocks cleaned quickly by the **Equatorial Current** and the incessant wind. They slow down to island time, and they begin to see the wisdom of this guide's constantly drummed advice: wait for weather, leave early, get in early, and never pass a safe anchorage. Hit all the stops on the way down. Some never get the message. They're the ones who write the whiny letters to the SSCA.

Georgetown abounds in fine anchorages, but unless you are in one of the holes in **Stocking Island** or in **Redshanks**, you will be moving from one to another in the winter months as fronts shift the winds. Redshanks, although remote and isolated, is only an 8-minute ride from town in a fast dinghy. To enter Redshanks with a 7-foot draft, run down the harbor on a line 126° magnetic on JR's house on **Man of War Cay**. This will carry you by the reef off **Sand Dollar Beach** anchorage and through the gap in the reef off the **Elizabeth Island a**nchorage.

The **Redshanks Yacht and Tennis Club** has a happy hour at its bar, located at the small beach near the bitter end of **Crab Cay** just at the head of the first anchorage. Non-members should get the Club Commodore's permission to enter. A lawn tennis facility is in the planning and may be available by the time this is published.

When abeam of the house on the middle of **Guana Cay**, turn onto 222° magnetic until you can distinguish a transit off the easternmost of the Redshanks and the bluff which bounds **Master Harbor** to the northeast. Keep these two features just kissing, neither open nor closed, and you will pass a large coral head to starboard which stands in the center of a 100-yard gap in the reef beyond.

Leave the last of the Redshanks 40 yards to starboard and steer to the bluff, rounding slowly to starboard so as to leave the bluff 100 yards to the southwest. Then steer west until you see the entrance to Redshanks anchorage and pick up the darker colors of the entrance channel's deeper water. Anchor southeast of a ridge-like shoal which runs the length of the harbor in a northeast line. Here deep draft vessels will find from 9-14 feet of water in coral sand. Enter 2 hours before high tide with drafts 6-7 feet.

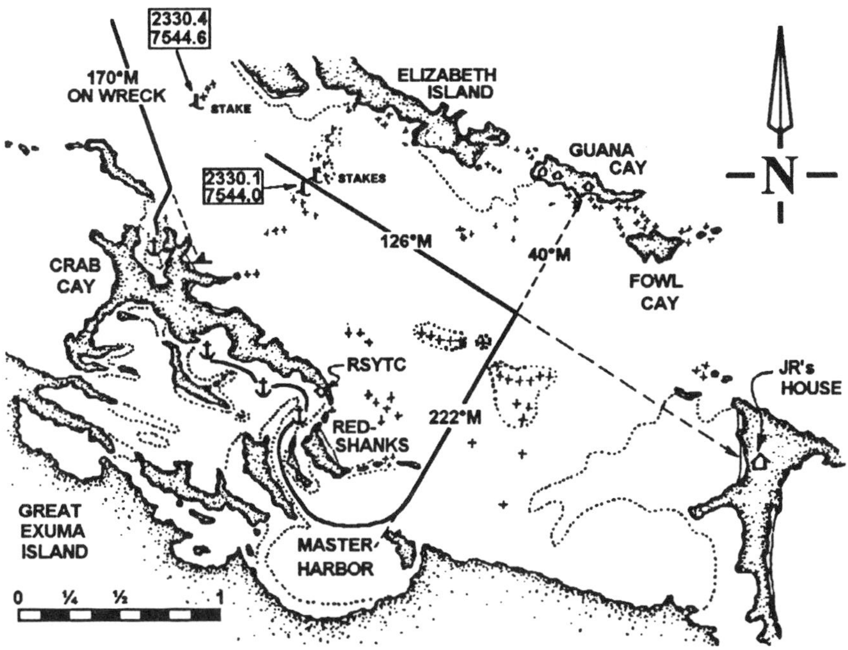

Georgetown Anchorage at Redshanks Yacht and Tennis Club

Drafts under 6 feet may round the northern extremity of the shoal close to **Crab Cay**. Vessels under 5 feet may try the anchorage even further to the east. The entrance is narrow and shallow, but there is reportedly up to 20 feet of water and the protection is extraordinary.

The leisure sailor following the Thornless Path may find it advisable to do **Long Island's** west coast, in order to get a leg up on the wind and the journey during the winter months. (See the example under Passage Elapse Times on page 28.) In any case, to leave Georgetown headed south you should position yourself at **Fowl Cay** first. Why? Review the section on Staging under Strategies for Passage Making.

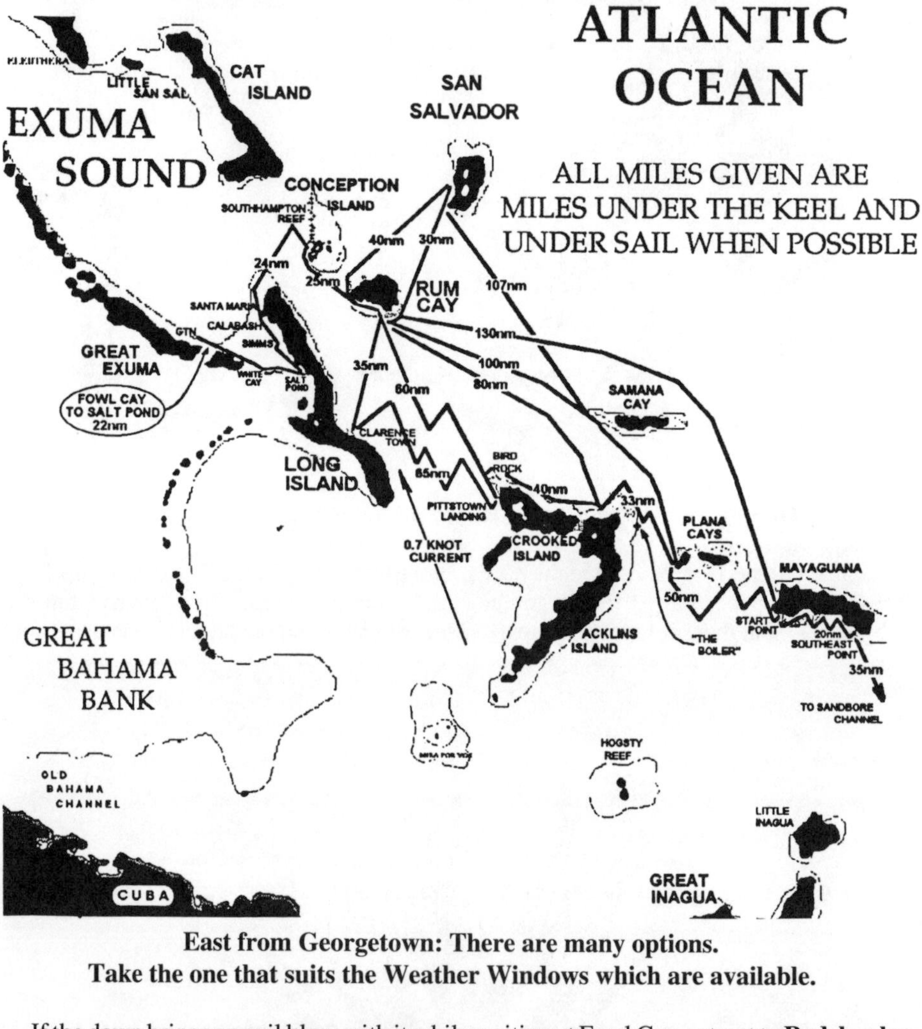

East from Georgetown: There are many options.
Take the one that suits the Weather Windows which are available.

If the dawn brings an evil blow with it while waiting at Fowl Cay, retreat to **Redshanks** for a day and attend the Redshanks Yacht and Tennis Club happy hour. Next evening wait back at Fowl Cay anchorage again.

A course of 35° magnetic through a point 30-50 yards from the last of the rocks which stretch northeast from Fowl Cay will carry you outside to **Exuma Sound**. The **North Channel Rocks** exit will be difficult in early morning light. If bound for **Calabash Bay** or **Cape Santa Maria**, take a course of 62° magnetic.

If going to **Salt Pond**, get well beyond the **Whelk Cay Reef** before turning to a course for **White Cay,** on the banks. The course to White Cay lies between **Black Rocks** and North

Channel Rocks. Watch set and leeway doesn't drift you onto Whelk Cay Reef as you round it going southeast.

If you are ready to leave **Georgetown,** yet the wind continues to blow briskly northeast, then don't hang around Georgetown gathering commitments. Take a sparkling sail over the banks to Salt Pond and say hello to John McKie *(Sunseeker)* in **Thompson's Bay**. John has helped countless boats along the *thorny* path over many years from his hilltop **BASRA** station and has detailed knowledge of the whole route.

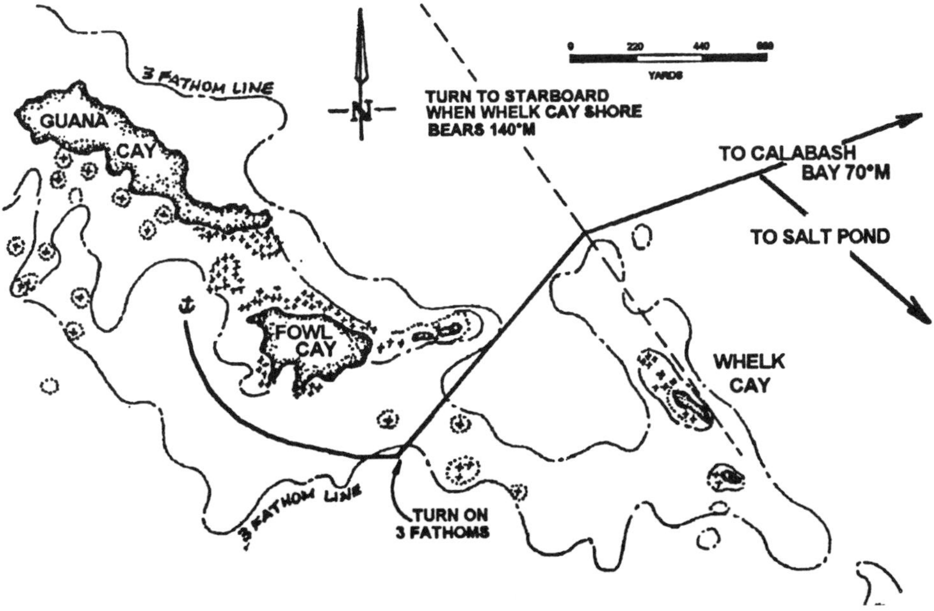

Fowl Cay Exit from Georgetown

The Fowl Cay exit from Elizabeth Harbour is a few miles nearer Cape Santa Maria **and has a better angle on the usual winds than the** Conch Cay Cut **exit. It also has a better angle on dawn light conditions than the North Channel Rocks exit. You may shorten a** Conception Island **landfall by several hours if you are already anchored at Fowl Cay at dawn rather than being in the middle of the harbor and taking Conch Cay Cut.**

Call Dorothy on the VHF *(Aquarius)* when you get to Salt Pond and order cracked conch dinner at Thompson's Bay Inn. Top up your water from the old plantation wells ashore.

The North Channel Rocks channel can be dangerous as it is directly against the light for anyone leaving Georgetown in the morning and directly up light for anyone entering in the evening. And those are usually the departure and arrival times of sailboats. The North Channel Rocks entrance is basically for power boats transiting in midday. The Fowl Cay entrance is never against the light, is short, and has landmarks close at hand with which to maintain a sure position while transiting.

Having positive, near-at-hand landmarks during piloting in dangerous cuts is of great importance. One season, we all listened to the breakup of a large and beautiful ferro cement yacht which, with two other yachts following her, wandered too far from the channel while going out the North Channel Rocks channel, against the light, early in the morning. There just isn't enough positive identification of whereabouts in that channel. It's all water that looks all the same, and a little drift you're not aware of can finish you.

If you leave from **Fowl Cay** around 7 a.m., you will have fair light south. By the time you have turned east along **White Cay** you will again have good light. Finally, the sun will be over your shoulder when making landfall at **Indian Hole Point**, the largest and darkest headland visible far to the south after passing White Cay. The tides on the banks between the **Exumas** and **Long Island** run east-west in the west and north-south in the east. Reckon on one knot at full ebb.

Trail a line for grouper and wigwag your way around the shoals between **Black Rocks** and **Forbes Hill**, dipping the lure onto them. To dip your lures onto heads and shoals, have about 80 yards of line out. Maneuver the boat, or use the wind to get the line over your target. Now put slack in the line by turning upwind or by putting the helm hard over in both directions several times to lose way. When the line drops almost to the bottom, fill sail and run away with the lure.

With practice you can dip and spiral a lure several times on one cluster of heads. The blue trench along the sandy bar east of White Cay has good trolling. Also, traveling the bar keeps you clear of the sand bores to the north. Round **Indian Hole Point** closely and proceed directly northeast to the **Thompson's Bay** anchorage.

Next day, sail north in the lee of **Long Island**, lunching with Mario at the Blue Chip in **Simms** and visit Mrs. Simm's for some stories of local history. From **Salt Pond** north to Simms, run point-to-point about 200 yards off each point. From Simms to **Calabash Bay** stand well off **Ferguson Point**, nearly a mile, and sail directly for **Dove Cay** until you can see the sandy bar west of it. A 50-foot-wide channel carrying 7 feet at low water will border the bar 280 yards west southwest of Dove Cay. Follow it 2 miles to deep water.

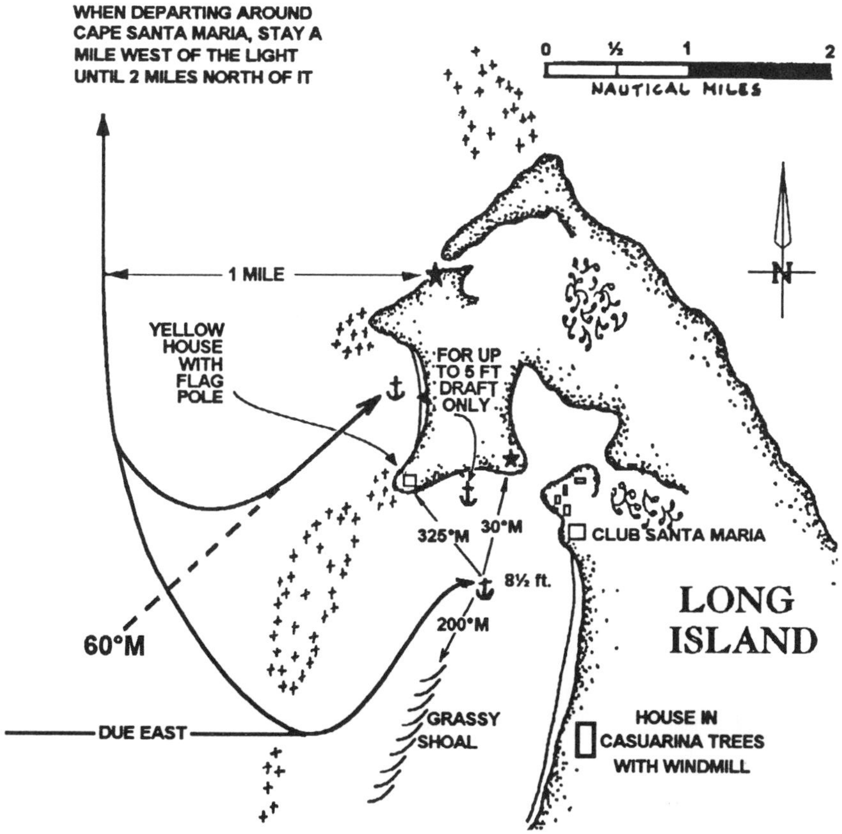

Calabash Bay and Santa Maria Anchorages

When you've left the banks and are in blue water making for **Calabash Bay**, trail and dip your lures over the deep heads a mile southwest of the anchorage before turning through the reef for the night. Calabash can be rolly in winds north of east or if there are large northeast swells forecast for the area. East or south of east it is a fine, smooth anchorage. If it looks like the northeast wind is about to go east, tuck in under **Cape Santa Maria** for an early takeoff to **Conception Island**, or fish the point in the morning and go in the afternoon. It's a short and easy sail.

After entering Calabash Bay through the reef, continue east to a grassy shoal which stretches blackly north and south in front of you. Turn to the lighthouse built at the west side of the inner basin entrance, turning in toward the houses slightly to a point which bears 325° magnetic to the point of land to the west, 030° to the lighthouse and 200° to the point of land to the south. There's 8½ feet here. Get out of Calabash if it blows anything but easterly. The chop and swell can be ferocious and will slam you on the bottom.

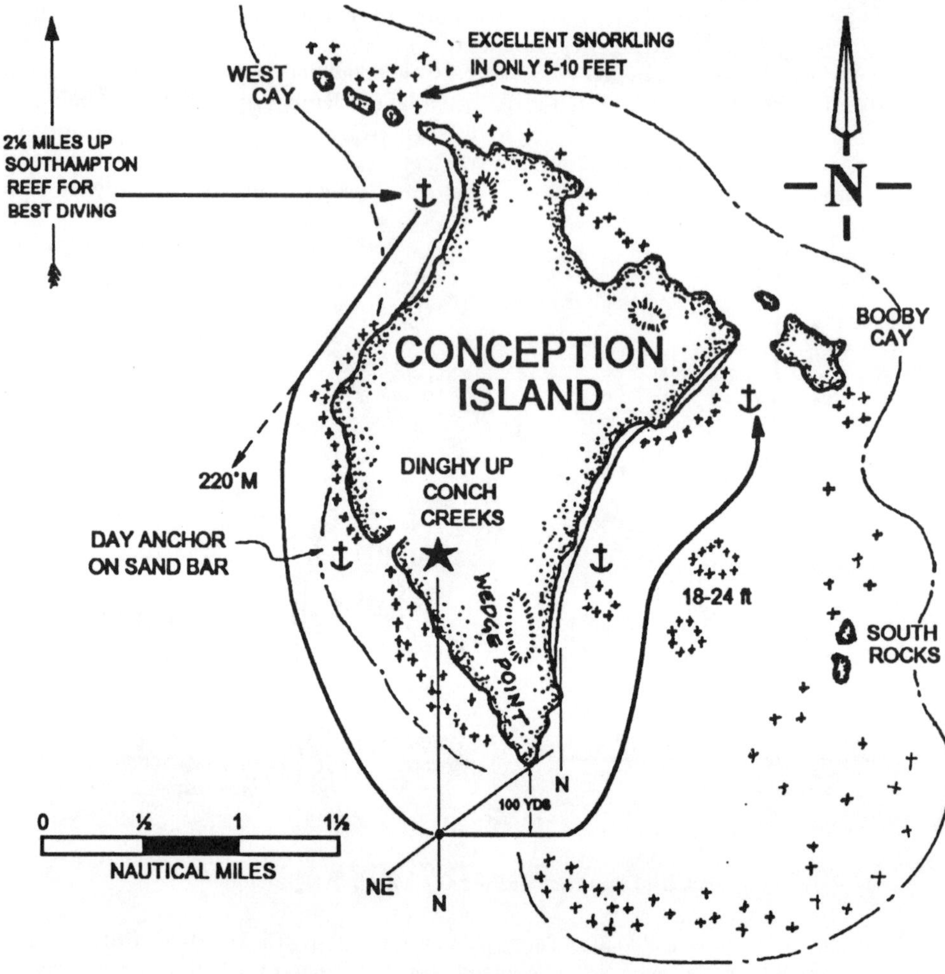

Conception Island: Use the east anchorage in a westerly.

If you have easterlies of Force 3 or less, make your landfall at **Conception Island** on **Southampton Reef**, anchoring in 20 feet of rock and sand around 2¼ miles north of **West Cay**. Dinghy over the reef for some of the most spectacular reef and wreck snorkeling available in the Bahamas, second only to **Rum Cay**. There are several square miles of reef diving here. With heads towering over 20 feet over white sand bottom, you'll feel like Superman flying between the skyscrapers of Gotham City. The bad guys on the streets below are 10-20 pound groupers, snapper and 5-10 pound lobsters.

Look long enough and you'll spot relics of the old wooden shipwrecks on this three-mile reef which is invisible from windward. Conception is now part of the Exuma land/sea park whose rules for taking of shells and wildlife are quite stringent. Hone up on actual enforcement policies at the time of your visit. You neither want to despoil this island and reef, prettiest of all the Bahamas, nor do you want to limit your enjoyment of it based on rumored restrictions or out-of-date publications.

Conception Island is the loveliest of islands in the Bahamas, bar none. Unfortunately, I meet folks every year who, having left **Georgetown**, feel they are now *en marche* and zip right by Conception, or use it only as a waypoint. In such a hurry to get to paradise, they rush right by, never knowing they were there.

Following the advice above, you can stay at Conception indefinitely, fronts and all, until a **Weather Window** opens which gives you a lay on **Rum Cay** or **San Salvador** as a Leisure Sail. Dinghy around the rocks to the shoal pocket east of **West Cay** and north of Conception. The snorkeling is absolutely outstanding, and this extensive area of sand and coral is shallow and safe for even non-swimmers in tubes. If you're not up to diving with the pros way out on **Southampton Reef**, don't miss this snorkeling kiddy park.

Other guides notwithstanding, the eastern anchorage has 18-24 feet of deep sand bottom and is an excellent refuge in westerlies. Coral shoals are few and easily seen. Anchor in the corner between **Booby Cay** and Conception. You can move from the northwest anchorage to the east anchorage and back during passage of a **front**, staying at Conception as long as you like. Enter the east anchorage from south of the light and southwest of **Wedge Point**, proceeding due east, 80-120 yards off the Point, and until the north-south line of beach is visible on the eastern shore. Proceed by eye even to the top of the harbor if you wish.

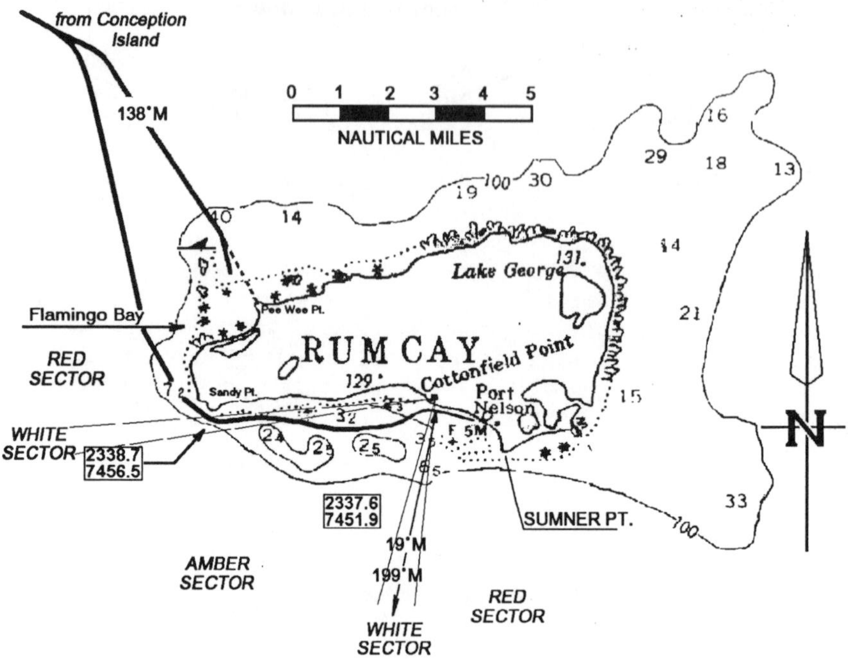

Rum Cay: Best Spot to Wait for a Front

Rum Cay is the best spot, all around, to **Wait for Weather** east of Georgetown—if you're well tucked in. It has the finest snorkeling, fishing and diving you can expect, a friendly little community of under a hundred souls, and good local restaurants and bars. It can roll a little unless you are well sheltered by **Point Sumner**. When *Jalan* tucks in with her 6½-foot draft she doesn't roll (see anchorages on chartlet). You can always jibsail over to the west coast beach or beautiful **Flamingo Bay** if your **wait for weather** becomes extended.

First time entrances here should be made from the south with high sun, or from the west with afternoon sun. For the experienced, a light with 8° white sectors on safe entrance is atop **Cottonfield Point**. Red sectors designate dangerous reefs while an amber sector covers an area with many coral heads. Upon approaching the Cottonfield Point take up a 110° Magnetic heading on a solitary house overlooking the marina between the town dock and **Sumner Point**. When the **Dive Club's** main house bears 15° Magnetic turn to it and proceed to a clear white sand anchorage in 8-10 feet. A larger anchorage, but slightly less sheltered by the points, can be had by continuing several hundred yards on the 110° course instead of turning toward the club. For longer stays, a hole of 10 feet can be found nearer the beach for a good sized sailboat by holding the 110° course even further.

Flamingo Bay on the northwest corner of the island is a beautiful anchorage in easterlies but a death trap in west and north winds. If you wait there, get out well in advance of any front. To enter **Flamingo Bay**, enter at 138° magnetic on **Pee Wee Point**, which appears from sea like a rock island, leaving the wreck at the tip of the northwest reef one-half mile to starboard. Once inside the bay, pick your way through the heads which only become numerous shoreward of a line between the points.

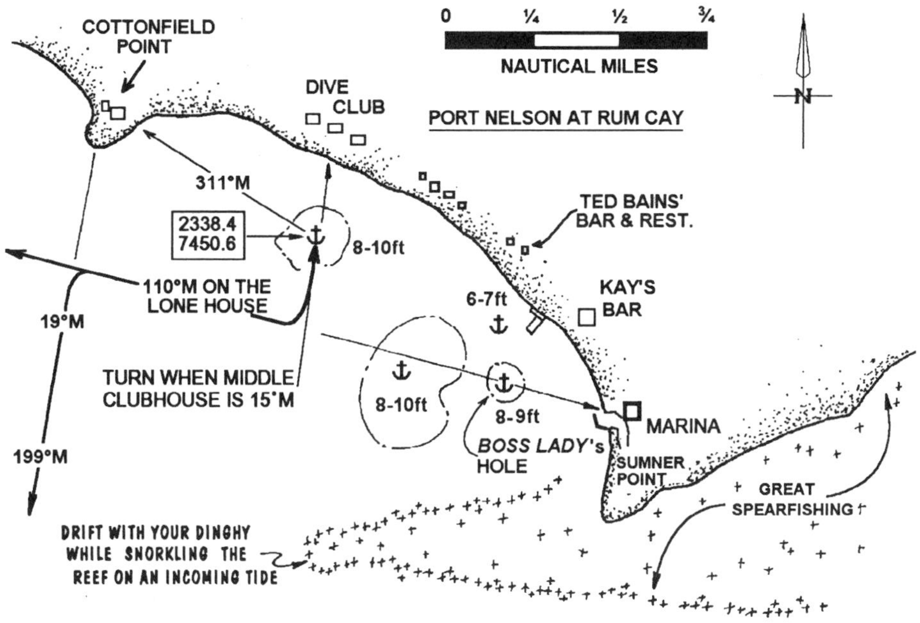

Anchorages at Rum Cay

The wreck northwest of the entrance to Flamingo Bay is a Haitian vessel which was delivering a load of Salvation Army clothes to Haiti. It's reported that the skipper ordered the Dominican helmsman to turn left to avoid the reef, which he did. Since the order wasn't countermanded, the helmsman held it left in a broad, circling sweep that ended back where he started but slightly south—where it is today. One used to be able to renew one's cruising wardrobe here, and it wasn't too shabby. Visiting the wreck may help you understand **Haiti** better before you actually go there. Thinking how it supposedly got up on the reef in the first place may enhance your enjoyment of the **Dominican Republic**: If you can empathize with the helmsman's "*no problema*" mentality, you'll *love* the DR.

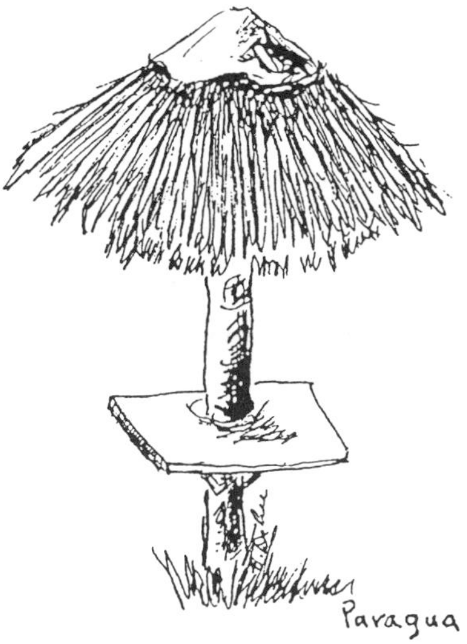

From **Rum Cay** you can strike various routes south. Bearing with the strategy to "Keep north to go south," however, it's best to try to make **Mayaguana** [*my-GUAH-nah*] direct with a **front** in winter, or **Attwood Harbor,** or **Plana Cays,** in light airs in summer (Force 4 or less).

A detour to **Clarence Town** or **Landrail Point** (same as **Pittstown Landing**, or **Portland Harbor**) may be in order. Once on **Crooked Island**, however, a day's motoring to Attwood is almost inevitable and you may stand in technical violation of the tenets of the Leisure Sailor. Review again: "Keep north to go south."

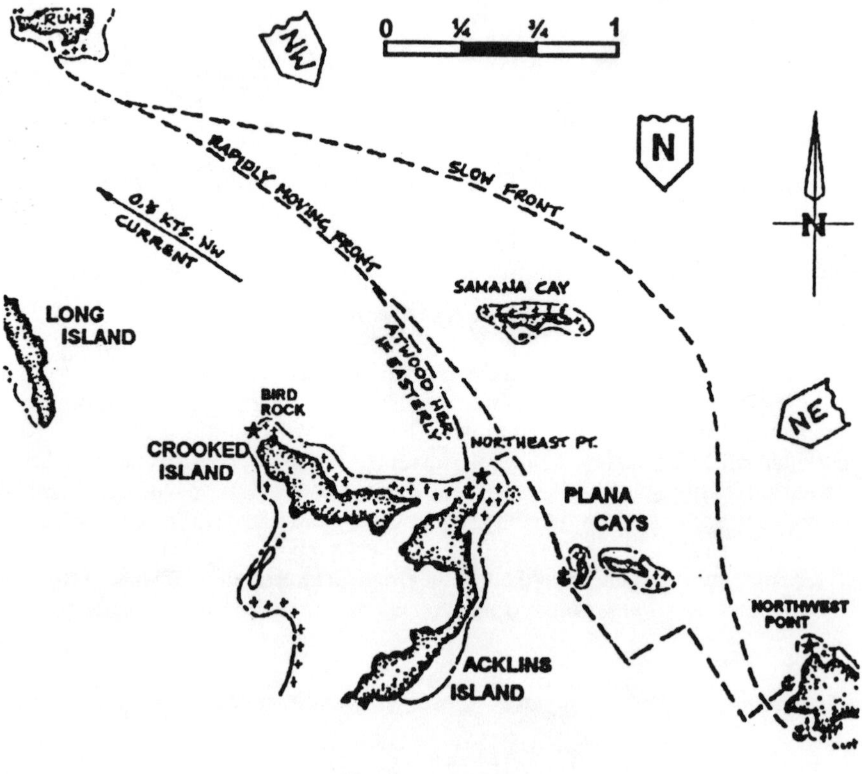

Riding a Front South

In following a front down to Mayaguana from Rum Cay, take off on the first breath of a southerly wind. By the time you are on a longitude with **Samana Cay** [*suh-MA-nuh,* not *sah-mah-NAH,* in the D.R.] you will be broad reaching north of the Plana Cays and can reach down the **Mayaguana Passage**, rounding up into **Start Bay** or **Betsy Bay.**

Later in the season, with the more rapid veering of the **front**al winds, you might not be able to turn the corner down the **Mayaguana Passage** before the wind goes east. In that case stop at **West Plana Cay**.

Once, when I approached **Samana Cay** from the south, conditions were just right to provide us with a mirror image of the island, in color, on the bottoms of the clouds of the coastal front above the island. It began, what for me was a series of discovery trips to this nearly unapproachable isolated jewel. If you want to know all about Samana Cay, read the November 1986 issue of the *National Geographic* (Vol.170, No.5). It is an intriguing piece which proposes Samana as the real landing site of **Columbus** in the new world.

Even in Columbus's day, Samana Cay was a site of temporary fishing camps where the **Arawak** inhabitants of **Acklins Island** to the south, could get away for awhile (for not always innocent reasons). They would hang out at Samana Cay, drying conch, crabbing and fishing until things cooled off at home and they could return to their settlements — or, as today, make a high speed outboard run over for cigarettes.

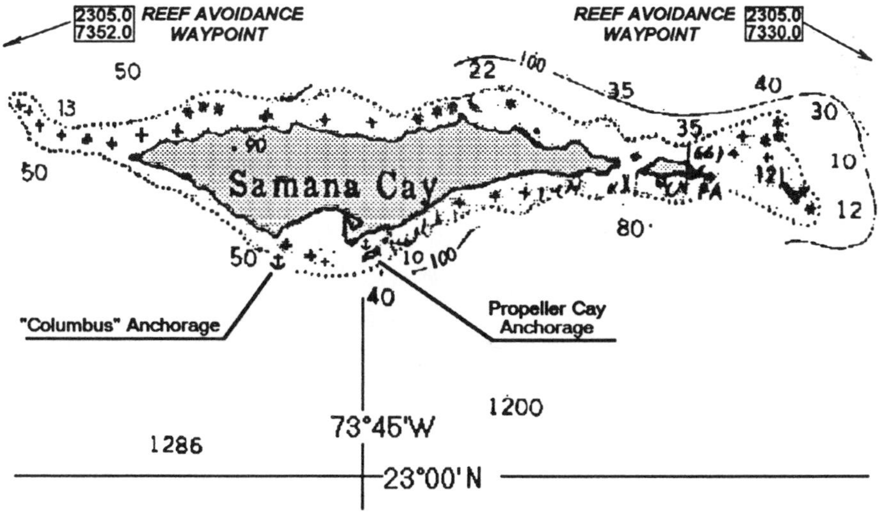

Samana Cay: Columbus's Landfall?

Anchor well tucked in at the supposed Columbus anchorage on the southwest and dinghy in. This is a very choppy anchorage on sand over rock. Have two anchors down and dive on them for inspection. If your draft is less than 5 feet, you might make it into the bay where the fishing camps are. Lead yourself in with the dinghy, however, and keep a kedge ready!

The holding is good. The 45-foot steel ketch *Stealaway* weathered a direct hit by Hurricane Klaus behind Propeller Cay, in deep sand, but surrounded by perilous rock. If you take this anchorage, enter in light wind only so there's little chop (Force 3) and in good light (10 a.m. to 2 p.m., sunny). Stay on the white sand, 15-foot-wide, 8-foot-deep, zigzag channel. The current runs east and west, *across* the channel.

SAMANA CAY

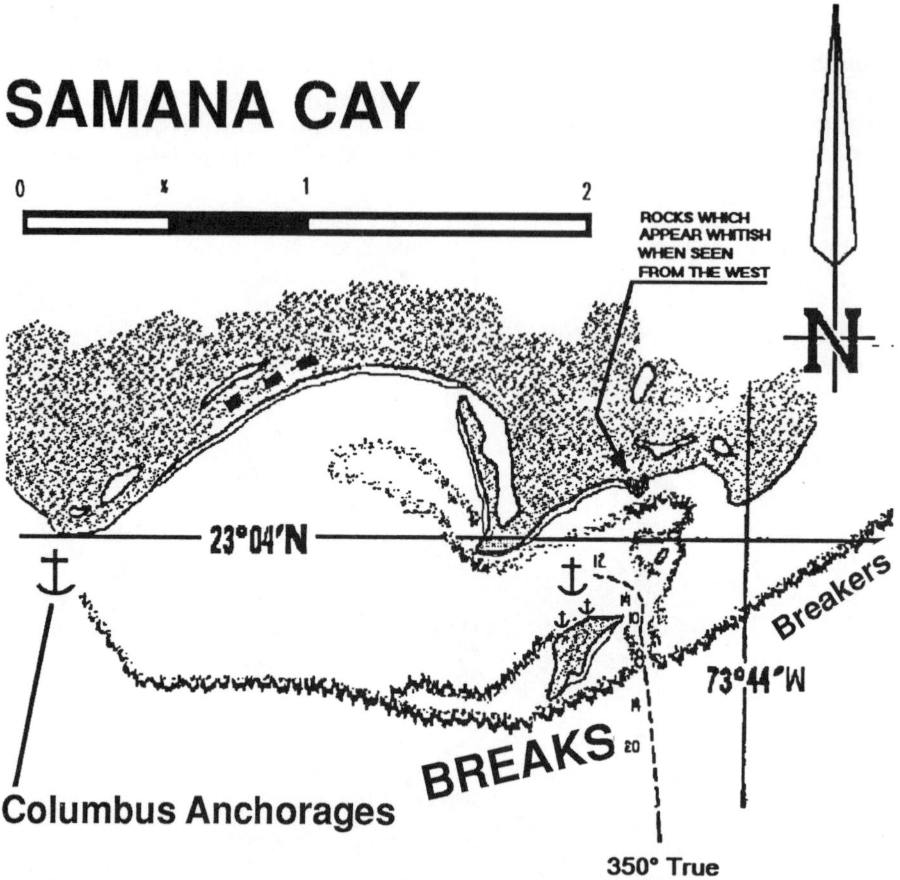

Anchorage at Propeller Cay, Samana Cay

To use this anchorage, you should do the following:

1. **Anchor off the entrance in Force 2 or below.**
   Otherwise take the **Columbus** anchorage and dinghy up to Propeller Cay.
2. **Swim the entire entrance channel underwater.**
   You may think it's sufficient to snorkel on the surface. The bottom is strewn rock and sand, making it difficult to distinguish the slightly deeper path of the channel.
3. **Buoy the channel before entering.**
   Plan your visit to Samana Cay well ahead and take 50-60 feet of polypropylene line and 4 or 5 floats. Secure the lines to rocks on either side of the channel in such a manner that they can be yanked free upon your departure.
   You might think, *at your peril*, that remnants of buoys already there are sufficient. Don't be foolish. Dive on them and reposition them or add to them as necessary.
4. **Take your buoys with you when you go.**
   Unless you put down stormproof buoys under permit from the Bahamian Government, don't think you're doing other yachtsmen, or the environment, any favors by leaving your flotsam behind you.

Sometimes a fast moving **front** will outrun you and the winds are too far east to continue on comfortably. In that case, head for **West Plana Cay**. An alternate harbor for longer waits is **Attwood Harbor** downwind, but that is not a good spot in northeast wind and a *deathtrap* in anything more northerly. The anchorage at Plana can roll a bit in southeasterlies but it is snug enough in stiff east and northeast blows.

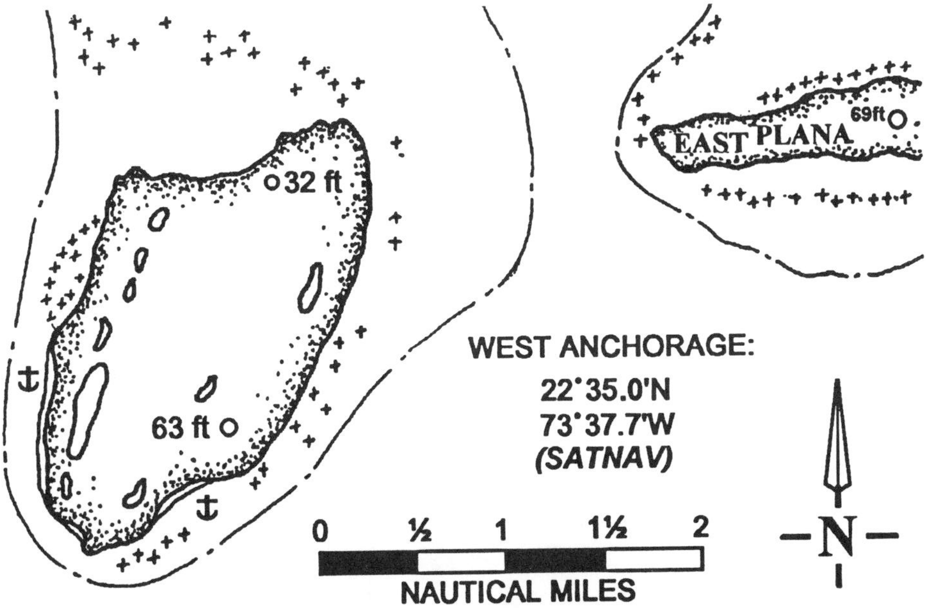

West Plana Cay Anchorage

Proceed due east to a point in the middle of the beach; the spot was once marked by 3 small palms planted by John McKie, though the plethora of Spanish bayonet and scrub will make them hard to distinguish if they're still there. There are many classic coral heads off the beach at Plana, widely separated and each hosting lively ecological communities of critters. Review the sketch on page 16 in Don't Be Afraid of Open Anchorages.

As you coast through the deep water up to the beach, keep a judicious eye on the heads which are clearly visible and deep enough. You want one not too deep and big enough to support a dinner-sized grouper, and, if in season, a lobster for appetizer. When you've chosen your head, anchor for the night about 150 feet dead to windward of it.

After the boat is snug for the night, let out enough scope to bring the bathing ladder over the coral head. While the mate sets out the **SG&Ts**, the skipper can harvest a bountiful dinner from the holes at the bottoms of these beauties.

If forced to wait a while at Plana, don't despair. The beachcombing on the windward shore is as good as at **Big Sand Cay** and there is good diving and fishing by dinghy, or off the beach on the north end of the island. It is possible to take your boat between the islands since there is almost an ocean passage there. You will be in basically uncharted waters, however, so, as with your first trip to **Samana Cay**, unless you're an old Bahamas hand, save the adventure for the dead calm days which occur once or twice a year.

When the wind moderates, take a sparkling and sporty ocean daysail over to **Betsy Bay** for a good lee over grouper rocks and a tour of the small and friendly village there. If you're lucky the wind will stay east or slightly north of east but still moderate. You can then sail directly to **Start Bay** or **Abraham's Bay** if you care to visit there, but don't waste a moderate east northeast. It won't last long.

As you round **West Plana Cay** on the south, the swells can be intimidating as the west northwest-going deep ocean current will be spoiling on the Plana shelf. But once out and away this is a delightful day-sail in clear weather and under Force 4 conditions.

MAYAGUANA TO CAICOS

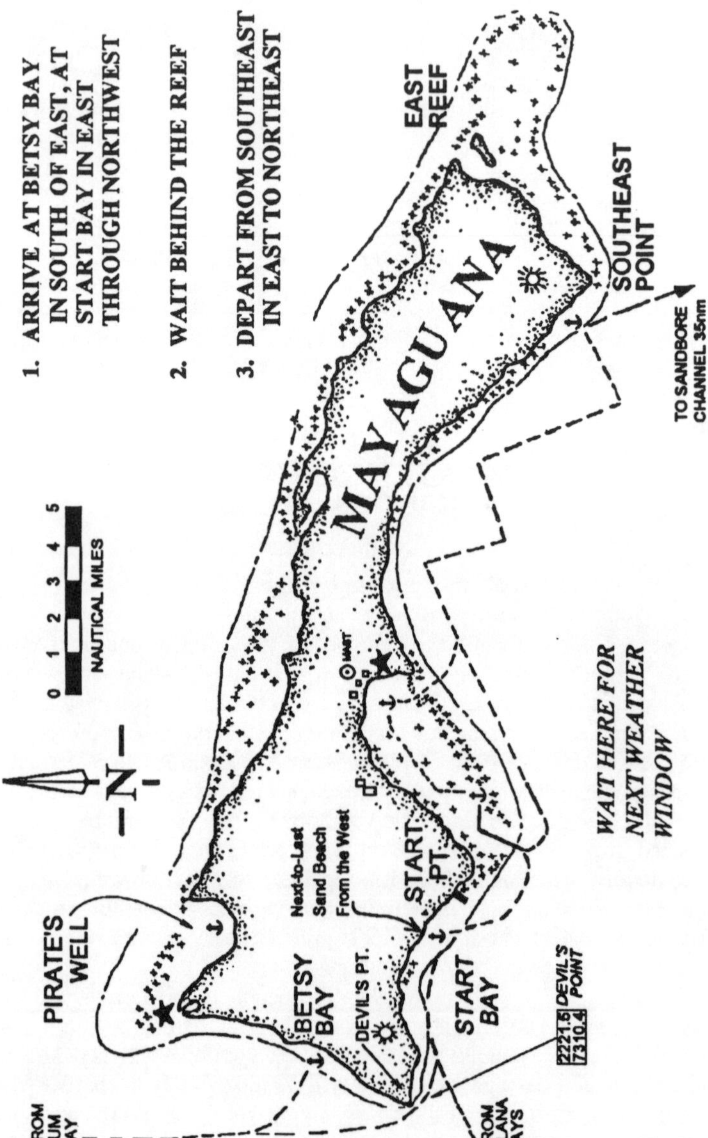

Anchorages at Mayaguana

When rounding Devil's Point, also known as Southwest Point, take it very close (40 yards) or the current may whip you out to sea again, and it's a long tacking process around it.

Betsy Bay is your anchorage in southeast wind, **Start Bay** in east to northwest winds. Both anchorages are good for bottom- or spear-fishing. If lucky, you can take northeast winds or westerlies directly to **Caicos** from your anchorage on the west end of **Mayaguana**. If you are faced with prevailing wind directions, however, you should start your way south from **Southeast Point**, even if you are in **Abraham Bay**.

All anchorages except **Pirate's Well** in southeasterlies, will roll as, indeed, will most anchorages in the **Far Out Islands.** If only overnighting, the anchorage at **Start Bay** is easily made and easily left. If the next day you decide to stay a while, move into **Abraham Bay** via the west entrance. Be careful to enter only in high afternoon light and beware of the shoals and coral extending more than a mile south of **Start Point**.

Proceed northeast through the blue water channel for ¼ mile beyond the reef entrance, then one mile east to a position 200 yards behind the protection of the reef in 2 fathoms of water. To avoid all chop, you must snug up to the reef. That also makes it easy to go snorkeling and diving. If you wish to visit the settlement, you can take up to a 7-foot draft up the bay on a rising tide. From the anchorage behind the reef, steer for the buildings to the north 3/4 mile, then for the settlement's radio mast, avoiding apparent heads and rocks.

Mayaguana is easy to leave if you're in **Start Bay**. Commit to go only in settled weather (defined to be when the **NWS Offshore Report** says "Today, tonight *and tomorrow...*"). When the winds have turned light easterly or north of east, take an afternoon sail over to **Southeast Point**. Arrive well before 5 p.m. in order to select a patch of deep sand in 12-20 feet at which to temporarily anchor. Do not snug up to the reef and coral heads to avoid the roll. Have your SG&T, read a little and catch a nap after dinner. Up anchor late evening to early morning, depending on conditions and your estimated time to make the 35 miles to the **Sandbore Channel** entrance to the **Caicos Banks**.

DMA charts and some guide editions to the contrary, the wreck of a freighter, which is really grounded high on the reef at the entrance to the **Sandbore Channel**, is about 2 miles east-northeast from the southwest corner of the reef bordering the north edge of the channel. Sail to the freighter in early morning light until you see the atoll-like reef with breaking seas dividing ocean blue from bright shoal green. Follow the reef south until you come to the half-mile broad ocean blue waters of the Sandbore Channel entrance. Can't miss it! Arrive early morning while the wind over 60 miles of banks to the east is still light.

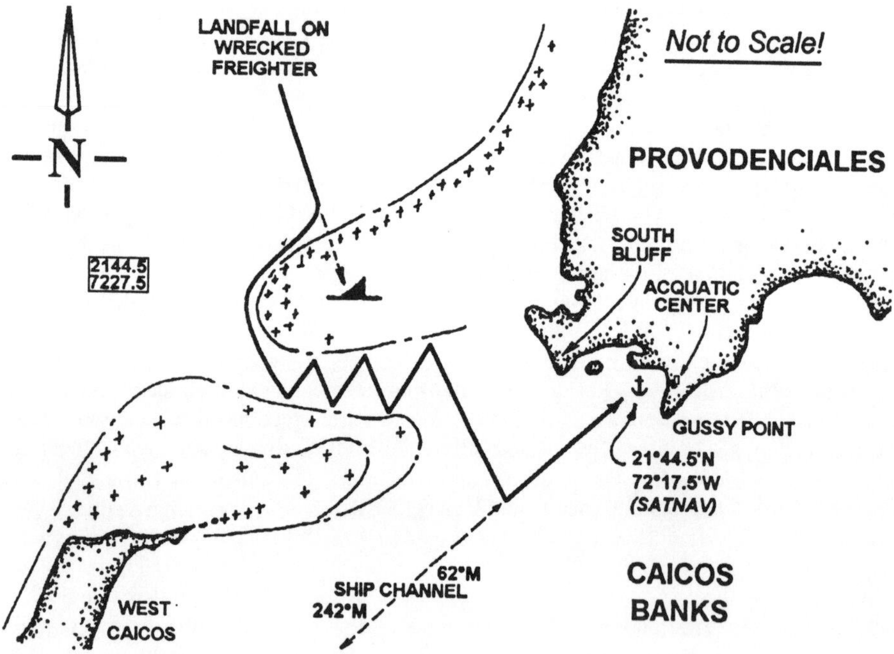

Sandbore Channel Entrance to Caicos Banks

Motoring or sailing, tack the 8 or 10 miles to the ship channel and enter **Sapodilla Bay**. You will meet supposed *cognizenti,* local and cruisers, who scoff at tacking the Sandbore in morning light. I've done this entrance many times. Nonetheless, I continue to take these precautions.

Why tack this channel even if you are motoring? The sun is ahead of you, but each tack permits good up-light visibility either side of the sun. Once on the banks, there are few real heads, but there are shoals of veggies and a few rocks, most of which are covered by 8-10 feet of water. Dodge them anyway for the sake of the odd rock which might be sticking up above the others, or the odd recently sunk skiff. Tacking slightly while motorsailing, you can also keep a watch over your shoulder to follow the trending of the shoals and extrapolate them eastward.

It looks scarier than it really is, but the above precautions can avoid mishap. Let the experts talk. I zigzag a morning up-light course over *any* shallows, *anywhere*. More fool you, if you don't, too. With or without tacks, the beat up to the anchorage could take several hours, so arrive early—*never* in the afternoon.

Sapodilla Bay

Cruisers on a budget can pass up **Turtle Cove** on the north coast of **Providenciales** ("**Provo**") and clear in at the Provo **Aquatic Center**, where you can sit over a cold beer while awaiting customs and immigration in comfort. Clearing yourself can lead to expensive hassles. The club is off and on again, open and closed under different owners. Officials will come down and clear you in, however. Call HARBORMASTER on VHF Channel 16.

Besides clearing in and out, the Aquatic Center can also help you with finding stuff in town. But be prepared for prices worse than Georgetown in the local stores. If you didn't get enough cash in Georgetown, there's a Barclay's here. And, believe it, you will need cash if you stay long in Provo.

Also, if you are planning to provision in **Puerto Plata, Santiago,** or **Luperón**, it is probably cheaper to get your cash here in Provo. The D.R. banks may charge a percentage fee on Visa. A visit to the **Conch Farm** at **Leeward Going Through** is well worthwhile.

Have your anchors well down. Holding's fair to good, but the occasional summer squall or winter front can have leading edges of up to 50 knots from the west. Otherwise this is usually a very good anchorage.

If bound for **Cap Haïtien or Manzanillo**, you might leave through the Provo ship channel and *stage* yourself the night before off **West Caicos**'s western shore for a 2-3 hours shorter passage. There are buoys there for the dive boats that are normally not used at night. Remember that hours cut from the beginning of a passage really come off the end.

Plan to be about 20 miles offshore of 'Cap' around 4 a.m. Any uncertainties of landfall will be made up for by the loom of the city in the predawn hours. Refer to the directions for sailing from **Big Sand Cay** to Puerto Plata or **Manzanillo**, and to the sections on Approaching Hispaniola, Manzanillo and Cap Haïtien for sailing directions.

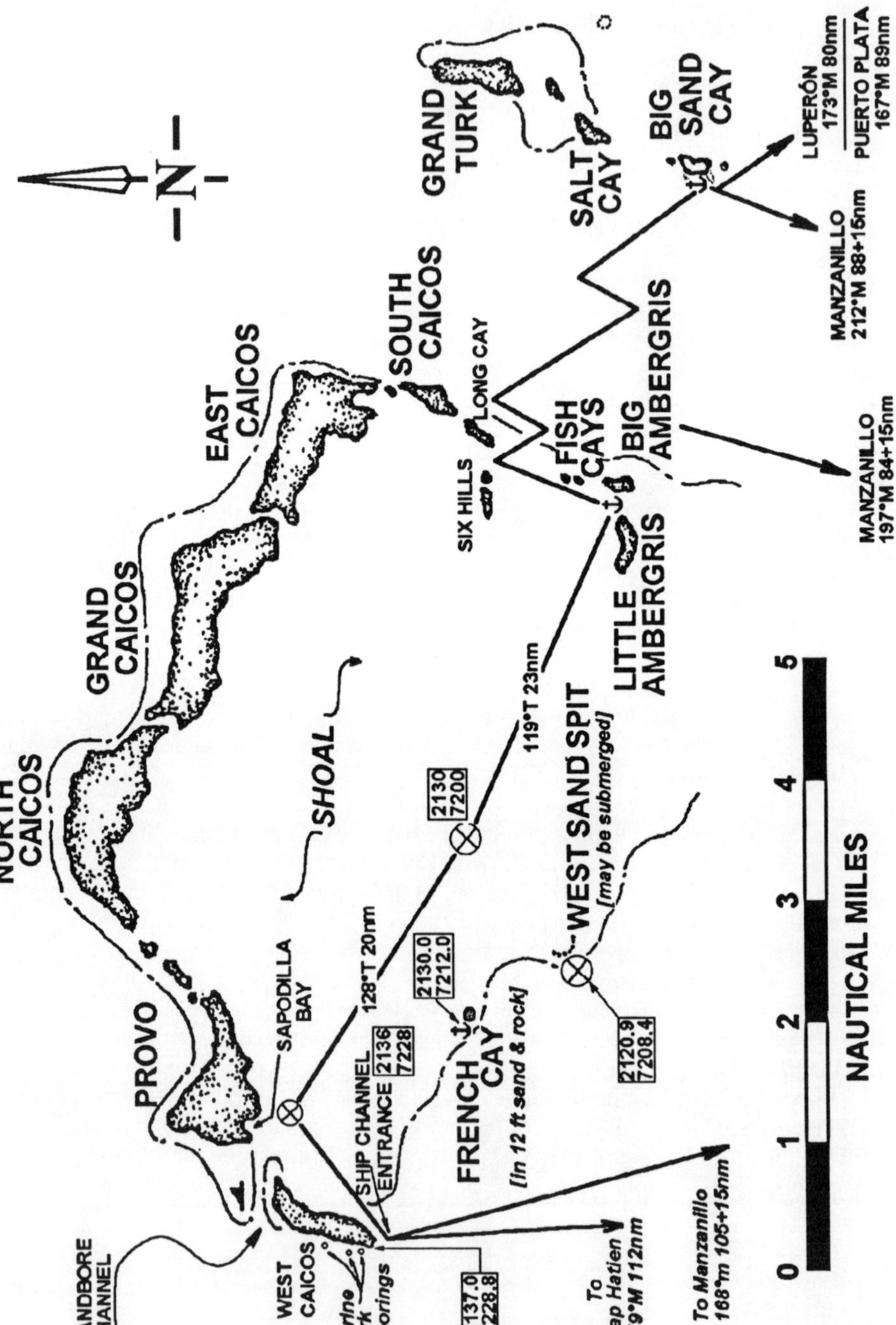

Crossing Caicos Banks

Over the Banks

From time to time there are reports of the central shoaly area having 'gone away.' These are probably started by cruisers who went more north than they intended, and having been lucky in their trip through the maze, they assume the shoals are overrated. From time to time you will hear cruisers give clever "new" routes to "safely" bypass the shoals. If they haven't sailed over their route at least a dozen times (ask them how many they have), ignore them. The route in this guide is chosen for easy-to-remember coordinates, for safety of the vessel without GPS, or with a frail engine in severe cross-tidal currents, and because it is tried and true. Other routes may save you a half-mile. You might do them safely a dozen times. Then again, maybe you'll hit the odd lump on the first try. Play it right. Play it safe.

Ignore recurrent rumors that the Banks' central shoal has "gone away."

Once, as an experiment, I took *Jalan Jalan* at 6½ foot draft across the banks to **Six Hills**, going *north* of the central shoals. I don't advise it, unless you draw less than 5 feet. Even so, it's like threading a maze and you most definitely will be caught out unless you're lucky or it's dead calm.

The slightly higher than the rest bulge in the middle of the northern half of the Banks has been there since, according to one theory, a northeast-going space rock slammed into it, forming the Turks & Caicos, zillions of years ago. I don't think it will go away so easily.

Though you may not think so, the **Caicos Banks** are on the **Thornless Path**. That is, it is easier to cross them than to go around them. Leave **Sapodilla Bay** at dawn on a day when the wind is north of east or else *under 15 knots for certain.* To clear out early you may be asked to pay overtime charges, even if the papers are done the day before during office hours. Pay it and go at daybreak. Don't delay departure. You don't want to be caught out on the banks. Leave Sapodilla Bay at *daybreak.*

Cross the banks with a 7-foot draft from a point 2 miles south of **Gussy Point**, proceeding along 128° true for 20 miles to a point 72°00'W, 21°30'N. Then motor lickety-damn in deeper water the 23 miles to **Ambergris** at 119° true.

Leave at dawn to arrive well before sundown. Reckon on a 1.2-knot northeast tide set at peak flood (northwest near the Ambergris islands) and use the **Rule of Twelfths** to interpolate your drift (see Glossary). Satnav may not help you here if there are no fixes for a while, and, of course, Loran is lousy this far from the U.S. So unless you have a GPS and full coverage, keep a good DR!

Even though the coral heads are far and few between, it doesn't pay to be complacent on this run either. Sailboats have been known to graze a coral head while in over 20 feet of water. So, with the Caicos Banks, as with the rice pudding in the school cafeteria, it's always best to avoid the dark spots.

If you have to anchor on the banks, do so at the risk of bending your anchor shanks, as I have done, while getting them up in a stiff chop the next morning. Best to start out at *daybreak.* But never, *never* proceed after sundown. How can you, anyway? You've got to have your **SG&T** to stay on the Thornless Path.

The round-the-world cruise for a family of four nearly ended here scarcely before it began. They rammed a rock just at sundown trying to make the anchorage at **Ambergris** before dark. So start out early and "arrive by 5" at Ambergris and anchor where shown, *not* near the land.

This anchorage looks too wide open, but it is good in most conditions and provides bountiful fishing. Anchor in 8 feet of water half way between the islands, one mile east of **Little Ambergris** and one mile west-southwest of some fishermen's shacks on **Big Ambergris**.

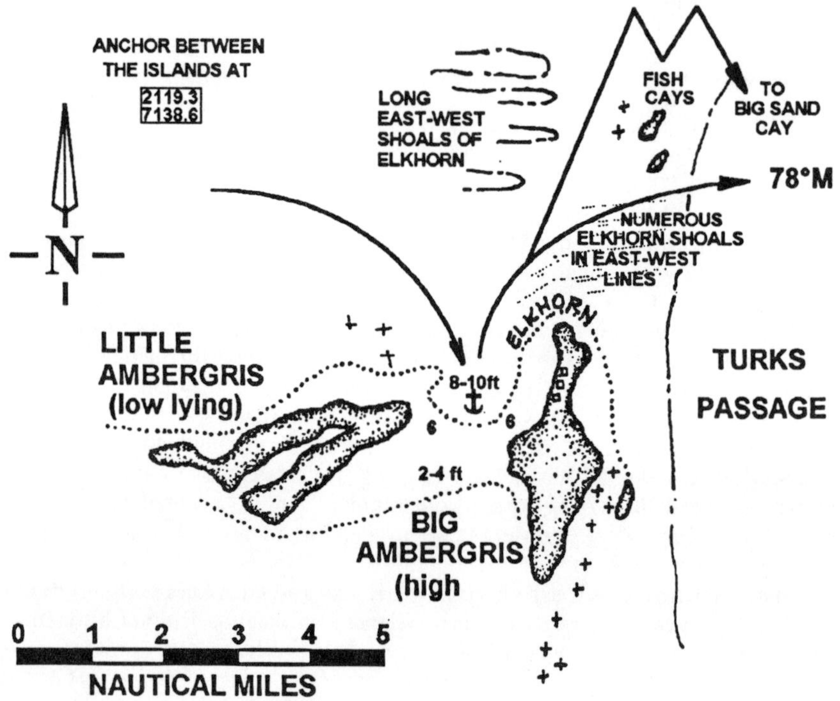

Ambergris Transient Anchorage

One cruiser accosted me down islands with a harrowing tale of how he spent the night in 4-foot seas amidst hull-tearing elkhorn coral. He thought this guide irresponsible for recommending Ambergris. When asked if he stayed at the anchorage recommended above, he replied, "No, we couldn't find it because it was getting dark and we had to anchor." So, as the night followed Polonius's day, I asked:

"What time did you leave Sapodilla Bay?"

"About 8:30 or 9:00."

"What were the winds like?"

"Oh, southeast, 15 to 20."

"Couldn't you leave earlier, say, *daybreak*?"

"Well, we were with some other boats."

"Couldn't you wait for a better Window, say, 15 knots east?"

"We really needed to get going. We'd spent too much time in the Bahamas, and we needed to get to the Virgins to earn some money."

Four violations! He didn't leave at daybreak. He left in a southeast Force 5 on the nose. He didn't captain his own boat. And he was in a hurry... The penalty almost came to fit the crime, but the perpetrator still saw himself as victim.

There are large fields of elkhorn and other coral in this area, and you need good afternoon light (before 5 p.m.) to identify them. The way into the anchorage from the Banks, however, is deep (10+ feet) and free of anything but obvious and black and only occasional heads. I have stayed at this anchorage during quite heavy blows, passing **storm cells** and steady, strong **trades**. It remained peaceful and serene with a light chop. Very surprising, since at first glance it appears wide open and not such good holding. Dive on your anchors, and of course, use two in case of widshift from showers.

From Ambergris proceed to **Big Sand Cay** to take up station on a **Wait for Weather** before jumping off to **Puerto Plata**. If proceeding south of the **Fish Cays**, watch out for the elkhorn north of the west coast of Big Ambergris. See the chartlet.

The first time you go south of the Fish Cays, go in good light only. There are east and west running "streets" of 3 fathoms depth, but in poor morning light you won't recognize them.

It's all around best not to go south of Fish Cays unless headed <u>west</u> in morning light the first time you do it. Until then, take the northern pass.

If you decide to go outside and avoid the Banks, you can reduce the agony by taking the ship channel out and nosing over to French Cay to anchor for the night, then following the reef until the punishment of the **Equatorial Current** and full trades start.

Upon leaving the banks either side of the **Fish Cays**, be prepared for steep and short seas. Wind with tide, you have the Atlantic Ocean trying to climb the wall onto Caicos Banks. Tide against wind, you've got cataracts underwater and overfalls above as the Banks empty themselves into the sea. Outside will be much smoother.

For purists, a good sail is north-northeast to the shoals south of **Long Cay**, thence southeast between Long Cay and Fish Cays, long-tacking and lee-bowing the current down to a western approach into **Big Sand Cay**. Do not tack as far south as dangerous **Endymion Rock**. If you short-tack, be prepared for an all-day sail, although Big Sand Cay is only 20 miles away.

The current in the Turks Passage can really rip north, so *lee-bow* it.

South Caicos is not worth a visit unless you are cruising the **Turks and Caicos**. For the sailor who is here *en route*, the anchorages are poor, shallow and rocky, with the exception of behind **Long Cay**. Even there there's not much room for boats with draft and it rolls badly in anything but southeast winds. If you need to jerry jug you will have to clear in and out again. Finally, stopping here can add a day to your sail south due to the current in the **Turks Passage**.

Big Sand Cay, though a bit rolly, has a large, deep sand anchorage. Thus the "Big Sand" name. Waiting here puts you 20 miles further to windward and up to a day's sail closer to **Hispaniola** than does any other route (e.g., **South Caicos** or direct from **Ambergris**). Being here also frees you from worry about **Endymion Rock**, 4 feet underwater and not always breaking.

Some DMA charts show Endymion Rock where Big Sand Cay is and other charts don't even show it. Kline's *Yachtsman's Guide to the Bahamas* shows it correctly on the chartlet

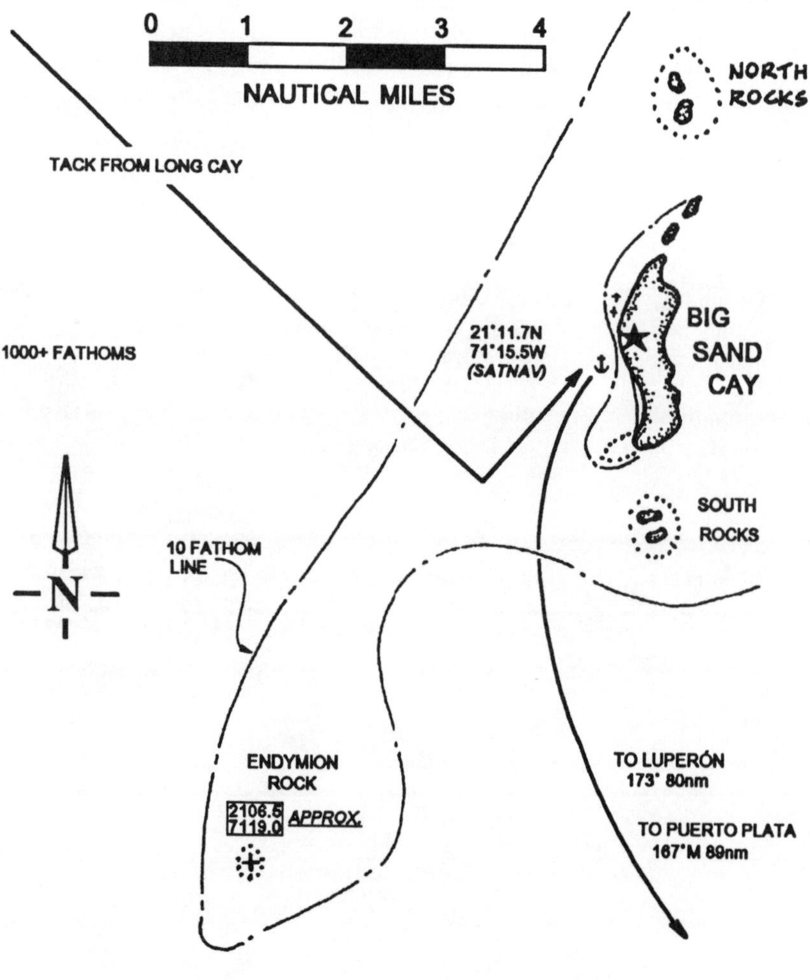

Big Sand Cay and Endymion Rock

of the **Turks and Caicos** as does the *Bahamas Chart Kit*, about 7 miles bearing 215° true from Big Sand Cay light, which is at 21°11.7'N and 71°15.5'W. Also note the clearly visible rocks, **South Rocks**, about a half-mile south of Big Sand Cay. If sailing the windward coast of Big Sand on a route from **Salt Cay**, you can safely sail between South Rocks and Big Sand, swinging wide of the sandy shoals off the southwest tip of Big Sand.

Getting to Big Sand Cay can be an all-day tacking sail due to the north-setting current in the **Turks Passage**. But those are hours shortened on the sail to Hispaniola, had you begun your trek from South Caicos or **Ambergris**. Approach the island from the west on the light, even in the dark, and anchor in 16 feet of deep sand, about 150 yards southwest of the light. The light is run by solar cells and is usually working. However, the switches often fail, leaving the light to work throughout the day, failing on dead batteries sometime around midnight. As with all lights south of Florida, assume they may not work. If they work, assume their characteristics are wrong because of poor power due to poor maintenance. It is actually all-round best to flat distrust all markers in the non-U.S. Caribbean and the Bahamas, navigating by pilotage. Transits of land features don't wear out.

The best beachcombing in the islands is on the windward shore of this uninhabited jewel. Watching **whales** is great in the month of February where the humpbacks gather to mate from **Samaná Bay** to the **Silver Banks**. In their once-a-year euphoria to get there the 40- and 50-footers will leap clear of the water, leaving echoes like cannon shots behind them.

Big Sand Cay can be departed by starlight with safety. Depart Big Sand, being sure to clear South Rocks well to your port, so as to arrive off the coast of Hispaniola just before daybreak. Your departure time can be as early as 3 a.m. and as late as 4 p.m., depending on conditions and your boat. Knock 20 percent and ten degrees off what you think your boat can do, however, unless you are facing a dead calm motor trip.

An alternate plan is to sail to **Salt Cay** for an overnight on the mooring there before proceeding to Big Sand Cay. It is worth the visit.

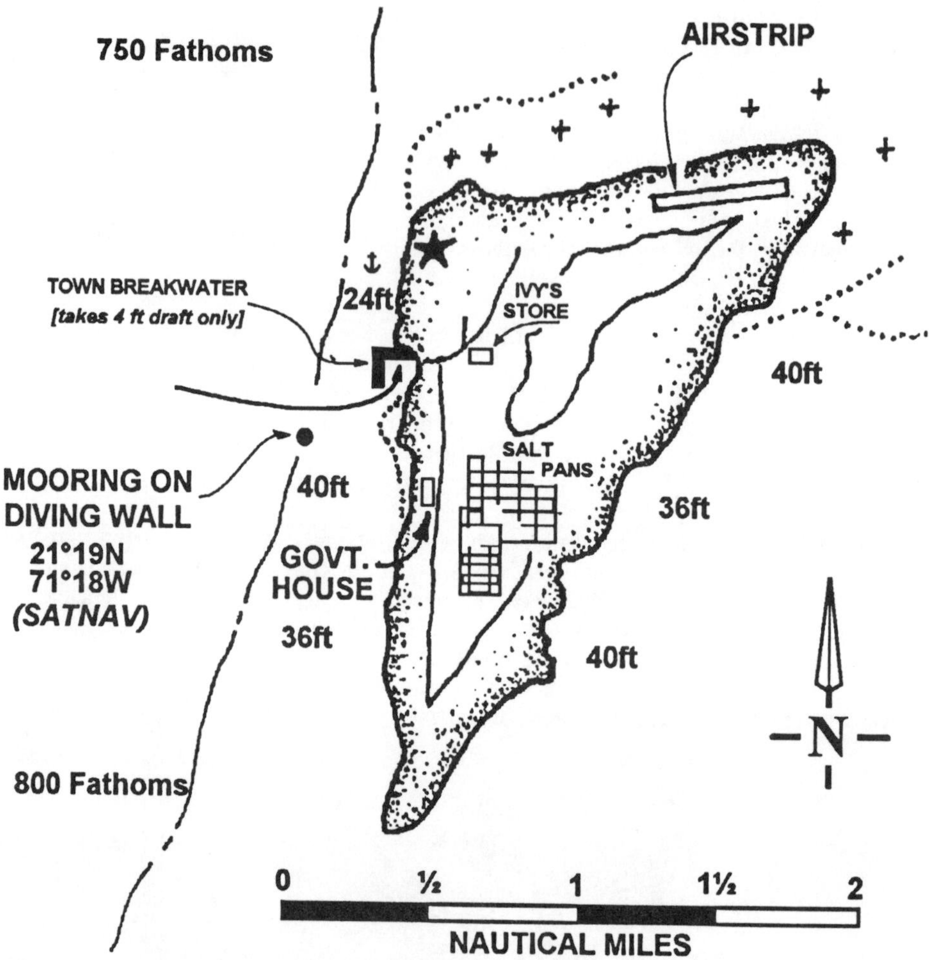

Salt Cay Mooring.

There is a mooring suitable for large freighters a third-mile southwest of the small boat breakwater at the town. It is a float with successively large messengers tied to a huge hawser attached to three large navy anchors. The mooring is in 40 feet atop a more than 300-foot wall. Scuba divers, don't miss it.

Don't anchor off the town. It's just a few inches of sand over rock. Same with the anchorage under the light. You'll bend your shanks in the chop if you don't drag the anchors into a crevice from which they cannot be tripped. Of course, in settled weather, these anchorages can be used with an eye to the wind.

The factotums at the Government House south of the dock have been known to clear one in and out when wheedled well. The people here are super nice. Be sure to bring Ivy some limes for her store and talk to Norman Tolbert about whales and the secrets of long life.

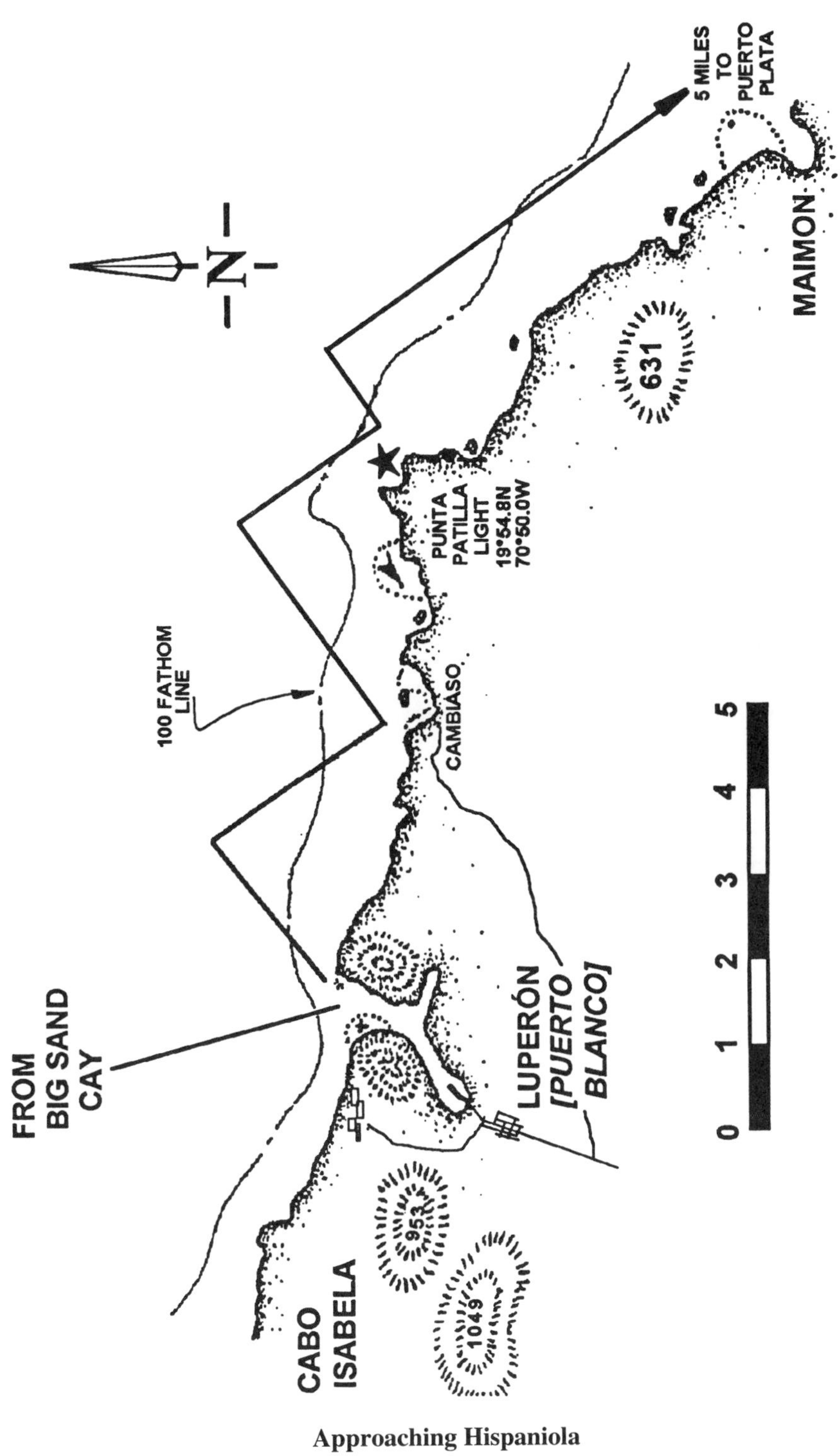

Approaching Hispaniola

Hispaniola extends a nighttime umbra of calm around itself which can reach as far as 30 miles offshore to the north and 20 to the east. Knowing how this phenomenon works can permit you to make a quicker and easier passage.

At night, the huge land mass of Hispaniola gives up the heat it accumulated during the day, while the sea, which has a much longer memory for heat, does not. Think of this as creating a "heat bubble" over the island, which shimmers away from the direction of the overall easterly flow. More north in the component of the **trade wind**, and the bubble shimmers south and west, shrinking the north shore's night lee. More southerly trades, and the bubble shimmers further off the north shore, providing sailors a larger lee.

Additionally, the **katabatic** wind, which is the cooling mountain air that slides downhill after nightfall, lifts the easterly flow off the island's coast. The katabatic wind adds to a possible **land breeze**, the opposite of the day's **sea breeze**. The land breeze is caused by the land cooling faster than the sea.

All of these effects create the **nocturnal** wind, which is offshore and can be light to moderate. The island's heat loss and the nocturnal wind redirect the flow of the trade winds over and around the island like a stream flowing around a rock. The effect will start earlier and last longer on light wind days, and start later and end earlier on days with strong winds. Similarly, the effect will extend itself further to sea on light wind days and stay inshore on hard wind days. The effect is greater after bright, hot days and weaker after overcast days.

After hot days you will feel the warm breath of the land on your cheek, and you will smell the aroma of black earth, cows, and charcoal fires up to 30 miles at sea!

Considering all the above factors, and observing the backing and veering of the winds from day to day, the shrewd **Leisure Sailor** waiting at **Big Sand Cay** to lay a course for **Luperón** or **Puerto Plata,** or waiting at **Sapodilla Bay** to jump off for **Cap Haitien**, or **Manzanillo**, will leave in 15 knots or less south of east to intersect this belt of flagging winds as far out to sea as possible. On the other hand, 15 knots north of east is a fine sail, despite a more narrow lee from the land. This calls for some iterative course planning to handle various assumptions of the land effects. After an overcast day of strong trades, stay in port. But after a bright, hot day of Force 4-5, consider giving it a shot.

If bound for Puerto Plata or Luperón, first sail or motorsail southeast, and eventually you may be motoring flat out for Puerto Plata in a slick, rolling calm. If winds strengthen or are not north of east, then ***don't beat into the seas,*** but <u>reach</u> across them for the island and tack up the coast in an early morning Force 3-4. Tuck under Cabo Isabela for the day if you get caught out when the trades start.

The deep bar south of **Big Sand** will give you a couple of more feet of sea than you imagine. Get out 5 miles before making definitive judgment of conditions. If you had planned one tack to Luperón, but conditions worsen to over 15 knots, don't be shy to change your plan in midstream. In such a case, sail comfortably south, <u>across</u> the waves, for the shelter of the coast. Don't continue to buck into it. Then motorsail up the coast in a lee. The trip will be faster and more comfortable than continuing to beat into seas. I don't know why, but year after year I see folks ignoring this advice as they often do the advice to avoid roll at **Rum Cay**. So once again:

When faced with bucking into current, wind and seas, slack sheets and bear off for lee of land where you can tack back up in comfort.

Bound for **Manzanillo**, sail for a waypoint 19°55'N, 72°00'W to ensure you clear the **Monte Cristi** shoals, then sail 18 miles southeast to Manzanillo. Thread the shoals in daylight by sailing due south on **El Morro** behind **Punta Granja**, then following backwards the instructions given in the chapter, *Monte Cristi and the Shoals*. El Morro is visible at night since it clearly interrupts the loom of Monte Cristi with its unmistakable mass.

Bound for **Cap Haïtien**, follow the same scheme as for **Luperón**. Plan to be off **Hispaniola** at dawn so as to be in port by 9 a.m., cleared in and squared away, before the **trades** renew. Leaving for Cap from **West Caicos** gives a little more beam wind than the **Big Sand Cay** to Luperón route, and the first 50 miles you have some lee from **Molasses Reef** to the east. The looms of **Monte Cristi** and Cap Haïtien can be visible up to 30 miles out if there are no power failures. Be careful not to confuse the two (as I did one year) and wind up in the **Monte Cristi Shoals**, thinking you are 10 miles out to sea off Cap.

Follow the **Provo ship channel** out through **Clear Sand Road**. Clear the southeast spit of West Caicos standing off the beach there about one-half mile. The lat-long of the Clear Sand Road, entrance to the banks is 21°36'N, 72°28'W, and the channel stretches 242° magnetic from **Gussy Point**. It's even easier to slip a mooring from the marine park west of West Caicos.

The **Equatorial Current** can sometimes be as high as 1½ knots in the heart of the stream, but it is usually ½ to ¾ knot. ½ knot west-northwest door-to-door always works. Enter the port at **Cap Haïtien** after 8 a.m. to ensure a non-defensive reception and proceed to the customs dock on the south side of the huge pier, which was constructed by "Baby Doc" to receive the cruise ships which have, so far, not returned.

Air

If you have been in the Bahamas several months, as far as your allergic reactions are concerned, you have been at sea several months. While at Hispaniola you will be bathed for 12 hours a day by air sliding down from the middle of the 250-kilometer-wide, high island. This air brings with it all the pollens and allergens of practically every type of flora known and then some. You haven't seen a deciduous tree or grasses in several months. Keep your antihistamines handy and double your vitamin intake.

Water

Most maladies reported by yachties arriving directly on Hispaniola from an extended stay in the Bahamas are due to these effects of climatic and allergen change. But, like the New Yorker visiting New Jersey in the summer, they blame everything on the water.

On the other hand, all developing countries are notorious for poor public sanitation coupled with poor or intermittent pressure in their town water lines. The H_2O from the mountains in the DR is delicious. Like in New Jersey, however, wait a couple of days after an outage before tanking up on the water. And, as in Florida, always treat it. (See the chapter on Doing Without Mr. Clean.)

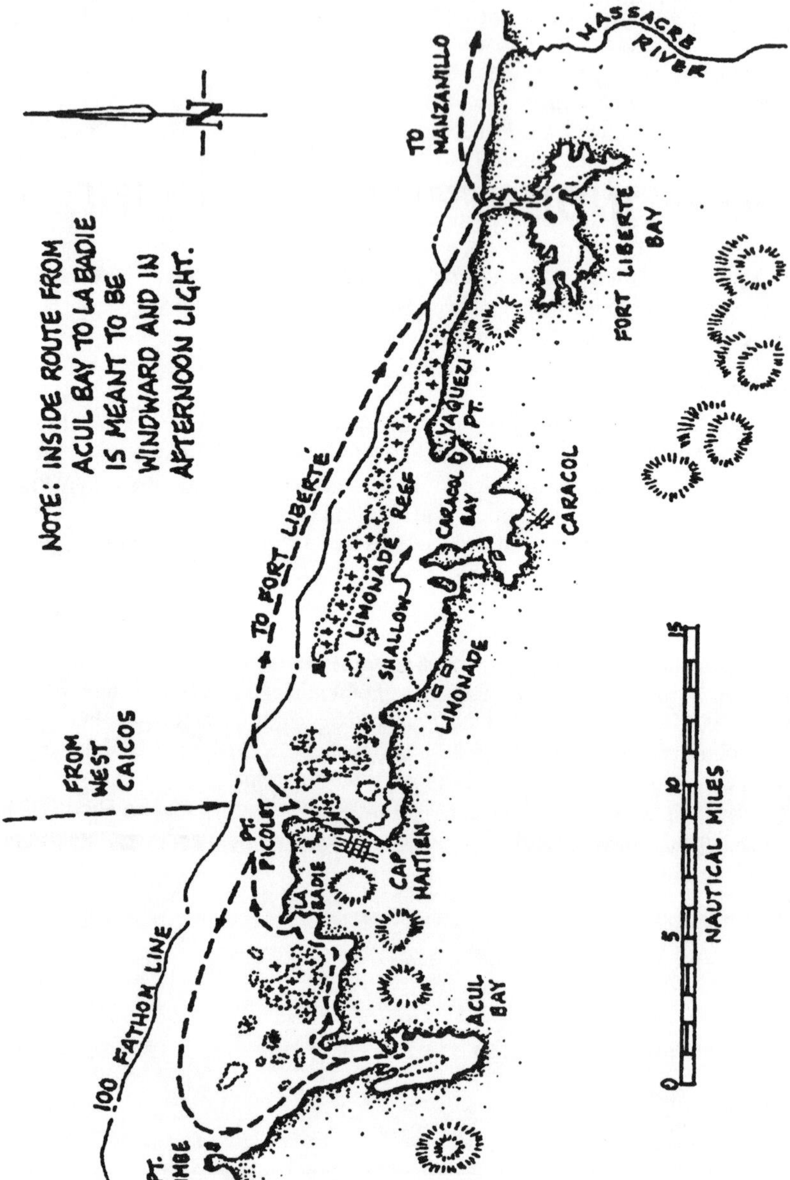

Haiti East from Acul Bay

After clearing in at **Cap Haïtien**, visiting the **Citadelle** or whatever else you find to do there, leave your arms, if any, with the authorities and clear out for **Acul Bay**. When coasting east from Acul Bay, you must stop again at Cap Haïtien to pick up a clearance for **Fort Liberté**, and, of course, in Fort Liberté, you need to pick one up for the **Dominican Republic**. Your first clearance from Cap Haïtien is for cruising the small bays to the west. Excepting ports of entry, in **Haiti**, one must be firm in allowing only one member from each bureaucracy aboard to inspect one's papers, else the whole town will be roosting on your settees.

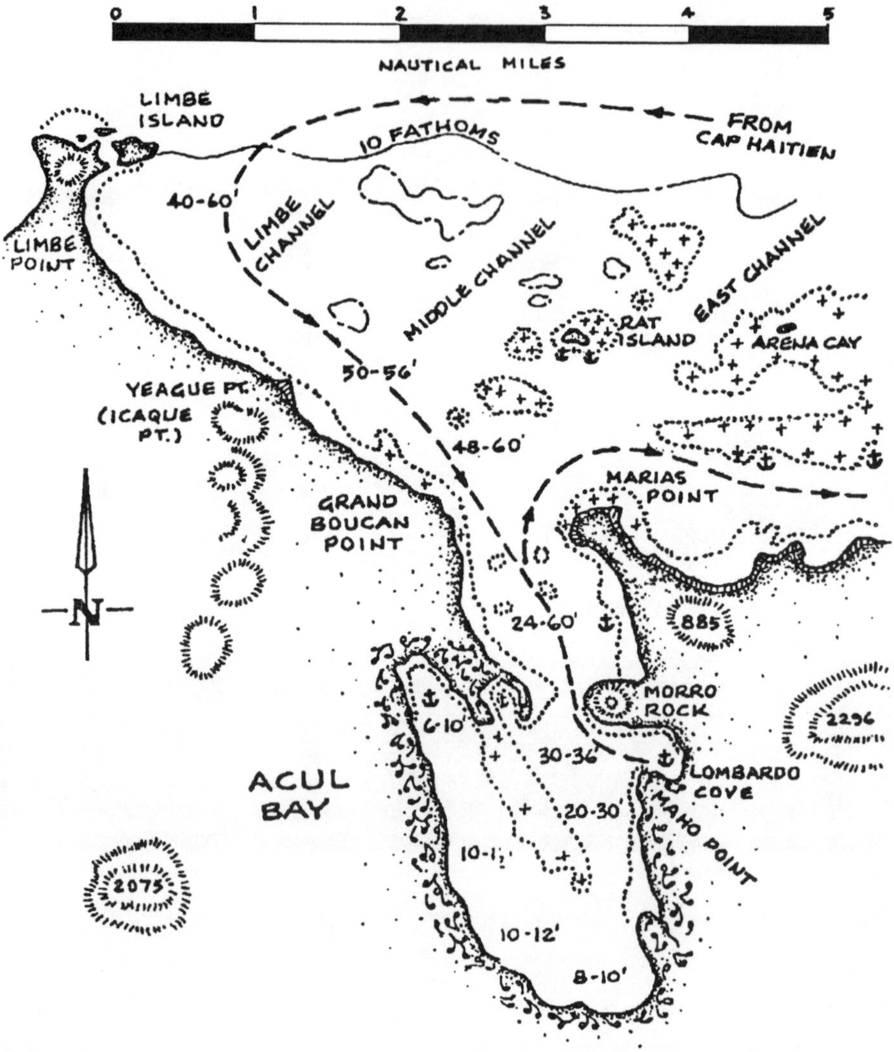

Acul Bay: A Fine Hurricane Hole

Follow the **Limbe Channel** down the west side of the bay, rounding **Grand Boucand Point** a half-mile off, then steer for **Morro Rock**. This will bring you safely up into a good anchorage deep inside **Lombardo Cove** by **Maho Point**. Ashore, see John and Mary (Jean et Marie) for great avocados, grapefruit and coconut. The Haïtien grapefruit are the world's best and run about an American nickel each. There's a fine hurricane hole up between **Lunetta Point** and **Belie Point**, and another behind Lunetta Point.

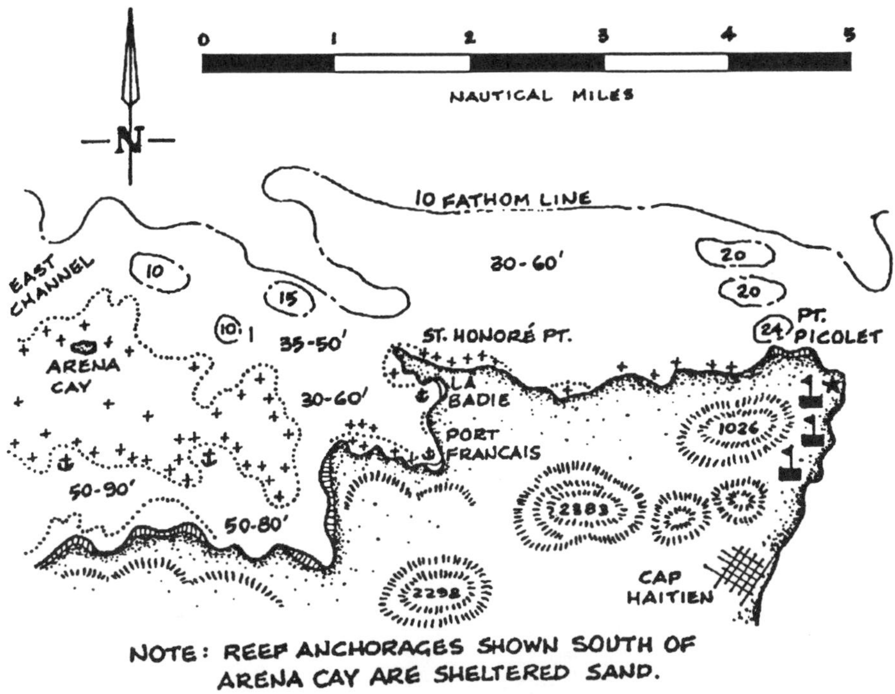

La Badie — Still a Pleasure

This whole coast, from **Ile de la Tortue** to **Puerto Plata** was for more than 200 years controlled by **corsaires** and **privateers** and the freebooters and buccaneers they left in their wake. **La Badie** was a famed watering hole and bordello in those days. Today it is host to a cruise ship whose passengers sun themselves and picnic on the white sand beaches once a week. **Rat Island**, in the middle of the bay, has good anchorages in clear water south and southwest of the island. You can snorkel and spearfish along the reefs around the island which is an overnight camp for local fishermen.

A Word About Security

There should be no problem cruising Haiti after the U.N. embargo is lifted. Until then, there should be no problem visiting by land, via the **Dajabón** bridge, while your boat lies at **Manzanillo**. You should not expect any personal threat in Haiti, although pestering from beggars may exasperate you.

Haitians, individually, are among the sweetest and most pacific people I have met in a lifetime of world travel. Collectively, however, Haitians have a penchant for screwing up what is the world's third-oldest republic (not counting that France is on its *sixth*). Unlike Latin Americans, however, Haitians cheerfully admit that they do it without outside assistance— you won't find Haitians blaming you for their plight. You will find them eager to share your resources, however, and squander them as they have their own. To prevent undue pressure on your purse, just practice what you do elsewhere, but industrial strength. Especially get all prices down firmly before accepting a service. It helps to speak French badly.

The course from the **Clear Sand Road** behind **West Caicos** is 172° true for a distance of 112 miles. Add a half knot of west-northwest current, stir in some leeway, variation and deviation, and add a pinch of caution: several degrees to ensure you aren't set onto the **Monte Cristi Shoals**.

The lights of the port may not be functioning but the buoyage is good. There are large red and green piles which follow the American "red right returning" rule. Make a daybreak landfall, sailing to within 500 yards east of the old lighthouse on **Picolet Point** on **Cap Haïtien** itself. Proceed down the well marked channel, turning right around the south end of the large pier. Midway down the long dock, between the freighters and the fishing boats, is the Harbor Master's office. Hail them and ask permission to tie up at the yacht dock across from them to do your clearing in since that maneuver may be difficult when the wind gets up later. Plan to clear in just after 8 a.m. to avoid overtime or transport charges.

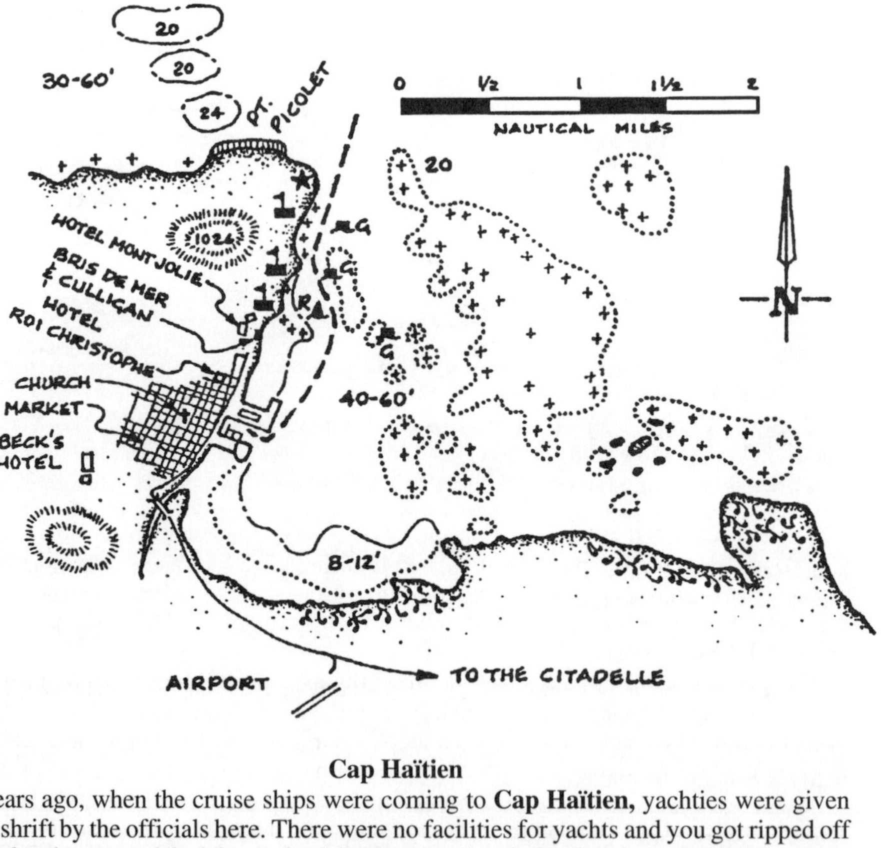

Cap Haïtien

Years ago, when the cruise ships were coming to **Cap Haïtien,** yachties were given short shrift by the officials here. There were no facilities for yachts and you got ripped off for fuel and water and the labor to fetch it. You were hassled endlessly by the kids "seeking work," but to whom a paint brush was a high tech tool. These harmless street urchins were used to scamming quick bucks from ship's passengers, taking them to the market, shopping the bric-a-brac and art stalls and generally misguiding them around. All that has changed.

There are no more cruise ships, although there is a new cruise ship dock and terminal. There is a new "marina" with sturdy steel pilings and bollards at a long dock. There are utility boxes for electricity and water, and a building with showers and a restaurant. Best of all, there are fewer, or no, kids pulling at you, no hassles, and, with no cruise ships, officials have time for yachts.

The bad news is that all of these facilities are non-functional or closed. They have been in sporadic use since being started in 1984. But recently there have been few yachts, no cruise ships and no (zero) tourists. Only two travel agencies are still open. Their only business is selling tickets *out*. During all the troubles **Haiti** has recently been through, the north coast plodded along with its usual serenity. There is no cause for alarm in visiting Cap.

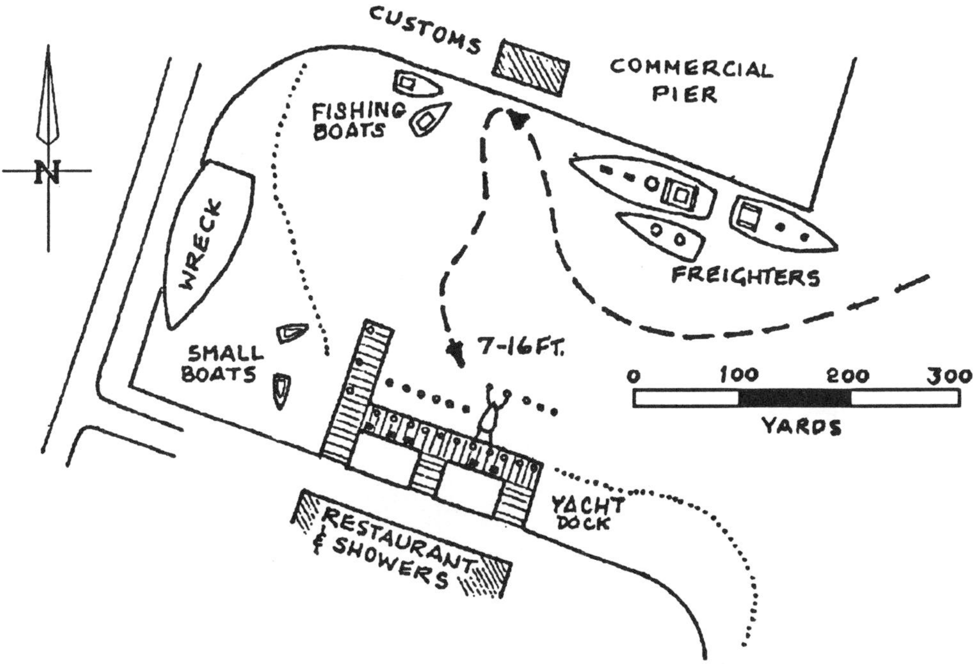

The marina at Cap Haïtien

Try to tie up to the yacht dock early or late, before the seabreeze comes up, or, after it dies. The dock is unaccountably built across the wind instead of into it. The docks are at what used to be an island. Since the land was filled to create the "marina," it can be assumed that lying across the wind was a specific design. Welcome to **Haiti**, the land of the inexplicable.

Haiti, founded in 1804 as the world's third republic since Rome, has a rich and dark history. Invest in a book on Haitian history. It will enhance your visit tenfold. Start your history lesson with an excellent dinner at the Roi Christoph, built to house the governor in 1724 with 2-foot walls and high, open rooms. Worm some invitations to some of the old residences in town. Go when the squalid streets and dingy facades are cloaked in the romantic luster of the fuel lamps in the evening. The interiors of the more maintained mansions will astound you with their elegance. Even those that are in half ruin will make an historian weep.

If you take a tour of the **Citadelle** and **San Souci**, you don't need to see the pyramids—first, because the experience is comparable, and second, because you will no longer be able to afford it: The con artists that take you there must have been trained in Egypt. A new cost will arise every step of the way.

Haiti is not cheap, despite its poverty. Perhaps therefore, the Haitians are accustomed to wringing every *sou* from the tourist. If you ask a price, be prepared to hear astronomical sums quoted by people who haven't seen a penny in months—not seeing it much, the ordinary Haitian hasn't got a grasp on reality when it comes to money.

Haitian money is called the *gourde*. That's right, as in gourds, like Indians used to trade. It is pronounced "goo." The first time you receive your change in a gooey ball of old one-gourde notes, you will understand everything.

To go to Citadelle, agree on a firm, all-inclusive price, due on completion of the tour, before setting out. If you're a good and patient bargainer, it's 15 to 20 bucks a head for 4 to 6 persons, half of which is transportation to the second parking level. Once I hired a car for 6 hours to run over to the Dominican frontier. After 15 minutes of a-hemming and a-hawing the first driver finally quoted his *discounted* fee of $150. Another gave us a quote of $60, and finally Gabriel, a member of the national police, gave us a "reasonable" price of $40—along with the security of having a cop as a driver, he noted, as he patted his monstrous .45!

The Hotel Mont Joli still has the loveliest deck in Haiti from which to enjoy your SG&T. Beck's and the Brise de Mer hotels are still open. The Hotel Universel, downtown, is both air conditioned and cheapest. Drinking water can be bought at Culligan's near the Brise de Mer, if you can find the owner. The best buy in the market, although not a great bargain, is still the charcoal-roasted cashews. Haitian art, usually cheap elsewhere, is, of course, even cheaper in Haiti. Do not, however, expect bargains in Haiti. The deposit alone on a bottle of beer may be more than a six-pack in the D.R. Never expect to find something like an engine part.

Fort Liberté

Leave **Cap Haïtien** the same way you came in. You want, of course, to leave as early as possible to avoid the hassle of the trades. To minimize any hassles from the officials, talk with them the day before leaving. Show up at the harbor master's office at first light with the yacht moored as instructed when you called on them the previous day. Then press hard for a quick clearance.

When close under the lighthouse at **Point Picolet**, turn on a course of 60° true for one mile or more, then east true for 3 miles. This should put you a mile or more north of **Limonade Reef,** where **Columbus** lost the **Santa Maria,** and well clear of danger. Now set a course of 105° true for the entrance to **Fort Liberté** 18 miles distant.

The entrance to Fort Liberté is difficult to spot from sea. This whole area is desert and sisal plantations and everything looks the same. For several miles east and west of it, however, you can sail up to ¼ mile offshore, so go close in to be sure not to miss it. The entrance to the bay is a narrow throat surrounded by low, red cliffs and nearly 100 feet deep everywhere. Once inside the bay, like the approach outside, everything looks the same again, but, instead of brown rock the color is mangrove green.

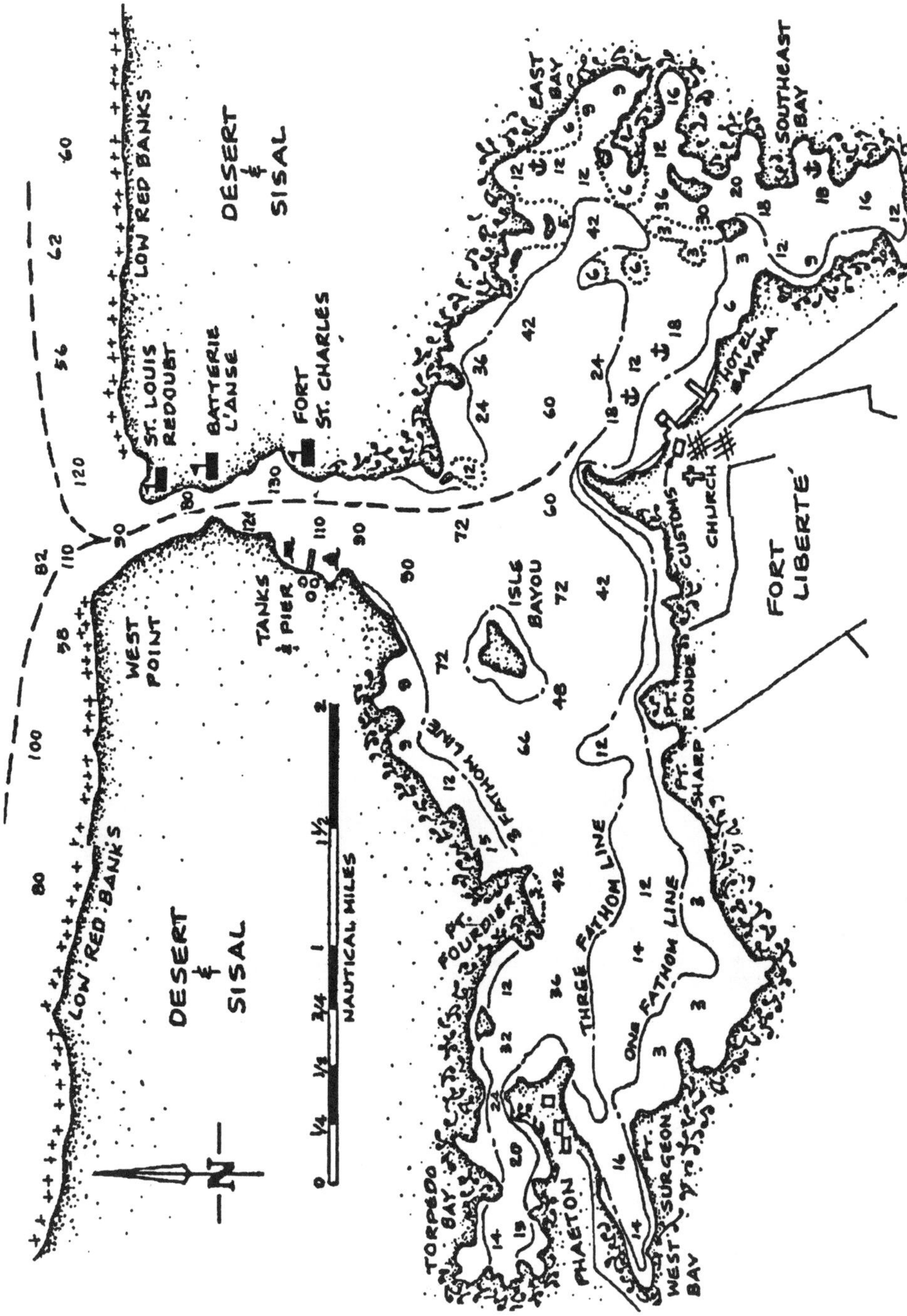

Fort Liberté: an easy and safe port of entry, as well as a fine hurricane hole.

The entire bay is lined with mangroves. Head for the large stone building with a concrete dock on the east side of the town. This is the Hotel Bayaha, run by M. et Mme. Nyll Calixte. The customs house is by the old town pier a couple of hundred yards seaward of the hotel. *Le Capitain du Port,* Herns Calixte, has been the boss here many years. He will organize the boarding party. Either dock has only a couple of feet of water. You will have to anchor well off and ferry the boarding party from either dock. The hotel dock is more convenient as it is new and has a good ladder.

There is a water point near the customs house, but it may not be functioning. Fuel can be purchased in gallon containers in the town. It is best to come here from either **Cap Haïtien** or **Manzanillo** with full tanks. See Mme. Calixte about jerry jugging water from a water point beside the hotel. The hotel has a verandah bar and restaurant overlooking the anchorage. Charges for clearing in depend on the boat, but should range to a few dollars only. After clearing you are free to anchor in any of the small coves and holes around the bay and stay as long as you like. Leave for Manzanillo, 6 miles to the east, to arrive there around 8 a.m. while it's still dead calm. Once again, do what you have to in order to get cleared and free of the harbor *early*.

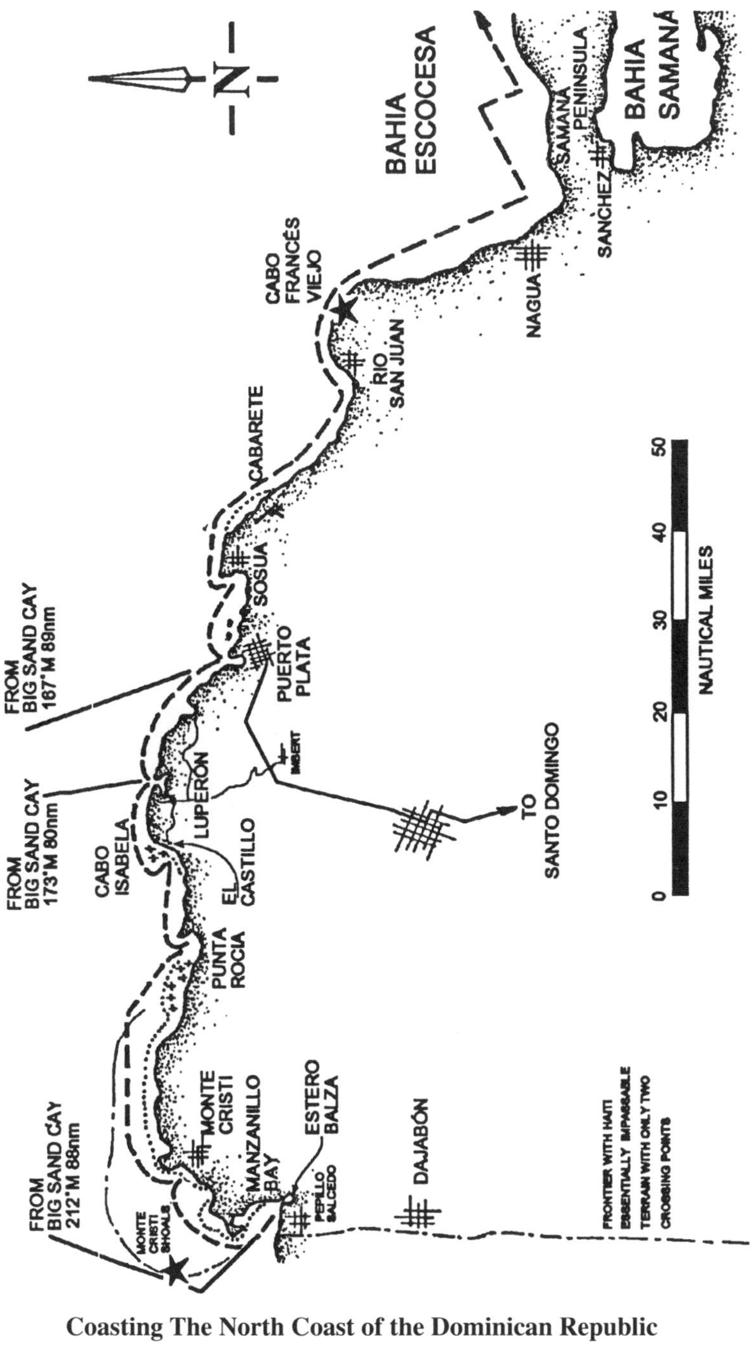

Coasting The North Coast of the Dominican Republic

The north coast of the **Dominican Republic** can be the roughest passage for yachts island hopping from North America to the Virgin Islands. But one of the oldest ploys in sailing can make it a quite pleasant trip.

For almost 500 years sailing vessels have navigated the north coast of **Hispaniola**, against the very strong winds and seas, by hiding behind the headlands and capes during the day and proceeding close to shore at night where more moderate conditions permit a slow progress against the wind.

Sailboats coasting against the wind have used this tactic all over the world for longer than recorded history. There doesn't seem to be much difference today, except whereas **Columbus** had to sometimes tow his ships at night with longboats under oars, you are lucky enough to have an auxiliary. The *Santa Maria,* Columbus's flagship, was lost on the reefs off **Caracol Bay**, east of **Cap Haïtien,** while being hauled in this fashion. After the ship touched they were unable to float her off. All the hoopla over efforts to find the *Santa Maria* notwithstanding, there shouldn't be much there, as Columbus's journal reveals they scavenged the ship down to her beams before leaving her to wave and rock. Even as you would do if you were on Mars and one of your three transports was disabled—you would have to make do there with whatever you had. Since **Martín Pinzón** had run off with the *Pinta* in the Ragged Islands, half the crew had to be left ashore. The *Santa Maria*'s materials went into construction of their new town.

The authorities in the **Dominican Republic** will seldom give yachts clearance to any port other than the official ports of entry: **Pepillo Salcedo** in **Manzanillo**, **Luperón**, **Puerto Plata** and **Samaná**. This is simply because the D.R. is a small and relatively poor country and cannot afford to place a customs house in every pokey little village for the odd cruising yacht to visit twice a year.

Don't be like the Swiss sailor I know who tried to cruise the United States. Being a good Swiss, he insisted everywhere on proper papers which followed the letter of the law. None of the American officials were quite certain of the rules relative to Swiss yachts, but he made them research them. My friend got as far as Rhode Island and fled directly to the Bahamas under the weight of harbor fees and the welter of regulations whose lines he felt he had to toe. Though a dear friend of mine, he dislikes Americans and America to this day.

One man, a HAMster, spent weeks chasing bureaucrats all over the Dominican Republic looking for a temporary license before using his SSB marine radio in their territorial waters. He finally received assurances that the usual treaty between the two countries in question provided for a 30-day grace period in which a visiting ship could use its radio. Armed with at least this verbal approval, he counted the days he had been in the country. They amounted to 31. He never did use his radio in the D.R. The usual Children's Hour and Breakfast Shows went on without him.

I *do not* recommend having improper papers, but, if you want to have pleasure out of your pleasure yacht, I do recommend you ease off on the expectations you place on officialdom and *go with the flow*. For instance, if you ask to be cleared into ports other than the official ports of entry in the Dominican Republic, you shall most certainly be told that you cannot do that. If you declare your plans to "stop at" **Sosua**, for instance, you will be told you can't be cleared for Sosua. True enough. With consideration for the language gap, a more careful communication would have you "pausing off" Sosua while the wind and seas around **Cabo Macoris** subside. I always coast with this strategy and have usually met understanding officials along the way. But some understanding of the officials by cruisers is called for as well. Read the section of this book on culture shock.

The only authority in a small village may be an 18-year-old soldier with a rusty rifle who has never seen a foreigner. His consternation at a great fleet of boats showing up on his beach is second only to that of the Nazis in Normandy on the morning of D-Day. When the brass in headquarters get his call for instructions, they'll next call the *Comandante* to find out what the hell is happening on his beat. The port *comandantes* won't be too fond of you after that.

I get a clearance "with intermediate ports" (*con puertos intermedios*) from **Manzanillo** and have no problems. I just waive the paper at each new *comandante*. For some reason, many American yachties find this procedure a lot of trouble, but it's actually less trouble than the Americans put the Canadians to, yet still it leads to a lot of grousing, which is quite unfair.

If traveling in company, do so modestly: no jilling about, yoo-hooing and mooning each other off the town beach. If you're there to rest and wait, then ghost up to anchor unobtrusively, slip below for a rest and wait. Also communicate your intention of not visiting the shore by anchoring well beyond the reach of any swimmers.

Departure Times

Coasting the north coast of the DR is much like coasting the south coast of Puerto Rico as far as departure times are concerned. The best strategy is to take the smallest hops possible between the staging harbors of **Manzanillo**, **Luperón** and **Samaná**, during 2-3 day **weather windows**, while making the best use of the night lees available, and ensuring good light landfalls. Consider the following examples of departures from Luperón.

Example 1: depart at daybreak for an afternoon at **Sosua** and an overnight at **Escondido**.

Example 2: depart at sundown for a full day and evening at **Rio San Juan** followed by an overnight at Escondido.

Differences between Haiti and the Dominican Republic

Although Americans are closer to Hispaniola by both heritage and geography, they are normally more confused than Europeans as to the differences between that island's two nations. The Dominican Republic occupies two-thirds of the land area but has less population than does Haiti. The Dominicans talk Spanish, Haitians talk Créole, an extremely corrupted French. Dominicans are Roman Catholic. Haitians are more animistic than catholic. Dominicans run the gamut of skin color, averaging a light cinnamon. Haitians are pitch black, with a few mulattos, some of whom are off-island as much as on. The history of the two countries is one of bitter rivalry: Haiti invading the DR, the DR slaughtering Haitian immigrants. Further distancing the two peoples is a practically impenetrable border with only two crossing points. The frontier that divides them is a 20-mile swath which alternates between desert in the north and the south, and *haïtises*, or jagged jungle hillocks, in the middle. The terrain surrounding the frontier has been unoccupied through the centuries due to its basic inhospitality to settlement. While fourth poorest in the hemisphere, the Dominican Republic is wealthy compared to Haiti. There are Dominican businessmen in Haiti, but in the Dominican Republic there are only Haitian migrant workers.

COASTING MANZANILLO TO LUPERÓN

There are 3 easy legs on this passage. The capes to hide behind are **Punta Granja**, or **El Morro**, the table-like mountain at **Monte Cristi**, **Punta Rocia** (also spelled Punta Rucia) and **Cabo Isabela**. Monte Cristi to Cabo Isabela should be an easy 36-mile motor trip in a flat calm before dawn, but I prefer to break this leg up into two or more stops. Monte Cristi is simple and safe to leave at night. Offshore dangers are more than a mile to starboard at any point in the trip. Short-leg this coast, stopping at Punta Rocia for its beauty and tranquillity, and Cabo Isabela to visit the penultimately historical site of **El Castillo**.

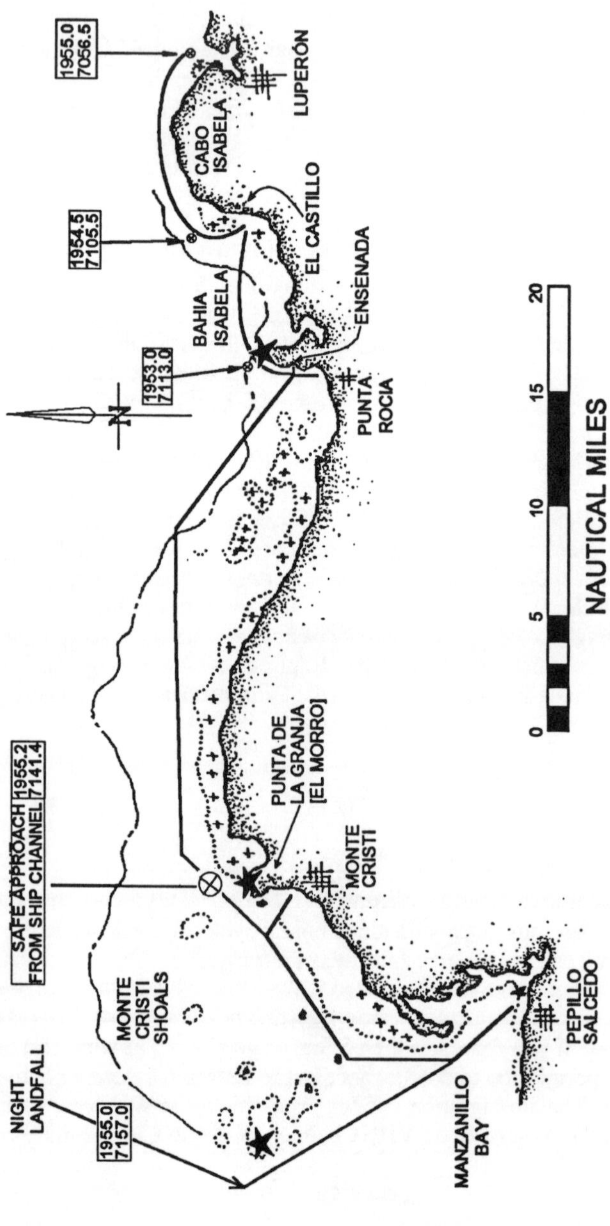

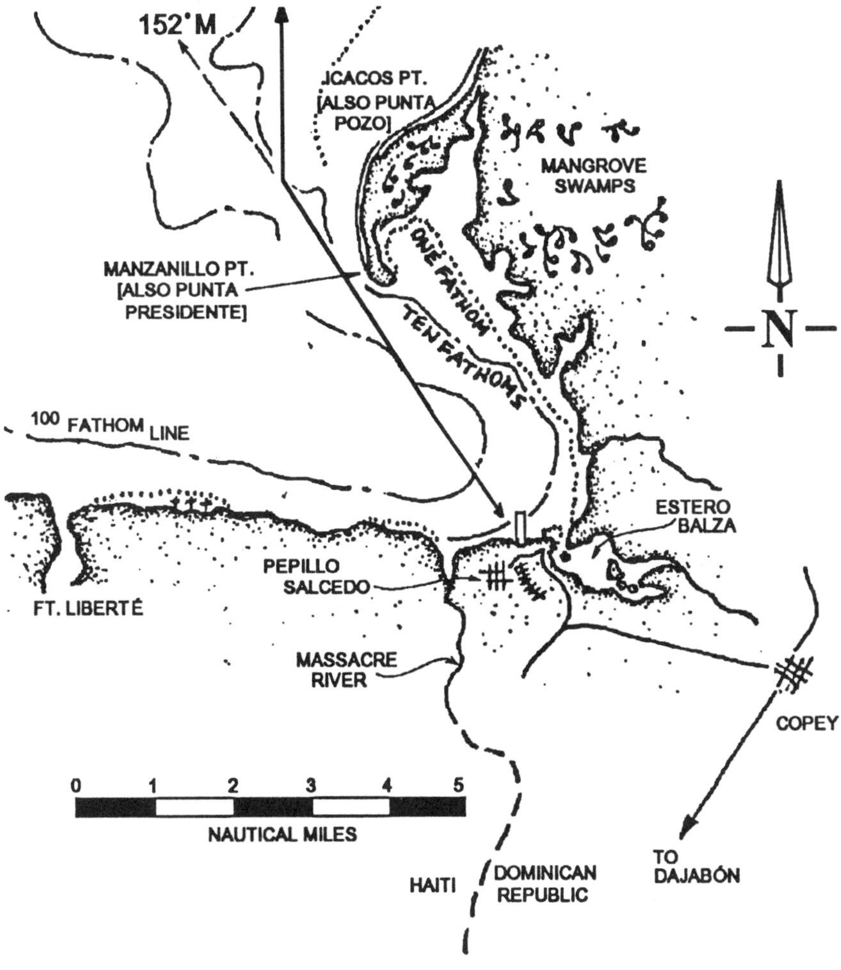

Try to be inside **Manzanillo Bay** in the early morning while the bay is calm. It is most convenient to clear in at the old company pier, but in the high chop and surge usual after midday, it is a dangerous place for a small boat. If you cannot arrive early, anchor off the *comandáncia* and ask to be cleared the next morning.

There is a fine hurricane hole in **Estero Balza,** the little estuary ¾ of a mile east of the large pier on the south shore. Seven-foot draft can be accommodated over the bar at high tide, 5 feet at low. If you draw less than 5 feet or you have fair wind and tide to enter the estuary, ask for permission to do clearance in the **Estero** (*ace-stair-oh*, or estuary) when the wind is up. The immigration officer, Fianchi (*fee-AHN-chee*), speaks very good American and will answer you on VHF Channel 16. North Caribbean Research (NCR), a treasure salvor, has put in a range of mangrove stakes at the entrance to the estuary. This is a fine hurricane hole and long-term anchorage from which to tour Haiti, especially when it's under blockade.

Pepillo Salcedo

Pepillo Salcedo (*pay-PEE-yo sal-SAY-doe*) is the name of the Grenada Company town built under the Trujillo regime in 1947 by United Fruit. It took three years to build the town and facilities before exporting one banana. During the political vacuum of 1965, when the United States Marines were invited in to pacify Santo Domingo, the Company gave up and pulled out, leaving factories, equipment, houses and the physical infrastructure of a sizable town. The government's Project Cruz, which was to have rehabilitated the enterprise, barely survives, and the town languishes with a few bananas being exported and fish being sent inland. The stone houses lining the wide curbed and sidewalked streets shelter hospitable but poor Dominicans. Some houses are for rent at a relative pittance. For shopping one needs to go into **Dajabón** (*dah-hah-BONE*), 20 minutes away in the foothills by the Haitian border.

The only other industry is the historical salvage and diving operation, **North Caribbean Research** (**NCR**), run by Rick Berry with his two sons, Chris and Scott, under license to the Dominican Republic. They are helpful to cruisers with limited Spanish.

Estero Balza

Estero Balza is a secure place at which to leave your yacht while touring the country, not as convenient as **Luperón**, but as good as **Samaná**. Take the **Caribe Tours** bus to **Santiago** and rent a car, or, for the more adventuresome, who want to meet the Dominican people and experience the country close up, rent a dirt bike or backpack with the variety of transportation available from pickup trucks to minibuses.

While at Estero Balza, see Don Nene (*NAYE-naye*) for transportation to Dajabón for provisioning or for trucking in fuel. See Don Bienvenido (*bee-ANE-vaye-NEE-doe*), who lives on the beach, for water, for watching your dinghy and for getting a cold beer.

There is a beach bar with the inevitable merengue dance floor at the entrance to the Estero Balza, and Jim Hickman runs the Hotel Galeón in town where the gringos gather. For bilge keels and multihulls of modest draft, there is a beaching operation in the estuary which can serve your haulout needs.

The seabreeze rises from the northwest around **Manzanillo Point**—also known as **Punta Presidente**—about 10 a.m., veers throughout the day, reaching 15 knots and above, and dies in the east toward 6 p.m. to make room for the gnats, or *gegenas* (*hey-HEN-na*s). The bugs are usually gone by 8 p.m., but, nonetheless, have your screens in or plenty of repellent handy.

If you draw more than 5 feet and don't have a fair tide in the early morning, or if you have arms which need to be delivered to the yacht, move the boat over to the anchorage off the *comandáncia* on the west side of the pier the day before leaving, and clear out that afternoon. Row in for your guns first thing in the morning and get underway immediately, crossing the bay before the wind gets up, or it will pen you into the bay for many hours. Motor across the flat *early* morning calm of **Manzanillo Bay**, north toward the little island of **Tororu**. When the wind rises, sail to **Monte Cristi**, tacking in the light morning airs.

Leave the bay in early morning calm or get penned in for a rough sail!

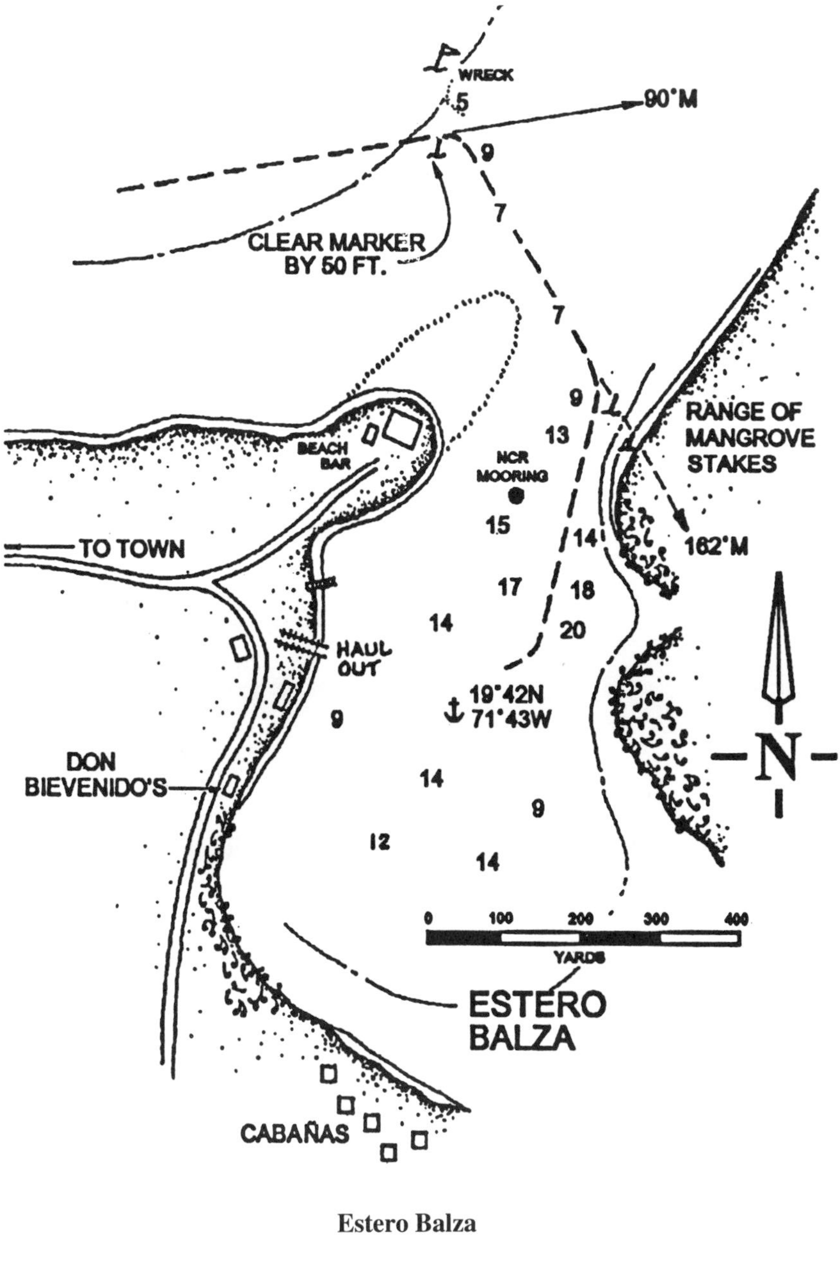

Estero Balza

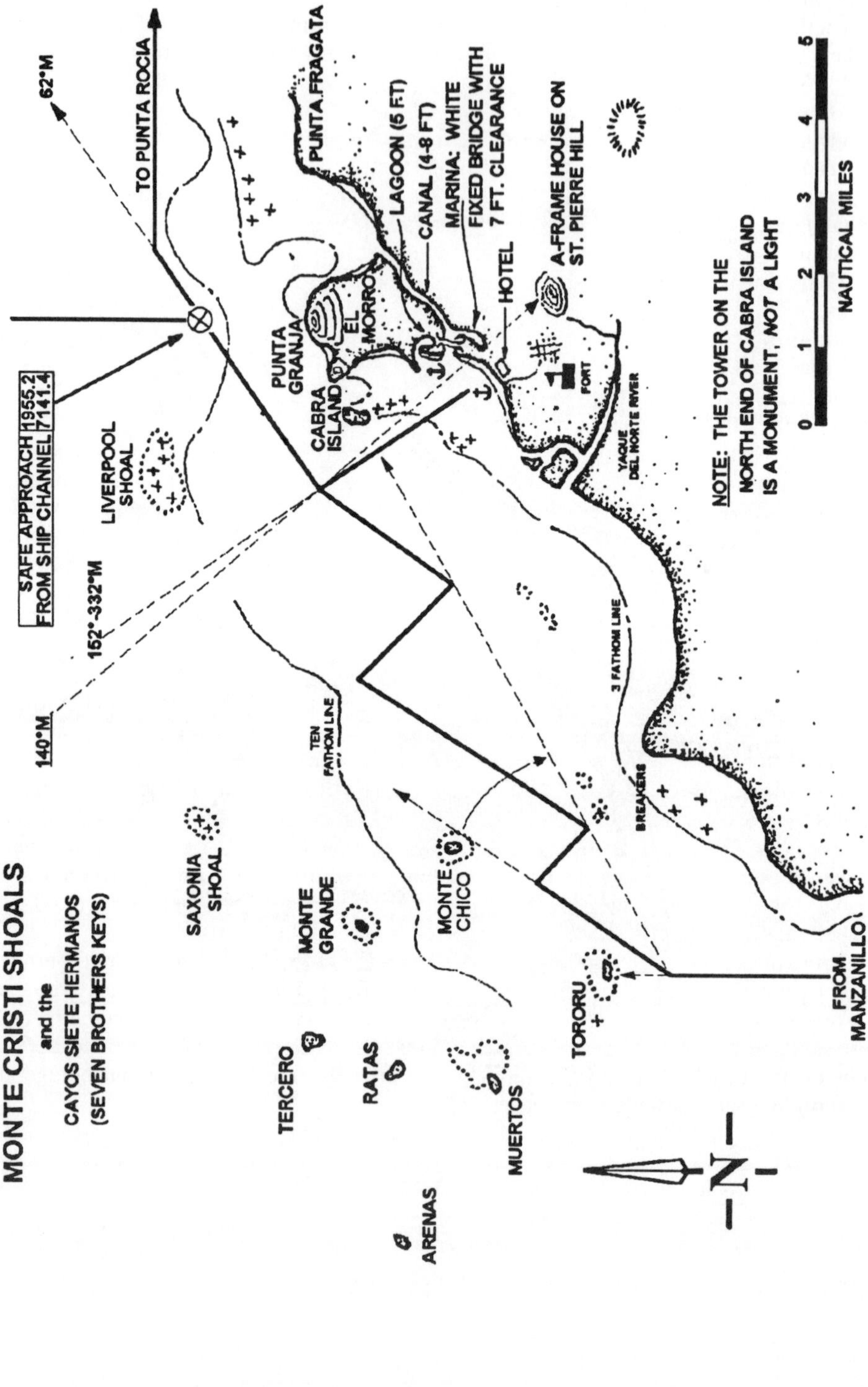
MONTE CRISTI SHOALS
and the
CAYOS SIETE HERMANOS
(SEVEN BROTHERS KEYS)
SAFE APPROACH 1955.2
FROM SHIP CHANNEL 7141.4
TO PUNTA ROCIA
62°M
140°M
152°-332°M
LIVERPOOL SHOAL
SAXONIA SHOAL
TEN FATHOM LINE
3 FATHOM LINE
BREAKERS
PUNTA FRAGATA
LAGOON (5 FT)
CANAL (4-8 FT)
MARINA: WHITE
FIXED BRIDGE WITH
7 FT. CLEARANCE
HOTEL
A-FRAME HOUSE ON
ST. PIERRE HILL
PUNTA GRANJA
EL MORRO
CABRA ISLAND
FORT
YAQUE DEL NORTE RIVER
NOTE: THE TOWER ON THE
NORTH END OF CABRA ISLAND
IS A MONUMENT, NOT A LIGHT
0 1 2 3 4 5
NAUTICAL MILES
TERCERO
RATAS
MUERTOS
ARENAS
MONTE GRANDE
MONTE CHICO
TORORU
FROM MANZANILLO
N

Stay on a longitude through **Tororu** to avoid the shoals off **Icacos Point** (also known as **Punta Pozo**) and **Yuna Point** (also known as **Punta Luna**). When one mile south of Tororu, tack northeast within the angle projected from the island of **Monte Chico** to the north and **Punta Granja** to the east. When ¼ mile west of **Cabra Island**, steer 152° magnetic onto the large white hotel on the beach, anchoring 500 yards off in 2 fathoms. Take a good look around on the way in—you will want your bearings for leaving in the dark. Not to worry, though: it's a wide cinch (DMA chart 26141 or 26142).

Many early morning departures are called for in this guide. But that's how it is on the windward way. Masochists can leave later than advised and slog against the **Equatorial Current** in Force 6 conditions and in the midst of the **Monte Cristi Shoals**. If you're a motorist, you can leave **Manzanillo** for **Monte Cristi** even later, but put the pedal to the metal, Gretel, if you want to get there before dark. If you leave Manzanillo at sunup and sail some, too, you'll be in the beach hotel at Monte Cristi for lunch, sucking on a cold beer.

Monte Cristi is a sizable town where most everything is available. For more difficult items, such as engine parts, you can take a *guagua* (gwah-gwah) for a few pesos to **Santiago**, the second city of the D.R. Take a look at **Mao**, a farming center, while en route. You may want to do some provisioning there. **Luperón** is a half-hour ride away from the bus terminal in Santiago. You may want to check it out by land.

Any extensive tripping around should really be done while at Luperón, however. Although the harbor at Monte Cristi is excellent in most conditions, it is wide open from the northwest, and weather can be expected from that quarter in the winter months.

Leave Monte Cristi for **Cabo Isabela** or **Punta Rocia** around midnight. A moon would be nice, but is not necessary. Follow a course of 332° magnetic from the beach hotel, passing close under **Cabra Island**, until you clear **Punta Granja** to the east. Steer 62° magnetic for 4 miles, to a point 3 miles north of **Punta Fragata**. Then steer true east for 14 miles to the 100-fathom line and go for either Punta Rocia or Cabo Isabela. Use DMA chart 25801 and radar or depth sounder to run even closer inshore.

Punta Rocia

Punta Rocia is a delightful Dominican vacation village with beautiful beaches and extensive opportunity for coral reef snorkeling and fishing. Unfortunately it is these extensive reefs that make it difficult to exit Punta Rocia in the dark—which would be necessary to sail a *Thornless* leg from here to **Luperón**. In settled easterly weather, however, one can stop here and, exiting at sunup, make the short 7-mile leg over to Cabo Isabela for another day's pleasure. If only hiding here from the Trades, move over to Cabo Isabela in the late afternoon and anchor there for your night departure.

Upon meeting the 100-fathom line on the eastward motor from Monte Cristi, turn to 122° magnetic for 9 miles to arrive off Punta Rocia at first light. Be careful not to go too close to the point itself, which is surrounded by a coral bottom 10 to 30 feet deep. Proceed true south, or 187° magnetic, from a point ½-mile west of the point's shoreline to a red zinc roof on the beach. Turn onto 120° magnetic after ⅓ mile to enter the anchorage at **Ensenada**. (See chartlet on next page.)

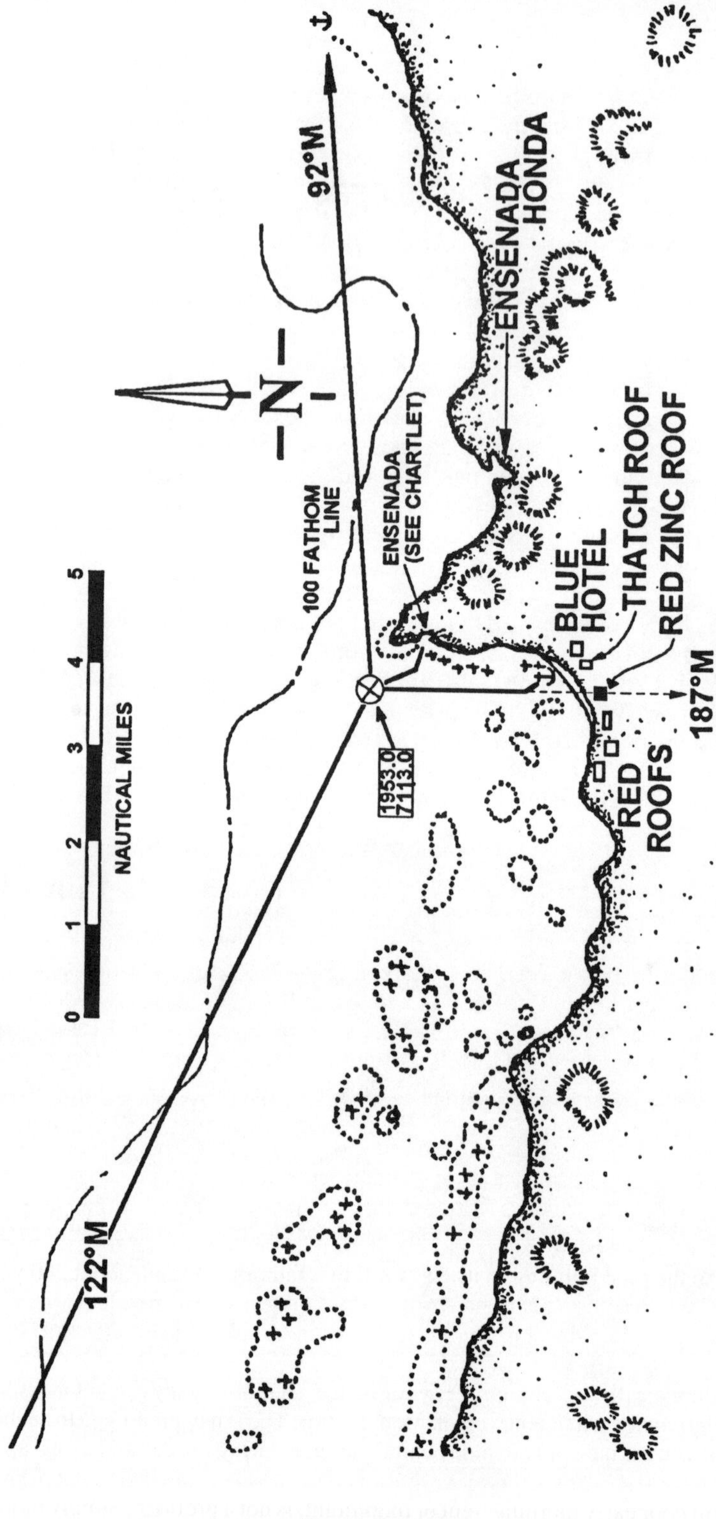
N
92°M
ENSENADA HONDA
100 FATHOM LINE
ENSENADA (SEE CHARTLET)
BLUE HOTEL
THATCH ROOF
RED ZINC ROOF
187°M (TRUE SOUTH)
RED ROOFS
1953.0
7113.0
0 1 2 3 4 5
NAUTICAL MILES
122°M

Punta Rocia

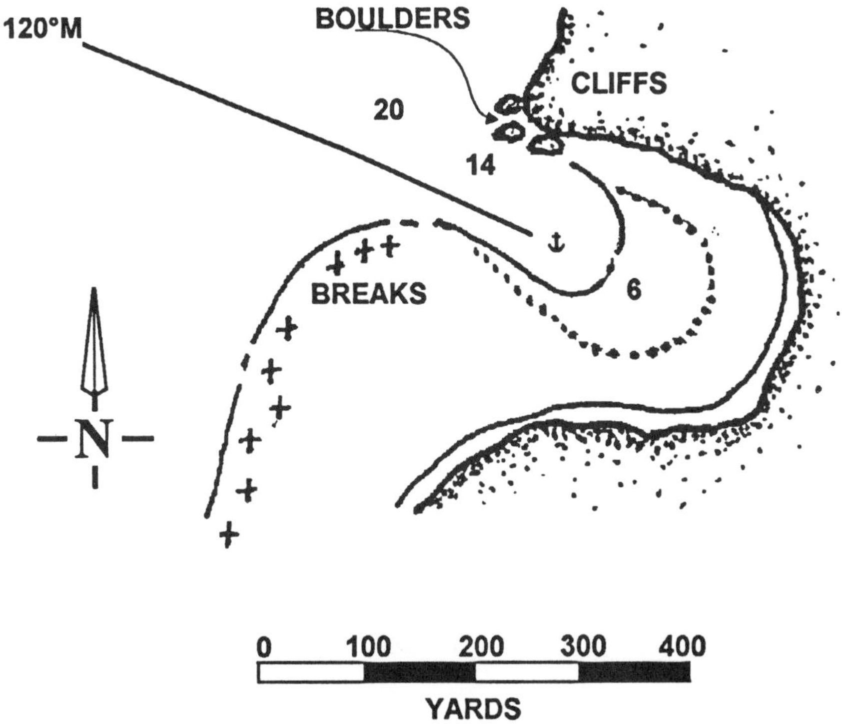

Ensenada

This is an easily recognizable landfall when you've got caught out too late in the morning while approaching **Hispaniola** from the north, and you want to give it up to continue in the next morning's calm. When entering the Ensenada anchorage, be careful to go exactly between the coral awash on the south side of the entrance and the boulders on the shore at the north side. When inside, pick a sandy patch between the grass and coral patches and get your anchors well down.

If staying here overnight, anchor off the town and leave at sunup for **Cabo Isabela**. To get to the town anchorage, proceed south on the red zinc roof for 1.6 miles from the point, then steer to the blue building to its east until in 2 fathoms of sand, about 200 yards from shore. The blue building and the thatch-roofed building next to it are part of a very nice hotel complex which attracts foreign tourists seeking a more simple scene than can be had at the great resort complexes further east.

The military will visit and inspect your papers (but no sweat, you got a *despacho con puertos intermedios* when you were in Manzanillo). They may prefer you to anchor off the town, but if you are here only to hide behind the cape during the day and to rest up, you will be exiting before sundown and there should be no problem in staying put. Exiting from Ensenada in poor early morning light or moonlight, is not a problem. Simply motor slowly for the half-mile on 300° magnetic, turn north for 1 mile and you're in the clear to head east.

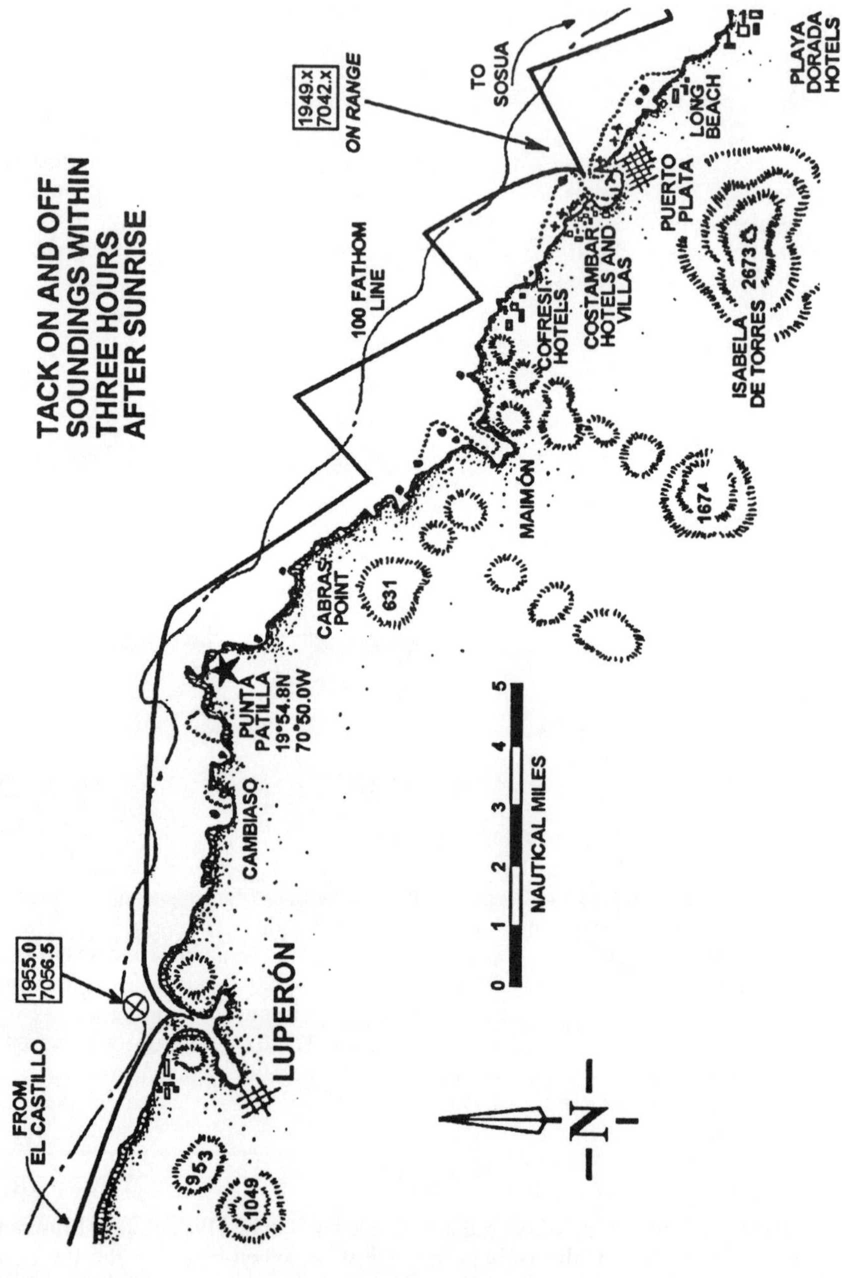

Cabo Isabela to Puerto Plata

This section of the coast is high and rugged, with the 100-fathom line being less than 2 miles off shore. If the offshore wind has been blowing 15 knots or less from east or south of east during the day, you usually will have a flat, calm motor sail in deep water close inshore before dawn.

The secret is to hide behind the capes in the daytime and transit the bays at night, taking the wind that is on a down-tick of a trade cycle. Go only when the forecast wind is 15 knots or less from behind the island (i.e., south of east), or in less than 15 knots if blowing east (along the coast), or in 10 knots or less if there is an onshore wind. Reduce these wind strengths by 5 knots if you want to coast in daylight.

Most cruisers, especially Pacific sailors, underestimate the Atlantic trades. Around the Greater Antilles there are great variations of depths through which pour voluminous, though not rapid, currents. Sailing or motoring to windward on this coast during full trades is flat out suicidal. For a truly thornless passage, the reader should study carefully the effects documented in the chapters: Wait for Weather, Hug the Shore Coasting to Windward, Don't Be Afraid of the Dark, Approaching Hispaniola, Harbor Telltales and Listening to the Weather, as well as each leg's chapter.

Cabo Isabela

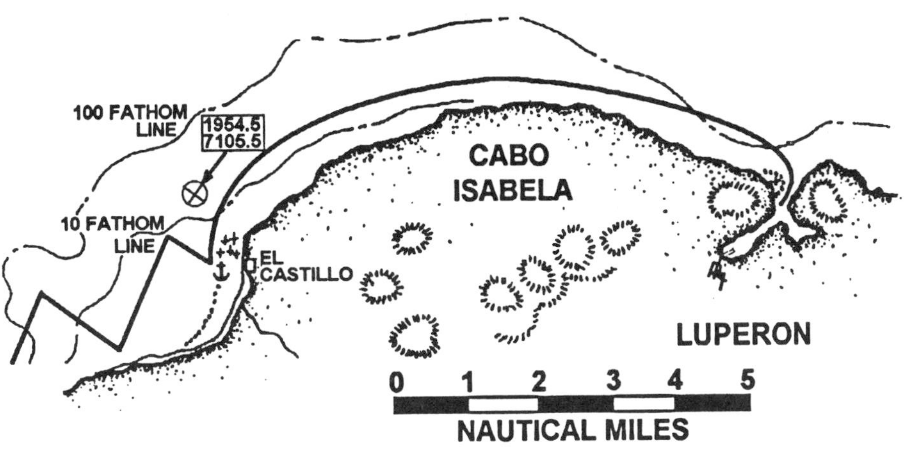

Cabo Isabela and the First New World Colony

The most thornless cruisers shall have made landfall on Hispaniola in **Manzanillo** and shall be approaching **Cabo Isabela** from the west. When you meet the 100-fathom line while motorsailing eastward from **Punta Rocia** in early light, strike an east-southeast course for **Isabela Bay**, about 10 miles west of Cabo Isabela to avoid the strong cape effects and get the most of the morning calm. Approach the beach anchorage from the west in good morning light just north of the mouth of the **Bajabonico**, also known as the **Isabela River**.

Your landfall will be **El Castillo**, a low, red rock promontory, which will stand out as the only variation in what is otherwise miles and miles of dark sand beach.

Approach El Castillo due east to avoid the reef a half-mile north of it. Anchor directly in front of El Castillo in 2 fathoms and await the arrival of the Navy. They are nice young men, full of smiles, stuck in a lonely outpost with no opportunity for advancement. If you don't offer a present right away, they will search your boat for suggestions. Better you offer first. Though an open roadstead, this is a calm and tranquil anchorage in prevailing conditions. Leave here at sunup for the 10 miles to Luperón, swinging wide of the rocks and reef projecting north of the anchorage.

El Castillo is the place where Columbus, on his second voyage, established the first surviving European settlement in the New World. After losing the *Santa Maria* on his first voyage, he had left his crew's troublemakers to establish the first European colony at **Navidad**, behind the **Limonade Reef**. The fact that no one survived cannot be blamed on the Admiral of the Ocean Seas. Based on the later behavior of the Spanish crews in Hispaniola, it's a safe bet they stirred up the Indians some and were probably the last of their breed to suffer due retribution.

The site selected for the first colony at **Isabela**, as you will see, presented free fields of fire on all sides, including over the rocky palisades to seaward. This was a snug redoubt fronted by a 1-by-2-mile patch of sand bottom in a harbor easy for a square rigger to make and leave in all conditions. Close to shore the bottom is shallow rock. There is a lovely hotel, restaurant and dive club just inside the reef which is run by a Belgian-Dominican couple, Herman and Sonia.

Don José María Cruxent, a Venezuelan archeologist, runs the digs at El Castillo, while the University of Florida tries to make sense of the findings. It is computerized archeology since back in the 1950's, when the dictator Trujillo ordered a crew to clean up the site in preparation for a visit by Spanish archeologists. They did what you might do if a dictator ordered you to clean up something: They bulldozed the remarkably intact ruins to a cleared depth of 80 cm. Nonetheless much has been done and the site makes for a very interesting afternoon's visit.

Due to current, landfalls are often off to the west when bound for **Luperón**, also called **Puerto Blanco** on some charts. The significant land feature to recognize will be **Cabo Isabela**. It should be near dawn and the coast is steep-to here, with the 100-fathom line less than a mile off the coast. After some time in the Bahamas you will be land-shy, and the mountainous coast will look very close at first. Remember that these mountains are quite high: 1049 feet at Cabo Isabela, which is backed up by a range almost 3000 feet high! You will see them, even on dark nights, as a high border of blacker against black.

These mile-deep bays provide the best yacht harbor on the island of Hispaniola. The cliff on the east side of the entrance provides a convenient transit with which to enter, headed due south. This cliff is where Martín Pinzón was found anchored with the stolen *Pinta* when Columbus's longboat rounded the point from Isabela looking for the *Niña*'s next anchorage. Leave the red ball buoy on your starboard and round into the western harbor favoring the southern shore. Do *not* trust the stakes I show or other markers cruisers will tell you about over the radio. Your benefit from this guide is my long-term experience with its harbors. I've watched these stakes be dragged around for various exercises and simply left where they fell. A casual cruiser would assume the marks were being carefully placed and had permanent status.

Again, treat all aids to navigation in the Caribbean with great suspicion.

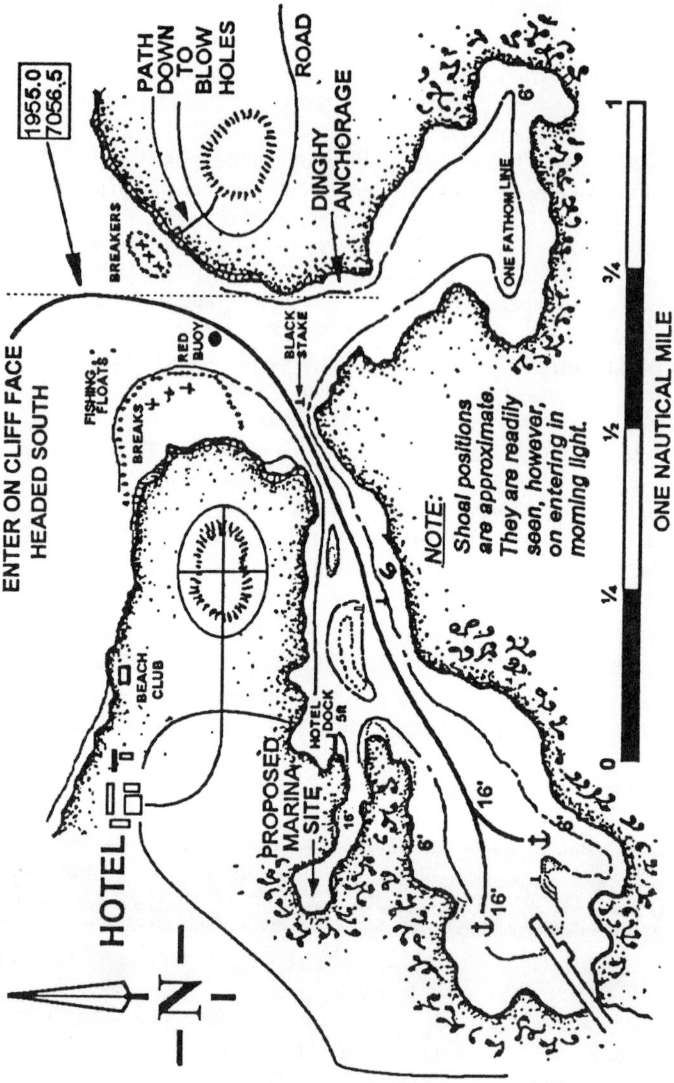

Luperón (Puerto Blanco)

Map the place with your eye on the way into **Luperón**—you may be coming out in the dark without a moon. Not to worry, it's dead calm at night. Motor slowly and if you nose into a mud bank you can slide right off into deep water. If you get stuck, you'll just have to prolong your stay in this lovely bay that looks more like a Swiss lake than a bay of the sea.

Clearing in here is easy. Motor by the gunboat at the dock to ensure they notice your arrival. Signal the uniformed men on the gunboat of your intention to anchor. A clearance party will arrive by dinghy when you are anchored. Anchor in 12 to 16 feet of sandy mud, far enough from the mangroves to be free from mosquitoes and *gegenas* (hey-HEN-ahs) or no-see-ums. (See the Dominican Republic section in the Appendix on Customs and Clearances.)

The water is good here, but add chlorine before filling your water tanks. Also, wait for the lines to clear after a drop in pressure caused by a break or a power outage. *Shame on you if you fail to take either of these measures, even in Florida.*

Guns are checked until departure and they may even get cleaned for you. The D.R. tries to be drug-free. Possession of illicit drugs will land you in jail and you will, properly, lose your boat for possessing them.

The north coast harbors leave your ground tackle a mud- and growth-encrusted mess. The cleanup job on the ground tackle will leave you exhausted and in an ill mood for a bad start to sea. You'll need a night's sleep after your labors. The day before leaving, get anchors unfouled and clean the rodes. Lay to a single fresh hook, and make ready for sea. Hire a boy, or use the Pinzón anchorage to scrub prop and bottom for the motoring ahead. This is also a good practice throughout the mangrove harbors in Puerto Rico.

The Town of Luperón

For the better part of two decades, Luperón has been the site of a tourist development project with villas, condos, hotels and marina. To put the best face possible on it, progress has been slow. There is a large hotel complex on the beach which is run on the Club Med all-inclusive plan. Many entrepreneurs have put up restaurants and bars in the town in expectation of a tourist boom which never came. As a result, local business people may be slow to see close-fisted cruisers as their economic salvation. Be cheerful and friendly yourself and you will find them willing to help you provision, jury-rig, travel, get medical help, or whatever. In the D.R., *smile*.

Luperón is a small rural town, it boasts markets and hardware stores, discos, hospital, police, dentists, and all the other amenities a civilized place needs including ice cream. Don't mistake lack of sophistication for lack of civilization. However, you will be restricted in what you can find in Luperón. A pharmacy catering to just a couple of hundred people will not likely have your specific brand of lipstick. Ask for what you want, and you will be surprised what a little persistence will produce. Otherwise, you may have to travel to Puerto Plata or Santiago, or even the capital, but usually anything can be had in the D.R. You just have to find it.

Transport

Buses leave Luperón daily at 1:30 p.m. for the capital (see map for bus stop). The same bus leaves Santo Domingo every day at 8:30 a.m. and will deliver you right to the dock, or muelle it (*mwaye-yaye*) in Luperón by 1 p.m. To get anywhere but the capital, take a *guagua* to **Imbert** from the *parquecito* (see map).

Imbert is a town on the highway that connects **Puerto Plata**, **Santiago** and **Santo Domingo**. To return to Luperón from anywhere but the capital, take a bus to Imbert. Your choice of transport ranges from motorcycles and pickup trucks to *guaguas* and large, air-conditioned buses with bar carts and two feature films. *Guaguas* are mini-vans, or tired buses, with fixed routes, open doors and a boy who collects the money and pushes the passengers into place. In Santo Domingo the *guaguas* run like conveyor belts at right angles to each other all over the city. If you know the X and the Y map coordinates to where you want to go, simply ride one *guagua* X blocks one way, then ride another Y blocks on the perpendicular, and you're there.

Getting to Puerto Plata and Santiago

Take the *guagua* (gwah-gwah) to **Imbert** from the *parquecito* in **Luperón**. The *guaguas* wait under the trees in the park until one is full, whereupon it takes off for Imbert, on the Puerto Plata to Imbert highway. If you don't want to wait for a *guagua* to fill up, you can always buy the remaining seats, thereby ensuring a more comfortable commute, as well as a faster one. These *guaguas* are vans. For max comfort, sit at the window behind the driver. Have change ready.

At Imbert there will be a stack of *guaguas* waiting to fill up to go to Luperón . They relay back and forth all day from 6 a.m. to 8 p.m. It's best to leave for Puerto Plata at 6:30 a.m. Much later and you hit the rush hour, but after 8:30 or 9 a.m. it slows down and you have to wait forever to get a full vehicle. Then you get to town and it's already siesta time when all the stores close from noon to 2 p.m. The 6:30 a.m. start gives you 4 hours' additional useful time in Puerto Plata. It's best not to plan on taking the 8 p.m. *guagua*: It may have left at 7:30, and you shall be stranded in Imbert overnight.

To get to **Puerto Plata** from Imbert, cross the highway and get into an east bound car (small cars this time, not vans) waiting to fill up with six passangers. These cars are called *carros publicos*, or more current some places, *carritos*. To get to Santiago, get into either a car or bus headed west. Car or bus to Santigo will be 17-25 pesos. *Carritos* to Puerto Plata will be 8-10 pesos. Arriving by car to Puerto Plata, the driver will take you whereever you wish in town. Go to *el Parque Central* if you aren't sure. Returning to Imbert from Puerto Plata, take a *motoconcho* (moped) to **La Rotonda** (lah roh-TONE-dah) which is the west bound terminal for *guaguas* and cars. Ask for the Luperón car and, once again, it will leave when it's loaded up. The *motoconcho* costs 5 pesos. Have it ready in change! If you don't, he may want more.

Lucas (LOO-cah) is the lady to know. She owns a good *tipico* (TEE-pee-coh) restaurant and discotheque a few blocks up the street from the pier (17). Her restaurant is the oldest in town and has the best kitchen and tipico cooks. It's where Dominican tourists eat. Lucas will have the propane truck fill your tanks if you drop them off with her. As tourism gains here, more upscale restaurants appear, but Lucas is still the choice for Dominican fare, price and quality.

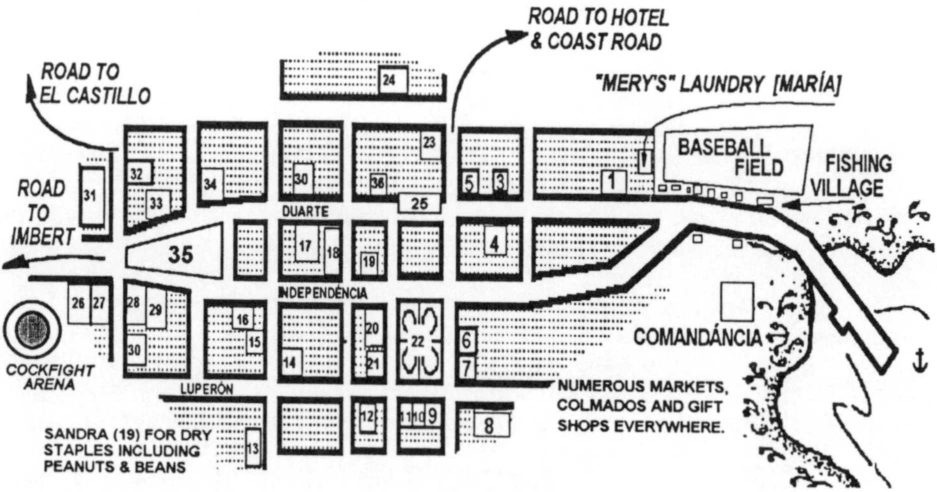

1 WELDING SHOP
2 ICE, FISH
3 CARPENTER
4 VIDEO THEATER
5 TERRAZZA RESTAURANT
6 BEVERAGE WHOLESALER
7 RESTAURANT/DISCO
8 NATIONAL GUARD
9 POST OFFICE
10 FIRE DEPARTMENT
11 FUTURE THEATER
12 CHURCH
13 HOSPITAL
14 STATIONER'S
15 BUS DRIVER'S HOUSE
16 PRIVATE CLINIC
17 LUCAS RESTAURANT
18 HOTEL
19 MARKET
20 MORROBEL'S STORE
21 COURTHOUSE
22 CENTRAL PARK
23 MARKET
24 WELDING
25 BUS STOP
26 HIGH SCHOOL
27 POLICE STATION
28 HOTEL
29 MARINA REST.
30 DENTIST
31 PRIMARY SCHOOL
32 TELEPHONE CO.
33 PHARMACY
34 NEWSPAPERS
35 GUAGUAS
36 SHOE REPAIR

The bank in Luperón is a farmer's savings and loan institution and does not change money. Individual tourist businesses, such as restaurants and gift shops, do change money. Strangely, the best rate is usually offered by the bicycle shop just beyond the high school, south of the *gallera*, or cockfight arena.

Welding (if you carry your own stainless rods) and carpentry work is available in Luperón. Once a local carpenter built my shower grating with a hand saw and pegs. I gave him the teak and the old one to copy. Go to Puerto Plata for machine shop work.

Buy singles of everything you think you *might like*, then cases of what you find you *really do* like. You can get rum, coke, tonic and beer by the case at the beverage wholesaler's (6) on the square, and what they don't have in stock you can order. Most everything is in local markets *if you ask*, but a trip to Puerto Plata markets won't hurt. Don Santiago Morrobel's store on the square (20) wholesales caselots and delivers them to the dock.

Traveling in the D.R.

Whether touring or seeking parts for your boat, **Luperón** is the preferred port at which to leave the boat to go inland in the Dominican Republic. If you fail to explore this wonderful country with its handsome and friendly people, you will have missed a major highlight of your cruise. Though many Americans do live in or visit the D.R., the preponderance of visitors are European or Canadian. Only 30 percent of foreign tourism comes from the United States. Americans tend to be timid travelers. If you are American, break the mold and see the D.R.! It has 18,800 square miles including lakes, forests, deserts and mountains over 11,700 feet. Visit it's museums of American culture (the Taino museum at *Altos de Chavón*, the *Museo del Hombre* and *Casa Real* in Santo Domingo), and get to know its gracious people, models of the American race.

The D.R. has tens of thousands of foreign residents and long-term visitors. All of them travel routinely and with safety. Many live in the north coast retirement communities. Many have built retreats and ranches throughout the island. Affluent visitors rent cars. Groups travel by bus. Young people, or others accustomed to foreign travel, simply wander the nation with backpacks, taking whatever local transport is available.

Hotels in Santo Domingo

If you go to Santo Domingo, it's most convenient, and most pleasant, to overnight at one of the old palaces such as Hostal Nicolas Nader, in the *zona colonial* at the corner of Calles Luperón and Duarte, just six blocks from where the bus from Luperón stops. There are big tourist Sheratons and Hiltons on Av. George Washington, also called the *malecón* (meaning dyke, or seawall). But the *paradors* are more comfortable and right in the heart of the old colonial city where the shopping and night life are, and, of interest to cruisers, cost about a third as much. Built in 1514 for General Alvarado, the Spanish military commander, this colonial palace served as headquarters in **Santo Domingo** for Cortez, Ponce de Leon and Pizarro.

There are other old *paradors* in the capital, the largest being the Nicolas Ovando, the palace of the first governor after Columbus. It is operated by the government and is therefore poorly maintained, less efficient and more expensive than the Nader. The Commercial on the Conde and Hostos, is a reasonably priced hotel, as is the Caribeño, just north of the bus stop. There are cheaper and more spartan pensions, with baths and fans instead of no air-conditioning, near the Parque de Independéncia. These cost about ¼ of the *paradors*. Europeans prefer the El Señorial.

While in **Santo Domingo** I do all the hardware stores and marine places, take care of medical visits, get new glasses, stock up the medicine chest, and so on. It often takes two nights. The first night I always stay at the Nader for both convenience and luxury. On the second or third nights I may take a cheaper and less commodious room at one of the neighborhood hotels near the hardware stores.

There are also accommodations for the less priggish cruiser. All over the world Chinese restaurants, like French cafes, often rent rooms upstairs for the economical traveler. The standard may vary. Often they have full bath and noisy a/c, and cost half what the pensions do. The D.R. is no exception. There may be large commodious beds, European baths and mirrors on the ceiling, when they're the type of room which is mostly used in the daytime. Anyhow, after 8 p.m. they sure are cheap. There's one with a not-so-firm mattress over a Chinese cafeteria near the best *Gallego* restaurant this side of Gallicia: Pepín on Avenida San Martín. For a dollar more there's a higher standard at the Londres Chinese restaurant down the street.

There's even a great ice cream store, and a newspaper and magazine vendor across the street from Pepín's. I run my errands all day, then go to Pepín's to read the paper over a drink. Late that night, after a great, leisurely Gallician feast accompanied by the Movie Channel, I scrub off the city dirt and crash on a king-size bed for the night (I try not to look up). No traveling commercial man ever had it better.

Using Guaguas in Santo Domingo

Santo Domingo is a huge Latin American city. It is dirty, noisy and confusing, like New York—but also like New York, you can get anything you want there if you know where to go. Look in the yellow pages (yes, they're the same as at home), get a map and go to it. The *guaguas* in Santo Domingo run west the length of Bolívar, Mella and San Martín, and east on Independencia, and both east and west on John F. Kennedy and 27 Febrero. They run both north and south on Máximo Gómez, Abraham Lincoln and Winston Churchill. This is a complete grid. You can hop two of these conveyances in just minutes and be within a block of your destination for 32 cents.

In Santiago, like in Santo Domingo, there is a "conveyor belt system" of cars marked "A", "B" and "M", which buzz all over town on fixed routes. Purchase a map of the town at any Librería or newsstand. The maps show the *carrito* routes. Ask for *carritos de M*, etc.

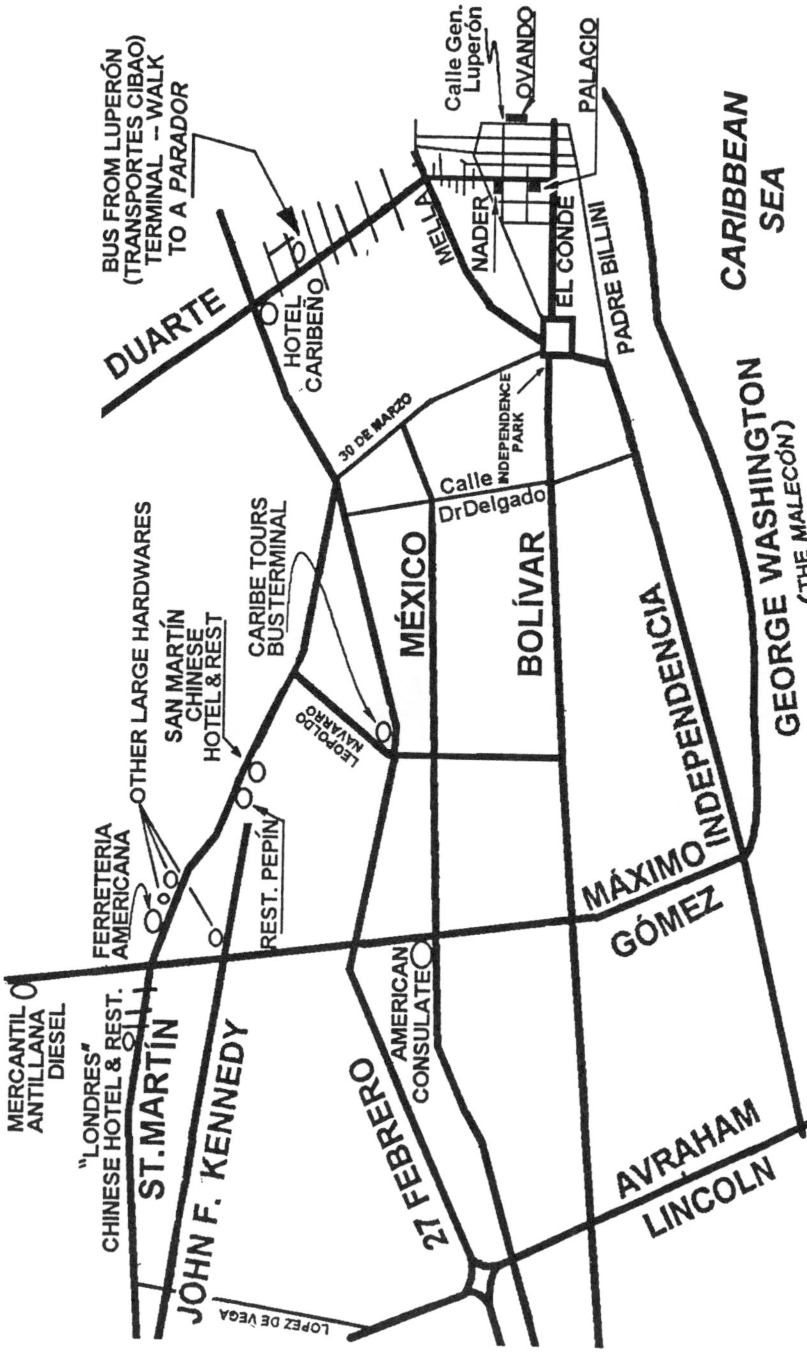
BUS FROM LUPERÓN (TRANSPORTES CIBAO) TERMINAL – WALK TO A PARADOR
Calle Gen. Luperón
OVANDO
PALACIO
DUARTE
HOTEL CARIBEÑO
MELLA
NADER
EL CONDE
PADRE BILLINI
CARIBBEAN SEA
30 DE MARZO
INDEPENDENCE PARK
Calle DrDelgado
GEORGE WASHINGTON
(THE MALECÓN)
OTHER LARGE HARDWARES
SAN MARTÍN CHINESE HOTEL & REST
CARIBE TOURS BUSTERMINAL
MÉXICO
BOLÍVAR
INDEPENDENCIA
LEOPOLDO NAVARRO
FERRETERIA AMERICANA
REST. PEPÍN
MÁXIMO GÓMEZ
MERCANTIL ANTILLANA DIESEL
"LONDRES" CHINESE HOTEL & REST.
ST. MARTÍN
JOHN F. KENNEDY
27 FEBRERO
AMERICAN CONSULATE
AVRAHAM LINCOLN
LOPEZ DE VEGA

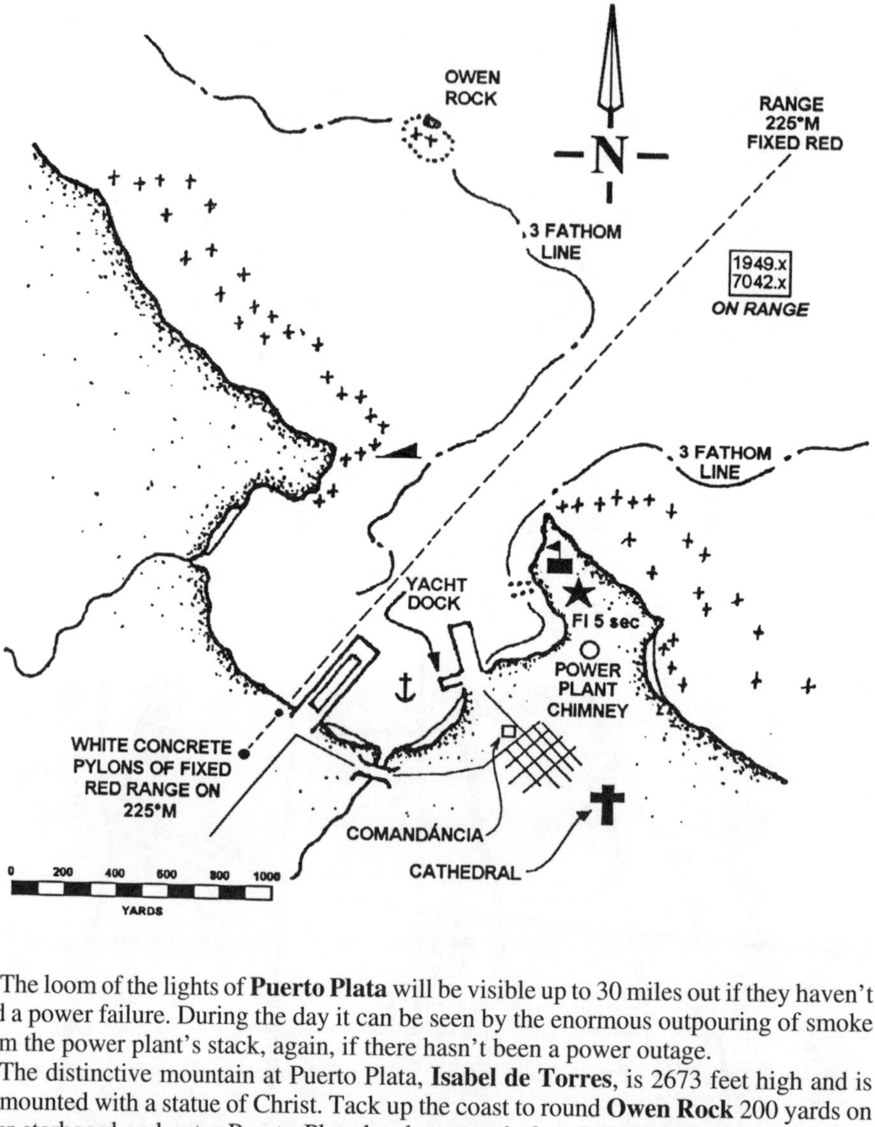

The loom of the lights of **Puerto Plata** will be visible up to 30 miles out if they haven't had a power failure. During the day it can be seen by the enormous outpouring of smoke from the power plant's stack, again, if there hasn't been a power outage.

The distinctive mountain at Puerto Plata, **Isabel de Torres**, is 2673 feet high and is surmounted with a statue of Christ. Tack up the coast to round **Owen Rock** 200 yards on your starboard and enter Puerto Plata by the range before 9 o'clock in the morning. If coming from **Luperón**, round **Punta Patilla** before 7 a.m. and two-tack in light easterlies down to Owen Rock. If you've had luck with the weather and arrive off the port at night, use the range. It consists of 2 fixed red lights at the west end of the harbor, just to the west of the long commercial dock at that end. I find this range easier to spot and follow than the range at the entrance to Europort, Rotterdam, the world's busiest port. A note of caution, the range lights, although large and bright, are well shrouded, as they should be, providing a narrow beam for you to follow. Keep a sharp lookout when picking it up and stay well off until you do. In daytime, the range can be seen as two white concrete pylons with orange tops.

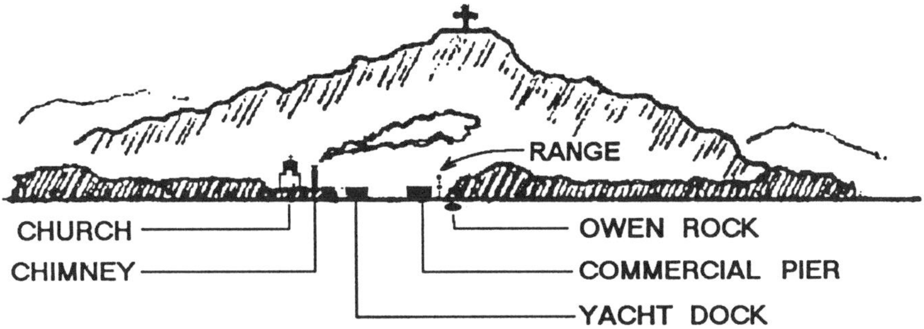

ISABEL DE TORRES
DUE SOUTH 3 MILES

Go to the dock in **Puerto Plata** only in Force 3 or less. If you don't want to lay to the dock upon arriving, anchor and row in with your papers to see the *comandante*. Move to the dock the next morning. Refer to the section on clearing customs in the Appendix for more details.

Boats often bunch up in the small anchorage and line the pier like sardines. Damage can occur from surge and big ship propwash. Security on the yacht dock doesn't seem to be anyone's responsibility. Lock up well and follow the anchoring advice below. **Luperón** is, of course, the preferred port of entry. Leave the boat there while seeing the D.R.

On entering Puerto Plata in the past, one found the dock was free, the electricity was free, the excellent mountain water was free and, when you walked through the gates to the nearby rum factory, the rum was free. Not a bad town at all! Then there's the harbor . . .

The harbor is congested and dirty and the dock is a nightmare. The dock is an abandoned concrete pier given to the yachties on an "as is" basis. "Med moor" to the dock with crisscrossed stern lines, two long springs, an anchor 150 or more feet ahead and slightly east, and another ahead and slightly west. Keep the boat from a half- to a full-boat length from the dock and use your dinghy to shuttle back and forth with a "telegraph" line.

Whether anchoring or "Med-mooring." let three days go by before trusting the anchor. It's in 20 to 35 feet of colloidal mud and will set itself fine after a spell. If at the dock, take up the slack for three mornings. Keep good slack in your stern and spring lines or you'll "rubber band" like a slingshot when a surge starts.

Jerry jug your fuel from the Texaco station around the corner if you can. Do major shopping yourself. (See the section on Major Reprovisioning En Route.) I have spent many months at this dock, both in summer and winter. Properly done, your mooring can be safe in all conditions—except from the "professional" delivery captains in power boats. They'll dig your anchors up at 10 knots while powering up their own.

The surge is less your enemy than are other boaters. Surge is mostly a winter phenomenon anyway. Be seaman-like when you up-anchor the day before leaving and maintain your bow over a vertical chain. That way you minimize the risk of breaking out your neighbor's anchor. (See the section entitled Anchoring in the Caribbean.)

The cinders from the power plant, dry and harmless, float out to sea and over the yachts, perpetually raining black dust. The commercial ship traffic in the small harbor causes the yachts at anchor to knot up dangerously close to each other, and often a seagoing tug will wash up anchors with its propeller. The least well-anchored yacht may tear loose and throw everyone against the pier like dominos.

The officials of the port handle yacht traffic with the left hand, so to speak. They often get fed up and can offer hassles of their own to the cruiser who loses his sense of humor. The **Puerto Plata** dock is a free-port area and Customs may inspect anything you take ashore. Don't be offended.

Puerto Plata Town

So! Puerto Plata harbor is crowded, dirty, and full of hassles. With Luperón only a bus ride away, there's no reason to take your boat there. Why go at all? Because the town and its people are fantastic and the DR is the best, if not the only, place to provision without going broke between Florida and Venezuela. And because the trip directly to **Samaná** can be very thorny. You could get a fair **Weather Window** to go directly for Samaná, but that is rare, indeed. Don't bet your boat on it. You can stop and anchor overnight at Puerto Plata.

Puerto Plata has the most character and the nicest people of any town in the Caribbean. It is the second-oldest town in the western World, **Santo Domingo** being eldest. From Puerto Plata you can get anything you need, sometimes via **Santiago**, a city of over a million souls, an hour away in the mountains, and Santo Domingo, the capital, a 4-hour bus ride away.

The bus terminals are near the central park. Some buses have video movies, a stewardess and a bar cart for just a few bucks. *El cheapo transporto* is also available in a range of flavors from flatbed trucks to village hopping *guaguas*. (See Traveling in the D.R.)

The people on the north coast of the D.R., besides being very handsome, are among the most hospitable people in the world. In genes and traditions they benefit from their pacific **Taino**, **Arawak**, pirate and **Hidalgo** ancestors. They have a 500-year-old tradition of independence from Santo Domingo, the island's big city of 2½ million people.

Despite its inherence to a Spanish colony, **Puerto Plata** was the main trading center for the fleets of *corsaires* and privateers who harassed the Spanish for two centuries. For trading with the crown's enemies, Puerto Plata was burned to the ground and sacked by the Spanish themselves. Unlike the stone city of Santo Domingo, wooden Puerto Plata has no monuments of architecture to survive fire and rot. Its heritage as the second-oldest town in the hemisphere resides in its fabulous people, not its buildings.

Violence is unheard of on the north coast and theft as here is rare. If you meet a cad, it's usually either a misunderstanding or an itinerant from the big city. Except for tourist shops, all prices are the same for everyone and there's normally no haggling. Treat these people as honest and trustworthy and you'll discover that that's exactly what they are.

Guides are available, official and unofficial, for the non-Spanish speaker. For official guides, see Hector or Anaima Echavarria, owners of the Las Palmas gift shop across from the rum factory. Hector is director of the Association of Tourist Guides.

Money is changed at various banks at virtually the same rate. You can get cash for credit cards but it's cheaper and easier to bring it with you.

Mail in Puerto Plata can be a problem. Reckon on a week to 10 days *from* the states and a week to 3 weeks *to* the states. If you have mail sent to the D.R., or any third world country, in envelopes that look like they may have checks enclosed—don't! Nor anything clearly of value. It all goes through Santo Domingo. There are courier services available, and Federal Express is on the island.

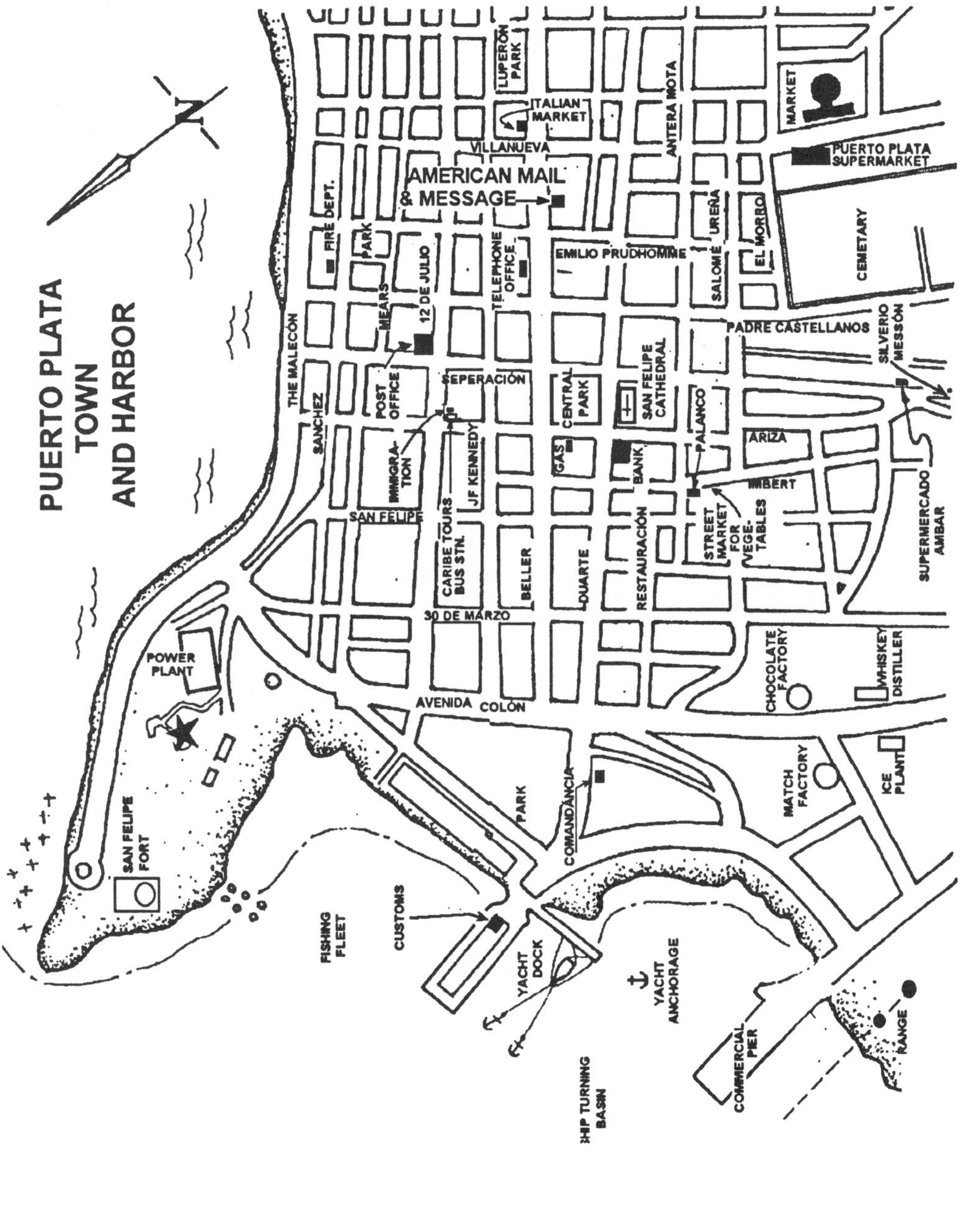

Puerto Plata Town and Harbor

Harbor Conditions

The Dominican ports are the first poor Caribbean country ports that cruisers from the north see. **Puerto Rico** and the **Virgins**, both deeply on the dole from their U.S. owner, are reasonably affluent. The **Leewards** and **Windwards** have sufficient charter and beach hotel operations around their ports to somewhat disguise their campestral nature. Not so the D.R. But if you wanted it like home, you could have stayed there.

The large province of Puerto Plata, which stretches from Luperón to Cabarete, where the wind surfing championships are held, has a pure tourist economy. There are more hotel rooms in this one province than there are in all of Puerto Rico. In 1992 there were 24,000 hotel rooms, mostly within the 50 mile long province east of **Cofresí** (name of a pirate who based himself there).

Cruisers in the D.R. contribute nothing to such an economy; therefore the situation in the D.R. harbors is unlikely to change. Less than 400 pleasure craft a year call, and half of those are on deliveries. The other half are penurious cruisers. Enjoy your stay, but don't waste your time grousing about the conditions of harbors to whose commerce you add little. Undeveloped ports are a growing rarity for the cruiser. Enjoy the D.R.'s.

"Dock Boys"

Throughout the Caribbean the loafers on the docks and in the harbors will hassle you for work which they may not do or errands they may not run. Some will ruin your laundry if you let them and gouge you in the bargain. The bad actors of the breed are guys who have been spoiled by "ugly Americans," mostly paid delivery crews in town for a crack at the red-light district. These crews push out their absent owners' dollars like Bible tracts at the airport. Therefore some of the dock boys respect neither your common sense nor your wallet. So sailor, beware!

Meanwhile, there are people who can do useful chores. You just have to find them. If you do employ someone for chores or errands—especially dock boys—specify short, specific tasks with firm, fixed prices. Have each task finished and paid for before going on to the next task, assuming you still want him to work for you. Finally, if a dock boy thinks you've agreed for a service from him, never change dock boys before the first one has been paid and discharged. You may find yourself in the middle of a labor dispute right out of Marlon Brando's *On the Waterfront*. The dock boys of Luperón are as yet unspoiled and they are the best you will encounter on your cruise south.

A Note About "Bribes"

Every season I hear the ridiculous chatter about *mordida* (Mexican for bribes) in the D.R. ports. It usually starts with the age-old Dominican expression for people returning to the island from abroad: "Did you bring any presents for me?" When adults say it, the response is usually something like "Half of what you have for me!" and there's a great deal of laughter. After a few $20 "presents," the surprised official becomes accustomed to the insolent response from the tourist and he goes with the flow, and accepting tips becomes routine. If you "tip" egregiously in Latin America, don't cover your bonehead behavior with wild tales of "being forced to pay bribes." That could be slanderous to your hosts and, under Napoleonic law, an arrestable offense. You won't get a bullet for not coughing up, but you will get respect. Just say a friendly "No," then share a beer or lunch with him next day. If you feel you must "tip" officials, do it as a delayed *favor*, not a *quid pro quo*. Regardless of what you've seen on old *Viva Zapata* movies, it is rude to offer a *bribe*. Doing *favors* for friends is different, however.

COASTING EAST FROM PUERTO PLATA

Once again, sailing or motoring to windward on this coast during full trades is flat out suicidal. For a truly thornless passage, the reader should study carefully the effects documented in the chapters: Wait for Weather, Hug the Shore Coasting to Windward, Don't Be Afraid of the Dark, and Approaching Hispaniola, as well as the specific advices given on each leg. In the following pages you will find some signs which tell the tale of a smooth exit when you are otherwise blinded from the conditions offshore by harbor and land effects. By making the tables and figures shown, and by listening to the Offshore Report each day, you can attune yourself to the music of the trades, and there will be no question when your window has arrived.

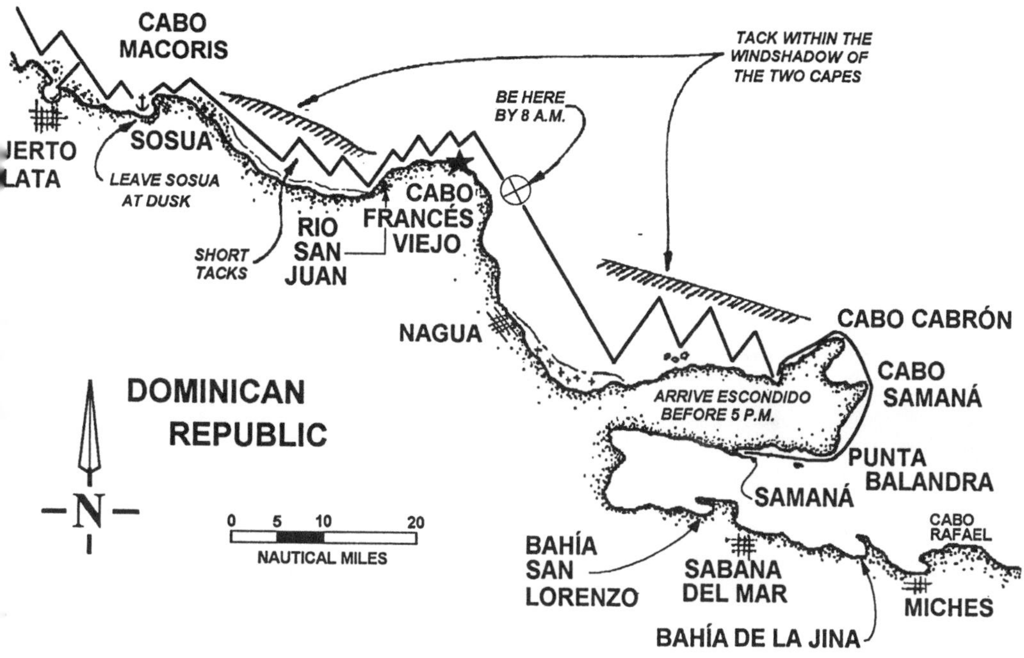

In this guide the unmodified word "wind" always refers to the overall flow forecast in the Offshore Report, not harbor wind and local effects.

It is not wise to guess the weather from harbor anywhere but the Bahamas. Even in some places in the Bahamas, where there are massive banks and land areas to weather of you, the real wind is not observed, for example, in **Landrail Point, West Caicos, Provodenciales**, and **Rum Cay's Flamingo Bay**, or **Georgetown**, in anything but north through east (southeast from there is a 60-mile fetch over land and banks). On the north and south coasts of the **Greater Antilles**, in prevailing conditions, the harbor wind can be at times greater (i.e., gustier) and at times much less than the wind just a half-mile offshore. In **Boquerón** it can blow 15 knots from the west, while, only five miles away on the south coast, it is blowing 20 knots from the east. In **Salinas** the wind may be zero at night, while outside the reef, only one mile away, it will be blowing 20 knots. Each anchorage and harbor has unique and complicated variables which contribute to its diminishing, increasing or changing of the direction of the real wind.

Ignore all harbor wind from Georgetown south, except for the telltales of the cycling of the Trades.

The point is to watch the cycling of the wind's direction and strength and take your exit only on a down-tick of a cycle, taking advantage of reduced wind speeds and southerly trends. Listen to both the Southwest North Atlantic and the Eastern Caribbean reports on the **National Weather Service** broadcasts on the NMN (see radio list in the Appendix) Portsmouth Coast Guard station, and go when the winds permit a comfortable and safe trip. On the north coast of the Dominican Republic, for instance, they should be less than 15 knots and south of east at best. The island shelters you from the eye of the wind, and the night effect is greatest.

To watch the winds, you should construct a table such as the one presented in the section on Crossing the Mona Passage. This is a good technique to track the winds and establish a baseline from which to discern "up-ticks" and "down-ticks" in the strength of the trades. (The data in that table are, of course, for departure from **Samaná**, not Puerto Plata or Luperón.) Always use the **NWS Offshore Forecast** winds. Apply "English" to the forecast winds only if you are in an area which is on the borderline of two forecasts, or near a significant weather feature.

Below are a few examples of harbor telltales I've found work. Coupled with your tracking of the cycles in the wind outside the harbor as given by the National Weather Service, the additional information you receive from these telltales will give you a sure indicator of your position on a cycle. You will have a confirmation of both the time of opening of your weather window and its possible duration.

EXAMPLE 1. If you have a forecast of W of 73W E15-20 kts. and E of 73W E-SE 20-25 kts., and you are situated at 73° west, then assume your winds are E 20 knots. Always, of course, leave harbor on the *beginning* of a downtrend in the wind strength cycle, never at the middle or near its end.

EXAMPLE 2. In Puerto Plata, one friend suggests watching the mountain. If the clouds haven't reached the mountain by 11 am, he says, you can go. In **Salinas**, watch the clocking of your flag from northeast to southeast in the morning. It will start earlier (or later) each day and take shorter (or longer) to finish clocking.

EXAMPLE 3. On the south and north coasts of the Greater Antilles, in normal trade weather, and in the absence of perturbing weather features such as fronts and waves, the trade cycles are indicated by the progression of the time of rise of the morning winds in harbor. There also are cycles in the endurance of the night wind over the daytime seabreeze. Here is a figure constructed in **Luperón** which clearly shows the regular cycle of the winds being masked, but not ultimately deformed, by a front.

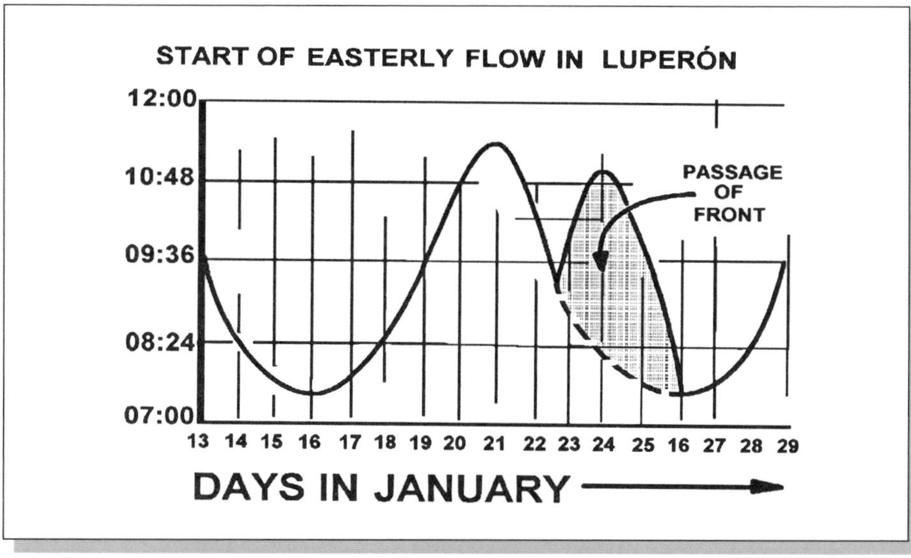

EXAMPLE 4. In either **Luperón** or **Puerto Plata**, unless you are going to ride a rare front directly to **Samaná**, observe the clocking of the winds each day and the cycle of their strengths day to day. The prevailing easterlies come back down to earth along about 9 in the morning along the coast, much earlier at sea, and farther out, they never lift. They reach a maximum between noon and 2 p.m., tapering off to a calm as early as 5 p.m. or as late as 10 p.m. If the maximum strength during the day is, say Force 5, and it's down to Force 3 by 3 p.m. (having raised to no more than Force 3 by 9 a.m.), get going! The rule, then is: "Force Three by Three." If it's Force 3 by 3 p.m. Monday, leave Tuesday a.m. so as to arrive in **Sosua** before noon.

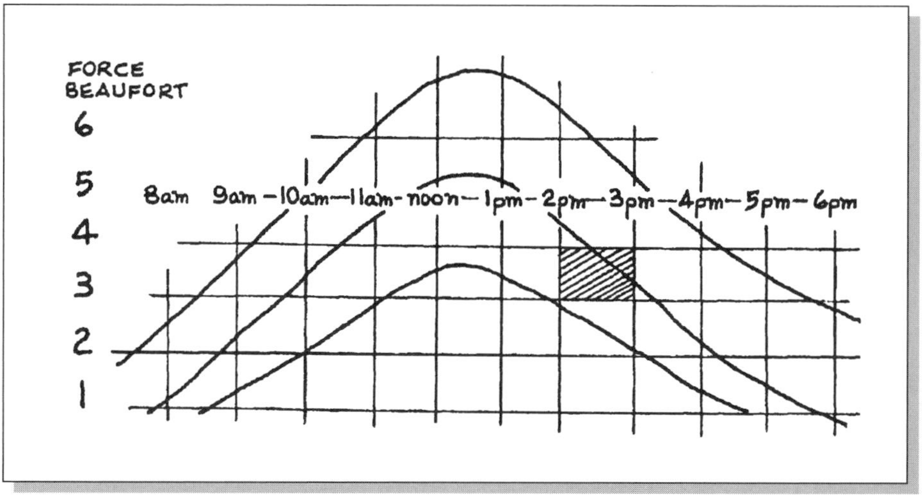

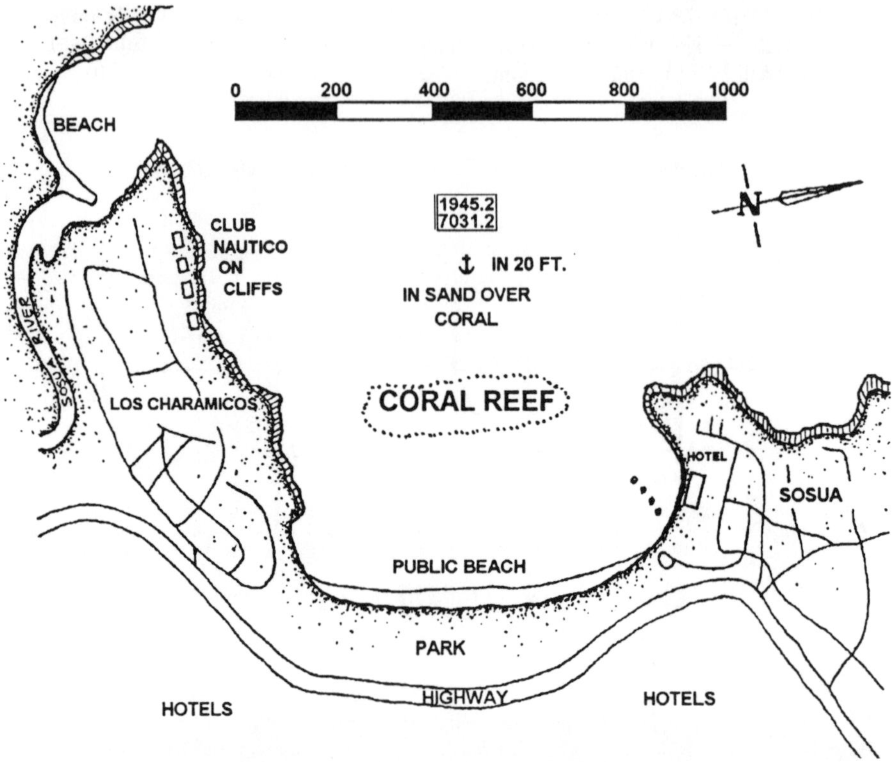

Sosua, a Transient Anchorage

Cleared from either **Puerto Plata** or **Luperón** "*con puertos intermedios*" for **Samaná**, take a **Leisure Sail** over to **Sosua**, standing well off the reefs along the shore. Leave Luperón at first light or a few hours earlier, anchoring overnight in the entrance, if necessary. As you approach the airport near Sosua, the cape effect around **Cabo Macoris** will be felt. Get closer inshore at this point to get cover from the stronger winds this effect produces. The reefs here are readily visible. These, and the surfing beaches off **Cabarete**, will be the last shoal shores on this passage. Anchor outside the public swimming beach at Sosua until 6 p.m., not going ashore or anchoring overnight, and forego your SG&T toward a safer voyage. Take a nap and prepare a thermos or two and a pressure cooker full of hot *burgoo* (see Glossary). Depart here at first light if daysailing to **Rio San Juan** on extremely light days.

Remember, great fleets of boats anchoring where they're not expected tend to draw more concern from local officials than do just one or two. Don't anchor close enough for swimmers to come out and hang onto your boat, thereby making a scene of yourself. If, despite your intentional low profile anchored way out there, a representative of the Puerto Plata *comandante* wakes you up, simply explain to him that you are sheltering under the headland until 6 p.m., and will be on your way when the seas permit.

One of the nicest parts of cruising the Thornless Path is that you see the same people again and again and, cruising in company, you can share your SG&T time with others. Headed south from Georgetown, I've often been in company with from 5 to 15 yachts. These trips weld friendships and make what is always a delightful trip south, even more enjoyable.

Staying Together

One thing I always make clear to sailing companions is that I paddle my own canoe, do my own navigation, select my own anchorages, and when I grab a **Weather Window** and go, it's my own decision for my boat. I encourage everyone else to do likewise. *Jalan Jalan* is my little universe on a savage sea, and she and I function as a team completely different from any other vessel and crew. This is no doubt true of all yachts and their crews. Unless there is an emergency at sea, we neither slow down to nor catch up with other boats, thus compromising our teamwork between crew and vessel, and forcing an unnatural rhythm to her functioning at sea. I suspect many problems on the path south are precipitated by this phenomenon, and by the subconscious reliance on other boats. (*Well, if I miss the weather, one of the other guys is sure to have it.*)

Fleets calling at **Sosua** will certainly be turned away. Proper respect for the sea and your vessel come first, demonstrations of camaraderie, second. When sailing in company, get advance permission to dawdle or leap ports ahead. Sail alone, even in company.

Buddy Channels

Many boats sailing in company stay tuned to a "buddy channel" instead of VHF Channel 16. I have seen one yacht sunk and many others suffer narrow escapes while the "buddy boats" blithely sailed on in ignorance of repeated warnings on Channel 16. Chatting on low power on Channel 16 while on the open sea will not bother ships in the area. On the contrary, you both will be glad to discover that you're within two miles of each other and didn't know it. Using buddy channels while underway in or near harbors, where dangers proliferate, is even more unwise.

Fleet Operations

One method of group cruising is to emulate a loose confederation of sovereign states. After all consultations are done, each captain must make his or her own decision, sharing it with the others out of courtesy, but not for approval. That's not to say, of course, that you can't change a decision upon hearing a wiser one made by someone else. Contact is maintained by radio and by common experiences in port.

If you are bound to stay together, then emulate the fascists whose emblem was the Roman faces, or bound bundle of spars. Appoint someone Navigator and someone else Admiral of the Fleet and make them responsible for putting voice to consensus. Democracy at sea can be dangerous. Picture a fleet of neophyte cruisers at sea, all strung out like a gaggle of geese, asking each other on the VHF whether to reef or tack while assuring each other of their like-mindedness, regardless of each vessel's differences. I see them every year. Each boat thinks another boat is leading. The one in the lead doesn't know he's leading. He thinks he made a wrong tack and left the group. Winnie The Pooh, off to discover the North Pole, was better organized than most cruising groups I've heard on the VHF.

Committee decisions, without a chairman to promulgate them, wind up not being made at all. If in port, preparing for a storm, that can be dangerous. At sea it is purely deadly.

Rounding the Capes

When making the usual nightsail between the two capes east of **Puerto Plata**, raise anchor at 6 p.m. and **Leisure Sail** around **Cabo Macoris** (CAH-boh mah-co-REES) until it's no fun anymore for lack of wind. This is usually an exciting sail in the ebb of the day's wind. But don't forget the cape effects. The wind blowing across a cape is squeezed by the cape. The same volume of air passing a smaller space must, of course, go faster, or the air behind would stack up clear back to Africa. The wind around Cabo Macoris and **Cabo Frances Viejo** (fran-SACE vee-AYE-ho) will be fiercer at the capes than well beyond them. Furthermore they will follow the contours of the cape and appear to be right on your nose all the way around. This occurs even in light night conditions. Don't despair—the real wind is less than what you see at the capes, and, if you start out to round a cape in the evening, the wind won't always be on your nose when you've left the cape behind.

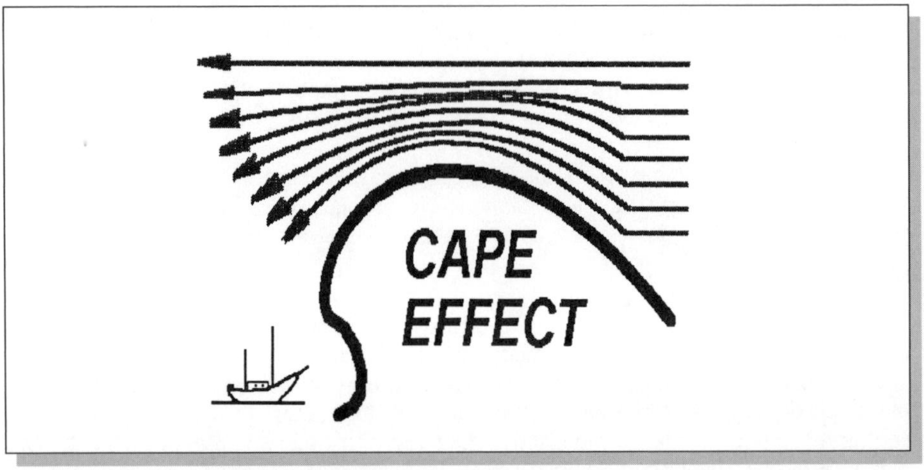

If there are some white horses, they will be the last you will see that night, and the wind will slacken beyond the cape, assuming, of course, that you picked a good window. If you got cheated on the window somehow, don't be shy of turning back to wait for another. Motorsail close along the capes themselves. If you don't stop at **Rio San Juan**, be sure to turn the corner and hoist sail east of Cabo Frances Viejo by 8 a.m., when the next day's easterly flow will hit.

One or two tacks south-southeast across the bay should carry you to the high offshore rocks east of **Nagua** and west of **Escondido**. From that point east the shore is fairly clear of reefs, and one can hug the shore and tack up to Escondido within a band of smooth sea. You should arrive at Escondido before 5 p.m. The harbor is difficult to spot from sea the first time. You will recognize it by the two rocks lying off the northwest arm of the bay. If it is your first time there, you will also need light while going in to convince yourself it is an easy night exit, which, of course, it is—as easy as a Norwegian fjord.

Sail with one or two tacks down the **Bahía Escocesa**. This is interesting territory. The bay is named The Scots Woman, while the two headlands surrounding her are named The Old Frenchman and The Cuckold. Furthermore, the bay is thought to be haunted. I've talked with sober and mature merchant seamen who have heard the crying of a woman while crossing the bay at night.

My first trip (westward) across the bay was at night, and we logged a peculiar melancholy that night, attributed at the time to the sorrow at leaving the Caribbean islands behind us. Only years later did I learn of the supposed haunting.

If, despite all the warnings in this guide to travel between the headlands only at night, you do get caught out in rough seas between **Cabo Macoris** and **Cabo Frances Viejo**, the little harbor of **Rio San Juan** is your escape hatch. On extremely light, settled days, it is possible to daysail here from **Sosua**, but don't count on getting those conditions without waiting more than you probably want.

This port offers a good lee in *prevailing conditions*: i.e., E-ESE wind with no large swells. Wait for nightfall before rounding Cabo Frances Viejo. Rules of good conduct while nosing around a harbor for which you have no explicit clearance prevail. If you are only one or two boats, you will heighten the prospect of the Puerto Plata *comandante's* representative inviting you to tour the botanical gardens by dinghy and dine in town. If the young man comes out to your boat on a jetski wearing a bikini and a tanktop, don't be surprised. Ask for his identification, which he will be proud to show. It's waterproof, because he carries it in the bikini.

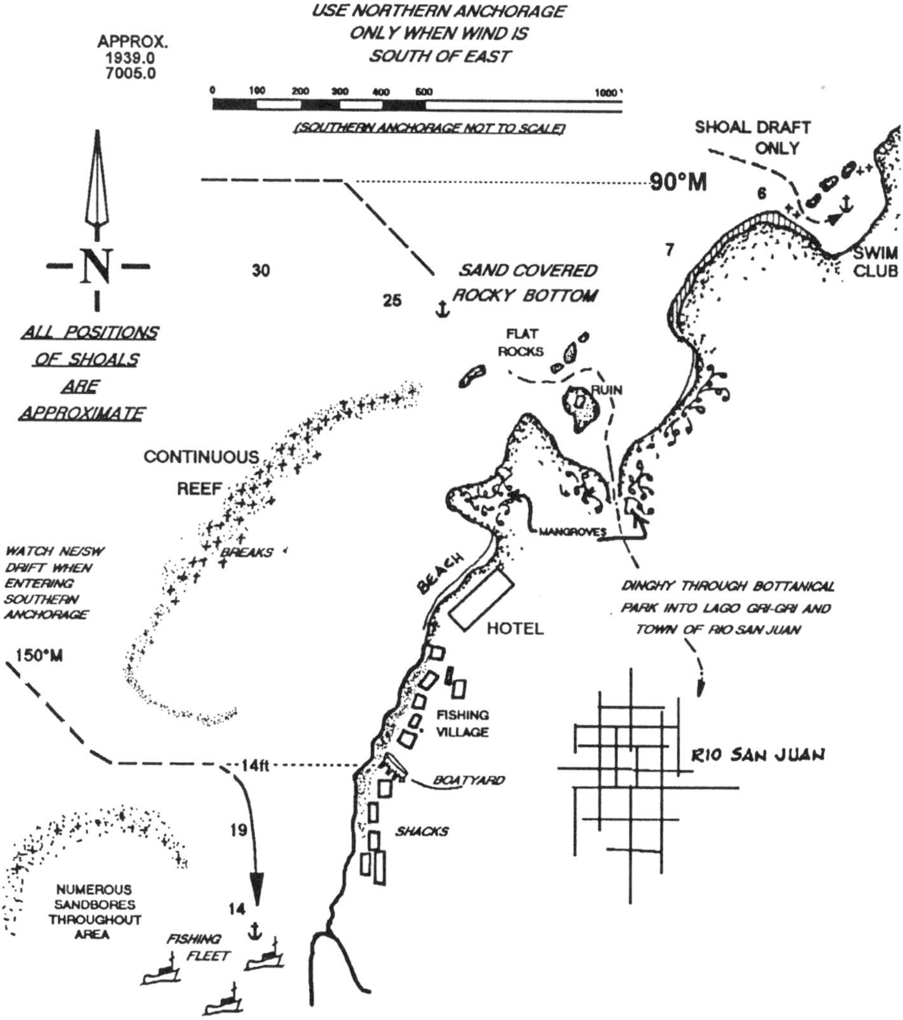

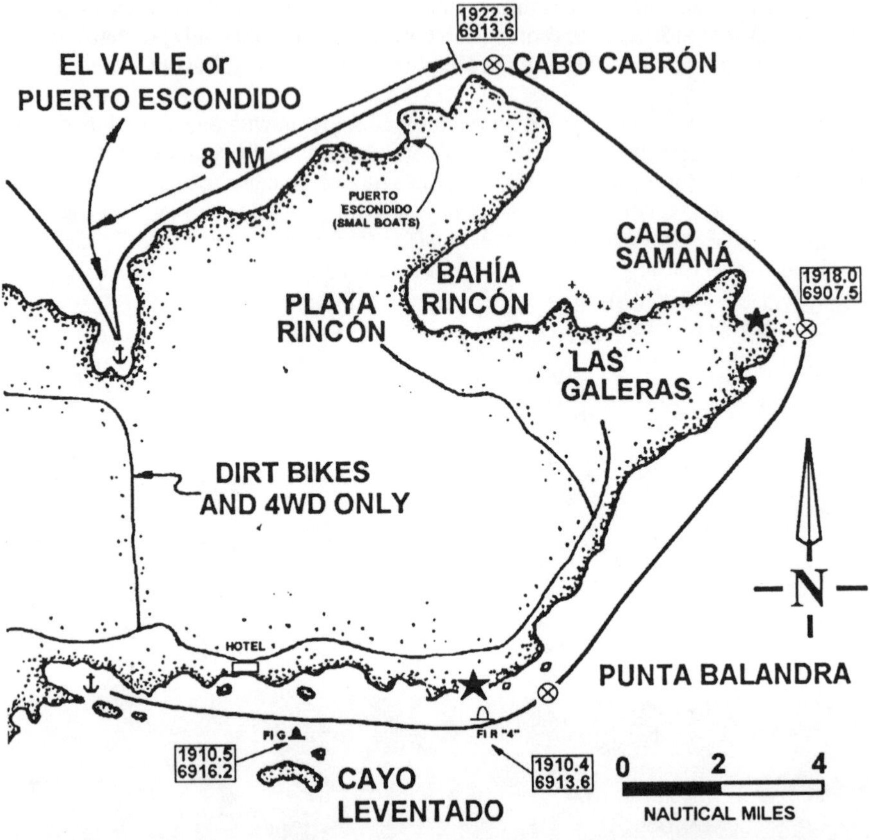

DMA chart 25723 taken from WGS72 datum and US Navy survey of 1977 show Puerto Escondido oriented east-west more than 3 miles to the east of what has come to be accepted by boat captains as Puerto Escondido at position 19° 19'N, 69° 19'W, where its fjord-like entrance is really oriented north-south. The chart's position is actually a refuge for fishing canoes. But the chart identifies the village correctly as El Valle.

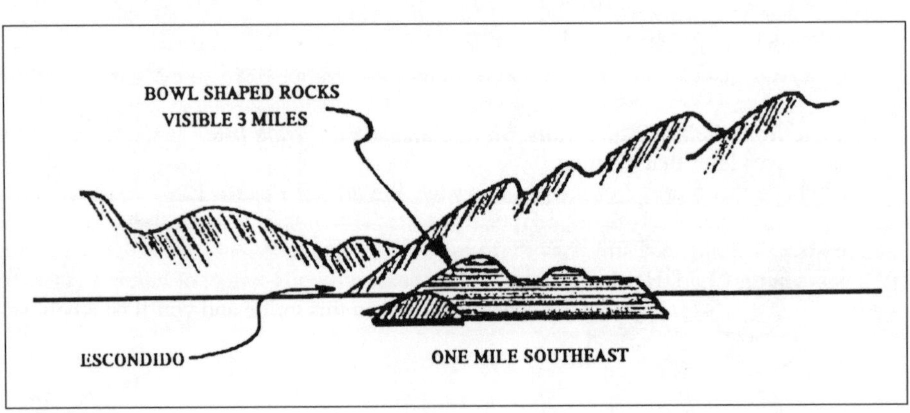

Engine breakdowns and other emergencies are, of course, legitimate reasons to be anchoring in Escondido for more than a few hours. If for any reason the wind has gone north of east, stand well off and take your lumps against the current for a night. Do not enter Escondido when there are large north swells running. Instead, sail down the edge of the **Mona Passage** about 2 miles offshore (a half-mile off in daylight) and enter **Samaná Bay**, heaving-to a mile south of the **Balandra Head** light, if necessary. Put out a lantern and go to sleep.

The local constable may try to chase you away. Treat him with dignity and friendliness and you can stay without going ashore. If you're having your SG&T when he comes, ask him to join you, perhaps by a small bottle of rum which he can share at home, since you won't be in the mood for onboard guests after your journey. Of course you purchased a case of small rum bottles while in Puerto Plata just for this purpose, didn't you?

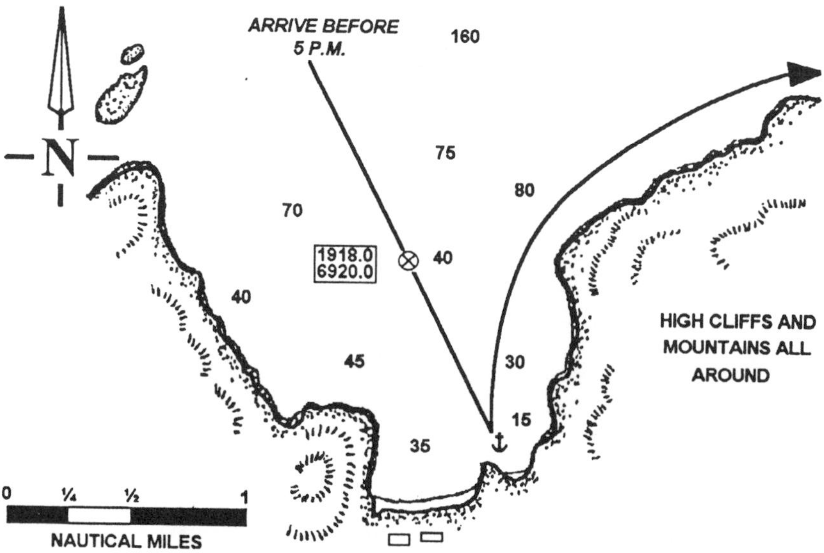

The next morning leave **Escondido**, a broad, deep fjord, between midnight and 4 a.m., following the east wall 200 yards off. If there is insufficient light, simply proceed due north out of the harbor. Motor hard against the cliffs in the flat calm, while scrambling eggs in the galley, up to **Cabo Cabrón**, cutting its cliffs as close as a boat length if you dare. Be sure to round **Cabo Samaná** well off (a half-mile) and be sailing south a half-mile offshore by 9 a.m. You'll sail into Samaná harbor before noontime. Have an early SG&T in the middle of the afternoon and toast all the slicker-clad yachties huffing and puffing into the anchorage from their offshore trials. Sit in Samaná Sam's and listen to their tales of the ultimate waves later that evening.

One year I met 5 crews exactly in this way. We all left **Puerto Plata** together. They motorsailed while I mostly sailed. I was the only single-hander. I had a comfortable, upright and dry trip. Their decks, strewn with drying slickers and cushions, attested to what kind of a passage they had. Hard to believe? Every season there's a fleet of hardnose cruisers who carry on offshore. Follow the coasting advice in this guide and you'll be a believer.

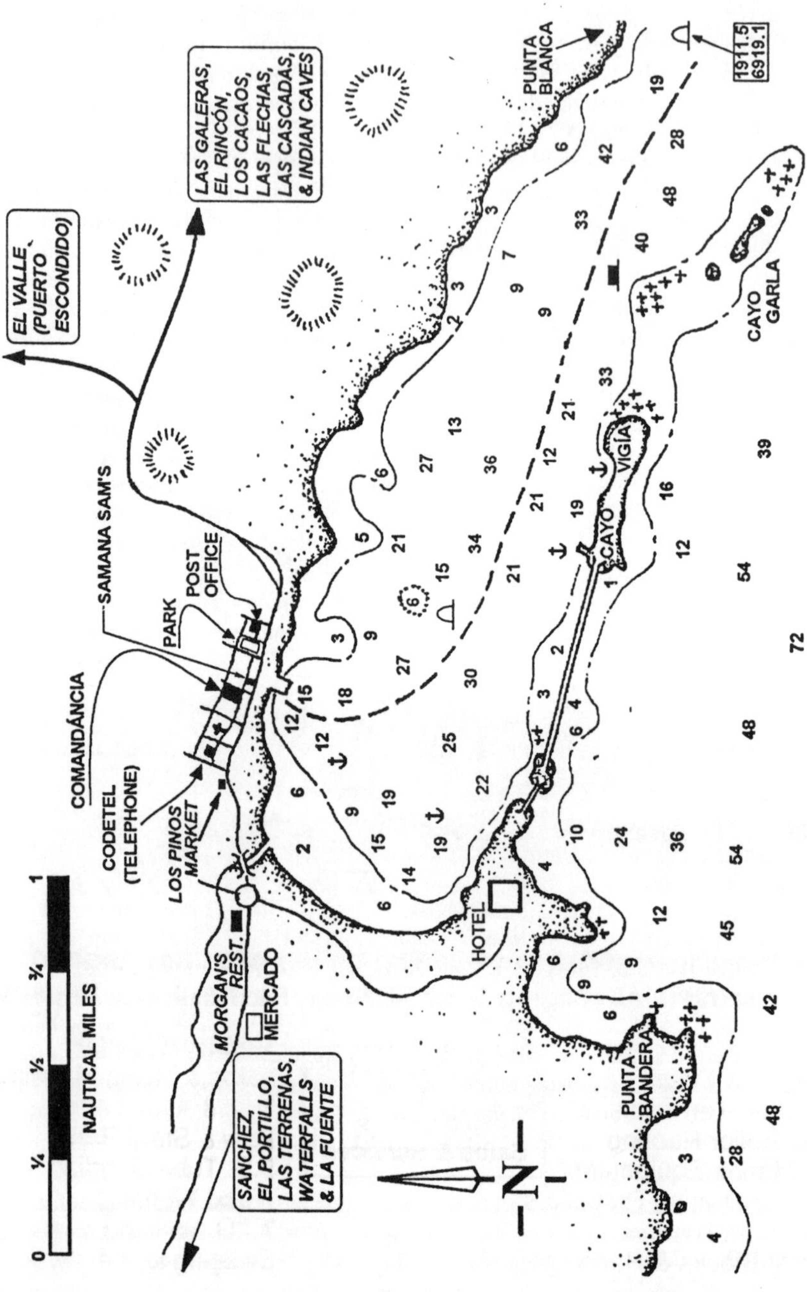
NAUTICAL MILES
0
¼
½
¾
1
EL VALLE (PUERTO ESCONDIDO)
LAS GALERAS, EL RINCÓN, LOS CACAOS, LAS FLECHAS, LAS CASCADAS, & INDIAN CAVES
SANCHEZ, EL PORTILLO, LAS TERRENAS, WATERFALLS & LA FUENTE
COMANDÁNCIA
CODETEL (TELEPHONE)
LOS PINOS MARKET
SAMANA SAM'S
PARK
POST OFFICE
MORGAN'S REST.
MERCADO
HOTEL
PUNTA BLANCA
PUNTA BANDERA
CAYO VIGÍA
CAYO GARLA
1911.5
6919.1
N

Samaná can be a place to leave the boat and tour the island, but **Luperón** is more convenient and more secure for that purpose. The bus to **Santo Domingo** has video but no bar cart. (See more on visiting Santo Domingo under the chapter Traveling in the D.R.)

You had better have done all your provisioning in **Puerto Plata** or **Santiago**, because you can't get there easily from Samaná. Major provisioning is impossible in Samaná, which is the Appalachia of the Dominican Republic. Some case lots are available at Minguitos hardware store or the distributor's behind the *mercado*. Samaná's remoteness is both its curse and its charm.

Mail and telephones work here, but recall that it's a very remote location and add a few days or even a week to Puerto Plata mail times. Nonetheless, there are times at which the service is surprisingly good. The personnel are friendly, anyway. Transportation in Samaná is very comfortable. Flag down a *motoconcho* which, in Samaná, is a motorized rickshaw carrying 6 passengers, with a canvas roof to keep you dry.

Samaná has some of the best scenery in the D.R. There are three spectacular waterfall sites. Take swimsuits to all. The cascades east of the town are like water chutes which drop to successive baths from a lovely tree-shaded river which runs along the ridge above. Take a motoconcho or *publico* (POO-blee-koh) to the falls, 8 kilometers west of town, where the 150-foot-wide falls slide into a treed gorge, and down a 100-foot cliff warmed by the sun. You can bathe in the cool lagoon below and shower under the hot waterfall. Before taking the path up to the falls, buy your lunch of cheese, salami, bread and ice-cold Presidente beer from the *colmado* (coal-MAH-doh) on the highway before taking the path to the falls.

Take a publico to La Fuente, west of **Sanchez**, for an excellent *tipico* (native style) lunch and a swim in the springs there. You can also organize boat trips to the grottos across the bay in the **Bahía de San Lorenzo**. Samaná is the closest you will come to Bora Bora while in the Caribbean. Some stay the whole hurricane season. Some go ashore and stay forever. But, like Bora Bora, Samaná is painfully remote, and likely to remain so, despite all claims to the contrary.

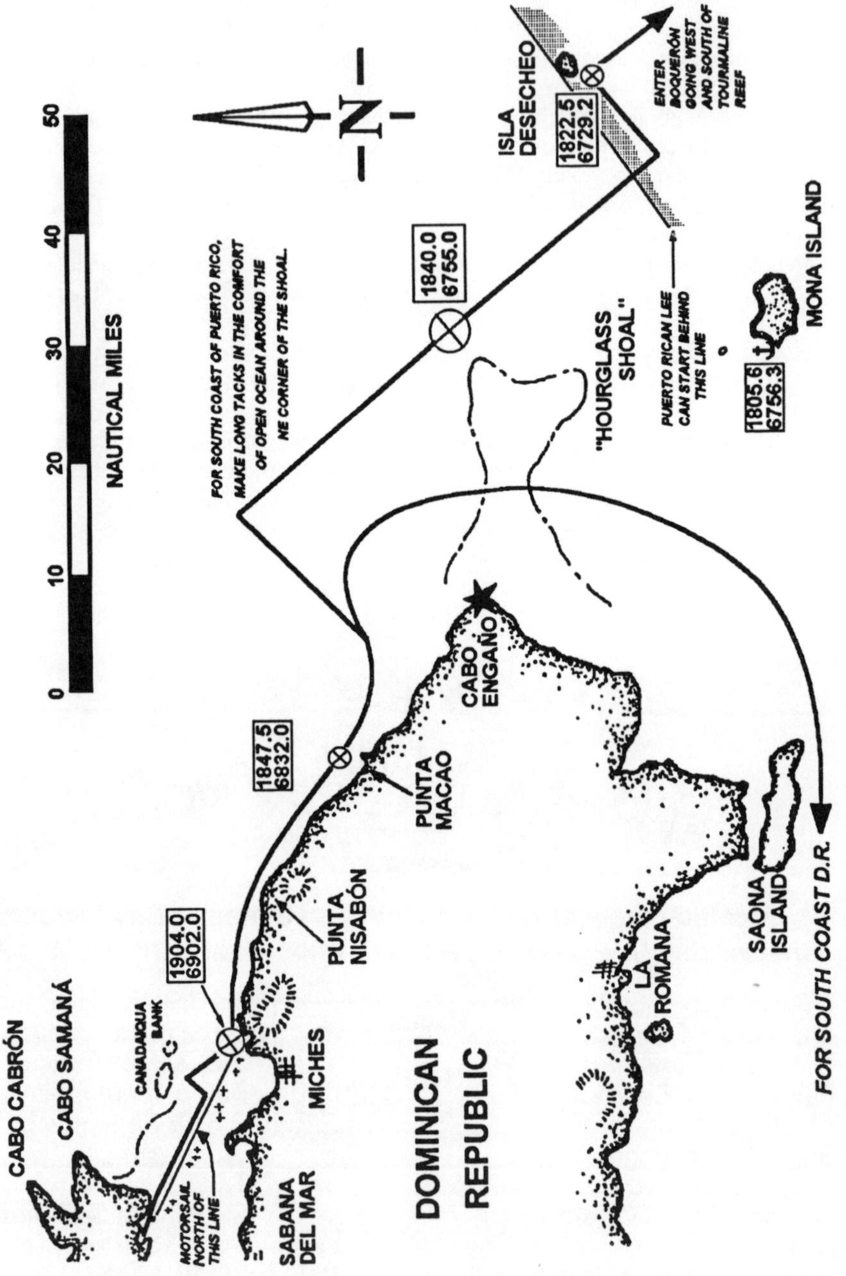
NAUTICAL MILES
0
10
20
30
40
50
N
ISLA DESECHEO
1822.5
6729.2
ENTER BOQUERÓN GOING WEST AND SOUTH OF TOURMALINE REEF
FOR SOUTH COAST OF PUERTO RICO, MAKE LONG TACKS IN THE COMFORT OF OPEN OCEAN AROUND THE NE CORNER OF THE SHOAL.
1840.0
6755.0
"HOURGLASS SHOAL"
PUERTO RICAN LEE CAN START BEHIND THIS LINE
1805.6
6756.3
MONA ISLAND
CABO CABRÓN
CABO SAMANÁ
1904.0
6902.0
MOTORSAIL NORTH OF THIS LINE
SABANA DEL MAR
MICHES
PUNTA NISABÓN
1847.5
6832.0
PUNTA MACAO
CABO ENGAÑO
DOMINICAN REPUBLIC
LA ROMANA
SAONA ISLAND
FOR SOUTH COAST D.R.

The **Mona Passage** has unpredictable currents and rough shoals off **Cabo Engaño** and **Balandra Point**. The fooler for newcomers to this area is that the shoals are deep and one doesn't expect rough water. Both areas can be avoided by the strategy below, which calls for coasting, then sailing. You don't have to sail the Mona, but if you motor it and you are the typical mom and pop yacht, then you will have to wait a month of Sundays to get your 30-hour calm. The way across is during a window of 36 to 48 hours of east 10 to 15 in summer. In the winter, a mild, or stalled front can provide light northerlies, or even westerlies.

It is best to plan no currents at all, just because they are unpredictable. A sailing crossing should use the nighttime lees on both sides of the passage. This takes 32-40 hours, depending on your draw of wind and wave. In a southeast Force 4 you can motorsail in that same time. In a calm you can motor across in just 24 hours or less. Count on leaving in 15 knots or less east, and not going over the windward side of the "hourglass shoal."

The Mona Passage's reputation comes from stories dished out with relish by:

1. Delivery skippers motoring dock to dock with someone else's property;
2. First time cruisers and power boaters who motor on a straight rhumb line in east-southeast 15 to 20 knots, right through the shoals; and
3. Others who collect their data over the bar (or on the SSB Breakfast Show) from cruisers who made the trip only once.

Neither class of seaman is ever a reliable source to the Leisure Sailor who can afford to **Wait for Weather**, and if cruising isn't Leisure Sailing, what is it? *Jalan* and I have crossed the Mona a couple of dozen times. The strategies for hugging the coast at night on the north shore of the D.R., and making little harbor hops at dawn on the south shore of P.R., are not *my* strategies; they are the *only* strategies that work. To do the Mona, you can choose from several strategies, one of which is mine. It is presented here for mom and pop on their 36-footer with the 25-hp. auxiliary, but anyone can use it with multiple benefits.

Many cruisers don't recognize the shoals on the **charts** because they may be several hundred feet deep and that does not, in their experience, mean shoal. However, the water these shoals are trying to contain comes from the **Equatorial Current** spilling into the **Puerto Rican Trench**, the second-deepest hole in the world. That's a lot of water and a lot of energy for the shoals to dissipate, and you don't want to be part of it. Stay clear of any area much more shallow than another if it lies west of the Puerto Rican Trench. This shoal, shaped like an hourglass on its side, lies directly on the motoring rhumb line from **Samaná** to **Boquerón**. Therefore, my thornless transit of the Mona Passage counts for comfort on a sailing tack around that area.

The hourglass-shaped shoals east of **Cabo Engaño** can be short-cut on your way to the south coast of the Dominican Republic by passing north-south through its "waist."

If you have more favorable winds than you had planned, you may make landfall in the dark. **Mayaguez** is an easy and well-marked open roadstead port. Heaving-to off Boquerón, south of the reefs to the northwest of the bay, is also simple and is in a good lee. Motoring less and sailing more gives you all the benefits discussed in earlier chapters of a morning arrival.

Some motorsailors can make the run in less than 24 hours in the right conditions. However, unless you have westerly winds or a speedboat, I strongly recommend using the nightly lees on both sides of the channel by taking two nights and a day to cross it. That is, two nights of lee sailing and one day of smooth, open-ocean sailing. Should you leave Samaná in the morning, trying to cross the Mona Passage in one day, there will be no margin for error or problems en route, and you probably will have the stuffing kicked out of you during the daytime on both sides of the passage.

Follow the advice below and you can do the Mona Passage in as little as two tacks with little or no roar of the motor and comfortable conditions.

1. Leave Samaná on a day when the winds are lighter than usual, preferably east or north of east, but never more than 15 knots and with no large swell running.

2. The ever-cyclic **Trade Winds** are switching back and forth like a cat's tail. Record them for a week or two until you have a handle on the cycle. Then take the first down-tick in the cycle that has sensible wind. (See also the chapter on Harbor Telltales.)

3. Up-anchor about dusk in 10 to 15 knots east in the summer months, or 15 knots north of east in the winter months. Halfway between Cayo Leventado and the mainland take up a 120° magnetic course.

   a. Leaving Samaná in the evening will take best advantage of whatever umbra of shelter the island extends eastward.

   b. After leaving the land behind, long tack southeast, tacking northeast before nearing the shoals off **Miches**, a small town on the south shore of **Bahía Samaná**, west of **Cape Rafael** in the **Bahía de la Finca**. The loom of Miches at night is quite clear as is that of **Sabana de la Mar** across the bay from Samaná. Don't confuse the two.

   c. The southern limit of a tack to avoid the shoals off Miches is on a line bearing 111° true to a point 19°04'N, 69°02'W. You may have to take a short tack or two out from the coast to maintain your course which should be 120° magnetic.

4. With luck, your first northeast tack can be your last and will be taken near **Cabo Engaño** itself as the lee you have been using all night begins to waiver on you.

5. Carry on northeast until able to lay a southeast tack to a safety waypoint well northeast of the northeast corner of the Cabo Engaño shoal's "hour-glass."

   a. This is at 18°40'N and 67°55'W.

   b. Carry this tack past a line from the northwest corner of Puerto Rico through **Isla Desecheo**. Conditions usually moderate southeast of that line, and the southeast tack usually can lay Boquerón early the next morning.

   c. You can pass Isla Desecheo on either side but, unless you choose to hug the shore down to Boquerón from **Mayaguez**, be sure to pass west of **Tourmaline Reef**.

   d. Buoys and lights here are good and U.S. standard..

Mayaguez

If you are a foreign vessel, or if you have non-resident aliens aboard, you probably will be asked to take the boat into Mayaguez. This is an industrial harbor with poor facilities for yachts. By noon the wind is up and your position might be uncomfortable. Arriving in the morning, or even before morning with the good ship's buoyage which marks the port, you will be able to clear in and get out to Boquerón or **Puerto Real** before the wind is up.

Tracking the Trades from Samaná

By following the **National Weather Service**'s *Eastern Caribbean Report*, you can predict when the **Trades** will be lightening up and favoring your tack.

While you **Wait for Weather** in Samaná, you may receive the Puerto Rico VHF weather channels (WX). *Use this information at your peril!* You will be crossing open Atlantic Ocean, not coasting the west coast of Puerto Rico.

Do not rely on data received by radio from friends in Puerto Rico. They are less able to gauge the weather from their lee harbors than you are in windward Samaná, and you can't do it very well there, either. You will hear reports of strong winds in **Ponce**, calms in Boquerón—even westerly winds which, in Boquerón, are common enough as a southeast Force 5 wraps around **Cabo Rojo** and backwinds the bay. These are all coastal effects in Puerto Rico which don't affect you.

Construct a decision table like the one below and update it after listening to the **National Weather Service** *Offshore Reports* for the Eastern Caribbean and the Southwest North Atlantic on **NMN** each morning.

DAY	WIND FROM	WIND SPEED IN KNOTS	WAVE HEIGHT IN FEET	QUALITATIVE CHANGE	GO/ NOGO
1	E	10-15	4-6	?	?
2	E	10-15	<5	better	go
3	E to SE	10-15	4-6	worse	nogo
4	E to SE	15-2	4-7	worse	nogo
5	E to SE	15-25	5-7	worse	nogo
6	E to SE	20	5-8	same	nogo
7	SE to E	15-20	4-7	better	nogo
8	SE to E	15	4-6	better	go
9	E	10-15	4-6	better	gone

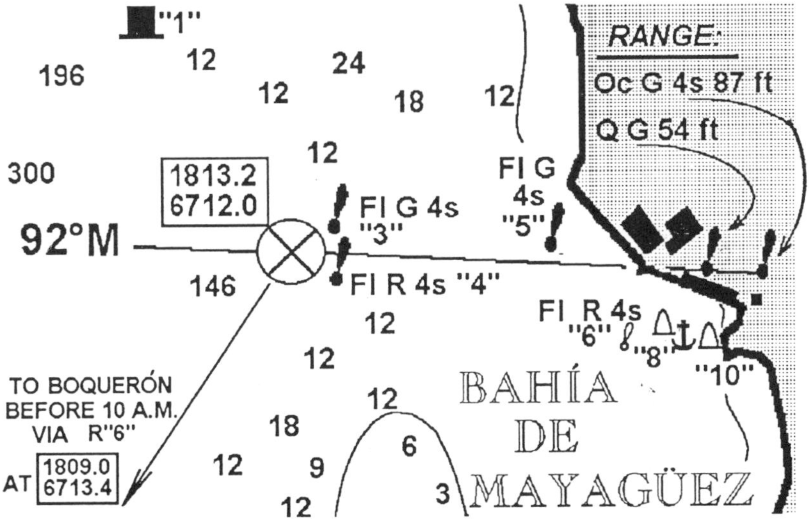

COASTING THE SOUTH COAST OF PUERTO RICO

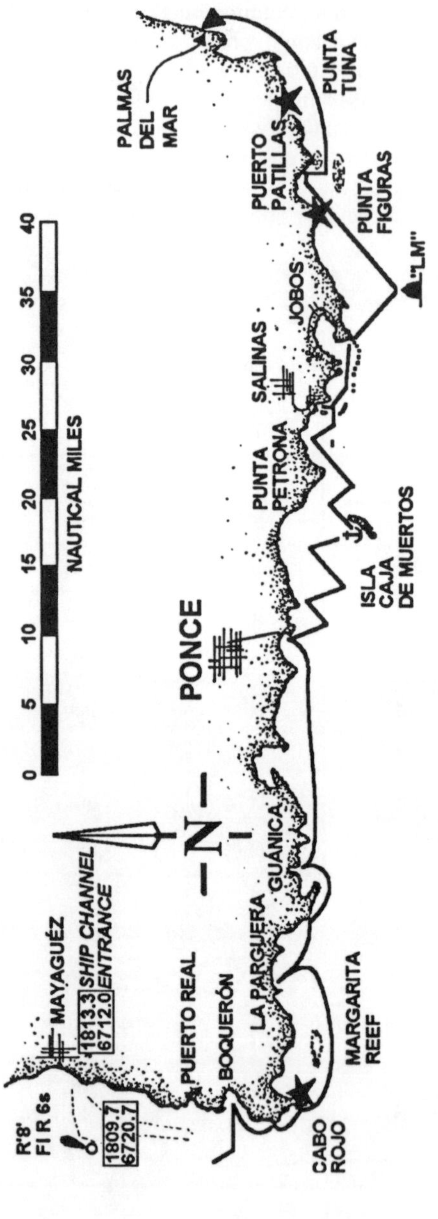

Jalan Jalan and I have learned the hard way to take at least *11 days* to transit the south coast of P.R. We prefer 2- to 4-hour pleasant motorsails at dawn to dancing the "Caribbean Two-Step" one minute. I begin my coasting by moving from the bay of **Boquerón** in the midmorning, after shopping, over to a beach anchorage (review the chapter on Staging). Short moonlit and dawn sails with lots of time to explore the small villages during the day, can be the highlight of your Caribbean cruise. Some anchorages could capture you for an entire season, so plan a slow cruise here.

As elsewhere, use all the cruising guides you can get for chart detail around the south coast of **Puerto Rico**. Detailed DMA or HO charts of this coast are hard to come by and expensive if you can get them. The **Imray** collection is excellent here, and provides the best detail available for the small keys around **La Parguera** and **Jobos**. There are also excellent waterproof charts of Puerto Rico available in the marine store in Boquerón. You can wait until Boquerón to get your Puerto Rico charts. If you are headed west, they are available in **St. Thomas** at either Marine Warehouse or Island Marine Supply.

The trick with this coast is to take advantage of the night conditions. Unlike the high north coast of the Dominican Republic, the south coast of Puerto Rico has wide coastal plains which further mitigate the already reduced calming effects of this smaller island. Look for a light offshore wind and a full moon. If you are lucky, or wait long enough, you can get both. If you're lucky it will be a moonlight sail on a flat sea with an offshore Force 3. If you are unlucky, tuck back into the next safe harbor, usually only 10 miles farther on. East winds and, in the winter, northeast winds, may become offshore at night as the central *cordilleras* (core-dee-YAIR-ahs) divide the wind. With the **katabatic** effects added to it, the wind slides downhill and offshore.

Don't look for much of a calm extension from Puerto Rico, however. It's a tiny island and you must stay close inshore to get any effect at all. Often the only effect you will get is a shifting of the daytime winds to slightly north of east which is, anyway, on the nose.

Don't be fooled by the apparent closeness of each objective. This coast will be your first encounter with the "Caribbean Two-Step": two steps forward, one step back. The Caribbean swell is usually from the southeast and 4 to 8 feet high, more like a chop than a swell. You will swear there are three swells within the length of your boat! With a clipper bow the Caribbean Two-Step becomes more like two back and two to the side. So, unless you get that rare offshore breeze, be prepared to motorsail close inshore with full main and no jib, while tacking.

If you are clever, you will be leaving each little harbor at dawn, or before, and arriving before 9 a.m., that is, before the trades come back. Row ashore to a cafe and have breakfast, reading a daily (English) newspaper. Go back to the boat for a late morning nap. If you decide to carry on, then before retiring in the evening, lay up a thermos of coffee and a pot of hot *burgoo* for breakfast.

When coasting Puerto Rico, look for an *Eastern Caribbean Forecast* on NMN (see radio list in the Appendix) of *east* 15 knots or less—*never southeast*! Late summer afternoon storm cells spawned by the **coastal front** may be intimidating, and local winds, especially the seabreezes, or beach winds, may be stronger than expected off the sea as a result of circulation around these towering cumulonimbuses. If you have a good offshore forecast, don't let these effects inhibit you. They will all dissipate by dusk, when the overall flow, as reported in the forecast, will reassert itself. If you listen to the **NOAA** forecasts over the San Juan VHF weather channels (WX Channels and AM broadcast, so-called "coastal reports: up to 20 miles offshore"), add 5 knots to the report. If you listen to the United States Coast Guard's Channel 22 reports, you may have to subtract a full day from their validity, as they often read the wrong report!

If you do this coast in the summer, take lots of time and hit every port. Summer in Puerto Rico is the season of the *Fiestas Patronales* (fee-ACE-tahs pah-tro-NAHL-ace). These are celebrations each town throws for itself (and, theoretically, for its patron saint) as a way to liven up the summer and the business doldrums.

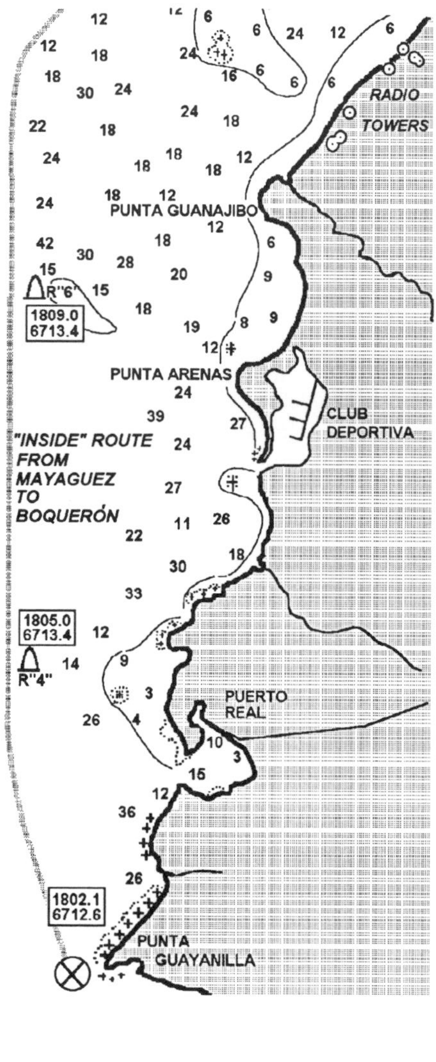

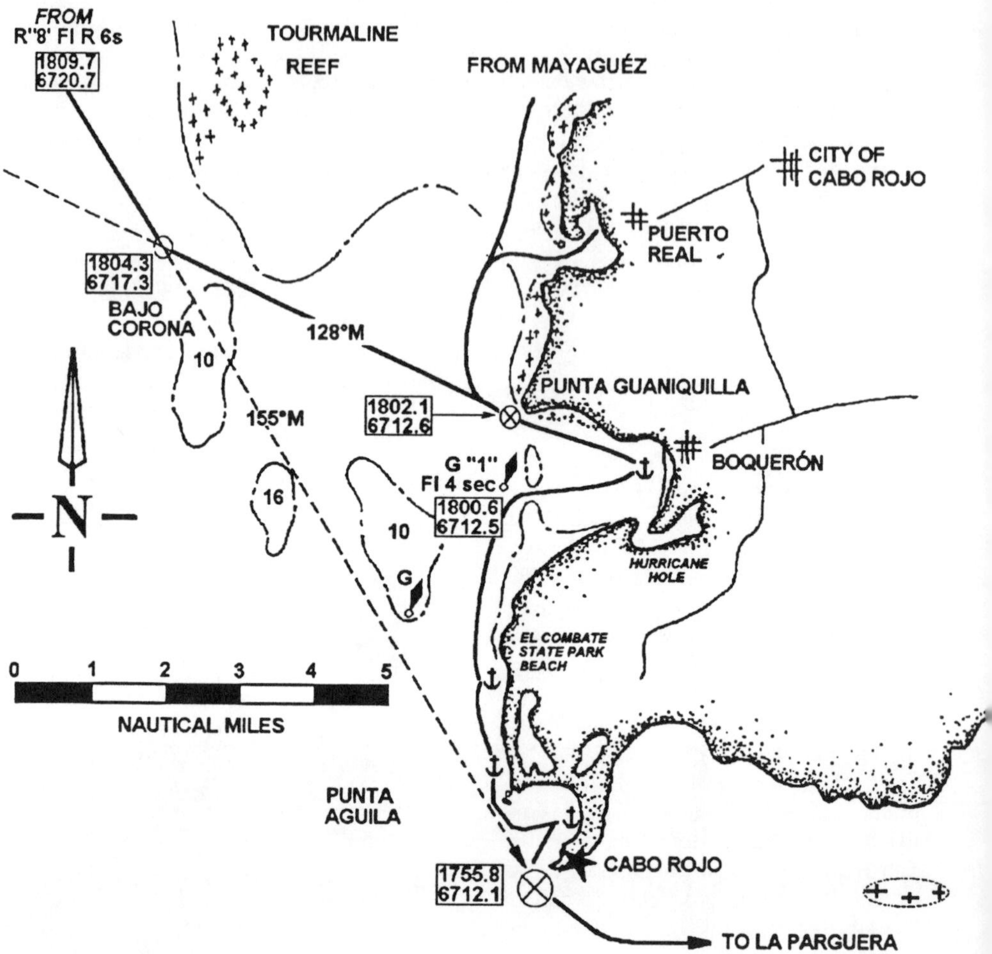

Entering Boquerón

Boquerón

Approach Boquerón along a line of 155° magnetic on **Punta Aguila**, by **Cabo Rojo**, turning onto 128° magnetic on **Punta Guaniquilla**, the northern point of the bay. Round the point 1/4-mile off and enter the bay, keeping 1/4-mile offshore right up to the anchorage off the town dock. With the shore close at hand as a guide, this is a deeper and safer entrance than the one through the reef and down the center of the bay.

Check in by phone in the little park (read carefully the chapter on clearing Puerto Rico under Customs and Clearances). Sears, K-Mart and Western Auto are a *publico* ride away at **Mayaguez**. So are Burger King, Kentucky Fried Chicken and Pizza Hut, if you're homesick to be sick.

Boquerón is a weekend haunt for Puerto Rican bohemians, and a beach and beer getaway for the Mayaguez University crowd. Weekends are wild, and the police force is very understanding. There are bars and restaurants everywhere with oysters, clams and tacos sold on the street. Try the conch salad at the Shamar beach bar or across the street. Conch is called *carrucho* (car-ROO-choh). If you never were a sophomore in college, or you were, but you miss it, you'll love Boquerón. Because you've been in the boonies in the Bahamas and the D.R. for the last months, you'll love this Latin version of Myrtle Beach.

But don't confuse this convenient and amusing landfall with the refit and reprovision point you need. Use all those 800 numbers to have stuff shipped in, but as far as provisioning, local parts procurement or mechanical work, wait until **Ponce** if you can. Case-lot stores, big malls, mechanics and parts are handier to the anchorage in Ponce than Mayaguez is to Boquerón. If you want to tour the island, do so from Salinas which is more central and convenient to Ponce, San Juan and Fajardo than is Boquerón.

Schafer & Brown Electronics, across from the dive shop have excellent cruiser services. In nearby **Puerto Real** they can haul you with their 35-ton Travelift and fix anything. The haul-out facility is a fisherman's cooperative with little room ashore, and working boats take preference.

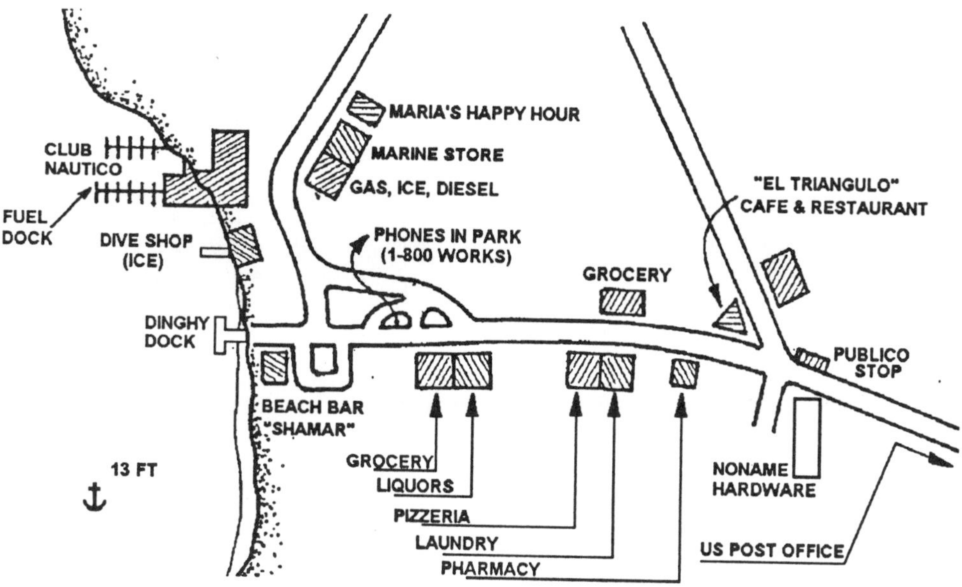

Boquerón, a Convenient and Happy Layover.

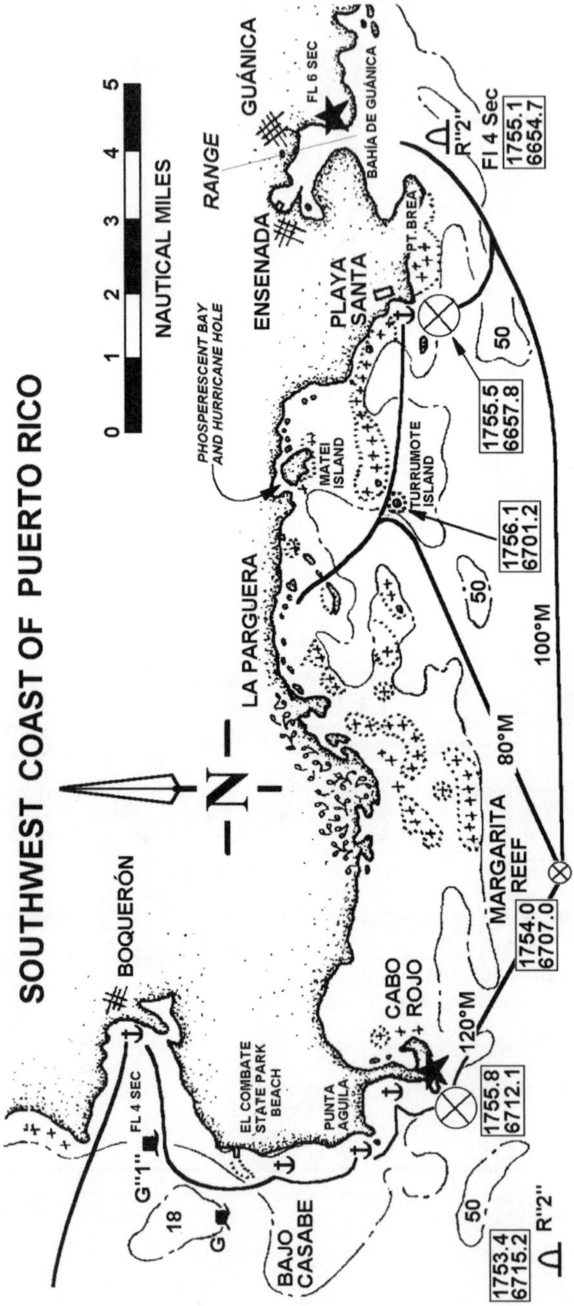

When hopping from Boquerón to **La Parguera**, it is best to shorten the passage into two or three smaller legs by moving out of Boquerón in the daytime to one of several anchorages along the public beaches off **El Combate** or **Punta Aguila**, or in the snug little mangrove anchorage immediately under **Cabo Rojo Light**. Pick your way to within a couple of hundred yards of the beach with a high sun. Do a bottom scrub in the clear water there.

The beaches at El Combate are a state park with many tourists on weekends. After scrubbing the bottom, I'll mingle with the crowds, buying beer and *empanadilla* for a late lunch and watching the monkeys, which inhabit the place. They're escapees from a research center and are breeding like rabbits. Watch it, they bite!

The next day, if a window hasn't firmed, I move all of two miles, into the mangrove anchorage under the light. There is room only for a couple of friendly boats, but I find this site ideal for watching the weather. The night wind over the point is an unmitigated ocean condition you may expect on rounding the cape.

Jump off for La Parguera at daybreak—never later! This is a shallow shore area. Leave the beach in the pre-dawn hours by hoisting anchor and drifting back due west, over the same ground you covered on the way in.

La Parguera

La Parguera is inadequately shown on almost all charts. Charts available in the Boquerón marine store, show this section of the coast with great accuracy, however. Enter between **Caracoles Cay** and **Enrique Cay** following the buoys, and anchor in the clear sand lagoon behind Enrique Cay, feeling your way through the reef in good light. This is a small but well protected anchorage for 6-foot drafts which some charts show as not having any depth at all. There is excellent snorkeling and fishing on the reefs lying offshore.

An alternate anchorage is near the 12-15 foot deep channel off the research station dock on **Magueyes Island**. Six-foot drafts can continue northwest down that channel, rounding between the second and third little cay, to arrive in a small anchorage in front of the town. An excellent Hurricane Hole is 2 miles to the east, northwest of **Matei Island**. In the right conditions this is also a highly phosphorescent bay.

To leave La Parguera by night, sail that afternoon over to **Playa Santa** and anchor and wait there for the nightly lee. Playa Santa is the public beach with condos just north of **Punta Jorobado** and 5+ miles to the east of La Parguera. Anchor in 8 to 10 feet of sand bottom and leave in the dark for **Guánica** or **Ponce** by sailing south midway between Punta Jorobado and the small cay ¾ mile to its west.

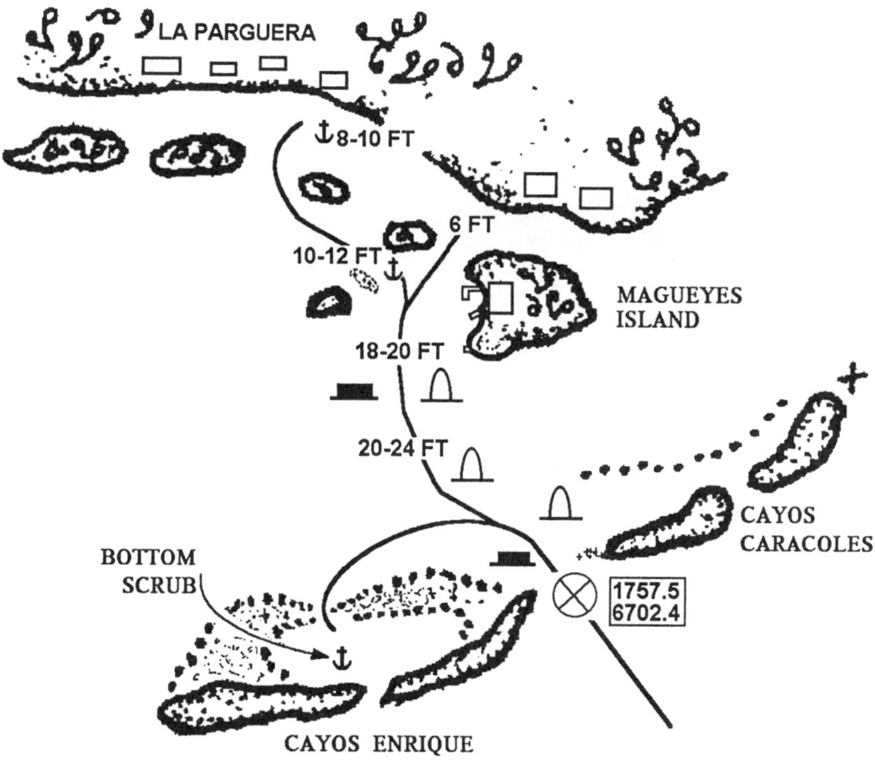

La Parguera

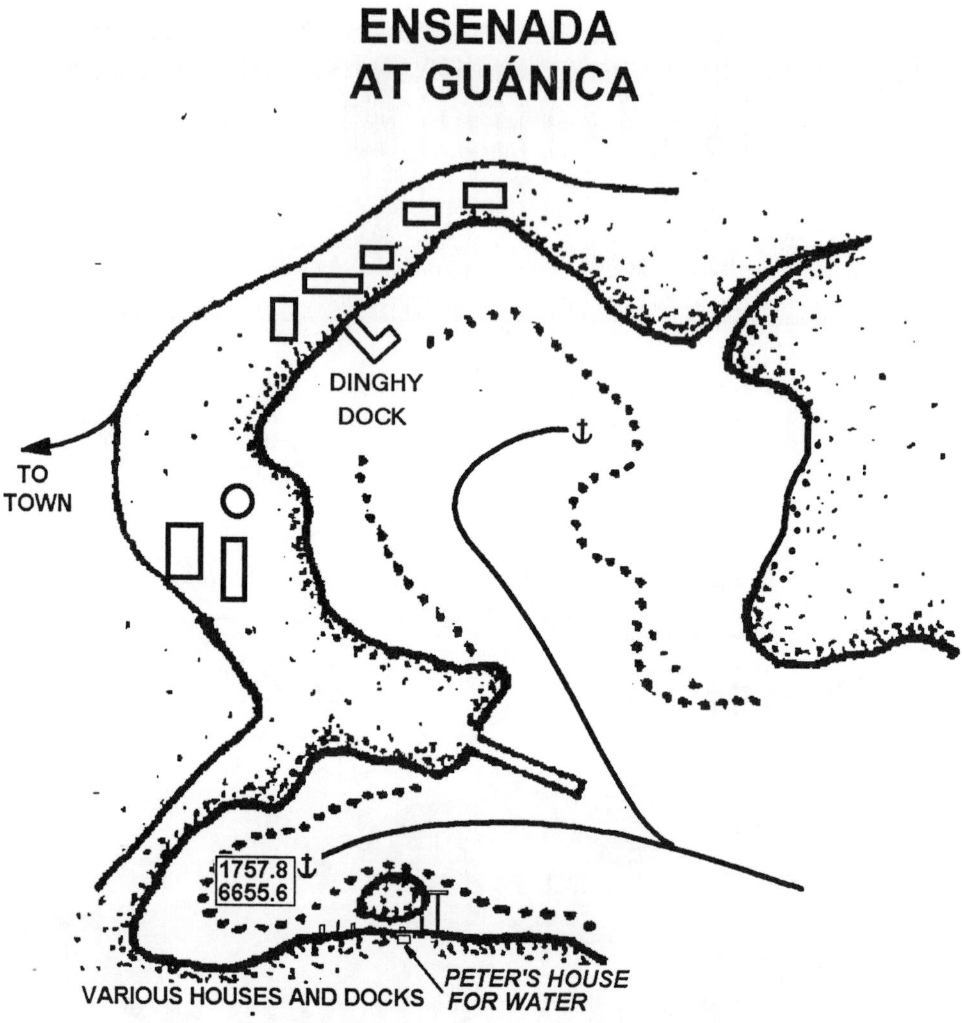

Anchorages at Ensenada in the Bay of Guánica

Guánica (GWAN-ee-kah)

The anchorage off the town of **Guánica**, north of the entrance, is no good. It suffers from heavy afternoon gusts directly through the gap at the entrance to the bay, especially in the summertime. Anytime the wind is south of east, it will combine with the onshore beach wind in the afternoon and roar through the cliffs at the entrance directly onto your anchorage. In addition, this anchorage has a foul bottom with construction material placed randomly, but surely, under your tackle. Finally, the old dock there is actually in use occasionally. When it's used, it's used to offload fertilizer—just about the time the wind picks up . Not to worry. There are excellent anchorages off the pleasant little town of **Ensenada**. The anchorage to the southwest can be used much closer to shore than shown in most charts, and the one to the northwest is an excellent **Hurricane Hole**. Exit at night is easy if you looked around on the way in. Leave Guánica at 3 a.m. to arrive in **Ponce** before 8 a.m. Follow the ship channel out. It is light buoyed, wide and deep.

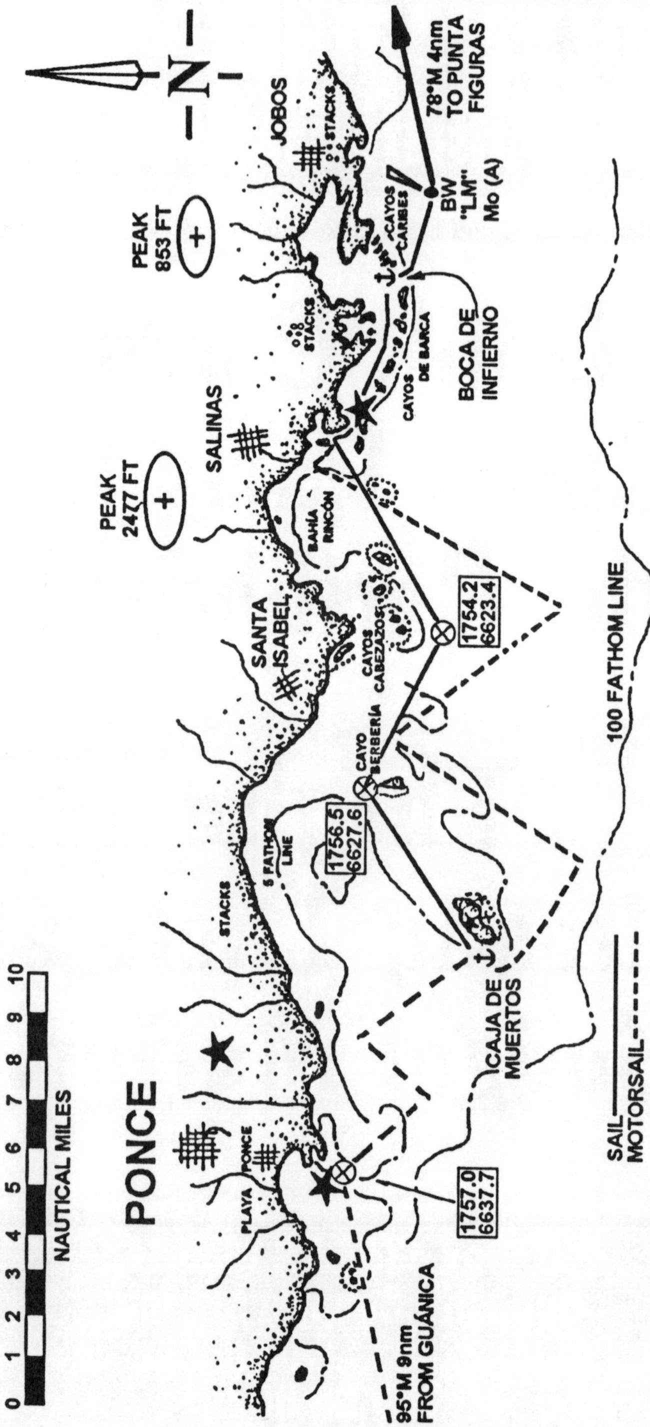

Ponce to Boca de Infierno

Ponce (PONE-say)

Ponce is a big industrial center with Sears, MacDonald's and everything in a neat and convenient downtown. XTRA is nearby and plans were recently underway for a Sam's and a Pace Membership Warehouse.

Ponce is **Puerto Rico**'s second city, and after **Boquerón** will seem quite serious. It's a working town and you can get just about anything done there. Some areas of town are worth a walking tour as they provide excellent renovated examples of Caribbean Victorian architecture at its most affluent. An excellent fine arts museum is also there.

Anchor in the Yacht Club anchorage. For a $5 charge per person per day you can enjoy their pool and facilities. The restaurant is open to all. **Salinas** is the best place to leave your boat to tour **Old San Juan**. You should be in Ponce purely for business: repair and reprovisioning.

Centro Nautico is a good marine store within walking distance from the Yacht Club. Ferreteria Merino, on the Ponce by-pass, a few blocks down from Sears on *Calle Hostos* has heavy-duty marine stuff including **packing, chain, Jabsco pumps**, etc. Around the corner from Merino is Ponce Gasket and Rubber, which has any kind of **hose** you want, sheet rubber, even sheets of Lexan. Everything can be had in Ponce, even **stainless** fabrication.

Buses leave regularly by the packing plant a short walk from the yacht club. The line is "Playa Ponce." While hunting for either breakfast or lunch stuff downtown, you will find great businessmen's specials at good prices in nice restaurants. To reprovision, tie the dinghy up at the yacht club dock. Walk a few blocks into the industrial park nearby. Down from the Centro Nautico marine store and across the street is Rafa's Cash and Carry. This is a case-lots warehouse for hotels and restaurants. Grab a dolly cart and heave on all the cases, sausages, cheeses and booze you want. Then drop a dime in the phone outside and call a taxi to deliver you and your provisions to the dinghy for only $3.

In keeping with my strategy of hitting every port on the south coast in order to ensure a peaceful and uneventful passage, I always leave Ponce from **Caja de Muertos** (Coffin Island). Caja de Muertos is a National Park and has four guys in Smokey-the-Bear hats that live over the beach. On weekends it is thronged by Puerto Ricans on family outings. The ferries leave from the Yacht Club anchorage and are themselves cause for loud weekend gatherings in the street and on the sidewalks around the yacht club anchorage. Join the throng at night and dine from the street vendors' *pinchos* (PEEN-chose), Latin-style shish-kabobs.

When leaving Ponce, take a midday sail out to Caja de Muertos. Anchor off the beach there and wait for a 3 a.m. departure to Salinas. The reason for leaving from Caja de Muertos, besides its fine, Bahamas-like, white-sand bottom where you can have a good scrub, is because it sits 6 miles offshore, astride the true conditions you will encounter upon leaving. This is one of only three spots on the south coast where you have this luxury. In addition, Ponce is in a deep bay. If you leave without knowledge of the conditions in the sea outside, you may get the colly wobbles kicked out of you east of Muertos, even though it's blowing less than 20 knots.

Salinas is a motorsail against easterlies. (Review the section on Coasting the South Coast of Puerto Rico for the conditions in which to leave.) The chartlet opposite shows both motoring and sailing routes from Muertos to Salinas. With a fast vessel one could motor direct from Ponce, proceeding east from **Isla de Cardona** light to a point 1 mile north of **Cayo Berberia** and thence 126° true to round the **Cayos Cabezazos** off of **Punta Petrona**. You may also sail on from Muertos to clear Berberia on the west, and tacking southeast between it and the Cabezazos.

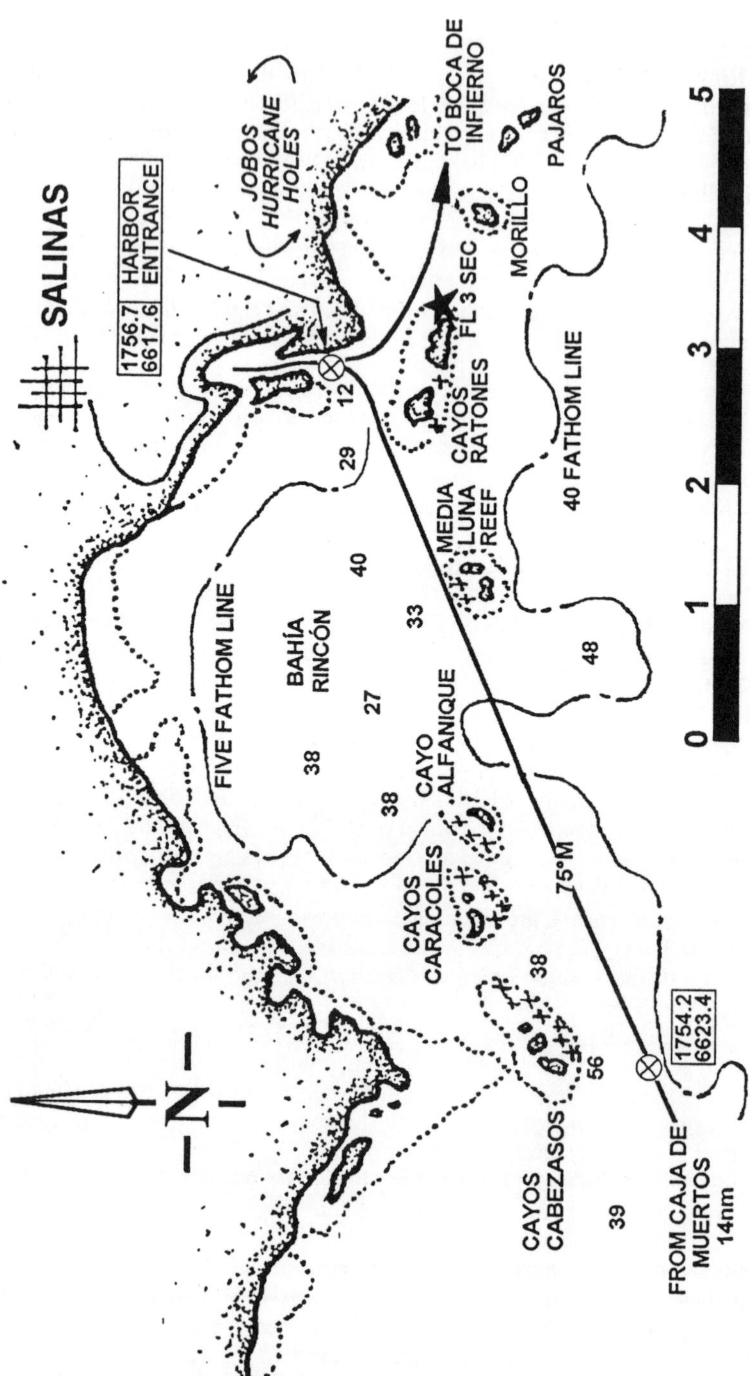

Entrance to Salinas

Salinas

With either the outside or the inside route to **Salinas** from **Caja de Muertos**, enter **Bahía de Rincón** on a northeast course which splits the difference between **Cayos Cabezazos** and the **Media Luna** reefs 2 miles further east. This will leave **Cayo Alfenique** one mile to port. Proceed east in the sheltered bay, rounding **Cayo Mata** into Salinas harbor. For drafts over 6 feet, when behind Cayo Mata, favor the channel slightly left of center until midway down the island, then favor the channel slightly right of center ("center"= midpoint of perpendicular from the shores).

It's better to commute to the shops and sights at **Ponce** or **San Juan** from safe moorings at Salinas than from any other harbor in Puerto Rico. There is a large new *publico* terminal in Ponce, two blocks off the main square, from which you can reach any destination. The trip to Ponce from Salinas is only one publico ride. Remember to return from the Ponce terminal early enough to catch the last publico. Find out when that is—it could be as early as 2 p.m..

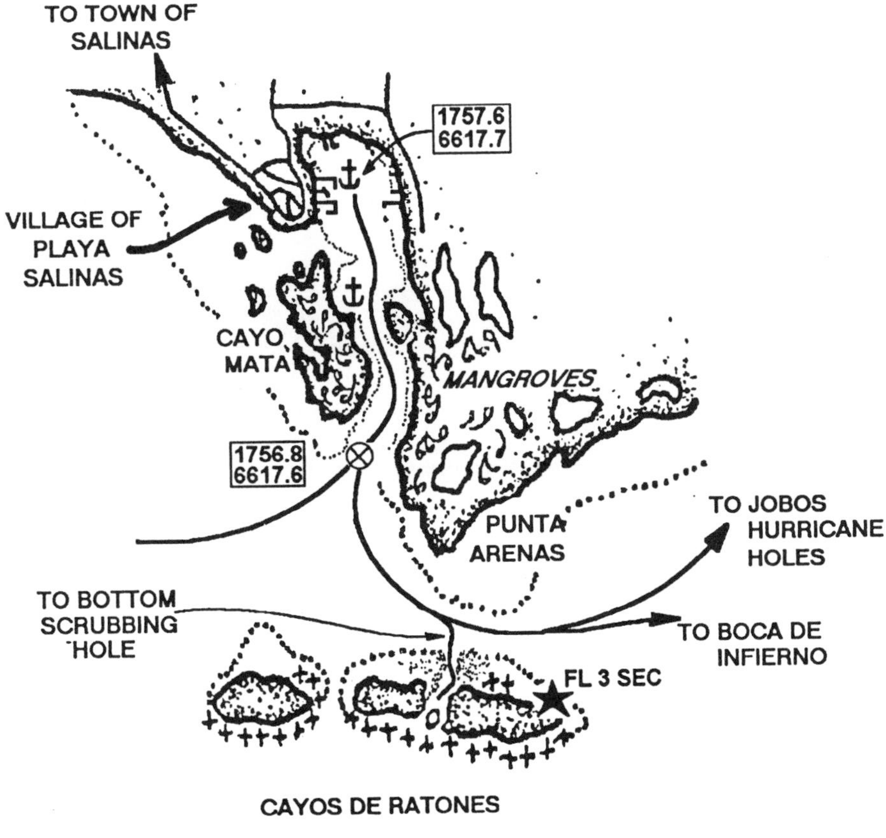

Salinas —stay for the summer.

Salinas is the best spot to leave the boat while touring Puerto Rico. It's a well-protected hurricane hole, has a convenient marina, post office, marine store, shopping and transportation. There's a good bottom cleaning anchorage between the two **Cayo Ratones**. The reefs and keys 5 miles east or west of Salinas provide good diving if you are the kind of diver who wants to eat your catch more than you want to look around. The water is typically mangrove murky.

If you know Salinas, you know it's the most convenient stop in Puerto Rico. If you don't know Salinas, this may not be apparent. If it's not apparent, you don't know Salinas. Talk with the gringo yachties who have gone ashore there, including Kirsti, at Tradewinds Sail and Canvas. Have your awnings and sails renewed by Kirsti while perusing the area.

Salinas, my favorite port in the Caribbean, and **Jobos**, next door, are both good **Hurricane Holes**. (See the chart for these holes in the chapter Watch Your Back.) For that reason alone it is becoming a summer yachting capital. Anchor in 10 feet of mud and sand (mostly sand) near the Marina de Salinas where the deck bar is built into the mangroves and yachties gather for happy hour after using the marina's laundromat. The marina has a modest weekly or monthly charge for using their facilities, including a pool.

Restaurants abound here both around the harbor and on the bay shore. The town of Salinas is a short, cheap publico ride away. In the village of **Playa Salinas** outside the gates of the marina there are no less than three hardware stores. The local *colmado*, Rodriguez, is really a marine store. It carries a wide variety of neat marine stuff—even stainless fasteners, fiberglass, polyester resin and 5200.

From Salinas you can finally get great weather reports on standard AM broadcast from **VI Radio** ("sailor's report" at 0630 and 0706). See the radio list in the appendix for other times and stations. Set your wake-up radio alarm and forget twiddling the SSB knobs. Listen, of course, for the *Eastern Caribbean Forecast* in the **Offshore Forecast** from the **NWS**. San Juan's English station, WOSO, or "El Oso" (the bear) has reports at 10 after the hour. Add 5 knots of wind to all coastal reports.

While in Salinas visit **Caño Matías** (CAHN-yo ma-TEE-us) with your dinghy. This is a pleasant bathing area behind the reef and between the **Cayos Ratones**. There is a small island between the two cayos with a hole on either side of it. The deeper water is on the western shore of either hole. Having gone in once by dinghy, you may also bring in the bigger boat. *Jalan Jalan* gets in at 6-1/2 feet. Go in at near high water and take the western fork.

If you sail nonstop for the east coast, leave **Salinas** at dusk to arrive in **Palmas del Mar** the next morning, being careful to not wander too far offshore, as the current and confused swells will make your northeast tack across **Point Tuna** difficult. Stay a good mile or more off Point Tuna to avoid the confused seas there as well.

The advice of this guide is, however, to continue this coast thornlessly. To do that you have at least two more stops before Palmas del Mar: **Jobos**, where you sit and watch the actual outside conditions from a snug mangrove anchorage, and **Puerto Patillas**. If conditions are settled and the wind from east or north of east 15 knots or less, you can also stop over at the little fishing port of **Arroyo**.

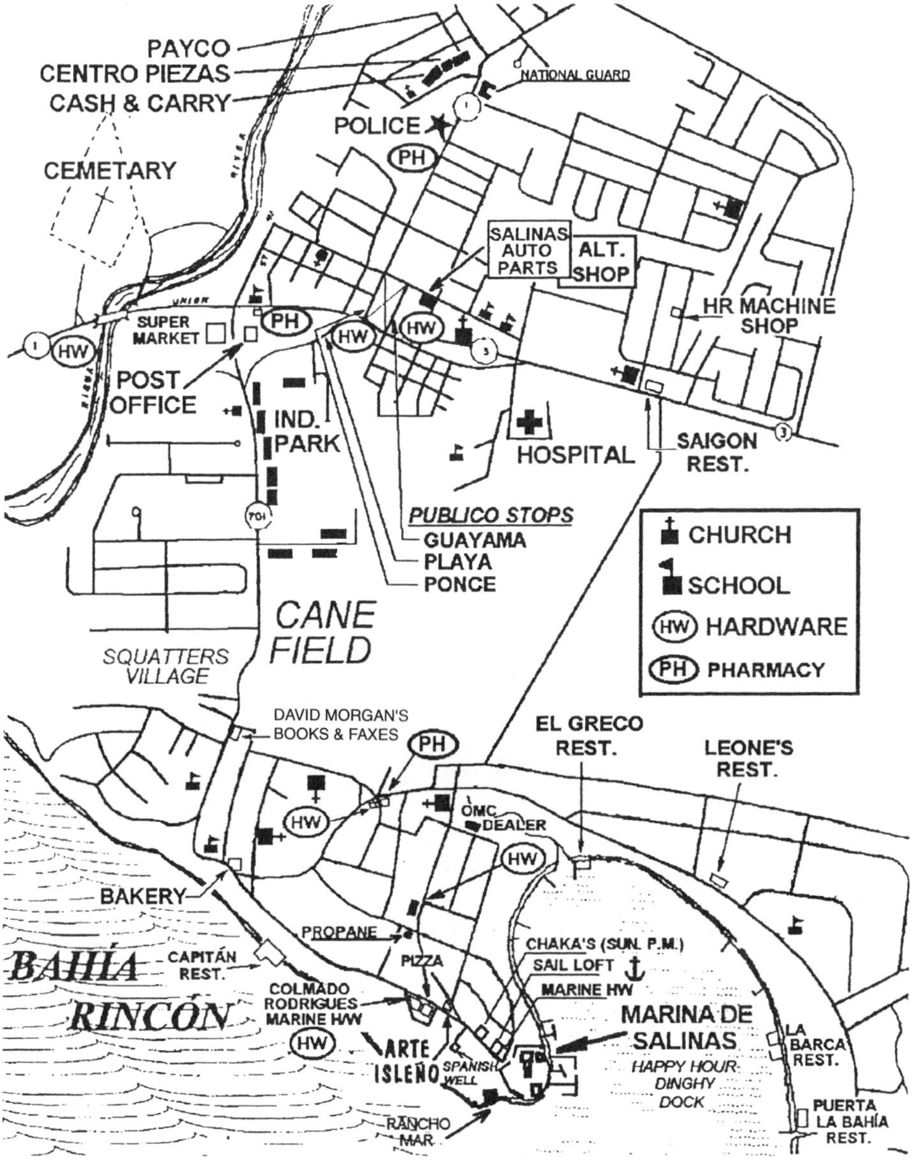

SALINAS & PLAYA SALINAS

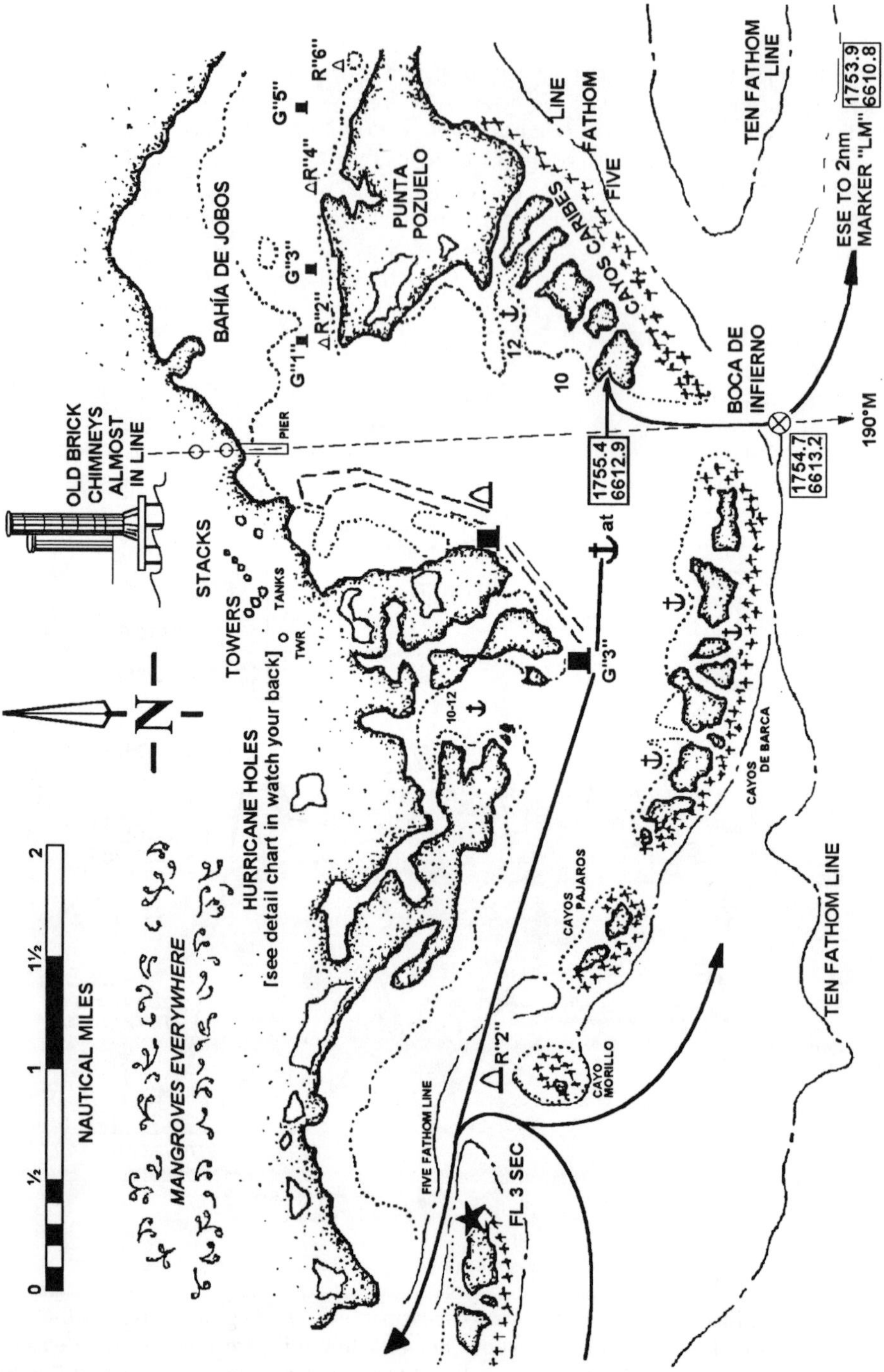

Boca de Infierno

Boca de Infierno

The long leg to the east coast can be a bear. For shorter, easier legs, position yourself at **Boca de Infierno** (BOH-kah day een-fee-AIR-noh). When approaching the anchorage, take bearings in good light of the *Central Aguirre* pier which is distinguished by two old-fashioned brick chimneys almost in line. Note also the breaking of the reef and the sea conditions outside. You should motor through this pass in early morning or light conditions. Ground swells on either side can be heavy in daytime conditions. As with the anchorage at **Caja de Muertos**, the benefit of waiting at Boca de Infierno is that you can see for yourself what the sea conditions are the morning of your departure. Depart through Boca de Infierno at first light, keeping the Central Aguirre pier at a 10° magnetic bearing. When a half-mile clear of the pass, head for the "Lima Mike" sea buoy 2 miles east southeast before taking up your next course.

To take another short leg, head for **Punta Figuras** and enter **Puerto Patillas**. I don't recommend bypassing Patillas, but if you do, keep **Guayama Reef**, off Punta Figuras, well to port. The sea buoy (FL R "2") off Punta Figuras has been missing and not replaced for several years.

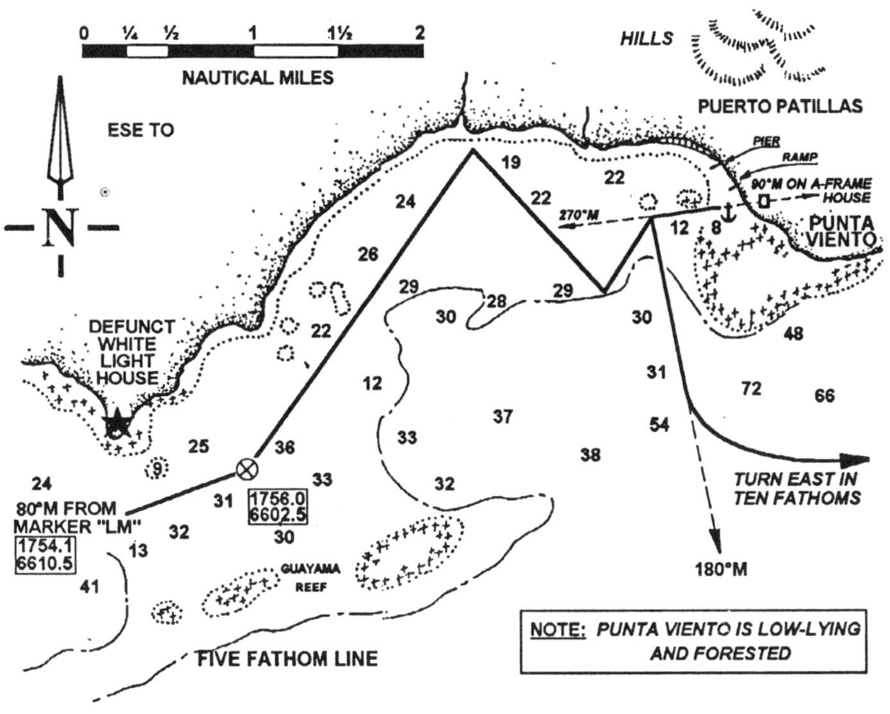

Puerto Patillas

Puerto Patillas is a small town, once a small boat fishing village supported by the reef 2 miles offshore. It lies northwest of Punta Viento, a low-lying treed point 3 mileseast of the **Punta Figuras** light (FL 6 seconds). In settled weather you can stay over at Puerto Patillas and dinghy in to enjoy the park beaches along the point and the restaurants on the harbor. Extending southward from the town one mile, to just beyond the point, there are rocky shoals. These shoals extend one-mile west of the beach as well. Approach for 11 miles on a heading of 70° true from the sea buoy [Mo(A) BW "LM"] off Boca de Infierno, leaving Punta Figuras 1/2 mile to port. Continue until high cliffs backed by hills are on the north and an A-frame house is to the east. You will be in 12 feet of water. Head east to the A-frame house and anchor in 7-8 feet of sand and mud bottom, 250 yards offshore and between the A-frame and a private boat ramp to the north of it. Go slow because of fish traps and old moorings in the area.

Leave Puerto Patillas before daylight to take advantage of the night lee. Be sure to stay south of the shoals by heading due west for 3/4 mile before turning south. Turn east in 10 fathoms for either **Punta de Arenas, Vieques**, or **Palmas del Mar**.

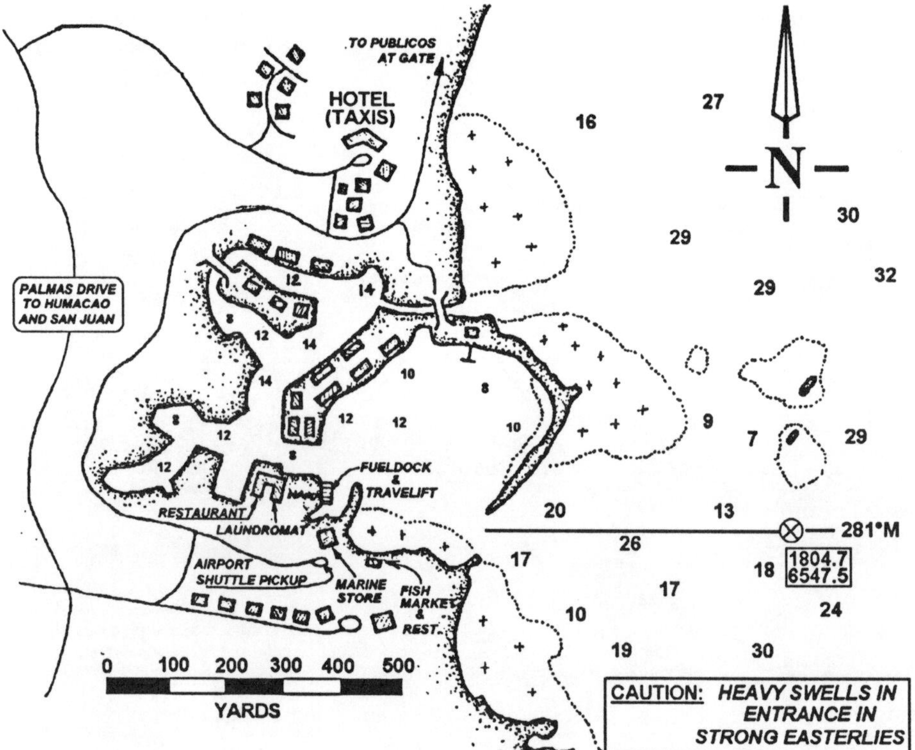

Palmas del Mar

Palmas del Mar

Enter in good water directly from the east. The anchorage may be temporarily used, some guides notwithstanding. It's good holding and deep all around. It may be possible to borrow or rent a slip from a condo owner under some circumstances. At a condo slip, in the marina, or laid up ashore at the yard, this harbor affords reasonable **hurricane** protection. Boats fared well here as hurricane Hugo passed by. If you lay up ashore, ensure for yourself that the jackstands are chained securely together. (See also the chapter on Hauling.)

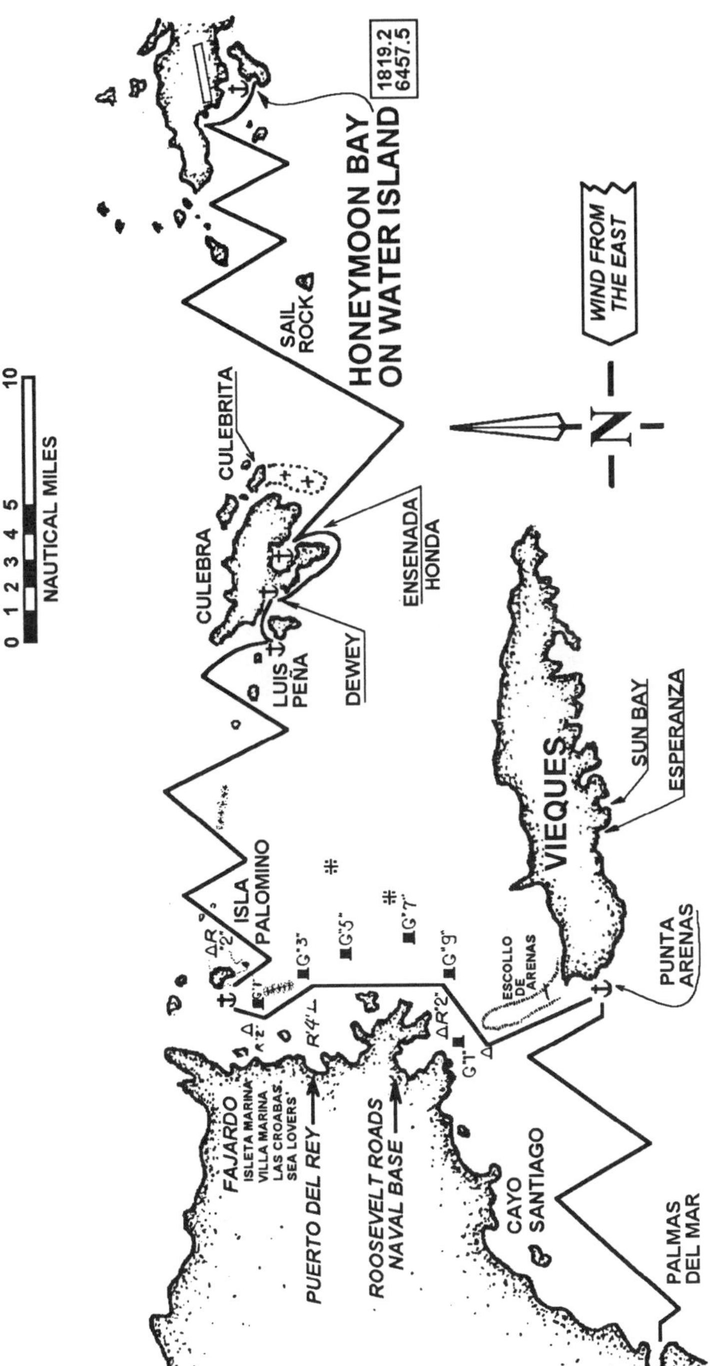

Vieques Sound, Not All Duck Pond

Once in Vieques Sound there is no need to do any passage planning until leaving the eastern end of the **British Virgin Islands**, since everything is within sight and only a short day-sail away. **Vieques Sound** is a duck pond compared to where you've been. Nonetheless, with a half knot of WNW current and a foul tide, you can get a full knot set in addition to a hindering chop. Newcomers always underestimate it. Yachties from the Virgins on their first trek to Puerto Rico and back are surprised to find a 6-hour sail to Puerto Rico becomes a 12-18 hour slog back. But breathe easy: Unless you try to cross the Sound in one bound, everything now is short day-sailing. Take whatever route you wish to get to **Culebra**, just not *direct*:

a. **Punta de Arenas** on the northwest tip of Vieques (Green Beach), then b, c or d,

b. **Roosevelt Roads** for retired militaries,

c. **Fajardo** boat yards for those not hauling in **Palmas del Mar**, or

d. **Isla Palominos** direct for those wanting to scrub their bottoms and enjoy a Bahamas-like respite before going eastward over the Sound.

Isla Palominos is the anchorage of preference whether coming from **Punta de Arenas** or the east coast of Puerto Rico. Despite the quality of their beaches, to find a really clear, white sand bottom in the Virgin Islands may require some searching. Isla Palominos may be the last clear sand bottom you'll see before **Tobago Keys** in the **Grenadines**.

A stop or two at **Culebra** is always required before pressing on to the hurly burly of the overly commercial U.S. Virgins. Anchor at the little beach behind Luis Peña. Carry on to Dewey or Ensenada Honda next day. Culebra is also a place to wait out summer storms and some cruisers make a pattern of summer in Culebra, winter in the Virgins, never moving their yachts more than a few miles east or west all year. They put down a hurricane mooring in a select spot before the seasonal rush can begin, and summer there in security, watching the fire drills when the exodus from the Virgins begins with each hurricane warning.

Cross the shoaly Sound with pleasantly short and easy trips, tried and true. See the figure opposite for an indication of the shoals to avoid. Notice that, to avoid a visit to Isla Palominos, one would have to go out of one's way and bash 12 hours to windward across Vieques Sound. From Palominos one can use the lee of Culebra and the keys west of it to pleasantly sneak—tack one's way to **Dewey** in only 6 to 8 hours.

Punta de Arenas

Punta de Arenas, on the northernmost end of the western shore of **Vieques**, is a good stopover either entering or leaving **Vieques Sound**. Depending on conditions and wind direction on leaving **Palmas del Mar**, Punta de Arenas may be a better first tack than Isla Palominos. Approach the anchorage only from the west. There are extensive sandbores with rock stretching north northwest from the northwest tip of Vieques with only 8-10 feet covering them. A good anchorage is 40 yards off a flat crescent beach, which the Navy calls **Green Beach**, and which is 1/2 mile south of the point. It is the third beach south of the point, and just south of a couple of large rusty tanks.

Head east to the point and turn to the anchorage when in 30 feet of water. Pick a *grassy* sand spot, avoiding the patches of sand-colored coral ledges here. The anchorage is isolated and the water is clear, great for bottom scrubbing and skinny dipping. Conch and an occasional lobster are available on the rocky shores to the south.

The **Escollo de Arenas** (be warned: *escollo* means trouble, thus, "troubled sands") can be crossed without incident. Each season some foolish yachtie tells me he's gone right across the Escollo and never saw less than 10 feet. Let him try it ten times in a row! Don't be fooled by these instant experts. Play it safe. Debris on the bottom can combine with 3-foot troughs to give you a nasty bump on some old wreck or steel tank. I usually go around the Escollo except in a calm. It is a pleasant, reaching sail, compared to motoring over the Escollo.

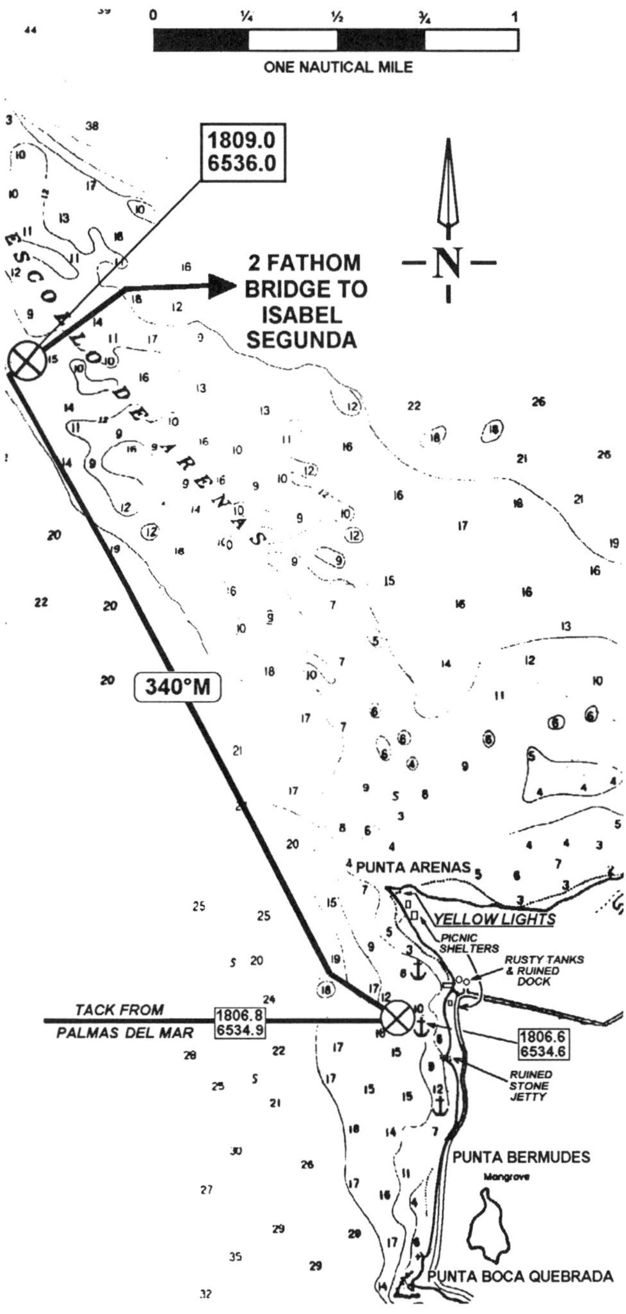

Green Beach at Punta de Arenas Anchorage, Vieques

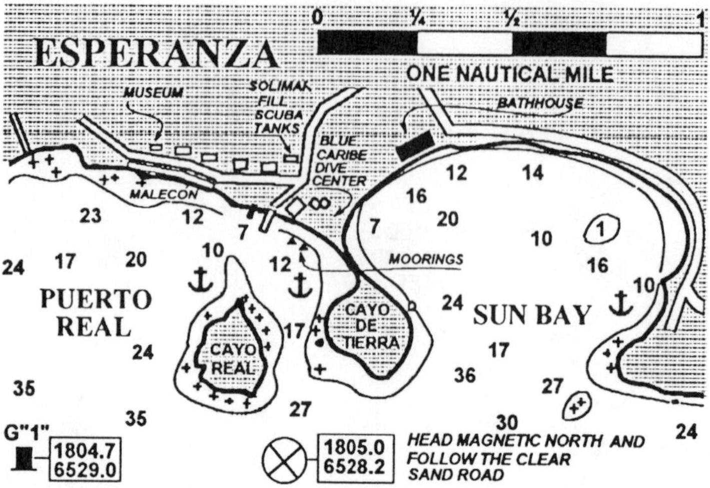

The south shore of **Vieques** is mostly a military target range. There is a fair hurricane hole in **Mosquito Bay** within the zone. You might seek permission to cross this area from VHF 16 "Vieques Range" unless you want to participate in the shooting exercises. Before the military zone is the little Vieques tourist town of **Esperanza** and the anchorage of **Sun Bay**. Both can be murder in southerlies. Sun Bay can be murder when they pump the septic tanks into it. Esperanza has little space for anchoring in thin sand. The shoreside restaurants and inns may be worth the slight slog to get there, but don't let the *Independentistas* get you.

Isla Palominos

Leaving Palmas del Mar or Punta de Arenas after breakfast, you should tack across Vieques Sound to Culebra with an overnight at Isla Palominos, where the clear water is great for bottom scrubbing. You can also overnight off the western beaches of Cayo Santiago, also called Isla Mono (the monkeys bite) 6 miles to the north of Palmas del Mar, breaking up the trip even more. Palominos is crowded with mainland boaters on weekends. In prevailing conditions you can anchor in 20-25 feet of protected water over coral sand. Arrive in good afternoon light in order to weave around the shallow areas to the anchorage. Next morning be sure to clear the bar extending almost a mile south of the island as you tack close-hauled toward the lee coast of Culebra.

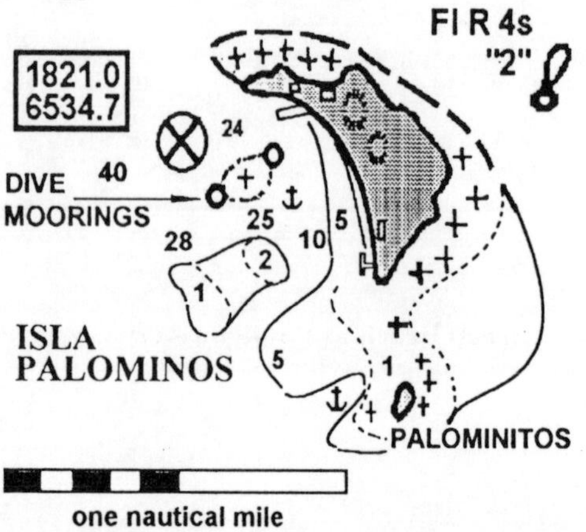

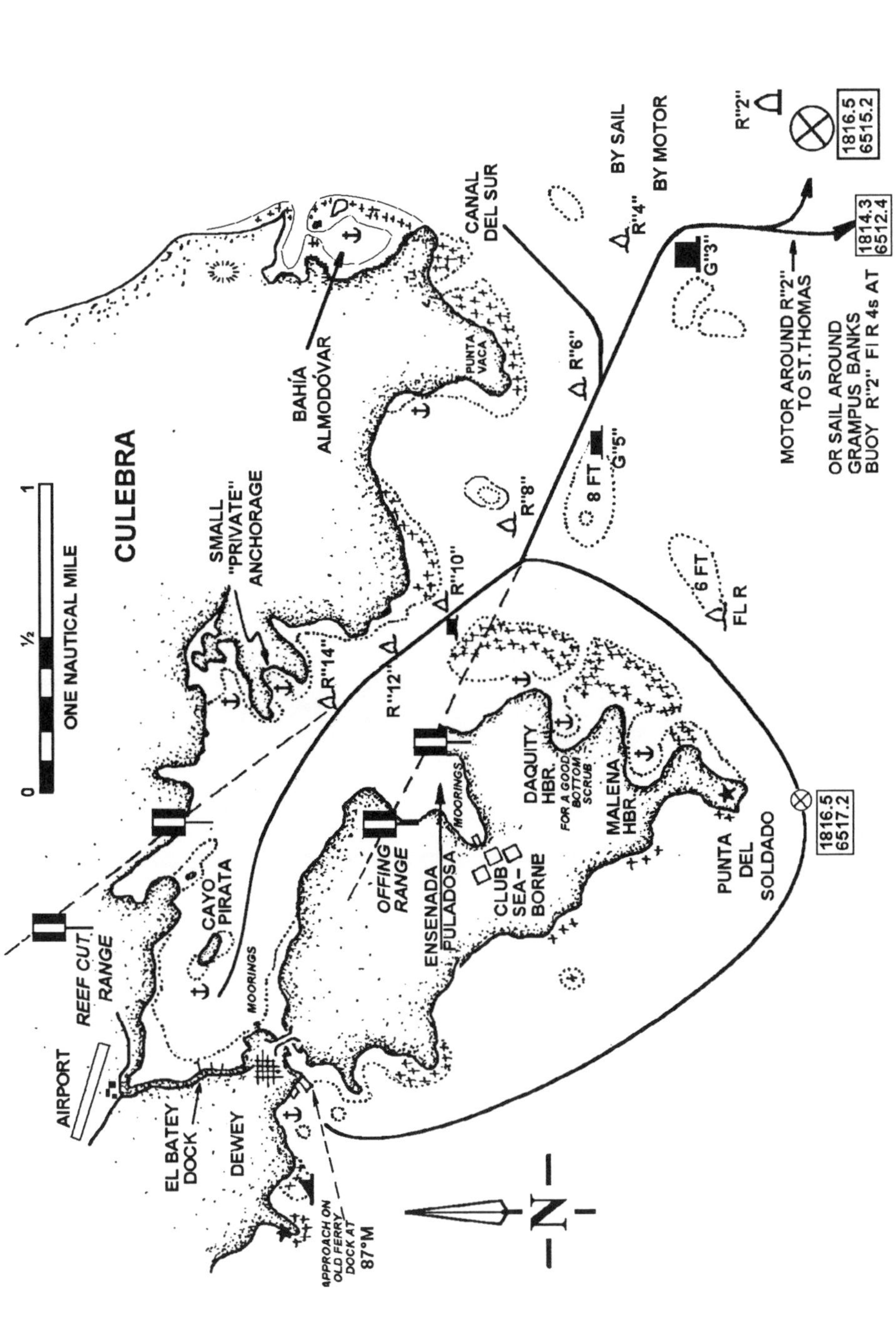

Ensenada Honda, Culebra

Your landfall and first anchorage here should have been Luis Peña. In case you didn't pay attention to the advice earlier to not try to cross **Vieques Sound** in one gulp, **Dewey** can be entered at night by positioning yourself 1/2 mile south of the flashing 7-second light marking the reefs west and north of the harbor entrance. From there take up a heading of 87° magnetic on the brightly lit old ferry dock on the south edge of town. Ferries to **Fajardo** run frequently from Dewey, if you choose to bypass Fajardo but want to visit from Culebra. There is a shopping area with a Sears and a K-Mart on the highway, a 20-minute walk from Fajardo, which is a 20-minute *publico* ride from the ferry landing at **Puerto Real**.

Next morning move around to one of the protected anchorages in **Ensenada Honda**. Do not anchor right off the town, where the holding is poor. The boats there look like they are at anchor, but they are really on moorings. In winter, anchor behind **Cayo Pirata**, but in the summer months go across to one of the fine **Hurricane Holes** on the east side of Ensenada Honda. Although a couple of hundred boats were lost here in hurricane Hugo, the mangrove hurricane holes on the eastern shore are quite secure. The problem, of course, is the sheer number of boats that try to come here, due to the proximity to the Virgins. The holes at **Jobos**, near **Salinas**, are the most extensive in the Caribbean. They are 24 hours downwind, but few avail themselves of these. (Read again the section on Hurricane Holes in the chapter Watch Your Back.)

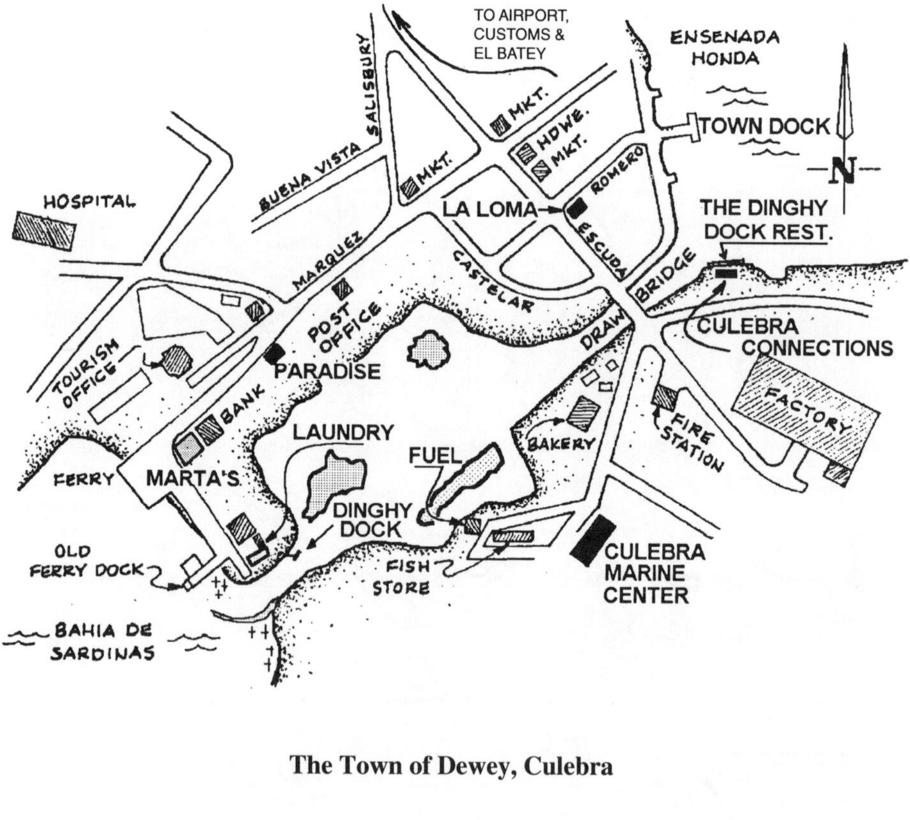

The Town of Dewey, Culebra

AlmodÓvar

Bahía de Almodóvar and **Dakity Harbor** are the most tranquil anchorages of **Culebra**. Round Culebra at **Punta Vaca** into **Canal del Sur**. Enter **Puerto Manglar** on a heading of 325xM to a large "wedding cake" of a house overlooking the bay, passing between small square red and green markers in 3 fathoms. Turn southwest around the double mangrove islet of **Pelaita** through a 10 foot deep channel and between another set of markers. Anchor west of the reef in 2-4 fathoms of white sand and clear water. Next morning do a pre-lunch snorkel northwest of **Culebrita**, and finish the day in that island's spectacular northern anchorage.

Culebrita

Within the northern arms of **Culebrita** is a 400 yard diameter basin with 7 to 25 feet of clear water bordered by white beaches. Hike to the seaward pools known locally as "the Jacuzzis".

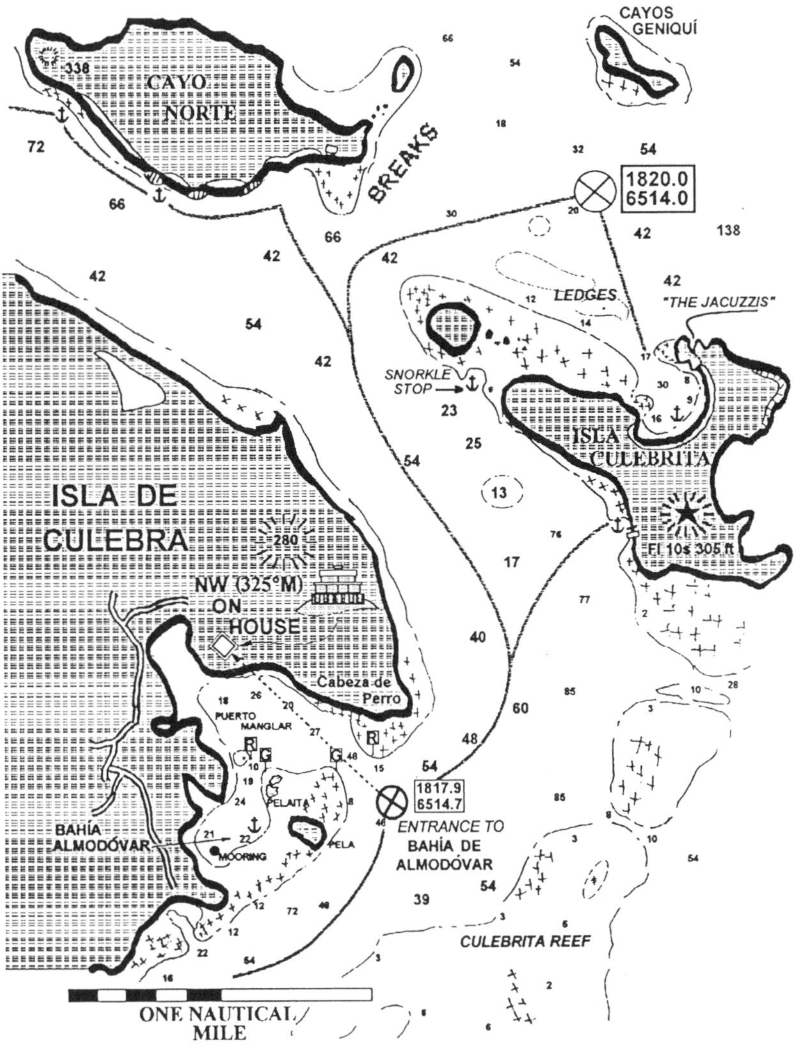

CROSSING TO THE LEEWARDS & WINDWARDS

1. Hard motorsail to St.Martin 80 nm. minimum
2. Beating to St.Kitts 120 nm.
3. Long tack to Martinique 300 nm.
4. Reaching to Venezuela 450 nm.

When selecting your route to **Venezuela**, don't make the mistake of many I've met who have crossed the Caribbean Sea from Hispaniola or Puerto Rico. If you are going to take your windward licks, take them up north rather than off Venezuela. The **Equatorial Current** down there runs up to 3 knots against you while its maximum up north is less than half that. (See also the section on The Virgin Islands to Venezuela.)

If you do end up in **Puerto Cabello** because you tried to sail to Venezuela from a point too far west, then treat the route eastward as though you were coasting Puerto Rico's south coast. That is, get some charts and do pre-dawn harbor hops of about 20 miles each from one little harbor to another. That can be a good trip, but you should have planned it that way.

For the entire **Eastern Caribbean** you need nothing but a few medium scale **Imray charts** and a good guide for harbor chartlets. Because of the transatlantic traffic in the winter months and the year-round charter businesses, there is a wealth of good information available on the routes from the **Virgin Islands** to **Grenada**. The Leeward and Windward Island groups are full of celebrating charter boats and fly-in tourists. Select your run across from **Virgin Gorda** to **St. Martin, Isla Margarita** or **Puerto La Cruz** in Venezuela. But when you get to the other side, always proceed by island hopping.

When crossing the Caribbean Sea from Virgin Gorda south to the Windward Islands, use 3/4 knots of west-northwest going current and reckon on leeway equaling, in degrees, the Force Beaufort encountered.

Virgin Gorda to St. Martin

This is a straight-forward motorsail. Leave **Bitter End** at 3 p.m., when the sun is high enough to guide you through the cut in the reef which bears 64° magnetic from **Saba Rock**. Sail next morning up into **Phillipsburg**, or stop at **Pelican Point** in **Simson's Bay**. The **Hurricane** Hole in **Simson's Lagoon** is enormous and the summer stop of many hard core cruisers. There are now slips available at the various condos and marinas in the lagoon. **St. Martin** provides shopping and touring as well as a miniature cruising area of its own. While in Simson's Bay you can dinghy through the lagoon to the French side at **Marigot** for lunch and shopping. Phillipsburg can be a rolly anchorage and it can be a *deathtrap* in strong southerly winds.

Virgin Gorda to St. Kitts

This can be a pleasant, close-hauled sail in light easterlies or winds north of east in winter. You haven't got the "Caribbean Two-Step" here. You are into longer Atlantic swells and this is ocean sailing at its best, assuming you go on light wind days only. **Wait for Weather** at **The Baths** in **Virgin Gorda**, or at **Peter Island**, and leave from **Round Rock Passage**. The anchorage at **Basseterre** on **St. Kitts** is rolly and busy with small freighter and ferry traffic. You can also make a stop en route at little **St. Eustatius (Statia)**. After a good night's sleep carry on to **Nevis**, anchoring off the beaches north of **Charlestown** over good sand holding.

Virgin Gorda to Martinique

As with the route to **St. Kitts**, leave **Virgin Gorda** through **Round Rock Passage**. The only trouble with this passage is that you miss **Guadeloupe** and my favorite anchorages of **Des Haies** and the **Iles des Saintes**. I like to make landfall at **St. Pierre** in **Martinique** and watch the villagers work their fish nets while I have coffee on deck early in the morning.

Virgin Gorda to Venezuela

Crossing the Caribbean from Virgin Gorda to Puerto La Cruz, Venezuela, use a west-northwest average set of 1/2 knot door-to-door. In the summer make sure you have a clear three-day forecast with no Tropical Waves or disturbances on the way over from Africa.

Puerto La Cruz is an easier destination to make and a rapid close reach under summer conditions. You can try to make **Pampatar** on **Isla Margarita**, but **Juan Griego**, on the northwest coast, would be easier. You can clear in there with a little more trouble than if you went to Pampatar where assistance is available with Customs and Immigration procedures. (Refer to the chapter on Customs and Clearances.)

PASSAGE TO VENEZUELA

Guides like Doyle's *Cruising Guide to the Leeward Islands,* Willensky's *Guide to the Windwards*, or Doyle's *A Sailor's Guide to the Windwards* and *Sailor's Guide to A Venezuelan Cruise*, as well as a hard-cover French guide to Venezuela, available in Martinique, are all you require. If you get **charts, Imray** charts are superior to the DMA charts.

ISLAND HOPPING TO GRENADA

While island hopping the **Leeward Islands** or the **Windward Islands**, it is important to get underway at daylight to avoid the midday squalls on arrival at your new anchorage. With an hour or two run in calm behind each island, you can make breakfast on the way. The boat is stable and upright as in a lee anchorage for all this time, and breakfasting underway will give you a couple of more hours to enjoy your next harbor in the afternoon. You may make a rapid transit down the islands in the hurricane season, or you may be cruising each one. In any case, when you are ready to move on, use the overnight anchorage closest to the pass you wish to hop: the southernmost on the way south, the northernmost on the way north.

All anchorages are lee anchorages, except if you are taking advantage of the excellent diving and fishing on the east coast of **Martinique**. Take every anchorage and you'll never sail more than a few hours each day. Try to be in by 1 or 2 p.m., or be prepared to turn up into the squalls coming down the mountains or through the passes as, for example, every 2 p.m. between **Guadeloupe** and **The Saints**.

Here's a list of easy hops I've taken several times for rapid transits. You can use this route for a fast, but pleasant passage, if you are not interested in seeing more of the islands on the way down. I certainly hope you would go slower on the way back, however.

Phillipsburg, St. Martin

See the discussion of Virgin Gorda to St. Martin, page 141.

Gustavia, St. Barts

Spots in the inner harbor are difficult to find. For only a day or two, anchor in the deeper water but good holding sand bottom of the outer harbor. **Customs** and **Immigration** are relaxed. Look for them but don't strain yourself. There is a mooring charge just to anchor.

Nevis

Anchor off the beaches north of **Charlestown**. Dinghy into the beach club there for a drink. If you're moving on the next day, fly a yellow flag and don't go ashore; or, if you do go ashore for a drink at the beach club, inquire after Customs and Immigration at the bar (after you order), and, once again, don't strain yourself to clear in.

Montserrat

Anchor under the hills of the northwest coast—the anchorage by the town dock further south is rolly and you'll love scanning the homes on the hillsides while having your **SG&T**. Fly the "Q" flag and move on at daybreak. This is the home of the "Big RA" transmitter (0930 AM).

Des Haies (day HEY), Guadeloupe

This is my favorite anchorage in the **Leeward Islands**. The people and the town are a delight in the daytime, and you would swear that the scene of the town at night, as seen from the calm of your anchorage, was set up by a Broadway stage designer. Fly your "Q" flag and don't expect Customs and Immigration to fall all over you. In general in the French islands, the officials are courteous and agreeable. They realize they have a tourist economy and do their best to make your touring pleasant. They are mostly French professionals and, usually, they see you before you see them. Make a modest effort to find them and clear in, but don't pound their tables. If you force them to shuffle your papers, they may insist your papers be in order (have your kids mailed you your new documentation stickers yet?). You must check in, of course, but it's better to go with the flow. Let them know you're there, but don't press them. If you decide to stay a while and haven't found the officials in a day or two, go up to the office during office hours and have a chat. They know you're there and will expect your visit.

Antigua (anne-TEE-gah)

This one is *not* my favorite place because of repeated insults from officials and locals over the years. If you go here from the west, do so by first following the route above to Guadaloupe, then close reaching *back up* to **Antigua**. Trying to get here in a straight line is murder, even from **Montserrat**. Besides, you get to see Guadaloupe twice that way, since you must come back to continue south.

Isles des Saintes (eel day SANT), Guadeloupe

Anchor on the north shore of the island west of **Bourg** one mile, sheltered on the east by a large, round rock. Clearing in isn't always necessary since **Customs**, or *Le Douane*, isn't always there. Dinghy in for a farewell to French cuisine here. Say hello to the *gendarmes*, but don't be surprised if they don't care you're there for one overnight.

Roseau (roo-SOH), Dominica (doh-mee-KNEE-kah)

Landfall going south is **Prince Rupert's Bay**. Anchor off the hotel on the south shore. Next morning truck on down to **Roseau**, the capital. You may tie stern-to to the hotel pier, but it is not necessary. You can anchor a boat-length from the shore as the nights are dead calm, and more than a boat-length away it drops off to China.. Dominicans (accent on the "ni," pronounced "knee") are among the nicest people in the Leewards or Windwards, and the island offers much to see. **Soufriere** is the pits, but it is the place to leave from.

St. Pierre, Martinique

(See the section on Virgin Gorda to Martinique.) As you proceed down the island, you will see blacktop "roads" climbing inland from the sea. They're not roads: This is the site of Mt. Pelée, which erupted in 1902, killing between 30 and 40 thousand, and wiping out a bay full of ships along with the capital of the Lesser Antilles.. Only one man survived—a drunk in the jail. There's a museum being stocked with finds from the digs.

Fort de France, Martinique

Good, but expensive, yacht chandlers and French cuisine will keep you here a while, even if you're a hell-bent for leather passage maker. **Martinique** is just about the only cruising-worthy island between **St. Martin** and **Venezuela**, as far as using your boat is concerned: little bays with their little villages and great restaurants; great diving on the east coast. Try the seafood restaurants at **Bourg du Robert**. Martinique also offers the best girl-watching between the **Dominican Republic** and **Brazil**. Hard-core cruisers hang out at **Anse Mitan** (aunt's me-TONG), or **Anse des Cocotiers** (aunt's day co-co-tee-AIRH) on the charts.

Rodney Bay, St. Lucia

Here is a fabulous marina with owner Arch Marez on site and hosting. Tie up or anchor out, this is the place from which to tour the island if you choose to do so. Rodney Bay Marina is still the best-equipped yard south of the **Virgin Islands**.

Marigot Bay, St. Lucia

Stop at this historic and scenic bay for lunch and press on to the **Pitons** well before dark, since you won't be able to count on room to overnight. Although a **Hurricane Hole**, it is doubtful you could use it profitably with the crush of charter boats all around. **Marigot Bay** is one of Lord Nelson's hidey holes. The man had genius for finding harbors where enemies literally at the entrance didn't know there was a harbor, much less ships, in front of them (e.g., Mahón in Minorca, English Harbor in Antigua).

Pitons, St. Lucia

A tricky spot in a blow. If you have all chain, you may find yourself with 200 feet of it hanging straight down after casting off next day. The beach boys used to behave quite ugly here, but recently they seem to have mellowed out and entered an establishmentarian phase of their Rastafarian lives. They do expect tips and they do provide a useful service. The size of the tip has been previously determined for broke cruisers by the bareboat charterers on vacation: $5—or so.

Chateau Belaire, St. Vincent

This is the unspoiled jewel of the island. Anchor 40 yards from shore in 20 feet of sand, just north of a little river at the north end of the bay (at the end of the line of beach). Unlike elsewhere, the kids will give you good service and not hassle you. Send them out for fresh fruits and veggies, but anchor your own boat. Use two anchors because of the nighttime swing. Boat boys are usually nice. Boy-Boy, in whites, will take your garbage. There is another good anchorage by the coconut trees just north of the bay.

Bequia, St. Vincent Grenadines

All the good shallow spots will be taken, so resolve to anchor in 40 feet and be done with it. Be here for Christmas. It's the meeting ground of the **Windward Islands** for cruisers from Mom and Pop to the maxis returning from the Mediterranean. One party after another.

The Grenadines

In the **Grenadines**, one initially has a certain temerity about bearing full sail, given the strength of the **Trade Winds**. The wind's rock-hard steadiness, however, and the fine lees available from the seas, let you carry a full rig. Your boat will perform as never before. Sailing the passes is exhilarating. No need to drop sail in a squall, just turn head to wind and let it rattle a while, then continue. If you don't head up, however, you could get knocked down since 50-knot leading edges are not unheard of.

Tyrell Bay, Carriacou, The Grenada Grenadines

Hillsboro is not a great harbor and a little out of the way for passage makers. The **Hurricane Hole** at **Tyrell Bay** is the best available since you left Puerto Rico. It is a pleasant little community with a rudimentary boatyard and gringos ashore, opening and closing restaurants.

St. Georges, Grenada

Anchor off the crumbling Yacht Services dock and clear in at their offices. (For further information on St. Georges, see the section on Customs and Clearances.) Doyle's *Sailor's Guide to A Venezuelan Cruise* can be purchased at the neat little bookstore below the Nutmeg restaurant, across the harbor. Rumor has it that this is the store where an Army lieutenant borrowed the phone to call the Pentagon to patch him into the Navy offshore to tell them to stop shelling him. So much for combined strike force technology. Another rumor is that yachties in the harbor were ignored when they volunteered use of their radios because they "weren't secure."

Grenada to the Testigos (test-TEE-gohs)

Depart **Grenada** from **St. Georges** or **Prickly Bay** at dusk to arrive at the **Testigos** for breakfast. Anchor north of **Isla Langoleta** to the west of **Isla Testigo Grande**. This can be a good spot for a bottom scrub.

On the crossing allow for 1.3 knots of current setting 300° true door-to-door. Have a full rig up, since you will encounter calms to Force 3 on this passage. There may be a belt of squalls 20 miles or so northeast of the Testigos, however. The **Equatorial Current** is really ripping around here, and this miniature weather system seems to always be there. The trip will doubtless be smooth and uneventful.

The *Testigos* (witnesses) are so called because they testified to the existence of the Equatorial Current for Columbus on his fourth voyage. The great navigator, having no knowledge of the Caribbean Sea, proceeded to make his new colony of **Santo Domingo** in one single tack. At the anchorage on Testigo Grande are the houses of five fishing families. They are the five sons from that island that married five of the six daughters born on the island across the bay. These families are the only inhabitants of the Testigos. Talk with Benjamin in the first house.

TESTIGOS TO PAMPATAR (PAHM-PAH-TAR)

Leave Testigos at first light for what probably will be a motor to **Pampatar**. Even though you have a fast boat, get going early so you can make your **SG&T** at your destination. Approaching **Isla Margarita** in the dark or in late afternoon, when there are often squalls with restricted visibility, could be a problem due to all the fishing activity around the island. It's best to sail overnight and arrive in the morning with good margin and good visibility. Anchor among the fleet of yachts and dinghy in to Shore Base Yacht Services, where you will be cleared in at a reasonable cost and with no hassle.

Trinidad

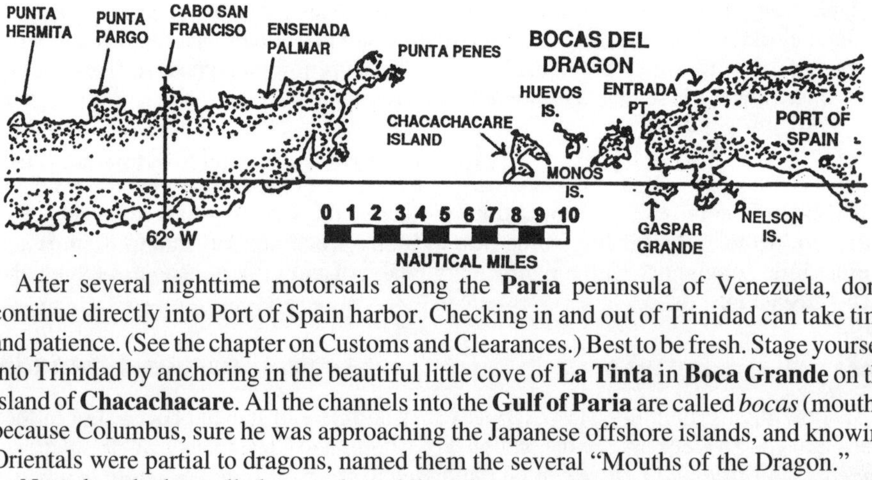

After several nighttime motorsails along the **Paria** peninsula of Venezuela, don't continue directly into Port of Spain harbor. Checking in and out of Trinidad can take time and patience. (See the chapter on Customs and Clearances.) Best to be fresh. Stage yourself into Trinidad by anchoring in the beautiful little cove of **La Tinta** in **Boca Grande** on the island of **Chacachacare**. All the channels into the **Gulf of Paria** are called *bocas* (mouths) because Columbus, sure he was approaching the Japanese offshore islands, and knowing Orientals were partial to dragons, named them the several "Mouths of the Dragon."

Next day, the boat all clean and sparkling, the crew all rested, bright eyed and bushy tailed, you can motor over to **Chaguaramas** to clear in. After the exit hassles, stage yourself out of Port of Spain by going over to **Scotland Bay** and anchoring on a shelf of sand all the way up the bay.

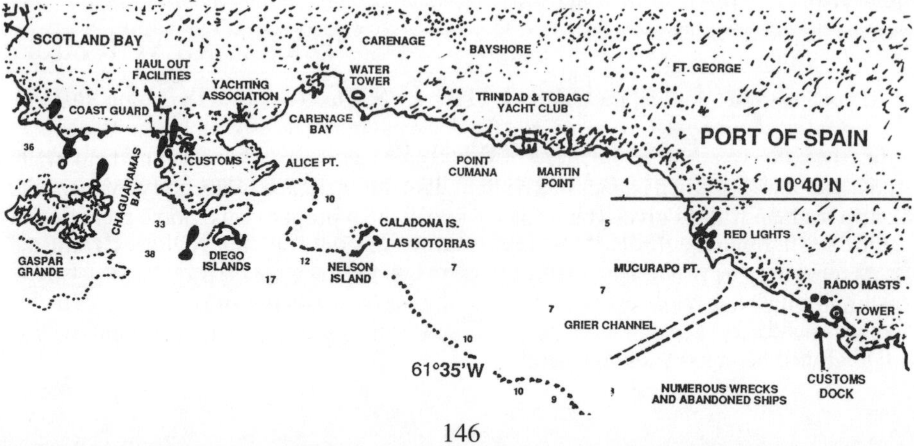

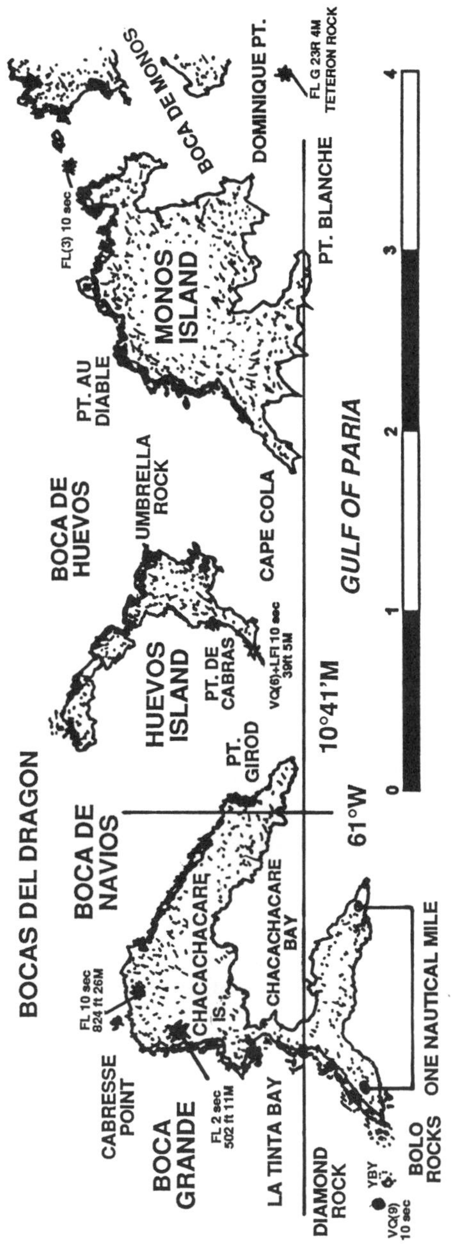

The way to *do* Trinidad is to be there in early to mid-December just to ensure a slip at the yacht club, or a mooring at the Yachting Association in **Carenage Bay**. The original of the steel band carnivals, Trinidad's **Carnival** gets going already in December with each band's preparation for Carnival being a cause to party. You must understand the jargon of Carnival in order to know how to best enjoy it. Just doing that will take a month. Trinidadians are an eclectic race of African, Indian, Chinese and European. The melange of customs, cuisines and beautiful people provide a tourist smorgasbord. By the time Carnival is actually staged in February, it will be an anticlimax, although it is a huge event.

Leave from **Scotland Bay** for an easy sail to **Grenada** in settled trades south of east. Alternatively, beat back up to **Martinique**. In either case, bear in mind the dictum you learned upon approaching Hispaniola (you did learn it, didn't you?) to ease sheets and run across the wind if the seas and wind begin to bite. *Do not* try to beat directly into it. So you arrive a few miles to leeward of Grenada. So what? Tack back up to the big island in its great lee. But don't blow out your sails and risk your hides doing a dumb rhumb just because it's programmed into your GPS!

Back from Venezuela

If you insist on Crossing the Caribbean, do so from **Los Roques** to the **Mona Passage**. Use a west-northwest average set of 1/2 knot door-to-door. The way back from **Venezuela** through the islands is preferable to croosing the Caribbean Sea. You get to vist them twice. And if you scurried down islands in a rush to get to the hurricane protection of Venezuela, the trip back up islands gives you a chance to pay them proper visits. Some great flotilla parties are thrown in the holiday season, which include all the returnees from the Mediterranean. Try **Bequia** for Christmas and **Petit St. Vincent** for New Year's—if you can't make the New Year's party at Foxy's on **Jost Van Dyke**, that is.

Crossing over to **Grenada**, you have to motor the coast almost to **Trinidad**, so you might as well call in at **Port of Spain**.

POINTERS ON THE PATH

Thornton Throckmorton Thorndike the Third was a gentleman sailor. While participating in the Thornypath Semifinals of 1933, Thornton discovered an entirely new method for heading south against the prevailing winds.

Skilled in the art of steering with his big toe while jigging for grouper over the stern, he and his long-keeled beamy yawl were totally unprepared for the cutthroat competition in the Thornypath Semifinals. The high-tech go-to-windward carbon filament keel-less burgee bearers backing and filling at the starting line awed him. Was his pokey little boat, *Rose*, up to it? Thornton thrilled at the threat and was ever more determined.

As the only member of the leisure class to compete, Thornton had a unique advantage: *leisure*. He laid on capers from Exuma Markets to gourmandize his usually superb Nassau Grouper *Au Vin Blanc*. He researched his Rolodex file of anchorages, fishing holes and recipes. He prepared his lists of dinner guests for each anchorage, being careful to invite each of the competing skippers on exactly three occasions, never having the same three twice. He underestimated his competition.

Four of the other yachts were crewed by professional delivery crews, only one of whose boats survived, but in such condition it was subsequently scrapped for spare parts for the Tortola charter fleet. Two contestants were on one-year sabbaticals to sail around the world. Two were on two week vacations. One had to meet a seaplane in St. Thomas. From this field of ten tough competitors there were five DNFs, three divorces and one case of road hypnosis who eventually ran ashore on the Cape Verdes.

And there was Thornton. Thornton won. This guide is an attempt to spell out his winning strategy: how to take the thorns out of the Thorny Path. Here are some of the pointers he's given me from his years of taking the Thornless Path, along with some I've picked up myself. I've been using them for years with good results. So can you.

Thornton Aboard His Yawl *Rose*

INTRUDERS

On two occasions I have been roused from my bunk by nighttime intruders while in a remote anchorage. The first time it happened I had not slept in two days.

When I finally made harbor, I doused the adrenaline level with a couple of **SG&Ts**, then dropped like an anchor into my bunk. At four in the morning I was shaken semiconscious by an unshaven, red-eyed, dirty and, except for old and holed jockey shorts, naked man. The hand not rousing me held an AR15 automatic.

In my befuddlement, I suspected that anyone, even naked, with a weapon like the AR15 had to be a Huk guerrilla, a dope smuggler or an official of a banana republic. Smugglers can afford clothes. I hadn't heard about any revolution, and this wasn't the Philippines.

Fortunately for me, I sleepily guessed that he must have a permit for the gun and that he represented some authority who had bought it for him, he not appearing to have the resources to buy one himself. I mumbled, "Buenos dias." And so my day began.

The intruder was the local part-time representative of the Navy, whose responsibility it was to inquire at the boat which had surreptitiously slid into the bay that night. He was out fishing all night with buddies in his little log canoe. Upon returning to port with the dawn, they had knocked on the hull to no avail. Being a serious man, he went the next step and stepped aboard. Still with no sign from me, he stepped inside.

Good thing I didn't grab my gun, a hand-sized automatic on the shelf over my pillow. Had I done so we would both have drowned from water pouring through the holes he'd have made in the hull with his machine gun.

Instead, we had an amiable beer together the next day and he warned me again not to go sneaking up on his beach like a Cuban fifth columnist. But he suggested that if I really wanted a special reception, I might try night anchoring unannounced in Cuba under Fidel's regime. Talk about stress!

Stress at any level has its price.

THE PRICE OF STRESS

Signs of normalcy in one culture may be alarm signals in another. For example, Latinos like to carry guns as a sign of authority. Why not?

Sometimes, the smaller the authority, the larger the guns. Larger guns are usually cheaper. Guns from the former eastern block are very cheap in quantity and, because you haven't seen them before, they look all the more sinister. Unless you are well traveled you are likely to suppose a revolution is in progress when you see poorly clad citizens roaming the streets with Russian machine guns and rifles.

Culturally transmitted visual stimuli and their culturally correct responses do not map easily from one culture to another. They can, in fact, be in direct opposition. The receiving organism—that's you—will undergo stress, depending on the extent to which responses expected by the two cultures to the same stimulus differ. If the conflict is mild and occasional, you giggle. If strong and continuous, you will undergo a stress reaction called **Culture Shock**.

You may have a repertoire of cocktail stories of what happened to you on your tour of Thailand. In that case, you understand the phenomenon being discussed, but you may never have experienced it in shock dimensions. If you have lived on the local economy of another nation for extended periods, and you have been forced to use their language exclusively as, say, a member of the Peace Corps, you know well the phenomenon at shock levels.

Roaming around the Caribbean on a small boat provides greater exposure to local people and their customs than does jetting in and out of well-protected resort complexes. If you haven't had the opportunity of experiencing culture shock before, you are about to learn on your own slow-moving sailboat. When it gets unpleasant you can't simply take a cab to the airport.

There are many symptoms of culture shock with which you should be familiar before leaving home. Your ability to communicate with or without language, your capacity to get what you want—say, an engine part—are dependent on your skill in cutting through the background noise of your culturally learned responses and creating a totally new set of responses which achieve your goal.

The better your skills in creating useful new responses to confusing stimuli, however, the higher stress levels you may suffer, due to the number of unsatisfied natural responses being accumulated.

You may be successful handling the customs guys, finding clean fuel, provisioning at fair prices, replacing a motor part, and so forth, but you will be left with a head of steam that's got to be blown off. It's the price you pay for coping successfully.

I've been known to blow my safety valve right in customs and get charged entrance fees others don't have to pay. I've seen others air-ship expensive parts from home with all the attendant hassles of telephoning, wiring funds, misdirection and delays, when they could have cut through the static of their learned responses and bought an equivalent (sometimes even superior) part locally in two days for less money.

In other words, it is possible to buy off culture shock with money or to mute it with anger: take it in the purse or in the gut. It is your decision how you pay the price of culture shock but pay it you will. Unfortunately, some people get others to pay it for them.

For example, the Albert Schweitzer in you might want to enfold the entire disadvantaged population of the Third World in his compassionate embrace. You settle for inviting a couple of homeless street urchins aboard for peanut butter and jelly sandwiches. Your finer instincts may be stroked by your behavior, but watch that the kids don't walk in uninvited with their friends later on. Your behavior may appear bizarre to them, remember, and they might expect you're going to adopt them and take them off to New York to pick gold up off the streets. Why otherwise would you usher them aboard what is as foreign to them as a spaceship would be to your kids? Obviously you're going to take them to Mars, if not New York, right?

Some years ago, I witnessed an incident that illustrates the point.

SPACESHIP YACHT

Two American couples in a motor yacht moored next to me brought some kids aboard their boat with results that were tragic for the children. The kids were given a tour of the yacht, an old classic motorboat once belonging to a famous man. They were then fed peanut butter and jelly sandwiches on deck. A few days later the couples discovered the kids had come back aboard and some costume jewelry was missing.

Seeing themselves as having participated directly, and with great humanity, in the work of *Save The Children* by their charitable invitation to peanut butter and jelly, the cruisers were justifiably outraged that the children had come back to *steal*. They complained to the police. Because offenses against tourists were quite a serious thing in their fragile tourist sector, the state security police, the dreaded *Ton Ton Macoute*, took direct charge of the situation.

As a result of their investigation one child was crippled and two were badly and bloodily injured. When asked if all her plastic bracelets had been returned, one of the women from the yacht, panicked by the beatings going on in the next room, cried, "No, but they don't matter, just, for God's sake, please stop beating them!" The beatings, of course, went on, since she said the property hadn't been fully recovered.

The child probably didn't want to give up his bit of brightly colored plastic because it was a link to the goddess-mother from the spaceship. She who had let him experience motherly warmth, perhaps for the first time in his life, along with peanut butter and jelly. She who seemed to promise to carry him off to another and better star.

So they broke his arm. He and the other children paid the price of the yachties' inappropriate responses. The yachties, blaming it all on the police, rushed to their boat and vroomed out of the harbor for home. I got one of the dock lines they left behind.

THE REMEDY

Culture Shock is responsible for the flocking syndrome of expatriates in any country—Latin Americans in the United States, for instance, or Americans in Latin America. While living in Paris I always noticed Americans *klatsching* with other Americans to whom they wouldn't speak while on their native soil. Matrons from Old Greenwich would eagerly trade recipes with the wives of North Sea oil roustabouts from Louisiana. They clutched together for the sole purpose of hearing their native tongue and badmouthing the Parisians.

Grumbling about the environment responsible for your stress is normal and even necessary. Frenchmen do it in America, Germans do it in Spain and Englishmen do it everywhere. But watch where you do your grouching. You are not in the private salons of Paris while on a cruising sailboat or sitting in a cheap restaurant. You are on display. Bitching about the local environment while under the gaze of petty port officials, dock boys and small time secret police, isn't too *suave*. Doing it in a restaurant where the couple at the next table run the local grocery store will get you higher prices on your veggies tomorrow.

It is best for you to find your own general remedy to the stress of culture shock which can be applied at an appropriate time and place. Whether yoga, expatriate kaffee *klatches*, or self-flagellation, a personalized remedy should permit daily satisfaction of personal and boat oriented goals while increasing your enjoyment of the different scenes.

Some boaters crawl into a VCR-induced haze, not leaving their boats for days at a time. Others meet every evening for a happy hour where they massage each other's spirits with spirits like the **SG&T**. While a dandy motivation to be at anchor early and safely, the G&T

is a poor remedy to the stress of culture shock. The ports of Asia and Latin America teem with besotted ex-pats who have taken this false remedy to their destructions.

Whether you go into frenzies of varnishing, practice meditation, write long letters to the kids or klatch on the SSB, your remedy should be a task you recognize as working off the stress of learning new responses. You will reduce the costs of making inappropriate responses in the future and increase your enjoyment of the cruising life.

Beware, though, that klatsching on the SSB has far-ranging effects, as did a story going around in Georgetown for years. Read on . . . .

PIRATES!

Returning to **Georgetown** from **Puerto Plata** one year, a friend grabbed me and said, "God, it's good to see you. I heard you had gone into **Abraham Bay** at **Mayaguana**!" After massaging the blood back into my arm, I learned that the SSB nets were full of tales of piracy in Mayaguana.

It was said that three boats were in the anchorage there. One boat was boarded by pirates in blue jumpsuits, masquerading as Bahamas customs officials. A fight ensued in which one of the boats was lost.

Over the Regatta period the essentials of the story changed little, but the details, for no one actually knew for sure, ranged from gory to grisly. After Regatta I returned home to Puerto Plata, stopping, of course, at Mayaguana. This time I bypassed my usual **Start Bay** and set anchor in Abraham Bay so I could visit the settlement and get the dirt first-hand.

The two constables on the island, one 22 years old, the other 20 and just out of the academy in Nassau, were wearing blue jumpsuits. Being in the Bahamas they, of course, had no guns. I chatted of various sea stories with them, including their recent unarmed arrest of eight Colombians with Uzzis. They were the crew of a freighter which grounded in Horse Pond Bay. The unarmed constables went to make the arrest in a little borrowed rowboat. The prisoners were put up in islanders' houses until Nassau could send a plane down for them. That's how life is in the Far Out Islands.

With a little conversational nudging on my part, a story gradually emerged about a power boat that had come in one evening while two sailboats were already in the anchorage. The boat didn't answer the constables' hails, so they borrowed a rowboat and stroked out to say "hi." The owner/skipper looked tired, perhaps even intoxicated.

Their queries as to where from and where bound were met with growls of "I don't want any," and "Get away," from the owner, a big florid-faced man.

Being good constables, the two young men smelled something awry. They asked if there were any arms aboard, the next question in the rote. When this was met with a surly shout, they decided this boat definitely didn't pass the smell test.

Instead of bidding the yachtsman a warm welcome to Mayaguana and paddling home, they started to tie their painter to the big gin palace and requested permission to come aboard. Not ever anticipating a negative response to this rote question, the younger of the two climbed aboard, whereupon the owner skittered into the saloon and emerged waving a gun. With a foaming roar of curses he shoved the young constable into the bay, where, given the sudden appearance of this maniac with a weapon, the young man was glad to be.

The yachtsman immediately upped his anchor and blasted out through the cut in the reef, even though the sun was nearly setting. He was soon lost to sight. The next morning's cruiser nets were ablaze with the story.

"Pirates masquerading as customs officials" probably was reported by the guy in the gin palace. The "fight" would naturally come from the sailboat captains observing from some distance away and hearing nothing but dim shouts, seeing the brandishing of guns and a body going overboard. The "three boats in the anchorage" was quite true. That one boat was "lost" might come from a mike switch being released too soon, untimely radio interference or simple embellishment.

The whole pirate story came about through the klatsching of the cruising community on their radios, sopping up their alienation and culture shock at the expense of two fine young Bahamian officers and the reputation of an island badly in need of visitors. Three years later I was still being approached at the Two Turtles barbecue with anxious queries as to piracy in Mayaguana.

Lately, at the barbecue, I heard a fellow at the next table authoritatively replaying one of the scarier versions of the old story, but, like all good stories, the essentials hadn't changed. Two guys in blue, a fight, a lost boat.

But I learned myself, long ago, the price of correcting a know-it-all in public is too high for me to pay. Instead of bringing them all down on my head, I ordered another gin and tonic. After all, no one likes a spoilsport and everyone likes a good story. Especially me!

Tales of rape, plunder and pillage in the Caribbean have titillated the minds of youngsters since the 1600s when the maraudings of L'Olenois the *Corsaire* and Morgan the Privateer, first were popularized in the British bookstalls. Most long-distance cruisers are adventurers and, to some extent, children at heart. Their titillation runs wild upon occasion and their stories of piracy and skullduggery on the Thornless Path are one of the many false dangers you cope with. Like cloud shadows on the banks, if you spend your time trying to avoid them you risk running into a real danger.

PERSONAL SECURITY

First, there are bad actors all over the world and "piracy," or bad guys potting at targets of opportunity upon the wastes of the sea, or in the alleys of the waterfronts, are everywhere as well. You're not in the Sulu Sea or the Red Sea, however. Your chances of running into a pirate in the Caribbean is about the same, or even less than, your chances of stumbling into one off **Key Biscayne**. Ask any European and you'll discover that most of the civilized world thinks America is among the most violent nations in the world. Unfortunately, there is much to substantiate that opinion, and your exposure to personal assault, on your boat or ashore, is less almost anywhere along the Thornless Path than it is in any yachting center in the United States. Having said that, there are yet some caveats which may make for a more pleasant cruise.

AFLOAT

Avoid pickup crew. The Caribbean is full of hitchhikers, both American and European, especially in the large yachting centers. Some are simply doing what used to be called *Le Grand Tour* between college and the start of a career. Others are simply doing you. If, after thorough investigation, you do take someone aboard, hold the person's passport and enough of his or her money to fly them back to their native country from your boat's destination. An even better filter of their real intentions is to do as the South Africans and some Europeans. Charge the crew for their room and board and the trip. Let the leeches pay or go get their own boat. Unbelievable folly has been met with pickup crew.

ASHORE

City waterfronts everywhere are close to rundown sections with poorer, sometimes desperate, inhabitants. Walking alone down unlit streets with flamboyant tourist garb, a bulging hip pocket and half a bag on from some happy hour isn't smart. In **Cumaná**, Venezuela, you're dead meat.

On the other hand, it's not always so grim in the Third World. It used to be that in **Puerto Plata** and Belize City, you could be a naked 16-year-old virgin with fistfuls of dollars and attract only admiration. And you should have seen the alleys of Belize City at night a dozen years ago! Times have been hard throughout the developing world. Skullduggery is up everywhere. Until you know for sure, act as prudently as you would at home. No more nor less.

FIREARMS

If you have firearms, be trained in their use and know when to use them. Never brandish a firearm. If you take one in hand, it should be to use it; its use is not to scare but to kill. Pretty serious stuff. Firearms aboard can be a hassle while clearing in and out. (See the Appendix on Customs and Clearances.)

The problem lies in threat assessment. Sober, nonprejudicial judgment is necessary. But that's rarely possible in a strange, poverty-stricken land where people speak a different language with excited jabbers and ominous overtones. It's hardly possible in a dirty town where everyone's a different color than you are and they all stare at you, point and whisper. It's certainly difficult when you're roused out of a sound SG&T-induced slumber after a long, hard, adrenaline-drenched beat to weather by someone who looks like a Huk guerrilla. Impulsive resort to a firearm is invitation to tragedy. Probably yours.

BOAT SECURITY

There are as few anchorages on the Thornless Path where I feel I must lock up my boat as there are towns in America where one can leave one's doors open. Most places, if a local inhabitant breaks through your locks he'll cause more loss through damage to teak joinery than he will through the trinkets he's likely to walk off with.

Only boaties take boaty things. Remember that when you anchor next to the dirtbag boat full of hippies in a lonely cove. Such "cruisers" do exist in the Caribbean. Avoid these boats and their crews. If they need a snatch block, they'll snatch yours. Unfortunately for world unity, some nationalities more than others tend to spawn boats like these.

In countries with acute economic stress, petty theft by locals can occur upon occasion. You can hire boat watchers while you're away, but they can sell you out to the pilferers—or pilfer for themselves. You may be asked to hire one anyway, like you're asked to hire a punk in New York City to "make sure nobody slashes your tires." But that's rare in the Caribbean. It could be you are in the wrong place to begin with.

How and where you moor the boat when you are away from it will provide you with more insurance than any insurance company or commercial guard service can offer. During extended absences, unless you can put up in a guarded marina, securely anchor the boat in a weather-safe anchorage, far enough from young swimmers from the shore, near enough to be seen by the casual observer, and in amongst other yachts whose owners you know and trust. Leave them instructions for access to the boat, as well as for charging the battery, feeding the parakeet or what-all else.

Alarm systems, like those in suburban America, turn in more false alarms than real. But if you're a gadgeteer and have the money, by all means, have the fun of installing them and spoofing your friends with all the hooting of horns and strobing of lights. Any local intruder, not knowing what to expect, is likely to think that this display is all quite normal boat behavior. One boater I know has a neat switch over his bunk. When he throws it, a brilliant floodlight mounted high forward in the saloon blinds anyone in the cockpit, the companion way, or messing around inside. Like a stun grenade: effective, simple and cheap.

DINGHY SECURITY

If you haven't learned dinghy security in the U.S. waters, here are some tips to help you from **Nassau**, onward. Motor and dinghy theft is not a problem where locals with a yacht dinghy would stand out like a dugout canoe in a Connecticut yacht club. Theft will occur where there is a ready market for either the motor or the dinghy.

First, use chain or coated stainless cable of minimum size 5/16", minimum length 12 feet. Alan's Rigging in Yacht Haven, St. Thomas, makes up superb dinghy security cables. Chain is better, as you will see below. Padlock or permanently secure the chain to a permanent steel fitting attached to a hard surface of the dink (transom, for instance), not the towing eye of an inflatable dinghy—thieves will simply cut them off. I know of one case where they even cut off the transom. Even if your motor is locked securely onto the transom, run the chain through the motor handle as well. Finally, lock the chain to some permanent fixture ashore with an eye to tide and current. You may want an anchor out to keep from sawing against a pier or going under one at low tide. You may come back to a crushed motor when the tide rises.

Lock your dinghy to the boat, coiling excess chain in a bunch on deck so it doesn't go overboard unless pulled upon. The thunk-thunk-thunk of the links going over the rail is your alarm system, and enables you to catch the varmint in the act. Depending on the sternness of your response, you won't have trouble at that anchorage for the rest of your stay. I've found flare guns neatly scare everyone in the anchorage as well as the varmint, and they certainly light up the scene of the crime well and call the attention of any law enforcement which may be around but pretending not to notice. Flares also continue to burn in the water, catching the crook in a ring of light. One friend prefers a "wrist rocket" slingshot with ball bearings. One fellow I know brought back a blowgun from South America with pretty serious darts.

If you have big motorized davits, use them to haul up your dinghy and motor every night. Another method is to arrange a three-point bridle with its lifting ring centered to keep the raised dinghy and motor level, as you haul them up to the rail with your halyard. Make the bridle out of stainless cable, or it may be chopped readily with a machete.

Plaster your dinghy and motor with reflective tape so you can find it when it drifts away at night. It also becomes a less attractive target for thieves. An inflatable in the Virgin Islands becomes less attractive to thieves (other boaters), if it is plastered with multicolored patches and 5200. One of my best dinghy trades was a flawless Avon RIB that looked like it had been through the battle of Trafalgar. I never had to lock that one up.

Finally, at crowded dinghy docks, leave your dink anchored well off with 30 or so feet of painter run to the dock. Neophyte cruisers often snug their painters to the dock and tip their motors up. As the tide changes their props become bucking and slashing scythes which will cut their bow section to ribbons. I usually make a dinghy dock with a stern anchor out, actually an undeployed grapnel. A rock does just as well. I land perpendicular to the dock a distance down from where I want the painter tied. The dinghy then lays off roughly that same distance, well free of the crowd. It can be retrieved at any point by dragging, since the anchor, or rock, isn't grabbing hard.

LAYING ANCHOR

Yachts that drag into you in the tight anchorages invariably seem to pay more attention to sailing than to seamanship. Ninety-five percent of seamanship lies in the art of keeping the boat from moving and only five percent in making it go. Here are some aphorisms which, when taken together, go some distance toward describing the art of anchoring between Florida and Venezuela.

1. Don't anchor near boats with damaged topsides.

2. Don't anchor near boats with performance hulls or rigs.

Chances are they are five-percenters and have only five feet of chain. They dance all over the harbor in any breeze. I watched one hull-sailing full circles all night long. He had two anchors, thank goodness, and the boat wound itself down like a cuckoo clock and took off on the other tack for another fifteen circles.

3. Small boats (under 50') are best anchored by one person.

In this way one person will know what was done at the time of anchoring and the knowledge will not reside somewhere between the wheel and the pulpit with neither station actually being responsible. This rule can save marriages as well.

Preparing the boat to fall off in the proper direction before laying the anchor is best the responsibility of the person who selects the spot and lays the anchor, not someone at the helm who doesn't quite know where the spot is or how the anchor shall lie. It also calls for knowledge of the boat's characteristics of way, its momentum, and how easily she faces or crosses the wind.

While anchoring single-handedly, however, it is essential that the maneuver to station the slowly swinging bow over the spot selected be well timed to enable the walk forward from the helm to the pulpit to be accomplished with a certain seaman-like decorum, rather than a headlong, cursing rush.

4. Anchors should be set by wind and current.

That is, not by someone behind 80 horses unable to see what's happening, unless, of course there is no wind or current. Anchors, especially burying types such as Bruces and plows, dig in by wiggling and worming with the action of the sea and tug of the chain. If you apply tractor power to them they will revert to kind and plow a furrow. Watch for drag by picking a range (not other boats) perpendicular to the extended rode. Also, a grasped rode can telegraph dragging to your hand. If the wind is up, it may be difficult to set even a Danforth in mangrove mud (e.g., Salinas, Luperón) or hard marl (e.g., Bequia). If you can't arrive early, before the wind comes up, you shall have to motor in such a fashion so as to maintain sternway slow enough to permit the anchor to set.

5. Anchors are to be laid, not dropped, thrown or swung.

Laying an anchor implies a smooth backward drift in the direction of the expected flow of wind or current, while *laying* the chain in a straight line behind the straightly laid anchor. Lay enough chain to ensure any pull on the anchor will be directed along the bottom before gently and gradually setting the anchor. Sailors who routinely talk about dropping the hook, you will find, often have hooks instead of proper anchors and usually do simply drop them, heavily entwined in a bundle of rope and chain.

6. Anchors should be selected for bottom and boat.

This guide includes tables which demonstrate the holding power of some anchors, some ground tackle strengths, and data which you can use to figure the loads generated on your anchors and rodes while riding out a Class-1 hurricane in a protected hole. The data may surprise you.

Use about a pound of anchor for every foot of the boat. A 45-pound Danforth would suit a 41-foot boat, but not as a single anchor if wind or current can switch. Danforths, while capable of tremendous holding power, do not reset themselves well and the stock can go afoul. Heavy burying type anchors such as the CQR or Bruce work well on almost all bottoms and tend to reset themselves. They don't foul as easily as Danforth types. Use Danforth types in mud or grassy bottoms, making well sure the points are dug in. In a blow, Danforths hold best pound for pound. No matter what the Danforth folks say, don't use a short length of chain. It may function in theory but, in the Caribbean, any nylon rode less than one inch shall most certainly be chafed through on the bottom, if not by coral, then by broken rum bottles.

For rocky bottoms use a heavy prayer.

7. Use enough chain: *long* enough and *big* enough.

Consider first that the chain's catenary must never be able to reach the anchor itself so as to exert upward drag on the shank—even in the most violent conditions—especially in the most violent conditions. Second, ensure that any rode attached cannot come into contact with the seabed or obstructions on it (coral heads, rocks, wrecks and broken rum bottles).

a. You might consider including enough chain so that chafe at deck level does not occur, i.e., all chain. Also, the catenary of an all chain rode makes a good shock absorber. If you use all chain, attach a nylon snubber which is one half the diameter of your rode, and as long as necessary to quiet the action. Absolute minimum chain length should be five feet for every 1/16" of chain size, i.e., 25 feet for 5/16" chain, 30 feet for 3/8, etc. An alternate rule of thumb is to use between 1 and 1 ½ boat lengths.

b. Roughly, add 1/16" in chain size for every 10 feet of boat's length above 20 feet. Thus, for LOA's 20-29 feet, use 5/16", for 30-39 feet use 3/8", for 40-49 feet use 7/16", and for 50-59 feet use ½".

c. For all chain use a scope of three to five times the depth of water *added to the distance from sea level to anchor roller.*

d. For chain and rode use a scope five to seven times the depth *added to the distance from sea level to anchor roller.*

e. To reduce the amount of scope required in tight anchorages, consider extending your anchor snubbers from a bow eye at the water line.

f. To reduce vertical snatching loads on the bow, buoy the rodes before leading them to the bow.

8. Almost always use two anchors.

The actual uses of the Bahamian Moor, one anchor against each expected change of current direction, are few: tidal bays, coves, creeks or rivers. These are places where currents can be strong and regularly reverse with the tide.

Nine out of ten of your anchorages will be in harbors or against beaches where these effects are minimal. So why use two anchors?

a. Because everyone around you does and if you don't you'll find your bow poking into someone's bedroom in the middle of the night.

b. Because you expect a switch in the wind or a front to come; or worse, because you don't expect it.

c. Because the harbor you're in goes absolutely calm at night and you want to prevent the boat from walking around your anchor, droodling chain all over and under it, so that when the morning wind rises you drag onto the beach, towing a ball of tackle.

d. Because you're the first one in harbor in the Virgins and you expect forty partying bareboaters to plunk balls of chain all around you in the middle of the night and you want to keep your elbows tucked in.

e. Because you don't want to wind your rode around a coral head.

f. Because you're in the anchorage for the first time and aren't quite sure about that wide open fetch to the Southwest.

g. Because you're leaving the boat unattended.

h. Because you're smarter than the average boater.

BUT, if everyone else is swinging on one anchor, go with the flow and set only one yourself so they don't bash you.

---

9. Let the yacht come to rest before paying out more tackle.

Pay out the final bit of scope, or, as the case may be, snug it in, only after securing the yacht and tidying up the deck. That will ensure more time for her to reach rest condition. The seaman who takes longest to get his yacht settled on her anchors is probably the sailor doing the best job of anchoring.

10. Dive on the anchor, if possible, to check it.

If necessary, set it by hand. While you are down there, check your neighbors' as well. I was cruising in company with a good friend who is a professional diver on the oil rigs. In deference to his skills and my taste, I started on the SG&Ts while he dived on the anchors. He found a neighbor's anchor lying sideways on the bottom. "Impossible!" shouted the salty-whiskered downeaster while posed cross-armed and bantam-like on his taffrail. "I set that anchor with 55 horses!" My friend set the fellow's anchor for him in order to protect our own boats.

11. Beware of local knowledge—the locals may not know.

For example, on the incredibly steep and rocky shores of some islands the conventional wisdom is to tie your stern to a palm tree with a bow anchor sort of resting on the slope a hundred or so feet below. Well, if you have a deep draft, barn door rudder, you may lose it. The boaters next to you with the expert advice may be down from New York on a one week charter and the boys on the bank never managed a boat anyway.

Anchoring and docking throughout the Caribbean you'll have a plethora of advice. But on the other hand, it's your boat, Skip.

The following may seem old hat. But sit any morning in harbor and watch the scene while folks up their anchors. Before observing too long, you'll want a tot of rum in your coffee.

1. When weighing anchor, keep the chain *vertical.*

Doing this ensures two things. First, you will approach the anchor along the chain's lie and in a pace commensurate with safety and the proper stowing of the tackle. Secondly, you are unlaying the links of chain right up to the anchor's shank, ensuring that you don't dislodge the anchor until ready and it won't skitter and roil around the seabed fouling things like other people's anchors.

The chain can be kept vertical under the bow by:

a. never powering beyond the catenary, instead *let the catenary pull the yacht forward*, and

b. using the windlass only to pull up slack links, NOT to pull the yacht.

The rule when walking the yacht up her ground tackle is: *let the "canary" pull it.*

2. Keep station until the anchor clears the water.

The bane of all anchorages is the morning clod who, upon sensing the anchor has broken loose, turns his head aft and yells "She's up!" and off the yacht drifts downwind, with a giant grappling hook beneath her soaring a few inches off the bottom, headed almost surely for your rode. Even bane-ier is the knucklehead who powers about the anchorage with an acute angle of chain stretched behind the bow while the crew tries to wrestle up the taut chain and anchor before they snag—you guessed it—*your rode*!

As mentioned in the chapter on Luperón, in the Dominican Republic, the mangrove anchorages in the Greater Antilles have a colloidal mud bottom which makes the anchors-up drill a messy, sweaty job. It's always best, as noted in the section on Staging, to do the cleanup the day before leaving. Wherever possible, depart fresh and rested from a clean, short rode.

This is a subject that ought to be under a heading of Marriage Counseling. Mom and Pop on their retirement cruise have never been so close for so long in 40 years. Now they're farthest apart only while they're anchoring. And that's only a matter of 30 feet or so.

Pop stands at the wheel because he's so technical, while Mom stands at the bow anchor because she's got stronger hands. One or the other signals and the miscommunication begins.

It can take another 40 years to develop hand signals and the concomitant divided responsibilities which are needed to choreograph the delicate ballet of anchoring successfully in all conditions and in front of the usual audiences who are pretending to look the other way. If you can't do it alone, at least follow these rules.

The bowman (-woman) should do all signaling from the same position always and with the same hand always while holding the forestay with the other hand to ensure its immobility even more than to ensure the bowman's stability. Signals needed are:

- **left**
- **hard left**
- **right**
- **hard right**
- **center wheel**
- **ahead**
- **astern**
- **more power**
- **less power**
- **stop**
- **@*~#-$*!**

There are already too many commands, so don't add any.

The last command is optional but preserves harmony in the more untested relationships. Roadman signals work fine. So do crane operator signals.

To avoid nasty equivocation keep all fingers together.

To really do it right get one of those walkie talkies on headsets. You can build them into beanies with the boat's name on them. That way they can't be seen by the audience who will think you're just plain proficient.

One couple I saw do this really looked great while silently anchoring with this advanced communications equipment. At least until Pop suddenly screamed at Mom from the bow, apparently apropos of nothing, "I said *starboard*, dammit!"

ANCHOR AND GROUND TACKLE SELECTION GUIDE

In the section Laying Anchor there are several rules of thumb included in the examples of trouble-free anchoring procedure for the Caribbean. Below are some facts gleaned from too many sources to be recounted. They are provided here for the reader who, like me, can't easily find the data compiled in one place.

These are my notes and calculations from which I make my purchasing decisions for my boat in the Caribbean. Were I in the South Pacific, my ground tackle, like my dinghy, would be a result of different choices due to a different cruising environment. Like all statistics these numbers can tell different stories to please the tale teller.

You may be coming from the Chesapeake Bay or the Los Angeles area. Though capable of holding your 38-foot boat quite happily at home, a 12-pound Danforth Deepset and a ½-inch nylon rode with 6 feet of chain will not suffice in the Caribbean. If the sun doesn't melt such thin rode, then bottom chafe will surely set you adrift some night.

BOTTOMS

Use Danforth-type anchors for coarse sand and mud bottoms. Heavy burying type anchors are better suited to grassy bottoms or hardpan, clay and shale. Both types of anchors can hook or wedge fast in rock and coral bottoms, but a heavy plow type will dislodge the easiest when you go to get it up in the morning, and it will have less chance of being bent if a you get caught in a high chop.

The following are pounds of cable tension necessary to drag different anchors when set with a 5:1 scope in soft mud before being well silted-in (which could take weeks). Note that this is different from some "holding powers" which may imply breaking strengths of the gear. Multiply by 5 to obtain figures for hard sand.

Weight of Anchor in Pounds	**10**	**20**	**30**	**40**	**50**	**60**
BRUCE	110	180	230	280	330	370
CQR (plow)	160	250	330	400	470	530
DANFORTH TYPE	460	730	960	1160	1350	1500

Lbs. Cable Tension to Drag in Soft Mud at 5:1 Scope

INCH DIAMETERS	1/4	5/16	3/8	7/16	1/2	5/8	3/4	7/8	1"
BBB CHAIN '3B'		1700	2320	3160	4120	6300			
PROOF COIL 'G3'	1250	1900	2650	3520	4500	6800			
HIGH-TEST 'G4'	2600	3900	5400	7200	9200				
STAINLESS CHAIN	2000	2850	3550	4300					
GALV. FALSE LINKS	1400	2000	2800	3720	4750	7250			
GALV. SHACKLES	1000	1500	2000	3000	4000	6500			
STAINL'S SHACKLES	1500	3000	4500	6000	7000	10000			
GALV. SWIVELS	850	1250	2250	-	3600	5200	7200	-	12500
STAINLESS SWIVELS	1750	2750	4750	-	9250				
NYLON 3-STRAND		240	340	470	520	620	1380	1880	2460
DACRON BRAID		230	330	500	640	700	1600	2300	2800

Safe Working Loads for Ground Tackle

Safe Working Loads (**SWL**) for chain is about 40% of the load under which chain links begin to elongate prior to breaking.

SWL of galvanized chain may be exceeded under shock load without permanent damage, but the chain should be replaced when elongation begins to occur. All galvanized chain will elongate up to 15% before breaking.

SWL of shackles and swivels should never be exceeded.

Proof Coil has been tested to 200% of SWL.

High Test chain is available which has from 2 to 3 times the SWL of Proof Coil, but the period between elongation and breaking of High Test chain is short compared to Proof Coil and **BBB**.

Ultimate Breaking Load (UBL) of Proof Coil and BBB chains are about 4 times the SWL.

UBL of **High Test** chain is about 3 times **SWL**.

UBL of **galvanized shackles and swivels** are up to 6 times their **SWL**.

UBL of **stainless shackles and swivels** are double their **SWL**.

Dacron Braid has no stretch and its **UBL** is up to 5 times the **SWL**.

Nylon 3-strand will stretch up to 33% and its **UBL** is up to 10 times the **SWL**, making it ideal anchor rode.

TYPE OF KNOT	% REDUCTION IN UBL
EYE SPLICE (4 tucks, 3 tapers, unfinished)	15
CLOVE HITCH	30
ROUND TURN and TWO HALF HITCHES	30
ROLLING HITCH	40
BOWLINE	50
OVERHAND KNOT	60
SQUARE KNOT, or REEF KNOT	60

Effect of Knots on Nylon Rode

The above values are the percentage reduction in Ultimate Breaking Load (UBL) in 3-strand nylon rope which is caused by using the indicated knots.

In addition, the strengths of nylon ropes are reduced by up to 15% while they are wet.

The table below shows pounds of drag exerted on various yacht configurations in 80 knots of wind. Wind is shown on the bow and on the beam while the yacht sheers.

Spars, standing and running rigging are included as well as stanchions and lifelines.

Sails are assumed to be furled on their booms while foresails are below.

Efficiency of hull streamlining is assumed to be 20% (30% is about maximum for a yacht).

The data does not consider the effects of seas or shock loads while sheering: the yacht is assumed to be in a secure hurricane hole with no wave action.

As can be seen, the stress on a yacht's ground tackle is severe indeed. After yanking around with great shock loads each link of chain should be inspected for elongation. Rodes subjected to severe and prolonged stretching should be replaced.

See also the table on the previous page for the weakening effects of using various knots on your anchor rode.

		AFT COCKPIT				CENTER COCKPIT			
		SLOOP		KETCH/YAWL		SLOOP		KETCH/YAWL	
Feet on deck (lod)	Feet on water line	Wind on the Bow	Wind on the Beam	Wind on the Bow	Wind on the Beam	Wind on the Bow	Wind on the Beam	Wind on the Bow	Wind on the Beam
28	23	1080	2460	1550	3100	1150	2890	1610	3520
30	25	1240	2820	1760	3540	1310	1310	1830	4020
32	27	1400	3210	1980	4010	1490	3770	2070	4560
34	28	1560	3600	2200	4480	1660	4220	2300	5100
36	30	1750	4030	2450	5010	1860	4740	2560	5710
38	32	1940	4500	2710	5570	2070	5280	2840	6360
41	34	2240	5200	3110	6430	2380	6110	3260	7340
43	36	2460	5730	3410	7070	2620	6730	3570	8070
45	38	2700	6280	3720	7730	2870	7380	3900	8830

LISTENING TO THE WEATHER

Knowing the weather is serious stuff, yet 99% of us just don't listen right. The following pages deserve serious study. Also review the chapter ***Harbor Telltales*** under the ***Passages*** section ***Coasting East from Puerto Plata***, and the section called ***Tracking the Trades from Samaná*** under the chapter ***Crossing the Mona Passage***. It might save you your boat.

THE MUSIC OF THE TRADES

If you think you're doing a good job of tracking the weather because you listen to the weather nets *most* of the time, when you are not out to dinner; because you listen to the Offshore Reports *almost* every morning, and make up for mornings slept in by catching the evening report; or because you jot down details of the conditions for your specific area. Try this:

1. Record a piece of music and

a. leave out one note per measure,

b. change the key on one chord per measure, then

c. delete the introduction, and the refrain.

2. Now ask anybody to name the tune.

That's exactly what 99 percent of all cruisers do. And they wonder where the windows are! Be smart. Write up NMN *every* 0600 (0735 on RTTY), and listen to the weather nets as well.

NWS OFFSHORE REPORT SCHEDULES

AST (EDST)	Station Call	Freq. 1	Freq. 2	Freq. 3	Freq. 4	Broadcast and Source (See Appendix A for more)
600	NMN	4426	6501	8764 13089	17314	NWS Offshore Forecast, USCG, Portsmouth, VA., every 6 hours
	WAH	4134	4381	8728	13077	St.Thomas,repeated 1000,1400,2200
		4357	6200	8240		(includes Tropical Weather Outlook)
630	WVWI	1000				AM VI Radio Sailor's Report (MTWTF)
655	ANT	930	AM	8:05	18:20	Antigua EC Forecasts
710	WVWI	1000	AM			VI Radio Sailor's Report (MTWTF)
	WOSO	1030	AM			San Juan, after hourly news
800	BON	800	AM			Bonaire, Caribbean Offshore
	WLO	6519	8515			NWS Offshore Rpts. (New Orleans)
	WOO	4387	8749			and at 1800, tfc. lists, even hours (NJ)
900	WOM	4363	8722	13092	17242	and at 1900, tfc. lists, odd hours (FLA)

Making Sense of the NWS Offshore Reports

For following the National Weather Service reports and the various cruiser nets you must have a radio capable of receiving Single Side Band, Upper Side Band (SSB-USB). A cheap portable with a "BFO" switch which can receive the frequencies is usually sufficient.

In the Bahamas, the Caribbean and the Gulf of Mexico, the forecast to listen to is the NWS's **Offshore Forecast**. These reports are updated and broadcast every six hours from the Coast Guard's NMN station at Portsmouth, Virginia. The Offshore Forecast is so named because these reporting zones are off the continental shore, not because you have to be 50 miles offshore to use it. The Bahamas and the Antilles are all included in these zones. NOAA or "Weather X Channel" coastal reports available in Puerto Rico and the Virgin Islands, and the NWS High Seas reports are not directly applicable to the cruiser making an interisland passage. The NOAA "20 mile out" coastal reports do not give the open sea conditions which, off these small islands, prevail within less than a mile of their north and south coasts. If you use coastal reports you can be buffaloed into going out into 8-foot seas since they report wave heights less swell. The High Seas report, on the other hand, includes a vastly larger area (essentially from Africa to Mexico and from the Equator to beyond Hudson's Bay). A great deal of detail is lost, and the forecasting periods are longer and further out. The Offshore Reports for the Caribbean, the Southwest North Atlantic and the Gulf of Mexico are also repeated on standard AM broadcasts out of Cap Haïtien, St.Thomas and Bonaire with additional local details (and occasional misreads).

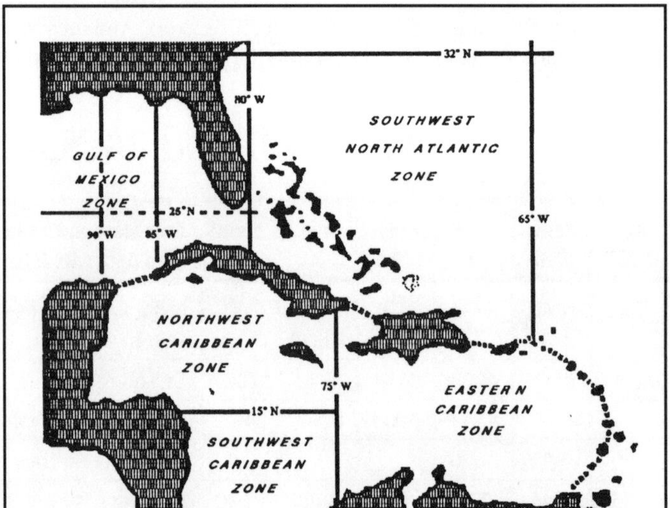

It is the day to day *changes* in the forecasts which should interest the mariner, not just the particulars of the forecasts themselves. Therefore it is necessary to have hardcopy of the reports for several days in succession. You can get the same "telex" the Coast Guard gets through telefax technology using either specialized equipment or a radio-computer link. You can also prepare it yourself by shorthanding the reports either directly from the radio report or from a recording playback. If you record and playback the weather to make your hardcopy, it must be done on dictating equipment or on a player with a "pause" switch. The mechanics of the ordinary AM/FM/Cassette machine make the copy process too cumbersome. I prefer to copy directly from the broadcast in my own private shorthand. I use the 3M Company's Post-It slips that can be stuck up on the bulkhead over the radio. Because the forecasts are repeated in the identical format every day, my shorthand notes have the same format and they can be rapidly scanned, showing a weather picture developing, or disintegrating.

If I've been in harbor awhile, I begin listening to the offshore zone reports ten days before leaving harbor. That ensures my listening and my shorthand are properly exercised before going to sea, but more importantly, since I listen every day at the same time, I develop a sense of rhythm and progression about the weather. In tropical trade wind areas, where the weather is ardently periodic, one can even develop a prescience for its cycles. I listen to the early morning report. That way I am guaranteed to be on the boat and never miss a report. I've seen no end of grief for cruisers simply because they listen to broadcasts at more convenient times such as the High Seas report (0730 AST), or they ate dinner in town and didn't catch the forecast at 1800. They lack a sense of progression since they listen at different times of day and not every day. Or worse, they rely on the guy anchored next to them. It boils down to just plain discipline.

Format and Structure of the Offshore Reports

The offshore reports use a fixed format and jargon which shall only be understood by repeatedly listening to the report for the same zone at the same time of day. If there are any warnings of tropical systems they are given at the beginning of the hour. Forecasts are read from the Boston and Washington, DC, offices of the NWS for the zones under their responsibility, followed by the Southwest North Atlantic and Caribbean reports from the Miami office. Last, the Gulf of Mexico forecast from the New Orleans office is read. Each office's report is begun with a time stamp, the time and date at which the report was released. This is normally just minutes before the broadcast, but if technical problems arise, the Coast Guard may broadcast a report 12 or more hours old. Always note the report's time stamp. The Caribbean forecast is given before the Southwest North Atlantic report. It is divided into three sub-zones which are reported in sequence: northwest, southwest and eastern Caribbean.

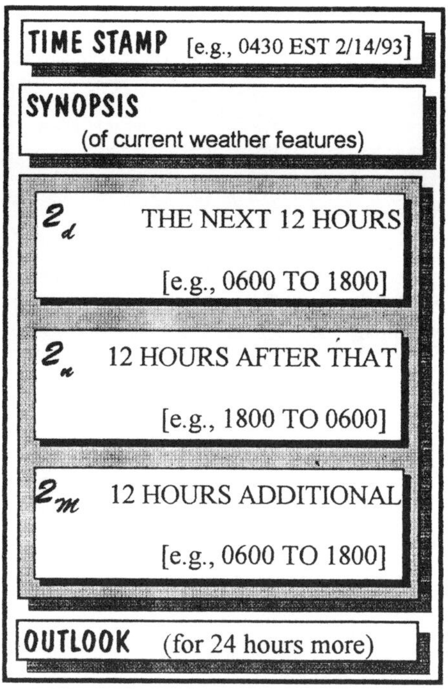

The forecaster begins with a synopsis of significant weather features in the zone, followed by three 12 hour periods beginning with the time given on the time stamp. Therefore, a new set of three 12-hour periods are forecast every six hours. Then comes an "outlook," or longer range forecast, for the 36-hour period following the 36 hours already covered. For example "Today, tonight and Tuesday:..." will be followed by "Outlook for Tuesday night and Wednesday." Reports at 1800 will of course begin "Tonight, Tuesday and Tuesday night," and so on. Each period is described with wind and sea conditions (wave+swell), including precipitation, in all parts of the zone relative to the weather features given in the synopsis. For example, "south of the front and west of 70° west, winds east to southeast 15 to 20 knots, seas 4 to 7 feet; elsewhere (meaning south of the front and east of 70° west to the end of the zone at 65° west) winds east 20 to 25 knots, seas 5 to 8 feet. Scattered thunderstorms west of 75x west." In shorthand this might be written as:

S_f W70 E-SE 15-20 4 7 ∃ E 20-25 5 8 SO W75

Shorthanding the Offshore Reports

RTTY Hardcopy from February 11 , 1992, MNM at 0615 AST on 4426 USB

00 KMIA 110915

OFFSHORE MARINE FORECAST NATIONAL WEATHER SERVICE MIAMI 0915UCT TUE FEB 11 1992

CARIBBEAN SEA AND SW N ATLC BEYOND 50 NM FROM SHORE.

. SW N ATLC S OF 32N AND W OF 65W

...GALE WARNING N OF 29N E OF 73W TODAY...

.SYNOPSIS...GALE CENTER ABOUT 150 NM SW OF BERMUDA EARLY THIS MORNING MOVING RAPIDLY NE. COLD FRONT WILL EXTEND S OF GALE CENTER TO _ MVOE TO NEAR 65W TONIGHT. ANOTHER COLD FRONT _ W EJ_CARLOINAS WED AFTERNOON.

.TODAY...N OF 29N E OF 73W WIND NE 35 TO 45 KTS. SEAS 12 TO 18 FT. E OF COLD FRONT WIND SE TO S 15 TO 25 KTS. SEAS 6 TO 9 FT. REMAINDER OF AREA WIND NE TO E 20 TO 30 KTS. SEAS 7 TO 10 FT WITH LARGE NE SWELLS. SCATTERED TO NUMEROUS SHOWERS AND TSTMS OVER THE NE PART. .TONIGHT...E OF 75W WIND NE 20 TO 30 KTS. SEAS 7 TO 10 FT WITH LARGE NE SWELLS. W OF 75W WIND NE TO E 15 TO 20 KTS. SEAS 4 TO 6 FT WITH LARGE NE SWELLS. WIDELY SCATTERED SHOWERS. .WED...WIND NE TO E 15 TO 20 KTS. SEAS 4 TO 6 FT WITH LARGE NE SWELLS. WIDELY SCATTERED SHOWERS MAINLY N PORTION.

OUTLOOK FOR WED NIGHT AND THU...LITTLE CHANGE.

Actual Copy of a Short-Handed Report

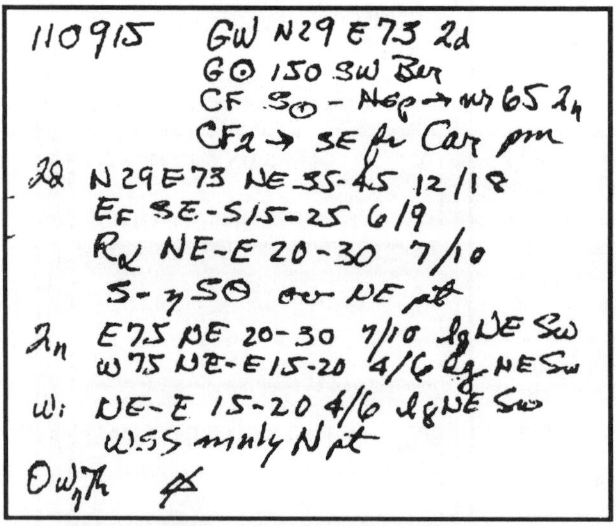

Shorthand Legend:

α	area, along
θ	through,thunderstorm
|	sea conditions
∃	elsewhere
▵	increasing
∨	decreasing
>>	moving
≈	drifting
⊕	center (low)
S_F	e.g., south of front
Δ	little change
CF	cold front
F	front
WF	warm front
R	ridge; remainder
G	gale (TD, TS, H)
Su M T W Th F Sa	
WS	widely scattered
2d	today
2n	tonight
2m	tomorrow
l8	late
lg	large
pm	afternoon
am	morning
C	Cuba
nr	near
fr	from
bld	building
bec	becoming
stn	stationary
few	few
bet	between
O	Outlook
Hsp	Hispaniola

Radio Teletype Copy vs. Shorthanded Audio Copy

Compare the two copies above, and you shall see that the shorthand version has picked up the garbled transmission that a second cold front is moving SE from the Carolinas in the afternoon. If you don't record the report, it often is worthwhile to listen to a later rebroadcast from commercial stations such as WLO or WOM just to double check your copy from the Coast Guard broadcast on NMN.

NOTE: On the east coast of Puerto Rico there is an 80-mile fetch to windward over small islands and shallow, heated water. Observed conditions here conform to the San Juan WX VHF reports. These reports are only good on the east and west coasts of P.R. The same as if you were parked in West Caicos in easterlies, the shallow banks to your east provide a land- like night effect. Don't be fooled; the real daytime wind will be what was forecast for the eastern Caribbean on the Offshore Report. Again, the NWS Offshore forecast wind, with *English* applied as required for local variations due to topography or conjuncture of weather features, is what you shall have, *not* the observed harbor wind.

Bear in Mind . . .

1. The boundaries of the reporting zones are implicit coordinates.

The NW Caribbean Offshore Zone lies west of 75W and north of 15N. If, in the report for that zone, the analyst says "North of the front wind NE 15 knots," that does not mean you have NE 15 knots at 20N. The zone stops at the south coast of Cuba. Pretend the analyst is a surgeon operating only on the zones described, and that there is an opaque sheet around the square of operating zone. Nothing outside the zone will be mentioned. An impinging frontal system, if not affecting the zone at this time, will not be mentioned, except possibly in the Outlook section of the report. If you want to know what's coming in more detail, listen to the zones to weather of you (east in the summer, west in the winter).

2. East to southeast is not the same as southeast to east...

... nor is it east-southeast. If the analyst has gone to the trouble of telling you "southeast to east," a movement counter to the diurnal flux of the trades, it's a fair bet it's not just a mistake. It means the wind is more likely to back than to veer. Usually this is a sign of strengthening trades. If, instead, "east to southeast" was used, you don't know if that's normal diurnal veer, simple convention to start with the main cardinal point of the compass, or pronounced veering. But that's why you listen every day, right? A veering trade usually portends weakening of the wind. Listen the same time each day, and always record the time stamp.

Reread the section on The Music of the Trades if you don't know why. Often the Coast Guard will replay an old report in the absence of a new one. During Hurricane Hugo this went on for 17 ½ hours. Many thought Hugo was stalled, and they began to venture out!

3. There is only one NWS.

Yachties often compare the value of different sources. Until Antigua or Martinique, the only source from which everyone starts is the NWS data and analyses.

4. Any report you hear not from NWS is an interpretation of their data.

When anyone but the USCG computer voice or radio teletype feeds you the analysis, you lose vital information that can cost you dearly. When "by Thursday" or "through Thursday" becomes just "Thursday" you lose 8-16 hours on calling a front. That can be a 160 to 320 nautical mile mistake! Beware of yachties, even some HAM net operators, who should know better, who repeat "east to southeast" as "east-southeast." You are losing a vital piece of data in your tracking of the cycling of the trades.

WHEN YOU CAN'T LISTEN TO THE WEATHER

If caught out without radio reception, or you just plain want to check on the old **NWS**, you may consider playing with the following rules to guess at the bearing, strength, direction and arrival time of a storm or hurricane.

1. You will first notice appearance of a long swell, mean period of 2 to 5 per minute (normal is 10-15 per minute).
2. If there is a clockwise change in swell direction, the storm will pass from left to right.
3. If there is an anti-clockwise change in swell direction, the storm will pass you right to left.
4. Swells travel from 2 to 3 times faster than the storm travels.
   a. To find the velocity of the swell in knots, take 60% of the ratio of the crest-to-crest length of the swell, in feet, to the swell's period expressed in seconds (V= 0.6 x L/P).
   b. Swell height is reduced by one third for every "X" miles traveled, where "X" is the crest-to-crest length of the swell in feet:

      Observed Height = 2/3 Height X miles away.
5. To find the center of the storm add 115° to the present wind direction.
6. Direction changes in the sustained wind betoken:
   a. If the wind veers you are in the dangerous semicircle: you should *put the wind on the starboard bow.*
   b. If the wind backs you are in the navigable semicircle: you should *put the wind on the starboard quarter.*
   c. If a steady but increasing wind, you are in the path: you should *put the wind aft of the starboard quarter* and pass out prayer books.

Predicting Storm Path

It is possible to make a fairly accurate guess as to storm path knowing its present bearing, its bearing at the time of promulgating the swell and the velocity of the swell.

For example, at 1200 you observe a swell from the south and you estimate the swell to be 200 yards long at 4 per minute. 200 yards are 600 feet. This means the swell's velocity is 0.6 x 600/15=24 knots. Therefore, the storm is moving about 10 knots, or one half to one third as fast as the swell. If you also observe the wind is east while the swell is south, then you know the storm lies along a bearing of 90°+115°, or 205° from your position.

Refer to the figure opposite for the following discussion. Lay off a swell vector of 24 knots with its head on your present position. Lay off the storm's bearing of 205°. Make a storm track vector of 10 knots with its head on a line of the storm's bearing. "Slide" the storm track vector's head on the storm's bearing until you can connect the tail with the tail of the swell vector. Adjust vector and bearing until you get a fit. You now have a guess at the current heading of the storm, and you know its bearing and velocity as of 1200. In the example, the swell is moving 360° at 24 knots. Therefore, the storm, which is moving at 10 knots, will be shown to be moving in a direction of 290°.

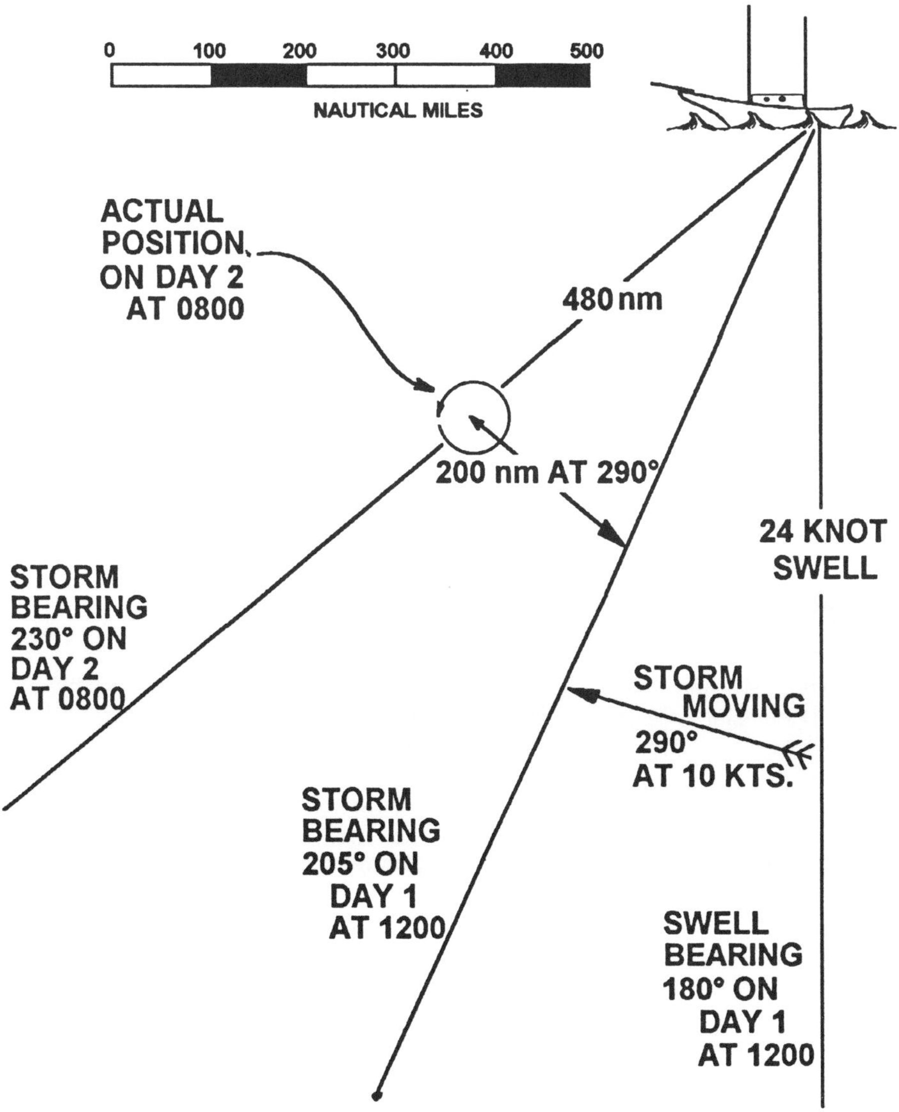

Storm Location, Path and Severity

Estimating Storm Severity

What can you guess about the storm's intensity? Let's say the swell you observe has a mean height of about 10 feet. Since the swell has a 600-foot length, you know that 600 nautical miles down the swell's bearing the swell had been 15 feet, or half again higher than now, having lost one-third of its height enroute. If, indeed, the swell traveled that far.

The force of the storm can be estimated by projecting the swell height back to its incidence. That is, you interpolate the original swell height at various distances off for the storm, then look at the **Beaufort** Scale to arrive at various storm forces for each assumed distance off.

For instance, if you assume the tails of the swell and storm vectors connect at a point 400 miles away then the original size of the swells, roughly speaking, would have to have been higher than they are now by 4 sixths of the 600 mile loss of 5 feet. That is, 10+(15-10)x(400/600)=13.3 feet. You will see the storm would have to have had a sustained strength of Force 7, and that would have been 17 hours ago (400 miles/24 knots).

Locating The Storm Center

The actual location of the storm is available through combining the results of two observations. Let's say that next day at 0800, 20 hours after the first observation, you see that the swell now comes from somewhere between 200° and 210° and the wind has veered two points (22.5°) to between 110° and 115°. This makes the storm's present bearing 115°+115°, or 230°.

Since you think the storm was traveling 290° at 10 knots you also know it covered 200 nautical miles during those 20 hours (Distance = Velocity x Time). There is only one spot on your chart where your dividers, spaced on the scale to 200 miles and set along a 290 degree line, will rest its points on the 205 and 230 degree lines radiating from your position. One point will be where the storm is now, at 230°, and the other will show where the storm was 20 hours ago, at 205°. You now know the storm is roughly 480 miles to the Southwest traveling at 10 knots toward the west northwest and blowing Force 7 because it is producing 10+5x480/600, or 14-foot waves.

Whatever **Force Beaufort** you estimate, remember that gusts in a severe storm can be 30% to 50% higher than the sustained winds. That means that even a baby 'cane (64 knots) can have gusts up to 96 knots.

If all the above discussion ruins your complacency, good! You are now ready to cruise!

What To Watch For

Squall lines and cumulo nimbus may sweep your area. These and their high altitude cirro-cumulus forerunners are "feeder bands," sometimes hundreds of miles in length, spiraling into the storm's center. If you are directly in the storm's path, there's no mistaking it's approach. The onslaught of the center of a major storm, or hurricane, will be heralded by the "bar": a long, low, intensely black area topped by dark and chaotic cumulo-nimbus and with torn patches of black strato-cumulus scudding in front. Prepare for the wind to gradually double in strength. If in the calm of the eye, prepare for the winds to strike from the opposite direction with sudden maximum force within a half hour. The "wall" will be frighteningly apparent in its approach.

FM Radio Telephony, or **VHF** signaling, has reached an interesting stage of development. The rules for using the VHF were developed for poor reception. When Alpha wants to call Bravo, Alpha should say "Bravo, Bravo, Bravo; Alpha, Alpha" and Bravo should reply "Alpha, Bravo; *nn*," where *nn* is the number of a working channel to which they both repair. Now that VHF provides high quality reception at a cheap price, every boob has one into which he speaks as would Thomas Alva Edison speak into the ear of Victrola's dog if he had expected the dog to speak back to him.

What's worse, today's Bravo has invented a lottery in which he asks Alpha to "Pick a channel." If he doesn't, then Alpha asks Bravo to do it. Although they call each other several times a day, they will usually pick channels which neither has. This is a noncommittal opening gambit used by VHF lottery players for whom tic-tac-toe is too advanced.

Bridge players will say "six eight" but not press the mike button until the word "eight," thus finessing the other guy into sitting on Channel 8 picking channels with no one. You can always tell a cruiser who plays chess. He will force Alpha to pick a channel first and then say "No, I don't have that, try another" until Alpha hits a good one. Then he talks in HAM codes and International Signals Code over the telephone. These guys also tend to call themselves "THE Bravo," which, incidentally, is against the rules in a few countries and not liked by the Coast Guard unless your transom says "THE Bravo." Guys that say "THIS IS THE Alpha" need severe correction. Guys that say "THIS IS THE SAILING VESSEL Alpha" should have their radios confiscated.

These are the same guys who play CAPCOM MCC (Capsule Communicator, Mission Control Center) and say "Affirmative" and "Negative" and "Roger That" 3 times each to a boat 200 yards away. Deke Slayton took endless ribbing when he slipped up on acknowledging a complex transmission from space with "Roger ... uh ... that." He never repeated it. But today there is a whole new generation of Captain Videos to repeat it and other airwaves eating clichés—endlessly. Myself, I pretend to be Glenn Ford at the controls of his screaming Saberjet calling to his wingman . . .

In most anchorages VHF users are in good hail of each other on low power. In **Provodenciales**, with 200 land stations and 50 boats, or worse, in **Georgetown** with 50 land stations and 400 boats, just following the normal rules with power down and squelch up will reduce traffic and hasten communications enormously.

The above discussion, as well as the following list of DOs and DON'Ts may be extended to the use of Marine SSB radios as well. Please don't clog the calling frequencies like this:

A: Bravo, Bravo, Bravo. Alpha.

B: Alpha, Alpha, Alpha. Bravo.

A: Bravo, Bravo. Good morning, Ted! Have you got a frequency?

B: Yeah. How about 6-delta? Let's go to 6-delta, 6-delta.

A: No. I haven't got that one programmed. Not programmed. Pick another.

B: Oh. OK. Just a minute. . . . . How about 6-charlie?

A: Yeah. We can try that. Let's try 6-charlie. What's the frequency?

Here's a list of some DOs rarely DONE.

- Turn your power down.
- Find an idle channel before talking.
- Talk normally, sideways to the mike.
- Wait thirty seconds for Bravo to answer.
- Get off Channel 16 with minimum chatter.
- Use the language your mother taught you.
- Make each transmission brief.
- Repeat only if asked.

Here are some DON'Ts which are DONE more often than not.

- Don't call yourself anything but your name.
- Don't talk HAM or CB, good buddy. QSL.
- Don't eat your microphone.
- Don't repeat everything twice.
- Don't use channels permanently assigned (e.g., bridges, taxis, hotels, USCG).
- Don't sit on your handheld's transmit switch, blocking all traffic for hours.

Don't be a Deputy Dawg. That's the guy who sits by his radio and busts in with chapter and verse of the Law of Using the VHF. He takes up more air time than casual abusers because his dictums are always followed by storms of support from the *Good Citizens* around and Bronx cheers from the *Outlaws and the Rowdies* in the harbor.

Unless Deputy Dawg is a duly authorized official of the country whose air you are using, you can tell him to take his Barstool Regulations and . . .

CAUTION: Never use "buddy channels" to the exclusion of Channel 16.

I recall the two yachts off Monte Cristi which crossed the steel cables of a 1500-foot tow at night while the tug's skipper bawled on Channel 16, and I desperately dialed around to find their buddy channel. The hawsers could have sawn the boats in halves, sintering fiberglass and flesh in a heartbeat. It took instead a small bite from a skeg.

American products are clever and useful and well packaged. When they are for the marine environment they're clever, useful, well packaged and expensive. In the Caribbean they're often unavailable. You can port around 50 bottles of each product and displace 10 cases of rum, or you can carry the following generic chemicals and refill the product bottle with a substitute solution which is sometimes better. Remember the first two principles of provisioning:

1. The Highest Utility for the Least Space, and

2. The Greatest Savings First.

In other words, a boat full of small bottles of cheap, but high quality rum, and a year's supply of cleaning agents packed into a few small chemical flasks is a happy boat as well as a clean one.

Remember also to store and handle all chemicals with the care they deserve. I use sturdy plastic containers, and I stow them in plastic milk crates to eliminate chafe. I use well-sealed plastic containers. I snugly wedge them into plastic milk cartons so they cannot move around. Never place plastic bottles against fiberglass mat or other rough surfaces. Stowage techniques which worked great while fattening the kitty from a mooring or a marina, suddenly can cause ghastly accidents at sea while cruising. Think of a container of muriatic acid leaking into the bilge together with a bottle of ammonia. You'll have a clean and bugfree bilge if you survive the gas.

Muriatic acid (HCl) mixed with lots of water will:

1. Eliminate rust stains and gelcoat chalking when mixed 1:10 in a spray bottle, costing a hundred times less than some products which are the same;
2. Make your corroded 12 Volt deck sockets work instantly if sprayed into them (or your brass boat horn as I once had to demonstrate to the USCG boarders);
3. Keep your coolers and heat exchangers bright and new inside when mixed 1:8 (stainless and copper only, not aluminum);
4. Keep your head clean and unclogged by calcium buildups when mixed 1:6 (rubber and neoprene seals only—no leathers);
5. Become Part B of two-part teak cleaners when mixed 1:5 with water. Plain old lye crystals and water become Part A (NaOH). Lye can be found in some toilet bowl or drain cleaners. Be sure you have pure lye and not some explosive mixture! In developing countries lye is readily available.

Of course, any muriatic mixture should not be allowed to react too long without being flushed away with water, salt or fresh.

Swimming pool shock treatment which comes in rapidly dissolving granules and has only chlorine as the active ingredient will provide you with a year or more supply of chlorine bleach for:

1. Treating the head
2. Pouring in the bilge
3. Doing your laundry
4. Killing black pin mold when sprayed on teak
5. Curing your water

To get normal strength bleach, put one to two tablespoons into a gallon of water and mix thoroughly.

Good quality mineral spirits will burn more cleanly in your oil lamps than specially concocted products. In addition it will thin your paints and varnishes, clean and oil your interior woods, start your fires and run in your diesel when you're out of fuel.

Besides all of that, mineral spirits is cheaper than any of the products whose use it can supplant.

FISHING

A plethora of pamphlets, books, fish identi-kits and even dowsing tools are available to anyone stopping at a gas dock or bait and tackle shop. Useful and serious information can be had in a good marine bookstore such as Bluewater Books & Charts in Fort Lauderdale (1-800-942-2583). In keeping with the rest of *The Gentleman's Guide to Passages South*, I will only give you here the information which strikes me as unique to the hard core cruiser and generally unavailable elsewhere.

I am indebted to my good friend and mentor, Bob Cockerham of *Moon Lady*, a beautifully maintained clipper ketch. Bob, known as "Grouper Bob" to Bahamians, has long experience fishing in the southern Bahamas. Some of his rules are:

1. First you have to decide if you're fishing for fun or you're fishing to feed yourself—hunger catches more fish than diversion.

2. You can't catch fish without a hook in the water. Hook time catches more fish than fancy lures or luck ever did.

3. Don't listen to the crybabies who complain the world is all fished out—the fish are where you find them.

SKIN DIVING

Fishing underwater is primarily a hunting expedition. To hunt, you have to take time. You have to watch the fish and learn their habits. You have to let them get used to your presence. If you missed a shot and spooked the fish, you have to give them time to get unspooked. All that adds up to time with you in the water just like hook fishing requires lots of time with the hook in the water. Wear a wet suit, even in the summer.

Some fish have skins which are extremely hard to penetrate with a spear. Before starting out make sure your spear tips are freshly sharpened. Coral rock will dull even your stainless points. Use a sharpening stone to shape a triangular point. Always the same triangle.

Good-tasting fish like grouper and snapper are usually under something. Sometimes you can spear them through a hole above, like a skylight to their living room. More often than not you have to get them through a side door down near the bottom. If they run into one door expect them to leave from another when they're ready. If they go around a rock, creep over the top and be prepared to shoot down on them. With time in the water you will observe and learn their habits and you can anticipate their response to your shots.

Only with many shots can you become good at it, so shoot lots. If you can't get that fat grouper you've been chasing and you're close to hypothermia, shoot a couple of small grunts or a trusting trigger fish. You should always come home with bait at least. If you're a novice at spear fishing you will be surprised to learn that you need to be very close to the fish to hit them. The tip of your spear should generally be no farther than two feet from your prey. Certainly this is true of a pole spear or a Hawaiian Sling.

For lobster, conch and whelk, swim low along the undercut shore ledges when the sunlight slants in under the ledge and lights it all up. For lobster around rocks and coral heads, swim with your cheek on the sand, looking into every crevice and hole. Wear gloves to protect yourself against skin reactions to various corals when you pull yourself along by grasping rocks.

The good eating, such as grouper, snapper and lobster, isn't always around coral heads, rocks and ledges. Often enough you will see sizable grouper playing 'possum in the branches of a bush while lobster are hidden in the roots. When all the jocks go roaring off in their Zodiac Grand Raids to dive the 40 feet on the windward side because the harbor is "all fished out," leisurely peruse your own anchorage and be ready for surprises. The anchorages are precisely the places where no one fishes and yet they are just the places where fish thrive due to the edible detritus falling from the boats above. This assumes a clean anchorage with good flow.

Take a catch immediately to the surface. Hold the thrashing animal still with both hands, or hold it above the surface of the water, until it is safely in the dinghy which is always nearby. Shark and barracuda, unjustly blamed for mythical mayhem to swimmers, cannot be held responsible for instinctual behavior. Especially the barracuda. The barracuda in the Bahamas and on the reefs of the Caribbean is a territorial garbage collector. It's his reef and when something dies and goes through the vibrations of extremis, the barracuda has the task of darting in and cleaning it up. You can get away with letting your dying catch slide down the spear and rest against your fist and never have an incident. But with low luck your catch will someday be met by a set of flying teeth which may, wholly unintended, carry away a few knuckles. Let the fish trail away from you until it's clear of the water.

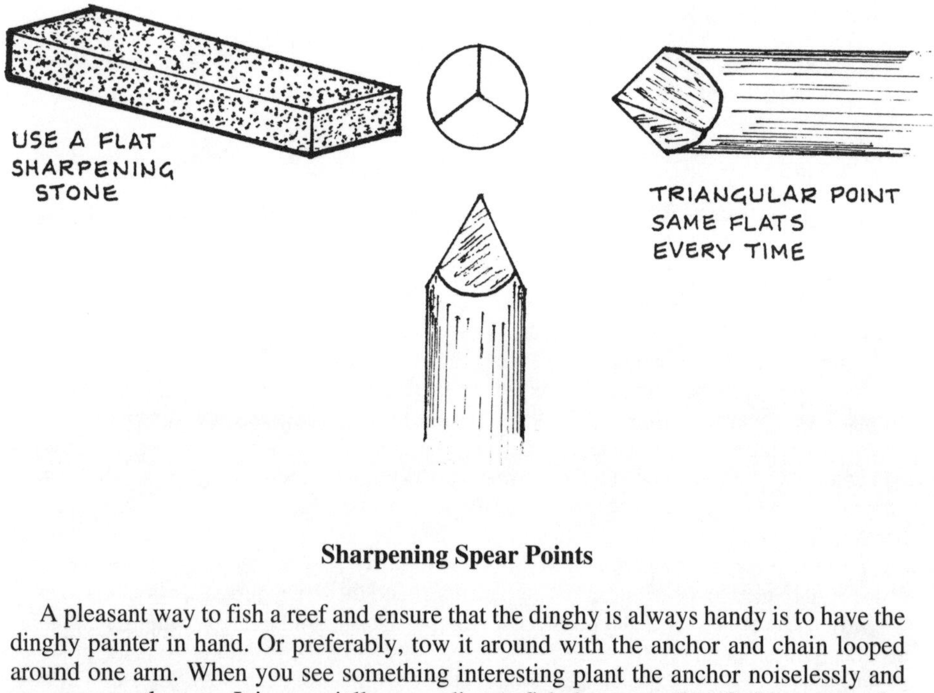

Sharpening Spear Points

A pleasant way to fish a reef and ensure that the dinghy is always handy is to have the dinghy painter in hand. Or preferably, tow it around with the anchor and chain looped around one arm. When you see something interesting plant the anchor noiselessly and pursue your pleasure. It is especially rewarding to fish the seaward reefs this way as, for example, at Rum Cay. Wait for slack low tide plus one hour. Then ride the tide back into harbor with dinghy in hand. The reef community will all be up to meet the incoming nutrients from Mother Ocean with their mouths agape, and won't they be surprised to see you and your spear instead.

If you get a coral fungus that won't heal, though it may not be in your spice rack, try monosodium glutamate (MSG). For cracked lips, try Preparation-H! But keep two separate tubes on hand.

When you have fed all your expensive lures to the lure monster, try making your own for free. The corner of a plastic garbage bag with appropriate slits can make an excellent squid, or skirt, lure. So does a small tube of Prell Shampoo Concentrate. Do you remember how to make those little yarn dolls that you hung on the Christmas tree when you were a kid? Make one out of the yarns from an old piece of nylon 3-strand rope. Wind the head of the doll around a 3-ounce oval lead and leave off the arms.

You don't need fancy equipment. The plastic doughnuts, or yo-yos, are great. Instead of a drag to alarm you to a bite, or more likely, seaweed, put a bight of the line through a clothespin spring and then around the clothespin. Then clamp the clothespin to a stay with a couple of yards of slack line behind it.

Use stainless clamps to clamp an old reel to the pushpit. Surprisingly, you can get many years of maintenance free operation out of an old reel exposed continuously to salt and sun.

Use 80 to 100 or more pounds test line. Have lots of large swivels and use lots of heavy stainless leader and big hooks. Run a line on each side of the boat. Four, if you like. Two short and skipping, two long and deep. Don't make sharp turns with the boat, though.

Now tend those lines. Keep them free of seaweed—a frustrating and monotonous task. People who complain they never catch any fish usually wait until they're in open sea before they put out a single puny line. Then they tow seaweed around and reel it in when they first sight their landfall.

Have your lines (plural) out while going through cuts or entering and leaving harbors. If you get a strike while going through a cut, ignore it, of course, and tend to your boat first. When you do reel in your catch it'll probably be drowned, saving you the trouble of dispatching it. Tending lines first and boat second was the cause of the death of a Newporter Ketch in **Conch Cay Cut** at **Georgetown** one year.

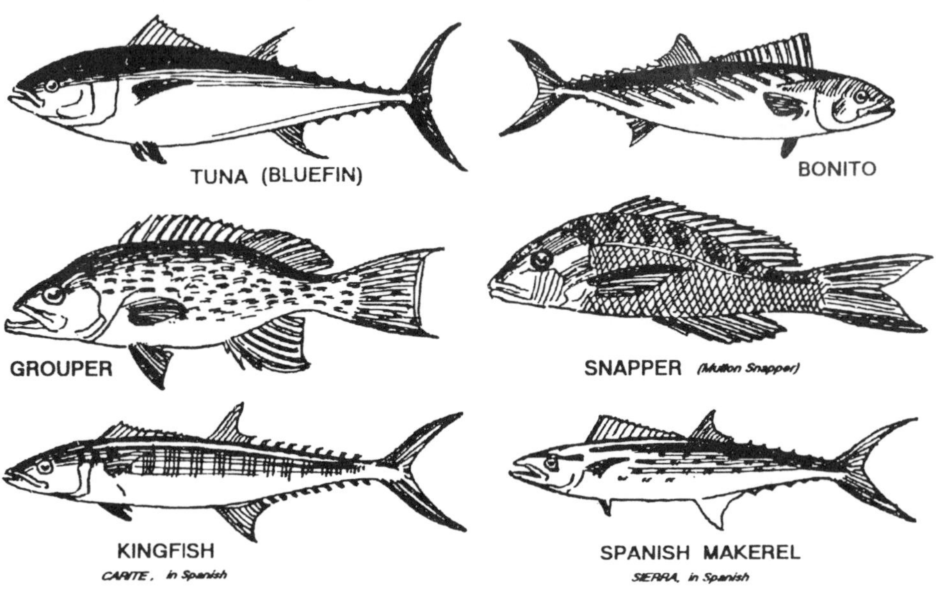

Good Eating Fish

Save the cadavers for bait after cleaning your fish. Swap your lure leader for a leader with bare hook and bury it in a fist size, or larger, hunk of bait. Before your second SG&T, walk to the bow with the baited line. Using large coils, hold a good boat length of line in one hand and, with the other, swing the baited hook in wide circles. Let go of the whole mess and the wind should bring it back to a boat length off your beam where the bait will rest on the bottom.

Sometime between your second SG&T and four in the morning your drag will go off like a siren. Nocturnal types, like grouper and snapper are out at this time grazing the anchorage. Sometimes you'll get a shark, sometimes a ray, but more often than not it will be a sizable, good-eating bottom fish.

MOTORING TO THE CARIBBEAN

The way south not only has lots of motoring opportunities but today's yachts have lots of motor to do it with. Motoring while cruising to windward, however, is a different kettle of fish than motoring out to the sea buoy to set sail on a Saturday afternoon. Half your motoring will be close to all out revolutions. Half will be low revs while generating zaps for your refrigerator to run on, unless you have an engine driven compressor. If you escape the daily drill of generating electricity because you've got a diesel generator aboard, you may be in for double trouble with two motors.

Many good books are available to help you with diesel problems and their prevention. Here are some tips how to avoid problems, or plan for the inevitable ones when they come. Once again, these tips are only associated with the special punishments a diesel takes while cruising to windward.

MORTORSAILING

Every year the Thorny Path claims its crop of sailing purists and sportsmen. The typical enthusiast starts from **Great Inagua**, or **Mayaguana**, for instance, and sails directly for **Samaná**. After an exciting morning's beat into 4- to 7-foot seas with 12-foot breaking rogues, our heroes return to a grueling afternoon's beat into the same. After going through the carefully posted watch schedules a couple of times the crew begins to realize there won't be any clubhouse showers at the end of the day nor will there be any prize banquets and parties. Just the sour bunk to return to, sodden by the seawater spurting through the crack caused by separation of hull and deck.

As the challenge of the whole thing melts into a funk with expensive repairs at the end, Captain Courageous flicks the starter switch and goes over to motorsailing. If he can. Chances are the incessant pounding has sloshed up the muck at the bottom of the fuel tank and the engine won't start. That's why it's called the Thorny Path, folks! And that's why you should know the Thornless way.

Now, Thornless Path adherents not only select their passages and their Weather Windows for short and easy legs (see "Strategies for Passage Making") but they know the following basic rules of motorsailing and don't cavil at applying their auxiliary.

1. Switch the motor on when you need it to maintain the minimum average speed you had assumed in planning your landfall. Purists plan low averages, motorists go for high average speed.

2. Keep the jib up only if it helps you point better.

3. Keep the main up and tack a bit if you're dead into the wind.

4. Know how much heeling you can take to avoid

   a. Sucking air through the raw water intake, causing an airlock in the cooling system and engine overheating;

   b. Siphoning seawater into the engine if you switch off while the anti-siphon valve is tipped under sea level.

5. Ensure the exhaust outlet is never under water while the engine is cooling. Following seas or heeling may cause seawater to be drawn up over the exhaust swan neck, flooding the engine. For downwind passages in the Trades, install a handy ball valve at the exhaust outlet. But remember to open it again when the engine is cool!

6. Always let the engine cool to its lowest operating temperature by running awhile at idle before cutting it off.
7. Ensure a goodly air supply to the engine by opening hatches if you have the usual tight and airless installation which was not meant to be high-revved for many hours in the tropics. Better yet, install ducted fans to carry additional air to the engine.

MOTOR MAINTENANCE

If you can't maintain your own diesel motor, stay home. There are few marinas and most of the "help" available is likely to leave you worse off than if you had done it yourself reading a shop manual.

Before You Leave Home

If you have been used to leaving the car for maintenance at the corner garage because business never left you the time to do your own maintenance, now is your chance to change. If you're really on the Thornless Path, you've got nothing but time. Get a shop manual before you leave home and do your own maintenance. When you screw up, you at least learn and won't do it again. If you let someone else do it, you will pay for the same screwup time after time. Review the next few pages. You may want to do some refit before leaving home.

The best preparation you can have is a course in diesel mechanics. Simple short courses are available almost everywhere through manufacturers such as Ford and Detroit (Perkins), or through your local adult education center. You can be independent of mechanics simply by going to your local high school one evening a week for 8 weeks. Some courses last only a single day. If you are not mechanically inclined, don't think you can't do it. Diesel engines are actually extremely simple. All you need is patience and a little logic to follow down and cure a problem.

The vast majority of engine problems on the Thorny Path come from contaminated fuel. You can finesse most of these problems by carrying a **Baja Filter** (see Glossary), using a good fungicide (not too much), and by preparing your installation with adequate filtration. What is adequate at home is not sufficient down south. Besides the manufacturer's engine mounted canister filter and the engine's lift pump filter, you should have at least one other filter and a water separator mounted between the tank and the engine. Make sure the filter elements are not decomposable by the fungicide you use.

It will be a good idea to mount a switchable fuel pump to get a few more hours of engine life when clogged fuel filters cause engine surging (fast RPM-ing) which is inevitably followed by engine death—the infamous Surge And Die syndrome (SAD). This installation also gives you a method of cleaning your tank without having to bucket out the fuel and strain it through T-shirts.

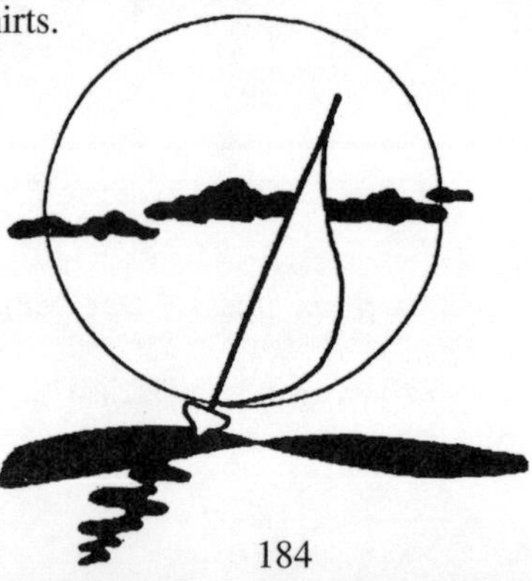

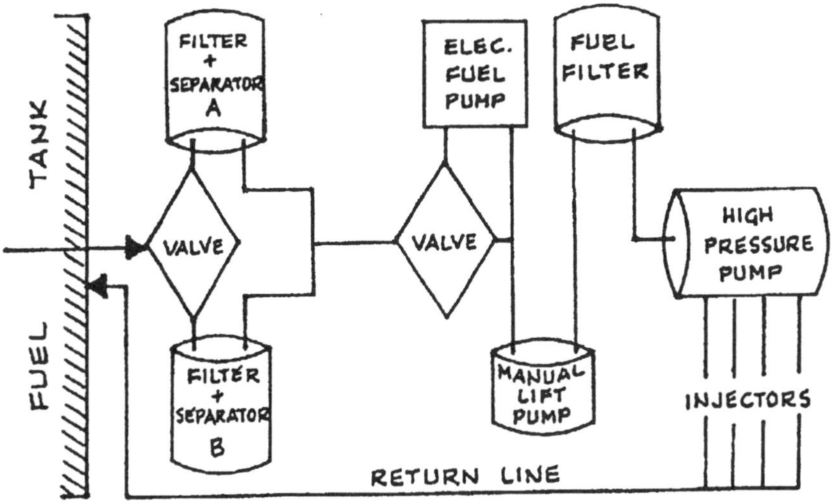

Keeping Your Fuel Clean

Not only does this installation give you better protection, but the electric fuel pump gives you the ability to overcome clogged filters in order to make port. When you hear the engine start to surge, put the fuel pump in-line and switch it on. Once in port, you can also use the installation to clean your tank.

Spare Parts

If you have recently installed a new engine you may consider saving key elements of your old engine for spares: head, high pressure pump, water pumps, injectors, delivery pipes, exhaust elbow, starter motor, alternator and instrument senders. However, the following minimum spares should be aboard before leaving home. Products which meet your engine specifications probably are not available until Santo Domingo or San Juan.

- Complete gasket set
- Alternator
- Fuel filters (6 each))
- Oil for 6 changes
- Fungicide for 300 gallons fuel
- Vee belts (3)
- Water pump impellers (2 each)
- Oil filters (8)

The Dirtiest Job In The World

Changing oil on a diesel engine is undoubtedly the nastiest part of cruising. The job can be made somewhat easier by thorough preparation before starting. Flipping settee cushions looking for the new oil filter is best done before your hands are covered with black goop.

Invest in a filter wrench and lots of 3-ply garbage bags before you leave. Also have a good stock of old newspapers and save those plastic gallon jugs with which to dump the old oil. If you don't have a scavenge pump, have a funnel standing by (a cut off bleach bottle top works fine). Even better, install a petcock in place of your pan drain plug.

Good, strong garbage bags are almost unobtainable outside U.S. territory. Have a year's supply on hand.

Scavenge pumps are fine for getting most of the old oil out but they don't get the gunk in the bottom of the pan. Accumulation of this stuff is what ruins your engine. It is usually best to get the last of the old oil out through the drain plug in the bottom of the pan. If your installation has an angle which prevents complete drainage you should consider having a new hole drilled and tapped in the pan.

It's a good idea to flush the engine from time to time. As an alternative to a mineral spirits flush every couple 100 hours you can flush each time you change oil by using one more quart of oil than necessary. After draining the old oil and before taking off the old filter, add one quart of fresh oil. With the fuel cut off (engine kill switch "on") run the starter for 20 seconds, pause a few minutes and do it again. Drain the engine again, change filters and add the new oil. This procedure will cost you a quart of oil every time you change but it may add thousands of hours to your engine's life.

As with many engine jobs, your cleanup is easier if you start the job with a little **Joy** dish soap rubbed under and around your nails.

Motor Failures

Every skipper has his own style going to windward. Some motor more than others. The trail south is littered by broken engines which were abused by skippers who didn't **Wait for Weather**, but bucked right into short, steep seas for dozens of hours with the throttle wide open. The boat manufacturers generally do not anticipate this use of the auxiliary engine when they install them. Neither do boat owners generally ask much of their engines until they meet the conditions going south. For instance, you should check your engine's specifications for the heel angle it will tolerate and don't exceed it for long periods.

Below are listed the usual engine failures one finds on the Thorny Path south. You can make it a Thornless Path for your engine by either modifying your installation before leaving home, or not leaving port in the conditions which abuse your engine. A true Leisure Sailor will do both.

FUEL SYSTEM

Motoring into heavy chop will thoroughly emulsify whatever is in your fuel tank and, if the tank is nearly empty, give your fuel pump a good gulp of air between sloshes.

The SAD syndrome (Surge And Die) will come from air being sucked into the system as well as clogged filters and water in the fuel.

If running dangerously low on fuel, you can supplement diesel with mineral spirits from your lamp oil supply. You can throw in some transmission oil to thicken the brew if you use more than a couple of gallons. I know a German engineer who made port with a mixture of vegetable oil, engine oil and gasoline. Shake well before using. And don't forget the oregano if your engine's Italian.

Dirty fuel is all you can buy in the Caribbean so plan on having it. Use a **Baja Filter** when adding fuel. See sketch on preceeding page for a description of a good filter and pump installation to combat the problem.

COOLING SYSTEM

Your engine can overheat for hundreds of reasons, but motoring to weather in tropical heat exposes you to all of them. When it happens, which it will, check:

- Weed-clogged raw water through-hull fitting
- Gulping air while heeling and pitching (airlock)
- Clogged raw water strainer
- Raw water strainer too small for flow volume
- Water pump impeller going or gone (salt or fresh)
- Water pump belt slipping or gone
- Heat exchanger clogged
- Thermostat jammed

Most manufacturers of raw water pumps provide a weep hole in the shaft housing between the pump seal and the oil seal on the engine side. If you don't have one, or if your pump is installed at the wrong angle, bore a good-sized one in the bottom of the shaft housing. This will prevent water from getting through your oil seal, which is meant to keep oil in, not water out, and ruining the engine. If you have a weep hole on your shaft housing and it is mounted to drain correctly, make the hole bigger. Most weep holes are small. Salt and corrosion will seal them up, preventing them from doing their job.

Powering off sandy ground in the Bahamas will etch pump shafts and undermine the seals. Volvo motors, especially, are fitted with high pressure raw water pumps, guaranteeing an effective sandblasting of the shaft. Water in your engine's oil, due to blown pump seals or blown gaskets, will show up as milky streaks in the otherwise jet black dirty diesel motor oil. If it has barely begun, look for drops of condensed steam clinging to the bottom of the oil filler cap after running hot awhile.

If you waited until you had a gully washer pouring into the oil galleries, watch for a fountain of hot gray oatmeal-like stuff to come foaming out of the blown oil filler cap. Better you check for the water droplets now and again.

The most dangerous prospect for your engine is intrusion of the sea into a cylinder through an open exhaust port. Water can get into your exhaust manifold by several means, not limited to those already discussed in the section on Motorsailing. Corrosion in the exhaust elbow's water injection jacket will not be noticeable from the outside but, with some installations, it is possible for water to drip back into the manifold this way. Know how your elbow is constructed and check it before leaving.

If you have a water muffler such as the wet exhaust VernaLift type, make sure the tank is large enough to hold all the water from a full swan neck. The volume of water in your swan neck is the length of hose to maximum rise multiplied by half the inside diameter squared **(Volume = Length x πR^2).**

Make sure your swan neck is high enough to motor heeled in high seas and your outlet won't spend a good deal of its life under water.

Throw away those bronze anti-siphon valves and replace them with plastic ones. While you're doing it, raise the anti-siphon valve and its U-fitting higher than the level of sea can conceivably come without your boat turning turtle.

Chafe, the bane of the windward yacht can hole your exhaust hose. That's not mortal but it sure is messy. One prevention that's easy is to always idle your engine until the operating temperature has bottomed out before cutting it off. If you attempt to start your engine and it doesn't budge, count your blessings. The attitude of the stroke when it stopped was such that the flooded cylinder compressed before another one fired. Water being basically incompressible, your starter can only sit there and hum a tune. Had a dry cylinder fired your engine would be scrap.

Many of these problems occur on yachts on their first real sea trials motorsailing the thorny path. If you must bash into it and cause these problems, it will be apparent by the time you reach the **Dominican Republic**. Get new parts out of **Santo Domingo** and fix it before going on. If you continue in the same style, the next 200 miles to Puerto Rico will be the *coup de grace* for your engine. You can find anything in the D.R. and the labor, if you use it, is cheap.

If you have seawater incursion do the same thing you did when you dropped the outboard motor overboard. If you haven't done that yet, not to worry, you will soon.

1. Take off the injectors until you find the flooded cylinder.
2. Crank to expunge the water.
3. Pour in some diesel or mineral spirits and crank again.
4. Put back the injectors, bleed the fuel system and get underway again.

Different from an outboard, you don't have to change the oil in your diesel's lower unit in this procedure. It doesn't have one.

ELECTRICAL SYSTEM

This guide does not intend to provide a treatise on boat electrics. Many fine reference works are readily available to thoroughly confuse you.

The intent here is to give you warning of what's unique to **Passage Making** south. What you will see for sure are charging problems and more charging problems. You can have wind generators, solar panels, automated battery charging systems and generators separate from the auxiliary. You'll still have charging problems. Especially if you have an electric refrigerator with less than 6 feet of insulation and more than one cube's ice making capacity. The wind won't blow, the sun won't shine, all your charging connections will corrode and generate more heat than they carry electricity, and your diodes will blow.

Also, there is a Parkinson's Law of boat electrics: Consumption expands to overfill the capacity to supply it.

Carry a spare alternator and get the burned out one fixed or rewound in the **Dominican Republic** or **Venezuela**. Anywhere else is prohibitively expensive if it can be done at all. In **Puerto Plata**, hop a *motoconcho* and tell the driver to take you to *Manuel, el Eléctrico* (man-WHALE, ail aye-LECK-tree-koh). *Don't* ask the dockboys.

The most frequent cause of electric failures will be chafe. Before you leave home do a thorough review of all wiring runs. Invest in good metal=jawed cable ties and install them everywhere. Make a detailed wiring diagram of the whole boat including motor and instrument panel.

Have a good multimeter and know how to use it to debug the system. If you rewire anything use one or two gauges heavier than called for and use tinned stranded wire. Label everything and turn square corners with the runs. In short, failures will happen. Have a system that can be quickly debugged. Have aboard *Spa Creek's 12 Volt Doctor's and Alternator Handbooks.*

Here's a gift: while cleaning up your engine's wiring, install a momentary switch on the hot line to the starter solenoid as it runs through the engine room. You'll use this for bleeding the fuel system at the injectors.

MAJOR REPROVISIONING EN ROUTE

Between Florida and Venezuela provisioning a yacht is expensive and often difficult. Puerto Rico and the Virgin Islands have American supermarkets with a limited selection of American goods available in the Virgins. Anyway, all you ever need from an American supermarket are **Joy** dish soap and Glad **garbage bags**. Joy is usually not available anywhere and garbage bags outside the U.S. are universally no good. Everywhere *en route* south will be more expensive than the U.S., sometimes 2 and 3 times more expensive. There is one exception to this bleak picture: the Dominican Republic. Venezuela can be better for many items but it is at the *end* of the route, not "*en*" it. See the section on Refitting for a discussion of provisioning in Venezuela. **Puerto Plata**, though an undesirable commercial harbor, is the provisioner's Mecca.

Actual prices will not be discussed in this guide because inflation and debasement of currencies cause prices to fluctuate within only a few months. Generally speaking, one can buy goods which are made locally in the Dominican Republic, and often for export to the U.S. market (Libby's, Victorina), for a percentage of the prices charged for the same items in standard U.S. retail outlets.

The actual price percentage you will find depends on many economic and political factors. It will almost always be somewhere between 33 and 67 percent. Knowing value before you even ask the price will keep you out of a lot of trouble.

First you have to find what the "provisions percentage" is before you can establish value. This percentage shall be more or less good to use in pricing almost anything of local origin. Restaurants, pizzas, Coca-Cola, etc., but not car rentals. They don't make cars in the D.R., and cars cost more than double the U.S. price because of import taxes.

Example: Linda Catsup is the equivalent of 40 cents U.S., and you paid $1.00 in the U.S. Ergo: 40/100 = 40 percent.

Example: If you got a beer and a pizza in the U.S. at a not-too-swank place for $8.95, then you should expect the same to cost a Linda Catsup percentage in the D.R., or, 40 percent of $8.95, or $3.58 equivalent in pesos.

Example: In any country in the world you can appraise the "oughta-be" value of goods by ratioing against the price of a standard cold beer in a workingman's bar. If it's a buck at home, and a good suit is 250 bucks at home, then a good suit where you are, barring any government interference with taxes and subsidies, shall cost you 250 cold beers.

The average yacht can easily save from $500 to $1500 in major provisioning here, and for cruisers, a dollar saved on provisions is a dollar earned. These savings cannot be realized unless you buy by the case in distributors' warehouses instead of at the pokey little *super mercados*. I've met many skippers kicking themselves all the way down islands because they didn't make room to buy in the **Dominican Republic**. If you don't speak Spanish, it may seem difficult for you, but it's really quite easy. Follow the instructions given below for single item and case-lot purchases.

CASH

Cash is available for **credit cards** in major tourist centers. *Not* **Samaná**. The **American Express** cards are good at any American Express office, and **Visa** and **MasterCard** at most commercial banks. In **Puerto Plata** they can charge up to 3 percent fees at the commercial banks to get cash from your plastic cards (the Banco Popular on the square does). You are always better off getting cash before entering the D.R. You can do this with a Visa card in **Georgetown** from Scotia Bank, however, with little or no fees. Last chance for Visa cash without fees may be Barclays at **Provodenciales**.

Currency exchange is regulated in the Dominican Republic. Both government and private banks, if chartered to exchange money, will do so within a point of each other. Exchanging on the street (an illegal practice) in **Santo Domingo**, you may run into fast-change artists, but not usually elsewhere.

If you carry a lot of cash, don't flash a roll. Keep it in separate pockets. Purses and "belly bags" may get ripped off with a razor in Venezuela—not too comfortable if it's in a tightly strapped belly bag. So travel light when out and about. Try wearing tight jeans.

TRANSPORTATION WHILE PROVISIONING

Take a *motoconcho* instead of walking. These are 80-cc. motorbikes, usually Suzukis for some reason, and sport a banana seat for a single passenger behind the driver. In **Samaná**, they tow a rickshaw sort of conveyance for six and try to put ten aboard. Flag one down with an arm motion which, in America, would mean "slow down," and pay per ride. A ride is a *bola*, (pronounced BOWL-la) and is any length run between two points in town. Each bola is just a few cents American, and it sure beats walking. In Venezuela it's easy. Take a taxi. But negotiate the fare before boarding!

Refer to the tips on transportation in each section, especially for the **Dominican Republic**.

FUEL AND WATER

Water and fuel should be taken on whenever available. Always bleach water with 1 tablespoon bleach per 30 gallons of water. Always filter the fuel with a **Baja Filter** (see Glossary) if you can get it, T-shirts if you can't. One year I had *five* motor stops at sea due to clogged fuel filters. In **Abraham Bay** I bucketed out all the fuel from the tank and gleaned 4 pounds of sand and gravel. The last fuel stops had been in Ft. Lauderdale, Nassau and Georgetown. The same thing happened to *Moon Lady* two years before in the same place.

If you count on catching water, you can be sure it won't rain for weeks, so load up when you can. I have found it convenient to have several 6-gallon jerry jugs for water and an 8-gallon jug for diesel. Larger sizes become unmanageable and smaller sizes make for too many trips. Some places, **Puerto Plata**, for example, you may pay several times more for your fuel if delivered at dockside. Often it is delivered in rusty barrels which are rolled down the dock to ensure you get a fine emulsion of fuel and iron oxide. In Puerto Plata you can jerry jug from the Texaco station and get filtered fuel at a fraction of the price charged at the dock. Better to wait for **Samaná**, where there is a dockside pump.

Jerry jugging can become a way of life. You should equip for it. We take one or two showers a day (albeit Navy showers) and wash dishes in fresh water. That means a little more than two gallons a day per person, or one jug run every three days with two people aboard. If you can afford it, here's a real back saver: use a 20- to 30-gallon flexible tank with a 12-volt in-line pump with which to shuttle water aboard via the dinghy. Look, Ma, no hands!

Treat your water with chlorine and never tank from a line that had a recent loss of pressure.

First of all, only you know what you want. I love French-cut green beans and I use them with mushrooms, onions and mayonnaise for great salads when I can't get fresh veggies. You may hate French-cut green beans and mushrooms.

The harbor is dirty, and you may get the itch to go before you've sampled the local goods. It is therefore important to forego restaurants for a couple of days early in your stay and shop single items from the *mercados* to find out what you like before shopping for case lots.

Buy only made-in-the-D.R. labels. The only exceptions to this rule are some occasionally good prices, due to trade concessions, on Spanish imports, some of which may be bottled in the D.R. (olives, mushrooms, fruit cocktail). The quality of local products may be uneven between brands, but not as dramatically uneven as in Venezuela.

Always sample several individual products before deciding what to buy by the case.

BUYING INDIVIDUAL ITEMS (NOT CASE LOTS)

In **Puerto Plata**, take a *motoconcho* to one of these supermarkets to look for the good buys when you need only one or two of each item or when you are sampling products before buying a case.

- The Italian Supermarket
- Super Mercado Ambar
- Puerto Plata Supermarket

These markets are relatively clean and provide a good selection of local products. The Italian Supermarket has some imported and gourmet items as well.

You must ask for what you want. One fellow complained to me that the D.R. had no bacon. He was too shy to ask. It's called *tocineta* (toe-see-NET-ah). He assumed it would be in a vacuum-packed package like Oscar Meyer's, with the slices of bacon splayed out like a poker hand. In the D.R., meats are usually kept the way they were when our mothers went shopping: They're wrapped in white butcher's paper among a bunch of amorphous packages in the cooler. The bacon is whole and requires slicing by the guy in the store. For that reason, it's usually also better tasting.

You also must ask to taste a slice. Certainly sample the cheese and salamis before buying.

Have a dictionary handy if what you want is not listed in the word list in this book. Here is a list of D.R. products which, when they are not entirely diverted to export, are usually high quality at low price in the D.R.:

- Dried milk
- Tinned hors d'oeuvres from Spain
- Worcestershire sauce (Salsa Inglesa)
- Vanilla
- Soy sauce (Salsa China)
- Strawberry jam
- Guava & pineapple marmalades
- Rum (Bermudez Añejo Especial)
- Gin (Bermudez is excellent)
- Fine rums (Bermudez Aniversario and "103")
- Local Scotch (McAlbert's—*caveat emptor*)

- Creme de Cacao and other liqueurs
- Cooking wines
- Cigarettes
- Very fine cigars
- Warm-stored margarine (Manicera)
- MasMas chocolate bars or others to your taste (for watch snacks)
- Salami (try the higher priced *Induveca* brands and taste first!)
- Large loaves of cheese called *Queso Danesa*
- Red ball Gouda cheeses (only Royal brand), can be warm-stored

Compared with large economies the reader might be used to, the economy of a small country like the Dominican Republic will fluctuate wildly with world conditions as well as with local policies. Even local goods may often be temporarily limited and therefore prices go up and shelves go bare. Seasonal production also reckons. Therefore, a buying trip is necessary for samples of both quality and price.

HOW TO SHOP FOR CASE-LOT GOODS

In **Puerto Plata** take a *motoconcho* to any of the *almacenes* for case lots. Almacén (alma-SANE) means warehouse. There are many wholesale warehouses in Puerto Plata or Santiago. Silverio Messon and Palanco are two in Puerto Plata that do a large business with hotels. In the larger almacenes there will be an old man or a kid to help you load up a cart. When entering, ask for a niño (NEE-nyo). He will follow you around with a great wheeled float and put on it whatever you point at. Take a look in any walk-in coolers in the almacenes. Remember they have a furious trade with the fancy foreign tourist hotels. You may be surprised and get fresh asparagus and artichokes for dinner.

First go into the broken case-lots section. Here you can buy items which you won't want in full cases and at the same time you get to see pretty much what they have in all those cases stacked outside. If there's something you want which is not there, ask, and they will break a case and give you a prorated case price on units. The *niño* will throw the stuff into a large supermarket cart.

Leave your full cart behind and go with the *niño* and his float out into the warehouse. If you don't see what you want, crawl back into the alleys of the boxes and look. If you don't understand what's in a case, ask the *niño* to break it open and show you.

When your float is full, go have someone make out a bill. The *niño* will call it all out and you can check it both before and after the guy on the stool writes it down.

Take your bill out to the cashier and pay it. Ask one of the guys at the desks who seems to know for a delivery time to the dock, the *Muelle de Yates* (MWAY-YEA day YAH-tace). He'll take your boat's name, give you a delivery time, and you can go out to the street without your stuff, your money or a receipt.

Not to worry. They'll be on the dock within a half-hour of the time given. The guys on the truck will have your bill and they will scrupulously check off all the items with you as they help you offload it onto the dock.

FRESH FRUITS AND VEGETABLES

The same should be said for fresh veggies that was said for fuel and water: Buy them whenever they're available. And wash them before putting them aboard. Also be sure to discard all cardboard, which may bring aboard cockroach eggs.

In Puerto Plata try the *Mercado Nuevo* (mare-CAH-doh NWAY-voh) (the spaceship look-alike building at the top of the hill over the cemetery). Mornings are best. Best quality is usually had on the market street downtown. In **Luperón** you will find varying quality in all the little shops and on the streets. Find the lady that has the best of what you want, then find out when she gets it in fresh. Don Santiago Morrobel's store on the square will bring in caselots and deliver them to the dock for you. Try out the different root vegetables that fed our ancestors before the Idaho white potato and mass production methods drove them from North America.

- Limes, Oranges
- Grapefruit
- Avocados
- Eggs
- All vegetables, especially root varieties
- Bananas & plantains
- Pineapples

The best buys are honey, peanuts, jewelry—and lunch.

For jewelry in **Puerto Plata**, go to the public market after 2 p.m. on cruise ship days. The suckers are gone and they need to shuck stock. Benita always has good stuff and a fair deal. For a huge, cheap lunch, go into the market kitchen where the workers eat and order up. You'll be aghast at the apparent lack of hygiene, but you won't be sorry.

DRY STAPLES

You will find rice, sugar, flour, beans, meal, and so on, readily available almost everywhere. And at prices better than those in the U.S. *Almacén Sandra* in **Luperón**, right behind Lucas' restaurant has good, clean, dry staples, including fresh shelled Spanish peanuts. Trying to store too much flour or rice will have you throwing it away when the insect eggs hatch, that is, unless you have pounds of laurel (bay leaves) to put in your canisters. You may need to clean the rice and beans of small stones and stems. This is true also of U.S. products, unless they are irradiated. In the Caribbean you will find that flour is not always "enriched," rice is not always "polished," sugar is not always "refined" and not much is "new and improved." But it just might be tasty and good for you.

GOOD BUYS IN CASE LOTS

The following items can also be purchased singly in the broken case-lots section for 1/24 (or 1/12, or 1/48) of the price of a case. Half-cases can also be purchased.

- Canned soups

  All types usually available. Be sure to buy local labels. Sometimes U.S. brands are available, but rather than being made for export to the U.S. they may be imported from the U.S. Ask the price on any U.S. labeled goods to be sure.

- Chocolate
- Candies
- Gum
- Instant cocoa
- Espresso ground coffee

  This comes in vacuum-packed tins. But for freshness aboard, you may want it in small, sealed packets good for several cups of coffee each morning. These are in the brown paper bags near the tins of coffee. It pays to peek into unmarked boxes and bags.

- Gin (Bermudez - other brands might be *aguardiente*, or gargle)
- Rum - *añejos* or extra *viejos* for 12-year dark. Try also the 15-year rums
- Beer
- Pear juice
- Pineapple juice
- Tomato juice - Victorina brand is closer to V8 Juice
- Tomato paste
- Tomato sauce
- Spaghetti sauce - Victorina *salsa condimentada* (condimented sauce) beats Ragu
- Mayonnaise - Baldom brand
- Knorr's dry soups
- Cigars & cigarettes
- All cleaning agents
- Canned pineapple
- "Scotch Brite" type green scratch pads (best buy)

I have fished cans out of the forward bilge after three years aboard in the tropics and found them still legibly labeled and delicious inside. Varnishing cans is a waste of time if yours is a basically dry boat.

I've had unrefrigerated eggs aboard as long as two months and found them delicious, although they don't foam as much when whipped if you don't turn them. Of course, you must buy only unrefrigerated, fresh eggs; refrigerated eggs go bad quicker. Unrefrigerated eggs are easy to spot: They have chicken poop on them.

Instead of waxing your eggs, try turning them once in a while to keep the yolks centered. Like many cruising customs of yore, the modern yacht and ubiquitous staples has eliminated varnishing tins and waxing eggs. A word about eggs and chickens in the D.R. You may see barbecued chicken for sale which is scrawny, and eggs which are more like bird eggs. If they are *huevos criollos* (WAVE-ose cree-OH-yose), or criole eggs or *pollo* (PO-yo), chicken, snap it up. They're more expensive but you'll find out what chicken and eggs were like in your grandfather's time, before factory methods.

BREADS AND DAIRY PRODUCTS

The bakery, Panadaria Dorado, is just a few blocks from the Puerto Plata dock and makes fresh French bread twice a day. More expensive, but sometimes of better quality, is Pépé Postre, even closer to the dock and with outlets all over the area. Pépé Postre also has delicious French pastries, so watch yourself. You will also find:

- Milk
- Yogurt
- Cheese
- Butter
- Bread
- *Pan del agua* ("Cuban" or small French breads)

The yogurt is great and extraordinarily cheap by the gallon! In Santiago, Puerto Plata, or in Luperón, from the truck, yogurt is available at Pépé Postre. Ask for yo-GOOR or *Baruga* (bah-ROO-gah), which is the brand.

MEATS AND SAUSAGES

The D.R. has the oldest beef culture in the western hemisphere. You will often get tough and tasteless beef in restaurants and in stores and come to the conclusion that D.R. meat is awful, a complaint often heard from yachties who just didn't know what to order and how.

Beef filet is often only sold by the entire filet, but at a price that you can't believe. Good filets are prepared the European way and are aged and blue. Other cuts of good beef are also European style and are lean looking to North Americans.

Cheap beef is called *res* (race) and is often tough. The secret to buying good meat is to not go cheap. It's already so cheap, there's no reason for shaving additional pennies which will only get you poor quality. Buy the most expensive filet, *filete lomillo* (fee-LAY-taye low-ME-yo), and you will be very pleased. Smoked ham, boiled ham and smoked pork chops are also good.

Best sources are Erica's butcher shop, next to the University, across from the Victorian Pub, or the Italian Super Market, or direct from the Induveca delivery van when you see it on the street.

If you can, get a Saronno ham to hang aboard. This is the Spanish version of the Italian Parma ham. It may cost you ten times as much in Spain as in the D.R., but the masters that make it in the D.R. all come from Spain.

MISCELLANEOUS

1. Old-time stuff hard to find in the States is readily available in the D.R.

You can find real sail canvas and blue denim for boat and personal use in the D.R.

2. You can eat fancy as well as *tipico* in the cities.

Fine dining is downtown at **Puerto Plata** or at **Long Beach**, a *motoconcho* ride east. In **Santiago**, it's at the Pes Dorado (the golden fish). **Luperón** is still trying.

3. Refurbish your medicine chest without prescriptions, often cheaply.

Like most small, poor countries, the **Dominican Republic** cannot afford to tie disease curing drugs to doctor's prescriptions, nor can the people afford to buy drugs abusively. Therefore pharmaceuticals are available without prescription, if you know what you want. The pharmacist will gladly show you the book so you can translate your antibiotic, or whatever, to generic, and back to product name as available there. The European seasickness pill, **Stugeron**, is sold here.

For immunity requirements, call the Atlanta C.D.C. at 404-332-4559. Drugs needed commonly for public health can be subsidized and cheap. Exotic items may be more expensive than at home. But if you need to replace drugs used up during treatment aboard, then this is the place. Also, pharmacies in Latin countries traditionally handle dangerous chemicals as well. You may be surprised to find acetone, muriatic and cooking alcohol available in quantity only through certain pharmacies.

4. Siesta (see-ACE-tah)

Shopping in Puerto Plata you will discover the noon-to-2 p.m. siesta when all the stores close. Take your lunch in the park. The central park, or *parque central*, (el PAR-KAY Cen-TRAHL) has a special flavor of its own. Watching the parade pass by is great entertainment while you: breakfast or lunch on the porch at Cafe Central; pig out in the ice cream parlor on the corner; eat 25-cent hamburgers from the street vendors (they're called Riki Takis (REEK-ee TACK-ees)); read The New York Times and The Wall Street Journal available at Libreria Félix; get your shoes shined; listen to the firemen's brass band at 8 p.m. on Sundays; fill your propane tanks next to Cafe Central.

5. Street food

I know I've got it coming to me, but in going on 30 years of living abroad in the strangest of places, I've been ill from food just once. That was a long time ago at the grand restaurant of the Palace hotel in Biarritz. In Arab countries or India, one might expect to become ill from the nazi balls (rice balls) the peddler rolls in his hands and pops into ancient hot grease. Not so. Perhaps it's the super hot oil that does it. Latin countries have superb little puffed, stuffed pastries—Puerto Ricans call them *empanadillas*, Dominicans call them *pastelitos* (pah-stay-LEE-toes), or "little pastries." Venezuelans call them *empanadas*. In Puerto Plata, buy your pastelitos from the baritone vendor who sings of his wares. He also says that the meat-filled ones have "mice meat" in them, but he means "mincemeat," I'm sure.

(P.S.: The wrinkled old lady who begs is crazy and really well-to-do.)

Possibilities to haul in the Dominican Republic exist but generally are not to be recommended. Multihulls and bilge keels can use the beaching facility at **Manzanillo** with good effect. Some materials are available in the hardware store in **Dajabón**, otherwise bring your own. Good labor is also available. A railroad lift exists in **Bahía de Cariñero** (Careener's Bay) in **Samaná**, Columbus's old careening spot. You'll be quite historical if you haul there. You will be hysterical by the time you launch. Of course, anything is possible with all materials and tools onboard and careful attention and guidance from the skipper.

Puerto Rico is dotted with boat yards. You will have no trouble finding one for a quick haul and paint. For more extensive work, as always, shop around before committing.

If leaving your boat for the summer, consider hauling out and leaving it at **Ponce** *Yacht Club* (expensive), or **Palmas del Mar**, near **Humacao**, or **Puerto del Rey**, in **Fajardo**. Puerto del Rey is the largest marina in the Caribbean and very well equipped, though it can be dear, depending.

Croabas, **Puerto Real**, **La Parguera** and **Isletta** have little or no facility for long-term storage, but are good and fast haulouts. At Palmas del Mar, your boat can be laid up either ashore or afloat and the yard has a marine store. Yard owner Hans Grossen is as helpful as can be. Las Croabas is do-it-yourself and usually cheapest.

The Yards in **Tortola**, Tortola Yacht Services at **Roadtown** and Nanny Cay Marina at **Nanny Cay** are quite professional, but likely to be busy, depending on the season, because of the charter fleets.

Further down island you will find Bobby's Marina in **Phillipsburg, St. Martin**, the Rodney Bay Marina in **St. Lucia**, Castries Yacht Service in St. Lucia and Prickly Bay Marina, **Grenada**. In the past, Castries has been most reasonably priced, and you will do most of your own work. Rodney Bay, on the other hand is undoubtedly the most well-equipped and convenient yard you will find in the Caribbean with host Arch Marez graciously officiating.

In the eastern cruising grounds of **Venezuela** there are two large commercial steel boat building yards in **Cumaná**, and regular yacht yards with Travelifts (Centro Marino de Oriente, and Amerigo Vespuccio Marina) in **Puerto La Cruz**.

The Astilleros de Oriente yard in Cumaná has a 100-ton Travelift, they do sand blasting in a pit dry dock so it doesn't usually spoil your brightwork, and they are capable of any work whatsoever. They are short on English, however, so most of the yachties wait in line to take the railroads up at Varadero Caribe, also in Cumaná, which sandblasts everywhere, but is long on English.

Xenophobia has cost yachties more money and trouble than has divorce.

Look in at Astilleros and ask for Tudor, a yard foreman raised in Chicago. Be aware, also, that security at Cumaná requires remaining in the *Cumanagoto* marina while you wait your turn to be hauled. Instead of waiting in the marina you may go across the gulf to anchor in the little bays and bayous. You may have better security there, but you will lose your place in the queue.

Both yards in **Puerto La Cruz** look great, but they often seem to be getting their act together, as though they were going into business almost any day soon. Beware of lax security if you park the boat on the *Amerigo Vespucci* side while waiting to be hauled there. Centro Marino de Oriente (CMO) security arrangements are quite impressive. There are three levels of secure storage with vicious dogs patrolling the third, or inner, level.

If **IMRON**-ing your boat, get your own paint at the DuPont store in either Cumaná or Puerto La Cruz. It will be cheaper than letting the yard get it, and you will be sure to have an exact match in the colors. Each store's personnel are extremely helpful. The yards are capable of beautiful paint work at half the costs found in the Virgins. Nonetheless, results can be quite uneven, perhaps dependent on the supervisory interest shown by the owner:

**Too much supervision may be worse than too little;
none can be disastrous**

Venezuela manufactures DuPont's IMRON. As a result of the local petroleum, the costs are less than half the U.S. costs. We brush ours on from the dinghy for only 2 percent of the yard costs (1 percent Virgins). From 10 feet away you would never know it wasn't sprayed. Use the lagoon at **Bahía Mangle** in **Chimana Grande**, Puerto La Cruz.

If you've been lucky there will be few broken and bent parts as a result of your travels. You can pick and choose what to refit at the terminus in Venezuela to prepare the yacht for going back or proceeding on to the Panama Canal. If you've been unlucky—a bent shaft, for instance—you will have a list of things to do which are absolute musts to make the yacht sea ready again.

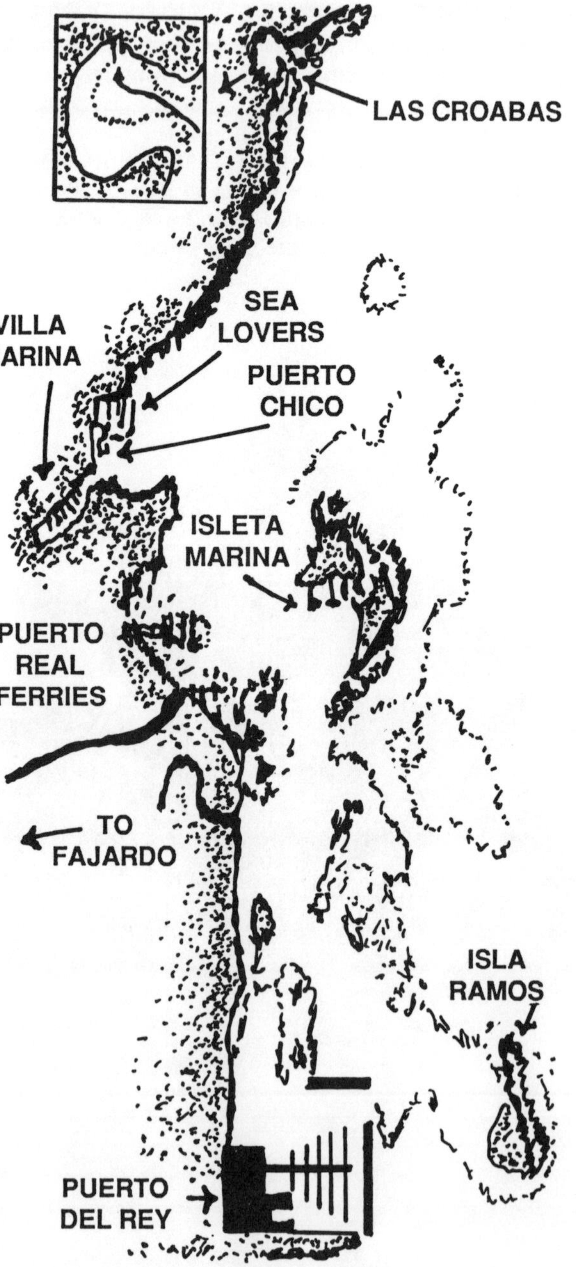

Yards and Marinas at Fajardo

Besides refitting at the end of the road, this section can also be used as guidelines for your decision making all along the route. **Venezuela** is the terminus for this guide and it is used in all examples. Nonetheless, the guidelines are valid for most of the Caribbean where most economies are in or close to crisis and shall undoubtedly remain so.

Recommendations of specific shops and services are not given. These tips rarely survive the test of a few months, so don't believe those you do get.

Specific prices are likewise not given. Prices go up, quality goes down and businesses go broke. Ten unthinking yachties in a row grinningly declaring, "Wow! That's cheap!" will make even the most straight arrow mechanic revise his pricing policies for *gringos*. He has kids to feed. So get your specific tips on shops and items to purchase (or not to purchase) from several cruisers with recent information, not from any book.

Transportation while refitting and reprovisioning is not a problem as long as taxis remain cheap or the dollar dear. Find out what each trip should cost in approximate terms before hailing a cab and find out what the driver will charge before entering the cab. *Always*.

DECIDING WHAT TO REFIT

If you are lucky and have only "wannas" instead of "haftas" to buy or fix, some generic advice will help. First of all, whether you seek services (awning repair?), workshops (straightening shafts?), retailers (awning material?) or groceries, go for the possible. Find out what's available and reasonable rather than pursuing preconceived goals which may get you in trouble.

For example, one cruiser I met thought **Venezuela** wasn't so cheap. They had to import their Sunbrella awning material. Had they investigated further they would have found the

British equivalent available at one-sixth the price, out of Hong Kong via Japan. Even if they had purchased normal canvas, they could have had several awnings done for the price they paid and those awnings together would have lasted at least as long as one made of Sunbrella.

To understand what's possible one must understand something of the Venezuelan economy. First of all, Venezuela is a large, rich country with undeveloped natural resources, excepting oil and aluminum. They nationalized these, along with all their subsidiary industries, from the Americans over the last 30 years and they have not developed a much wider industrial infrastructure since. The chances of doing so faded with the world oil glut and the dive in oil prices in the early 1980s.

So here you have a modern country the size of a good chunk of the United States with 20 or so million relatively educated (if only by television) souls expecting the good life promised by the beer ads and not finding it.

Carlos Caraqueño (car-ah-KAY-nyo: a resident of Caracas) can't get his shaft straightened because it's too expensive for him. He's told his depressed economy is due to the bloodsucking usurious northern bankers (that's you, by the way) to whom his country's reduced revenue must go in payment of the old high interest rates on ancient loans which didn't help their infrastructure anyway. Agree with him or not, that's the reality he lives in.

Meanwhile, due to the accident of currency markets, Bob Boatie stands beside Carlos Caraqueño in the prop shop in Cumaná and shouts, "Wow! That's cheap!" 'Way to go, Bob. When Carlos goes back to his awning shop, if he's like you or I, he'll really gig the foreign yachts with his prices, and perhaps, with his quality as well. Therefore…

RULE ONE: Use non-yachtie sources wherever possible.

EXAMPLE 1. Go to the hardware store farthest from the marina.

EXAMPLE 2. Get your dinghy anchor at the fishermen's supply store.

EXAMPLE 3. Don't wear white shorts with a regatta tee shirt when you go shopping.

EXAMPLE 4. If you can, grow a Pancho Villa mustache and talk Venezuelan.

Venezuela is a favorite source of Japan's oil for which contracts are negotiated with increasing creativity on a rolling basis almost monthly. Since oil and aluminum are about the only commodities Venezuela can sell, and they need to import just about everything else, the mixture of currency and trade concessions gets frenetic. For example, if you give me a break on your fixed (oil-based) exchange rate, I'll sell you outboards for your fishermen on that rate instead of the floating rate. Or how about I set up a fiberglass boat factory in the mountains to use your petroleum stocks to make boats for your fishermen with Indian labor so the mountain folk don't continue to jam the slums in the cities where there are no jobs for them? If you were Carlos Caraqueño I'd bet you'd go for that.

However, when Carlos sees you, the usurious banker, carrying away one of those neat Yamaha fiberglass boats bought at prices subsidized by his labor and resources, and he still sees you demanding your interest, he might get mad and call the militia. When the militia boards your boat they may not be too courteous since they're not always recruited from the best Venezuelan families and they may lack your sophistication and education. The various militias are, after all, like the American CCC in the Great American Depression, a source of employment for the unemployable during the Great Venezuelan Depression. They will understand, however, that you are double dipping in their wounded economy and that you are avoiding the export tax on subsidized articles. The export tax would have paid back the subsidy and brought prices of your purchases up to world levels. In their eyes you can be quite a scoundrel. Try grinning at their combat boots and shouting, "Wow! It was so cheap!" Or, you could have followed...

RULE TWO: Know current export restrictions.

The economic trials in Venezuela make it a great refitting spot and many opportunities exist for bargains. Understanding their problem better will not only protect you from doing something illegal but will also open up some purchasing opportunities you might not have thought about.

Buying and towing five dinghies behind your boat will surely attract the rancor of a Venezuelan, but giving work to the many well qualified craftsmen there will guarantee good results.

EXAMPLE 1. Ever wanted to replace your charging wires with good "00" gauge battery cable but 20 feet of cable made up into 4 different lengths with small ring connectors cost too much money since the battery shop in Fort Lauderdale took $35 an hour to make them up? Battery cable is one of the hidden resources in the bottom of the Venezuelan heap of heavy and light industries supporting mining and drilling.

EXAMPLE 2. Need pipe? Tools? Stainless welding? Been thinking of a "jungle gym" to support all the stuff you need to mount high up aft? Awning supports? Take a look at the fabulous grades of polished and corrosion resistant aluminum tubing available and the high tech welding methods they use.

Therefore . . .

RULE THREE: Refit from the strengths of the economy.

While in Venezuela, consume the products and labor of the land. As in Phoenix, Arizona, they will not be yacht oriented. As a matter of fact, outside of Cowes, La Rochelle and Fort Lauderdale, very few places are. Aluminum, oil (a year's supply of 2-stroke oil) and oil stocks products (Imron, polyester resin, enamels, urethane varnish). If electronics were on your agenda, go back to the US or to a free port and order from Europe where you'll get decent quality.

Furthermore, think of all the things you have been doing yourself and not purchasing due to unavailability of qualified labor and materials throughout the islands to the north. You may be in a mental set, normally good for a cruiser, that says "do it yourself, don't be a consumer." This may not be good for you in Venezuela.

Therefore . . .

RULE FOUR: Let the Venezuelans do it, and consume like a Venezuelan.

EXAMPLE 1. You sew your own courtesy flags? You may be spending more by using your own thread and machine. A couple of years ago I had my curtains replaced with beautiful cloth backed with reflective coating for $6. The seamstress was the wife of a restaurant owner who also did children's clothes.

EXAMPLE 2. A can of tuna in the store is made in Venezuela and may cost a small fraction of what you paid for each can of tuna on board.

EXAMPLE 3. How about your personalized stationery? Your yacht's visiting cards? Visit a commercial print shop and be amazed at both quality and price, and you will also get the copper printing blocks to reuse in the future.

EXAMPLE 4. T-shirts with your yacht's logo? The artwork and the silk screens are delivered to you with the shirts.

EXAMPLE 5. Say you don't use fancy restaurants? Try one and you may be eating out every night for less than what it would cost to consume your own stores. Please tip the musicians moderately and don't shout, "Wow! That was cheap!" Your patronage of their businesses is appreciated without insulting their currency.

Currency in Venezuela has certain complexities. When I was there in 1972 it was enormously expensive for someone with dollars and the Venezuelans thought nothing of hopping a jet for a shopping trip to Miami to hunt bargains among their poorer cousins to the north. I remember admiring the Venezuelans then for their industriousness and success. How times change!

Now that the shoe is on the other foot, don't expect to be admired for the industriousness which made you a successful cruiser. Latin pride, or *orgullo* (or-GOO-yo) mitigates against it. Furthermore, not all Venezuelans have benefited equally from their country's bounty. As in your own urban societies there always lurks the alienated or conscienceless few to take advantage of what they can. These days the lurking is pretty good.

Therefore . . .

RULE SIX: Don't flash your money.

When going to the bank to exchange cash or to get cash from a credit card, pretend you're in a spy movie and case things out pretty thoroughly. Sit a while on the sometimes sumptuous sofas in the bank lobby both before and after your transaction. Watch for loiterers in the street or even in the bank lobby. Upon leaving the bank, stop to do what shopping you can to divest yourself of some of the cash. Leave stores by entrances other than ones through which you entered and use devious routes back to your boat, throwing in a couple of changes of public transportation.

Think I'm exaggerating? What do you think all those gun slits outside and inside the banks are for?

Finally,

RULE SEVEN: Leave high finance to the Swiss gnomes.

If you think you understand how the currency game works and you place your bets at the bank accordingly, changing nothing this week and lots of it the next, be aware that how you spend your cruising chips doesn't attract attention in Zurich.

The quoted floating exchange rate doesn't tell a tenth of the story. The government is committed to stabilizing the economy at the risk of eliminating some subsidies. The Bolivar may cheapen against the dollar by a factor of 3, but if inflation raises prices by 4 you've just lost 33 percent of your money. Government controls make timing of purchases which depend on import materials bought with hard currency (e.g., rubber dinghies) very difficult. If you wait for a point more on the exchange you risk running into a sudden order backlog which puts delivery off beyond your **Visa** expiration.

If, like I did one year, you decide to gain the billing time of your credit card, effectively buying the Bolivar short, you may run into what I did. The Central Bank decided to hold all Visa transactions until a more favorable exchange rate was available and after debt renegotiation. That was *four months* later. Not allowed under the Visa rules? Call Chase Manhattan and while you're at it, call up the central bank of this sovereign nation and tell them you heard they can't do it. Otherwise, follow . . .

THE GOLDEN RULE : Take cash and convert it as needed.

That way you'll average out your gains and losses and you'll avoid institutional interference with your transactions. You'll buy only the things you can use and won't be suspected of profiteering. You'll consume more on the local market, such as restaurants, and you will be happier. So will the Venezuelans.

REFITTING AND REPROVISIONING IN VENEZUELA

Enough examples are given in the previous pages that you should have a good idea of what kind of opportunities may exist and how you can go about identifying the specific ones available during the time frame of your visit.

Shafts can be straightened in **Cumaná**, by the way, as well as propellers repitched. Haulout work is addressed in the "Hauling" chapter. As already mentioned, the opportunities for reasonably priced and quality refit jobs will change from time to time with the swings in the troubled economy and the government efforts to regulate them.

Simply using those opportunities which the economy and the government conspire to make attractive will more than occupy your time without trying the impossible, or worse, the illegal.

Some bargains will not change, such as **Margarita** for clothes and duty-free jug wine, Cumaná for industrial supplies and services, **Puerto La Cruz** for consumer products, restaurants and entertainment, and, shades of a younger America, travel by any means which requires great amounts of fossil fuels.

Jet air fare in Venezuela, despite recent price increases, will continue to be one of the greatest bargains around. Firstly, because they have oil and it is relatively cheap. Secondly, because there are enormous distances to travel in South America and thirdly, because there is so much worth touring.

One cruiser I know put the boat up in the marina in **Puerto La Cruz** and spent 6 months touring South America. Even if you don't go so far afield, a trip to **Mérida** and **Angel's Falls** is too good to pass up if you're at all a tourist. By all means leave your boat in a marina while you are gone if you are on the mainland. From Margarita you can have friends look after the yacht in the **Porlamar** anchorage in front of the Concorde Hotel.

A neat way to visit the mainland from Margarita is to take a ferry over and a plane back. Now you've sampled travel in Venezuela with minimum investment and without later having to take time out from your stay on the mainland which might be a busy one if you've got a lot of refit to do.

Reprovisioning edible stores can be slightly cheaper on the mainland because you avoid the transport costs of bringing the goods to **Margarita**.

Because shortages will come and go, hitting almost all items but rum and tobacco, it's best to provision wherever you can. The supermarkets are large, convenient and "Americanized." For example, veggies are Saran-wrapped in little ozone-destroying green plastic trays. The better products are in a deli section where you pick a number. Shopping carts are huge and so are the women in curlers compulsively grabbing the impulse buyers' goodies in the check out lines. Very Americanized indeed.

CaDa supermarkets are ubiquitous and on Margarita, CM (Centro Madeireño) is very large and has a great bakery next door. As in the Dominican Republic, you can get *Pan de Agua* here but they call it *Pan Francés* (PAHN frahn-SACE), which makes sense. If in **Pampatar**, there is an excellent little bakery right by the anchorage. As in the D.R., *you must sample each brand before buying a bunch.* Unlike the D.R., however, where there is a fairly consistent level of quality, Venezuela is a large market with worldwide sources and quality (or taste, if you prefer) can be a problem.

Try a couple of different brands of corned beef for a test. One will be worse than dog food and the other better than Hormel. And both the same price! Coffee is excellent and cheap, but don't get caught by the troops with 30 pounds aboard if it's on their list.

In Venezuela I've found it more convenient to provision a little at a time while eating out lots. By the time your visa is up your boat is full, and you never had the hassle of major provisioning nor attracted undue attention.

Finally, as in the Dominican Republic, if you need to replace drugs used up during treatment aboard, then this is the place. Also, you will find acetone, muriatic and cooking alcohol available in quantity only through certain pharmacies.

Plantains

What do you do with them? Anything you would do with a potato. But plantains don't taste for those of us not raised on them. Here's how to make them taste.

The simplest method is to wait until they're yellow. They then taste slightly banana flavored. Let them get black spots and they do taste like bananas. Let them turn black entirely and they are bananas but not rotten. Think of it this way: bananas mature (or rot) from the inside out while plantains mature from the outside in.

To make excellent French fries, use a yellow plantain. If slicing disks instead of matchsticks, slice thinner for more taste. Douse with good old salt and ketchup and go to it.

To make tostones (toast-TONE-ace) slice up a plantain, or plátanos (PLAH-tah-nose) in Spanish. Spread the slices into very hot grease, seasoned with garlic salt (and hot pepper if that's you're style) in the Puerto Rican style, turning them over and squashing them with a spoon when they're half done. Blot on paper and serve hot or cold with a dip, doused in ketchup or as is.

Again, use more mature plantains for more sweetness and slice thinner for more taste. Foreigners living in the Dominican Republic learn to like their plantains and are therefore called "plantainized," or platanisado (plah-tah-knee-SAH-doh).

Black Bean Soup

For 12 ounces of dried black beans, or "turtle beans," use:

- 4 ounces ham bone
- ¼ cup olive oil
- ½ cup wine vinegar
- ½ large onion
- 2 green peppers
- 1 crushed pod of garlic
- 1 bay leaf
- 1 quart of water
- ½ tablespoon salt

Clean the beans and soak them overnight. Add all ingredients but oil and vinegar and simmer covered for 3 hours, stirring occasionally. Add the oil and vinegar and simmer covered for one more hour.

Keep up the water level while boiling so you have a rich, black soup. Ideally, the beans should be mostly disintegrating. But this comes from restocking a pot which is kept going all week, and that isn't easy to do on a boat.

Serve over rice with side garnishes of finely chopped onion and fresh green peppers.

For a quick method, stick everything all at once into a pressure cooker and cook for 1 hour. For an even faster method, buy cans of black beans.

Spanish for black beans is *habichuelas negras* (ah-bitch-WAY-lahs NAY-grahs). In Venezuela, *caraotas* (car-ah-OH-tas). Buen provecho (bwayne pro-VAYE-choh)!

English Muffins

For simple stovetop English Muffins which keep without refrigeration, try the following recipe. It will make 10 2½" muffins.

1 cup warm water

1 tablespoon dry yeast

1 teaspoon sugar (and honey if desired)

2 teaspoons salt (or less)

¼ cup liquid shortening

3 cups flour (up to 1 cup may be whole wheat)

Sprinkle the yeast over the water in a large bowl and let sit a few minutes. Thoroughly combine the dry ingredients. Mix them gradually into the bowl with the water.

Roll out the dough to one third of an inch thickness. Cut it into 2 ½ inch circles and lay them on a surface sprinkled with cornmeal. Sprinkle the tops with cornmeal and allow the muffins to rise—about double in 2 hours.

"Bake" on a preheated griddle with medium flame until brown on both sides—about 5 to 7 minutes each side. Put away until ready to serve.

To serve, split with a fork and toast each half face down on a buttered griddle. These are as good as the Thomas's English Muffins made in America.

Englishmen, by the way, don't know what they are.

Beer Bread

For a tasty sour-dough type of bread with no kneading necessary, try mixing:

1 can of warm beer

3 cups of flour

2 tablespoons baking powder and

3 tablespoons sugar (for the beer to eat)

Allow the dough to set up in a greased pan for 1 hour and bake until it looks done. Simple. Add raisins, citrus, bananas and so on, to make it complex.

Thornton's Grouper au Vin Blanc

2 pounds fresh grouper fillet (must be fresh)

2 tablespoons olive oil

½ fresh garlic clove

8 oz. mushroom slices

¼ cup dry vermouth

¼ cup evaporated milk

1 teaspoon dill weed

Sauté the mushrooms and paper-thin garlic slices in one tablespoon olive oil. Lightly fry the fish fillets in one tablespoon olive oil mixed with dill until white all the way through. Turn the fillets several times.

Turn off the heat, add the vermouth and cover the fish.

Pour off the water from the mushrooms into water for rice.

When ready to serve, pour the wine and juices from the fish into the mushrooms and continue to sauté, agitating briskly with a fork while dripping in the milk. If the sauce is too thin, continue sautéing until thick as desired. *Never* thicken artificially.

Serve the fish with the sauce on the side.

APPENDIX A: RADIO TIMES AND FREQUENCIES

Atlantic Standard Time (UTC-4)	Station Call Sign	Freq. 1	Freq. 2	Freq. 3	Freq. 4	Broadcast and Source [see also *Listening to the Weather*]
600	NMN	4426	6501	8764		NWS Offshore Forecast, from Portsmouth
	WAH	4357	4381	8728	13077	NWS Offshore Forecast (plus), St.Thomas
	VOA	5980	6095	9590	7405	Voice Of America with news to 0800
	CSM	9495	7395			Christian Science Monitor World News to 0800
630	WVWI	1000				VI Radio Sailor's Report (MTWTF)
645	HAM	7163	LSB			Antilles HAM weather net (LSB) also at 1830
700	BBC	6195	15220			World News to 0930, main news at 0900
	HAM	7237	(alternate 7230)			Caribbean HAM weather update - **LSB**
705	4VEH	1030				NWS Offshore Forecasts, from Haiti
	WOSO	1030				San Juan weather report hourly after news
	BAR	790				Radio Barbados forecast
720	HAM	7103	changes with EDST			HAM Bahamas weather roundup - **LSB**
730	SSB	6215				Antilles Cruisers net (all the way down)
745	HAM	7268	changes with EDST			HAM waterway net (begins with weather) - **LSB**
800	BON	800				Caribbean forecast, Bonaire
	WLO	6519	8515			NWS Offshore weather reports (New Orleans)
	WOO	4387	8749			NWS reports (and at 1800), tfc list even hours-N.J.
805	ZNS1	810	1240	1540		Nassau weather (after news some hours)
830	ANT	930				Antigua EC Forecasts (also at 18:25)
900	WOM	4363	8722	13092	17242	NWS reports (and at 1900), tfc list odd hours-Fla
1000	WAH	4357	4381	13077		NWS Offshore Forecast (plus), St.Thomas
1200	NMN	13089	6501	8764		NWS Offshore Forecast, from Portsmouth
1400	WAH	13077				NWS Offshore Forecast (plus), St Thomas
1600	BBC	5975	6175	6195	7325	World News every hour to 2400
		9590	9915	15215		....................other BBC frequencies
1800	NMN	6501	13089	8764		NWS Offshore Forecast, from Portsmouth
	CSM	7465	9440			Christian Science Monitor World News to 2000
1905	BBC	5975	6195	9915	9590	excellent financial news, again at 2005
2000	VOA	5995	7405	9455	15205	US news with Caribbean slant
2200	WAH	4357	4381	8728	13077	NWS Offshore Forecast (plus), St.Thomas
2400	NMN	4426	6501	8764		NWS Offshore Forecast, from Portsmouth

Distress and Calling:	2182	4125	6215	8291	12290	16420		HAM Hurricane Net: 14325
working 1 (Alpha):	2065	4146	6224	8294	12353	16528	22159	WLO WX Radio TeleType Broacasts:
working 2 (Bravo):	2079	4149	6227	8297	12356	16531	22162	MORSE: Hour FEC: Hour + 35 min.
working 3 (Charlie):	2638	4417	6230		12359	16534	22165	Nov-May: 4343 6416 8514 12886.5
working 4 (Delta):	2738		6516				22168	Jun-Oct.: 4462.5 6344 8534 12992

Epanded Ship to Ship Frequencies: 4 MHz: *from-to* 4000-4057 *every 3KHz.*
8 MHz: *from-to* 8101-8110, 8116-8122, 8125, 8131-8191 *every 3KHz.*

Other/Miscellaneous: 18840, 18843 18 Alpha-Bravo
22171 22 Echo
25115, 25118 25 Alpha-Bravo

APPENDIX B: NAVIGATION AIDS

CHARTS AND GUIDES

Modern yachtsmen are confronted with the problem of too much information being available. Years of cruising in the Third World where documented navigation aids are few, and Europe, where there are too many, have led me to make the following recommendations which are listed in priority order.

1. Yachting Guides

Guides, this one included, are out of date the moment they are printed. Look for guides that give you less tips on where to do your drinking and more detail on anchorages, landfall marks, sea conditions, etc. The fathom lines rarely change but, except for Lerman in the Peace and Plenty, bartenders change every three months.

Guides like Nancy and Simon Scott's *Cruising Guide to the Virgin Islands*, Doyle's *Cruising Guide to the Leeward Islands*, Doyle's *Sailor's Guide to the Windward Islands*, or Doyle's *Sailor's Guide to A Venezuela Cruise*, are essential. The venerable Hart and Stone, now Hart and Hayes, *A Cruising Guide to the Caribbean and Bahamas* is still a great book. The more guides, the better, since each author has a slightly different viewpoint. Land guides such as *Island Expedition* (Bahamas), are also invaluable for getting more out of your visits. If you cruise to Trinidad, get Doyle's Cruising *Guide to Trinidad, Tobago and Venezuela (available in January, 1994).*

2. Medium Scale Charts

These are the **charts** which get you between guides, or guide sections. For instance, if you already have a guidebook, a single chart each of the **Leeward Islands** and the **Windward Islands** is sufficient. A single chart covering all of the **Virgin Islands** is all that's needed in addition to the guidebook. A single chart of **Hispaniola** is sufficient and a chart of the **Mona Passage**, showing **Cabo Engano** on one side and **Puerto Rico**'s West Coast on the other, is desirable (DMA 25700). This latter is available, along with charts of Puerto Rico in a waterproof yachtsman's version.

The scope and shallows of the **Bahamas** requires good charts in addition to the guides. Fortunately, the *Bahamas Chart Kit* is all that you will require.

Imray charts are superior to **DMA** charts because they offer the scale a yachtsman is interested in. They often show landmarks of interest to the small boat skipper making for small harbors. They also have a format which better fits small boat nav tables, and they have excellent color contrasts.

3. Pilot Charts (or Routing Charts)

I keep a pilot chart on my chart table at all times. It is used only occasionally for plotting Caribbean crossings, tracking **Tropical Storms**. and planning passages with the current and wind data it provides. However, it is used every morning in the Bahamas to plot the **Cold Fronts** and every morning in the **Caribbean** to plot the **Tropical Waves**. It is the single most used chart aboard and is covered with pencil marks and coffee rings. The best buy the U.S. Government ever offered is the chart table-sized book of 12 *Pilot Charts of the Central American Waters* at the price of only one regular chart.

4. Large Scale Charts (covering small geographic areas)

Except in the Bahamas, these charts are only necessary where you intend exploring areas not shown in available guides. The *Bahamas Chart Kit*, along with a guidebook, is sufficient for all navigation in the Bahamas. Recent versions of the *Virgins Chart Kit*, on the other hand, provide little information beyond what is available in one medium scale chart and the Scott guide book.

5. Almanacs

Almanacs are of great use as reference works aboard. (What is the breaking strength of 5/16" BBB chain, anyway?) I have found that a single copy of *Reed's Nautical Almanac* from any year provides more useful information than *Chapman*'s and *Bowditch*'s combined. In the English Channel I was never without my tide tables and current guides. The tides were, after all, 34 feet at my moorings, and the currents reached 9 knots! In the Caribbean there's nothing to know outside the information on the Pilot Charts which basically doesn't vary year to year. In the Bahamas the daily tides are broadcast several times a day on standard AM broadcast radio. The tidal differences on Nassau rarely exceed ½ hour in the anchorages and details on tidal banks are all "local knowledge," some of which are given in this guide. High tide is at 8 o'clock local time everywhere in open sea on the day of a full moon. So add 52 minutes a day and do without current local tide tables.

6. Small Scale Charts (covering large geographical areas)

These make great wall decorations at home; at sea, I have only those needed to plot crossings and major passages. The *Bahamas Chart Kit* is sufficient for both large and small scale needs. Its chart of **Turks and Caicos** is as good as you can get. A chart of the entire Caribbean, like a Pilot Chart, does nicely for the rest.

7. Lists of Lights

These are not usually necessary to a yachtsman since the same information is on the charts and in the guides. To keep these up-to-date is an expensive and near impossible task. The sensible policy is always to assume all land and sea mark data is suspect, even if you think you're up-to-date. The marks and lights which exist in the **Bahamas** and **Caribbean** are, in fact, definitely suspect. Save the book space for fish handbooks and a good medical and pharmaceutical guide.

Compass

I had sailed for years with no more than a **compass** and **a log**. After cruising a while I found that even the log was a luxury. Knowledge of your boat's speed settles into your bones after only a few weeks of cruising. You can navigate surely and safely forever with only a compass by careful and frequent position plotting, attention to leeway, current and tidal currents, and by introducing intentional errors in order to be sure which side of a feature you make your landfall. Even the compass needn't be all that accurate, since who can hold a perfect course anyway, what with all that bobbing around?

Your compass should be mounted where you can see it comfortably from your sailing position on either tack while cruising. Bolt upright behind or beside the wheel is a racing position. The cruising steering position has a little more Zen in it. For instance, I sail scrunched up in a ball in the same corner of the cockpit on both tacks, never behind the wheel. Therefore I use a bulkhead compass.

The compass should have a large, legible scale which is well illuminated, not just bright. Some compass lights illuminate everything but the card's scale. Ideally you should have a compass which is rapidly damped. This usually means a larger and more expensive model, but not always.

Old-fashioned binnacles look nice and are useful for taking bearings of ships. But they are rarely visible from comfortable positions while seated.

Swing your compass from time to time to confirm your compass's deviation table and make sure you are using this year's variation.

Log

Mechanical sumlogs, taffrail logs, or any device which keeps a digital track of miles run is a great check on the navigator. They all fail, however, and there is no substitute for the skipper knowing intuitively how fast his yacht is going through the water.

Before the impeller is tangled in seaweed or a shark eats the rotor, take the time to calibrate your sense of the boat's speed by the old chip log method. Select a fixed length of deck viewed from your sailing position. Do a slow count on bits of foam as they pass perpendiculars of that length, checking results with actual speedo readings. Speed in knots is twice the meters travelled divided by the seconds taken.

$$\text{Knots} = \frac{2 \times \text{Meters}}{\text{seconds}}$$

Practice makes perfect and eventually you will know with a glance how fast your boat is going in all conditions.

It is an old principle of navigation that the more regular and frequent your plots are, the more sure your course. Without a sumlog, plotting intervals should become shorter. This is due to the fact that you have got to estimate average speed over the last interval and, the shorter the interval, the more accurate your estimate will be.

Sextant

The last time I used my **sextant** was crossing the Atlantic in 1979. In the Bahamas and the Caribbean they're only useful if you really know how to use them on clear and starry nights. I have a friend who is able to pull off a 3-star fix faster than a Satnav can prepare one, and be just as accurate (he can't beat a GPS). Solar and lunar sights, however, don't usually provide the kind of precision required to navigate among islands. If you are island hopping, the distances are not great and landfalls are unmistakable and inevitable in the Caribbean. On the other hand, if you are crossing the Caribbean Sea, or you are masochistically beating over the ocean to **St.Thomas**, great accuracy isn't really called for, but the sextant can be useful to confirm drift. I'm afraid sextants have gone the way of the sliderule. Still, they're neat. Every skipper should have one to play with.

In the passages described by this guide, your time and money is better spent on chart work and a good compass. You don't want to be like the "professional" delivery crew who gave up their charge on East Reef, Mayaguana, having spent all their time playing with their sextants and none of it on avoiding a lee reef. The day after the paid crew of 3 deserted their ship, by the way, it was taken off the reef whole by one salvor using the boat's own ground tackle. He turned the key and motored off with the boat.

ELECTRONIC NAVIGATION AIDS

If all you really need is a chart and a compass, then why spend the money on fancy electronic navigation aids? Well, the older I get, the mistakier I get. Once I missed the Dry Tortugas entirely because a pair of pliers left under the compass gave me a deviation of 17 degrees . . .

Nature also makes mistakes, often enhanced by the bureaucracy.. Each year there is a budgetary wrangle between the Air Force, NASA, and the Department of Commerce over hurricane surveilance responsibilities. It usually isn't resolved, but they begin to cooperate by late summer and cease abruptly on November 1st. If you don't believe it, watch the newpapers carefully as June 1 approaches.

December 19th, 1984, the **NWS** forecast continuing fine weather. We up-anchored and sailed for Georgetown from the north shore of Caicos. They came back 6 hours later with a hurricane warning for ***hurricane** Lilly* which they placed exactly 90 miles off my stern and blowing me northwest into the islands. *Lilly* was a small, tight 'cane, out of season and bearing no telltale feeder trails. She broke up early but spawned several days of gales throughout the area. *Lilly* was only a hiccup for Mother Nature, of no interest on Capitol Hill, but a major surprise to small boats.

When that hurricane forecast was received I was already on the run before it, surfing down ten footers with the log pegged at eight knots, and me, between curses, wondering what the heck was going on. For 36 hours we slowed our progress toward Exuma Sound, which, with only raging cuts to leeward, would be a **deathtrap** in those conditions, by zig-zagging down breaking waves in continual darkness.

My oval of navigational uncertainty became so big, I still don't know if we passed the Plana Cays and the surrounding reefs on the west or the east. Three months later I had a **Satnav** on board.

In general, the more navigation aids, electronic or not, the better. Bless you for being affluent enough to afford them, clever enough to select the right ones from the welter of black boxes on the market, and patient enough to maintain them. Which devices will serve you the most on the way south?

Radio

VHF, AM/FM

VHF is required. Get an international switch and lots of channels. See the chapter on "Using the Radio." Of course you have AM/FM aboard with cassette or CD player. You should also have a hand-sized portable with a fishing rod type extendable antennae in the emergency locker with full batteries. If you have to abandon ship you can listen to all the religious stations that dot the Caribbean. But more important, you can use it as a highly reliable radio direction finder, homing in on the rock stations. Perhaps the combination of direction and religion will save you.

SSB RECEIVER

For following the **National Weather Service** reports and the various cruiser nets you must have a radio capable of receiving **SSB**. A cheap portable with a "BFO" switch which can receive the frequencies is usually sufficient. Before you pay $300 for a Sony, look at more professional gear which may even be cheaper and much better.

SINGLE SIDEBAND (SSB) TRANSCEIVER

If sailing in company and leap frogging each other this helps you keep in touch with your friends. It also helps you keep up with the rumor mill which is grinding between the cruisers on your path so you don't feel such a stranger when you arrive. Be careful about weather information received, however, as well as talk of piracy, revolutions, the sky falling in, and so on. Remember this is an entertainment medium. Pure marine SSBs with fixed channels are usually very powerful. The new breed of synthesized digital ham transceivers are less powerful but can be modified to permit marine transmission. See Appendix A: Radio Frequencies.

HAM

It certainly gets you invited to a lot of hamfests. And think of the telephone bills you'll save if you were going to have any. Whether a Rowdy or a Good Citizen, you will find a team to root for on the morning Deputy Dawg Show out of **St. Croix** on 14313. During emergencies the HAM nets are of great help.

RADIO DIRECTION FINDERS

Unless you have a double loop, mast-mounted antennae tunable to AM, FM and VHF, forget it. In the Caribbean, there aren't enough airports and no marine beacons. Anyway, those low frequencies are only good for homing on as any fix available from three shore based senders will have a cocked hat larger than the gap between you and the shore. I buried my last RDF in the North Sea.

RADAR

As with all electronics, think of your ampere usage and make sure you can handle it. Some can suck juice like a water maker. An old radar, properly installed on robust mountings with indestructible, high fidelity waveguides, or a modern unit with data communication from a dome-mounted computer, can be a dream come true for coastal cruising. In the Caribbean, the radar isn't for fog, it's for confirming landfalls, finding buoys (whenever there are any), and "lordy, lordy," plying a windward coast so close you can shake hands with the natives. I haven't got one but I am indeed envious. I'm waiting until they're made tiny—and cheap.

For the single-hander, a well-tuned four-mile radar with a "fence" function can help keep watch on crossings.

RADAR DETECTORS

They work, but ships often don't use their radar in the open sea, and if you're coasting or in a shipping lane, you better darn well keep your own lookout. Besides, these things chirp at such distances that you're never free of an alarm despite no ships in sight. If you squelch them to eliminate ships over the horizon, the controls are so rinky-dink you will squelch out the guy who is about to run you down.

RADAR REFLECTORS

Yachting Monthly showed the futility of anything but welded radar reflectors and the Japanese "goat's eye" solid type in a study done in 1978. We repeated their tests in Antibes the next year and got equally dismal results. Even the manufacturers produce reflectors that can't be mounted in the proper "catch water" attitude. I had used a fender full of aluminum chaff once until I discovered my mast steps were a better target. Radar transponders would be great if only you could get the radar officers to look at the radar within the time you've got between acquisition and collision. There is a Norwegian reflector out which is in a small tube, and reportly, it is quite good.

To calibrate your boat as a target, talk to seagoing tugs. They usually keep a good radar watch and the ones I've met will enjoy helping you.

If you haven't got a tiki aboard you might as well hoist the old radar reflector, it's marginally more effective in avoiding collisions. Better to keep a good watch.

LORAN

Great for finding Ft. Lauderdale. Super for crossing the Great Bahama Bank. Depending on your machine's algorithms and tuner fidelity, Loran's can be reasonably accurate in the Exumas by using the TD's with corrections. (Though it's beyond me why anyone would want a machine to tell them where they might be when they can simply look out their window to know for sure.) Below the Exumas, the Loran stations, like Voice of America, if received at all, can give biased information and that's dangerous. An acquaintance swears his worked all the way to St. Thomas. But he also claims to sail 35 degrees to the real wind. Systems are available which receive corrections from a linked Satnav with each satellite fix. The Loran then will provide accurate Lat/Long output between Satnav fixes in case you can't do a DR that's good for 90 minutes.

GPS

Outside of a compass light and a depth sounder, the single, most valuable electronic aid to navigation available. They come in a variety of models. Cheap is best. You both save money and eliminate confusion during operation. All GPS units seem to have the worst human factors built into their consoles since spark advance was eliminated from steering wheels. "Hoo-boy!," says the engineer, "if we connect the freemis to the gizzis, and you press these six buttons at once, you'll get the Gregorian date expressed in hexidecimal." "Grrreat!" explodes the marketeer, and into the machine it goes.

The more expensive models are loaded up with inane "functional add-ons." These are doo-hickeys the manufacturers make to keep up unit price in an expanding market. As an example consider 900 waypoints. Unless you're a fisherman or a smuggler on regular and complicated routes, you shouldn't need more than a few waypoints. Where you came from, where you're going (with a couple of options), a couple of real waypoints, and the location of a weather feature you may want range and bearing on. Leave one or 2 waypoints to play with and you've justified 10.

When road-based transportation and shipping fleets install GPS receivers en masse, then relatively low-cost, low-function units will be available to the yachtsman. Until then, these are expensive devices.

Plugging in your auto pilot for following routes of waypoints can be hazardous to your health. Course alterations should remain the captain's prerogative even in these modern times.

LIST OF GPS CAUTIONS

a. While coasting, make your own fixes regularly by compass bearings and confirm with the GPS.

b. While crossing, keep estimated positions, *not* DR's, which should include current, leeway, tide, variation and deviation.

c. Ignore entrance waypoints given by "helpful" yachties down to the hundredth of a mile (20 yards). The future will see many yachts motored onto reefs while headed to waypoint of an entrance or seabouy. Get out your chart. Step up to a mile off of the entrance, and make that your waypoint, from where you will go on visual.

DEPTH SOUNDER

The depth sounder, or **fathometer**, is a much under-used tool among yachties. This navigation aid is second only to the compass. A reliable digital depthfinder in the cockpit is great for coasting. Tack in to 20 fathoms, tack out to 50, and so on, while coasting. Additionally, there is good evidence that sounders left on even when off soundings, deter broaching marlins and whales from coming up under the boat.

Finding your position off a coast where everything looks the same is child's play by using the **Chain of Soundings** method.

CHAIN OF SOUNDINGS METHOD

This is a method of navigation that many of us use unconsciously while coasting in order to confirm the boat's position. With chart in hand, keep mental track of the soundings shown on the fathometer. If the readings of the fathometer do not agree with your expectations gained from the chart, you have reason to wonder where you really are.

By sailing a straight line and taking soundings at regular intervals one can arrive at a "signature" of the bottom which usually identifies only that line over that bottom. A somewhat complex, but unequivocal, way of doing it is to plot the readings to scale on a piece of clear plastic or tracing paper. Then move the tracing about on the chart until you have a match. Of course the bottom must vary, and sometimes the line is be very long and you have to get it all done before you've left the area and become lost again. As long as I am on soundings I prefer to just make mental note of the fathom lines as I cross them and never lose my chain of soundings in the first place.

AUTOPILOT

The **autopilot** is an absolutely necessary piece of equipment on any cruising boat. The trip to windward can be tiring enough without having to face the tyranny of the wheel. Autopilots are available today for ampere-poor sailing craft which have minimal current requirements: 3-5 amperes on duty, negligible current draw on standby. Most sailboats can sail themselves close-hauled with a lashed helm and balanced rig, but the autopilot handles motor sailing better than a crew could. For returning downwind you might want to snap on a self steering device such as the Aries wind vane. If you have both refrigeration and an autopilot, a fixed mount wind generator can handle the load to windward if the motor isn't running. Downwind you may not get the zaps from either alternator or wind generator to keep both the autopilot and the refrigerator going.

WEATHERFAX

There is too much information made available through the fax and even the scheduling problem can turn into a nightmare (upper level charts, suface charts, satellite photos). If at all possible go for a solution which combines the fax with a computer (as if your life wasn't complicated enough already). With a connection to a database you will be able to store only the images which relate to your navigational problem. Your computer will enable you to escape the machine while it regurgitates its endless rigamaroles on unusual sectors of the planet.

Compared to the **NWS** radio advisories, the fax data tends to cover very large areas. In reality **weatherfaxes** transmit the source materials of the NWS forecasters you hear on the radio. Those guys have studied for years and went on to earn an incredible buck reducing their macro plots of micro data to a carefully considered verbal report with which mariners can make decisions within local areas. To try to second guess their interpretations seems dangerous. To do so at the exclusion of their summarized analyses may be deadly.

If you do have a computer, you can receive and store weather charts, satellite pictures (2 US, 12 Russian), and even the telexes of the Offshore Reports. Finally, if you're a HAM, you can participate in bulletin-boarding through your SSB radio. Devices and software to do this are on the market. I use Software Systems Consulting's product (telephone 714-498-5784).

Once again, gadgets are great. If you can afford them and if you can use them, go to it. But listen to the NWS reports on NMN anyway, huh?

MAIL

It is always best to use **General Delivery**, the Virgin Islands notably excepted. Cafés, bars and marinas go out of business, change owners and policies. With the possible exception of the U.S. Virgins, it is best to let the official postal system hold your mail for pickup. They are generally incorruptible, provide sorting and secure warehousing services which are their business. They are reasonably conscious of an obligation to you with respect to your mail. These things cannot be said about a bar, restaurant or hotel where your mail will be pawed over by hundreds of anxious cruisers, each one dripping wet and anxious to get to the bottom of the pile.

Your mail will be more conscientiously looked for by postal officials around the world if you follow this simple routine the first and every time you ask for it.

> Face the clerk squarely and look directly into his or her eyes. Smile brightly. Say "Good morning. How are you?" Pause and look like you're about to say good-bye, that you had only come there to make them happy. Then, with a shrug, remember you had minor business and, regretfully, wonder if they couldn't help you find your mail. Give them a card with your name written in large block letters. If your name is Van Somethingorother, tell them sometimes it's filed under *Ess*. This gambit works miracles everywhere. Even in the U.S. Virgins.

In the **Dominican Republic** and **Venezuela** it's *Lista de Correos* (LEE-stah day koh-RAY-ohs). In Puerto Rico use "General Delivery." Since P.R. is bilingual, the clerk will be scanning for General Delivery, not Lista de Correos, after he sees your gringo face. In the U.S. Virgin Islands it's safest to use a business address. Try one of the services like Business World or Home Port.

Reckon with U.S. to Bahamas, one week, unless it looks like a parcel; U.S. to Puerto Rico, 4 days; U.S. to Puerto Plata, one to 2 weeks; U.S. to the Virgin Islands, maybe never. The U.S.P.O. General Delivery will hold U.S. mail only 10 days, foreign mail one month. Other countries are more or less stringent (several weeks in France, Venezuela indefinite), so be there!

HOW TO SEND MAIL

Never make letter mail in bunches look like a parcel! Tell your forwarder to separate the mail into two or three small envelopes so yours doesn't get shuffled off as a package to customs or parcel post for three weeks. This is especially possible in **Nassau**. You should know exactly how many envelopes are coming so you don't wait around for the third packet that never comes. If Aunt Lizzy rebels at sending two empty envelopes because there's only one letter to send, but your instructions are always send 3, then fire Aunt Lizzy and hire Uncle Claude.

A tip about avoiding local taxes on parts shipped into **Puerto Rico**: send it Priority Mail or Air Parcel Post. UPS has, in the past, been difficult to deal with. Federal Express will not charge taxes if your shipping address includes the words "BOAT IN TRANSIT" and you give the driver a copy of your ship's registration. Priority Mail may also help ensure delivery in the Virgins. Never, *never* send checks so they can be seen by handlers. *Anywhere*. If they can't be cashed, they can always be sold at discount to someone who thinks they can be cashed.

It may sound nautical to address yourself as:

Captain John J. Courageous
Aboard the good ship S/Y *Chicken Little*
General Delivery

Your mail will almost certainly be stacked under Captain, or Aboard, or sent to the Littles' household. Try this for better results:

John Courageous
General Delivery

Aside from the pretentiousness of such nautical addressing, it makes you an easy mark. What do yacht people ever get except checks and bills? Their kids never write!

As you paw through the mail boxes yourself at the various bars and hotels along your route, you will notice how non-uniform all those yachtie addresses are and how difficult they are to sort sensibly. If you have problems, then think about the Third World postal employees who might not spell as well as you, nor scan as well as you, nor have an inkling that addresses can be so complicated.

In Latin America, the middle name is often the main name for sorting. So leave out middle names unless you are John X. Smith.

TELEPHONE

It's usually easiest and cheaper to call collect or with **credit card**. You can dial direct from any street booth almost anywhere, including the **Dominican Republic**. It is now possible to obtain telephone credit cards in the U.S. without having a permanent home phone installation. You are billed according to usage, but there may be monthly limits, such as $100. This is sufficient for most cruisers unless, like Superman, they're running a business from the phone booths of the world.

The area code in the Caribbean is 809 and the country code is the North American code: 1. However, some of the islands and **Venezuela** use local area codes for intra-Caribbean direct services, so don't be confused by these. The system in the **Dominican Republic** operates like the U.S. system but they don't accept credit cards over the phone. If you start speaking in English they will answer you in English. The booths in **Puerto Rico** have instructions in English.

Most telephone companies in the islands are offering facsimile services, putting telex/telegrams out of style. When you strip your calls of all the howdy-dos, you usually have only a message to transmit and the tele-fax is unequivocal and lots cheaper.

TELEPHONES IN THE DOMINICAN REPUBLIC

Telephone communications are excellent in big cities. Use any street booth to dial direct (0 + area code + number) and speak in English when the operator comes on to give your call instructions. Use the phone company's office (CODETEL) if you want to pay. Every CODETEL office has booths which direct-dial anywhere in the world. Just dial 1 and your number. When you hang up, an English bill will be prepared for you by computer. CODETEL also has Telefax service at their offices that's too cheap not to use. Buy your kids a fax machine for Christmas, and save money on your phone bills.

TELEPHONES IN VENEZUELA

As in St. Lucia and Martinique, the phones in Venezuela are becoming credit card oriented. You buy a thin, plastic card with magnetic stripe at various outlets, mostly tourist locations. You insert this card into the phone machines in lieu of coins. A digital display tells you how much money the card has left on it as the time of your call ticks away. Neat.

Also neat and useful is the fact that the decrement by which your card is ticked down is left on the card when you're done, never decrementing to zero. Don't throw away those used up large denomination cards. They're worth local calls. On the other hand, they're at least worth a pile of local calls which, of course, have smaller decrements.

On the mainland in Venezuela or other than at a tourist resort these phones are hard to find. One must usually go to an IPOSTEL office and wait in line to place the call. The personnel are usually friendly and helpful but the system has its shortcomings. I recall Moscow being better equipped and organized in 1973—and that's saying something.

APPENDIX D: CUSTOMS AND CLEARANCES

TIPS ON CLEARING CUSTOMS EASILY

In general, your experience with clearance officials will be dependent on your presentation. Have your boat and yourselves presentable. Have your papers in order. Smile, be honest, friendly and courteous. Never bribe. You may get in trouble and, once started, it never stops.

The customs guys all over the world are trained to use their sixth senses. If you're tired from the trip and harried by the hassle of mooring in a strange place, you may give odd responses to them. Get some sleep before dealing with guys who are just doing a job. Re-read the section on Pirates! Clear into ports which "specialize" in yachts, or anchor around the corner with your yellow Q-flag flying, and get a good night's sleep before entering.

In places where they don't have many yachts, you must realize that you are an intrusion on their management of a busy port and are a pain in the neck for low-paid working men. If you think the Dominican Republic, for instance, is in dire need of your big time cruising kitty bucks and they should receive you like a major relief to the national debt, then think again. Puerto Plata Province has more hotel rooms than all of Puerto Rico, for which they get up to $200 a night from each passenger aboard the constant stream of jumbo jets laden with European and Canadian tourists. Some waiting may be required, as there is only one man available from each of the Customs, Port Authority and Immigration Services. They may be handling a freighter or a cruise ship or be at lunch or a girlfriend's, so just be patient.

THE BAHAMAS

Clearing into the **Bahamas** is getting more expensive. Coming from the south it's usually a freebie. Recently, however, the anti-drug smuggling effort has required boardings and charges have been added for use of marina docks. Clearing in at the **Nassau** fuel docks while watering up and refueling can be cheaper. Clearing out of the Bahamas isn't necessary and they don't want to do it. Refer to the Gun Cay and Cat Cay sections for more Customs and Immigration recommendations relative to the Bahamas.

TURKS AND CAICOS

The procedures in these islands vary from season to season, and even from island to island. Once, coming from the south, I was cleared in by a lovely young lady of high school age in the government house on **Salt Cay**. Often I was charged nothing at all in **Sapodilla Bay**. Once, in **Turtle Cove**, I was charged $49 for a 16-hour visit to the country to pick up a crew member. The founder of the Sapodilla Bay Acquatic Center asked me to accompany him to a meeting with the head of immigration. He wanted to discuss the rules for clearance and the requirements of the yachts using his facility. We were told that the rule was to charge overtime and transportation for officials (even if you transported yourself to them and not vice-versa) if your boat, upon arrival, was within their territorial limits outside their office working hours of 0830-1200 and 1300-1630. A little arithmetic and chart work will show these conditions shall be met 100 percent of the time. He grinned, and the meeting was over. My host left the island not long after.

The officials, the inhabitants and the yachties at **Provo** will all press on you the *inflexible gospel* of how it really works the day you arrive, as though it always has and always will work that way. They'll tell you, "Oh, that's just one person's experience one time." It's been my experience a dozen times or more. Just smile and pay. See also the section on **Sapodilla Bay**.

HAITI

Ports of entry on the north coast are **Cap Haïtien** and **Fort Liberté**. At each port you will be boarded by 4 or 5 officials. Coffee in the morning or a cold drink in the afternoon is appropriate while all the paperwork gets accomplished. Any firearms will be taken for safe keeping until you leave. The costs of clearing in will depend on the yacht, but in any case should be only a few dollars unless you arrive on a Sunday or outside office hours, which are variable. There are no costs for clearing out.

Cap Haïtien is a large commercial port which has seen busier days. A yacht will have no problem getting full attention clearing in. Moor on the south side of the main pier between any freighters on the east end of the long quai and small fishing vessels on the west end.

Fort Liberté has had the same *Capitain du Port* for many years, M. Herns Calixte, whose office is at the foot of the old town dock. The skipper should dinghy in with his papers and ferry out the officials if they haven't already found transport. The dinghy dock of the Bayaha Hotel, 200 yards to the south, may also be used and offers the convenience of a good ladder.

THE DOMINICAN REPUBLIC

Bear in mind that the D.R. is not a yachting country. For many years it maintained itself drug- and violence-free by applying maritime conventions rigorously. As far as procedures are concerned, your yacht is a tanker. Like the U.S., they clear foreign vessels in and out of every port and, theoretically, you are allowed to go ashore only where a customs house exists.

If you can't manage the dock in a stiff breeze, the skipper should row ashore alone with all his papers and without his firearms and follow the instructions of the uniformed, and normally armed, person in charge (i.e., not a khaki-clad dock worker hoping to get a job washing your boat).

With courtesy and understanding it will all be handled easily. For instance, don't wave at them and go below for an extended time. Stay in sight and use your actions to communicate by clearly showing your preparations to come ashore to the official doing the waving.

I heard a yachtie complain that the *Commandante* was irritated at him. No wonder! He interrupted his breakfast to do them a courtesy between visiting a tanker and a cruise ship and the idiot yachtie went below to have a shower and his own breakfast before coming ashore. Needless to say, under those circumstances the Commandante and his officers wander off out of the sun and don't eagerly come back for you.

Anyway, if you follow this guide you arrive in **Luperón, Puerto Plata** or **Manzanillo** in the early morning and can easily back up to the pier in the prevailing calm. To stay at the dock is your decision. They might even prefer you anchor out.

The little cards they gave you when you came into the Bahamas work as Bahamian clearance out devices while entering the D.R., but if you go into Caicos, you should have clearance out from there.

There is a tourist card charge of $10 for each passport entering the country by any means. Sometimes they run out of forms. Then it may become $5, or even be free. Of course the SSB nets will report it was free, so the next yachties to pay $10 a head can report up and down the islands that they got ripped off by gun-toting officials. There is a port fee for each boat entering the country. In Luperón it was recently $10.

To extend your visa, simply take it to the immigration officers *before* it expires. They'll extend it without question as often as you like, unless you are an undesirable. They're nonchalant about how long you and your boat are there because (a) you spend money, and (b) if you're a bad actor, they'll find out and make you wish you'd never come. See also each section on the individual D.R. ports.

PUERTO RICO AND THE VIRGIN ISLANDS

Non-US vessels, and vessels with non-resident aliens aboard (what Americans call foreigners, I'm afraid), must check into Puerto Rico at **Mayaguez**. The harbor at Mayaguez is for large ships. The pier may cause damages to your yacht. Holding is poor in the dredged channel. Anchor between red buoys numbers 8 and 10 on the spoil bank, which is poor holding by definition, but shallower. Leave for **Boquerón** before the wind comes up. It can be gusty and on-shore in this wide open bay. Arrive before 8 a.m. to be at Customs when they open in order to be under way by 10 a.m.

US vessels can clear Customs in **Puerto Rico** by phone from their landfall. On the west coast call 831-3342,43; on the south coast call 841-3130,31; on the east coast call 863-0950, 4075, 0811, or 0102; in **Vieques** call 741-8366; and in **Culebra** call 742-3531. Outside office hours call the Customs office in **San Juan** at 253-4533,34,35, or 36. US vessels coming from Puerto Rico don't need to clear into the US **Virgin Islands**, but going back to Puerto Rico they do.

While Customs, a profitable bureaucracy, goes out of its way to provide courteous and efficient service at the convenience of the returning citizen, US Immigration maintains a confusing, often belligerent, stance despite many attempts to obtain clarification. Specifically, Immigration states they have "the right to inspect the passports" of returning citizens. The officer in Mayaguez interprets this to require the physical presence of crew and boat in Mayaguez harbor, though he does not leave his office to see the boat. His policy is unwritten, unique in my experience, and it is arbitrarily enforced.

In the **British Virgin Islands** check in at **Jost Van Dyke** or at the Virgin Gorda Yacht Harbour at **Spanish Town**. Never check in at **Roadtown** and avoid the Customs at **West End, Tortola**, like the plague. In both of these places, 2 out of 3 trips will go smooth, but 1 of the 3 will find you tangled in a fine mess of charter people and cops. There are various official money-making schemes afoot in the BVI's which may catch yachts in charter boat snares. Get all the current stories in the USVIs before leaving, and, check in at my recommended spots of Spanish Town or Jost Van Dyke to avoid hassle and extra expense.

THE LEEWARD AND WINDWARD ISLANDS

The British islands give the most hassle, the French and Dutch are ok.

Clearing in and out from the English-speaking islands is a new procedure every year. At best, the officials in the main harbors are brusque. At worst, they intentionally hassle you, not for money, but for the fun of it. This is only true in the English-speaking islands, however. It's best to steer clear of commercial harbors and their official hassles. Go instead to the tourist harbors like **English Harbor**, **Antiqua**, or **Rodney Bay**, **St. Lucia**. There you will usually be greeted by less antagonistic and more tourist-friendly officials.

If making a rapid passage down the islands and not going ashore, there is no need to check in. Fly a Q-flag all the way down as a declaration that you haven't cleared in. No one can accuse you of sneaking around if, by chance, an official with his hand out boards you while you are at an overnight anchorage.

Costs for cruising permits seem to vary each year, or perhaps with the official. Some countries choose to levy these, others don't. Some levy "cruising permit" charges, depending on your estimate of the time you will spend there. Going ashore one night only while passing **St. Vincent** could cost you some bucks. Once again, check into the tourist spots. In St. Vincent that would be **Bequia**. Current information should be sought from a current guidebook for the area, but for the official policy ask an official for a brochure describing the procedure and costs.

GRENADA

Get your Venezuelan visa almost anywhere, but if you do it in **St. Georges, Grenada**, you won't be faced with a rush to get there before it expires because you spent more time than you had reckoned with visiting other islands. Clearing in and out of Grenada is simple and can be done at the crumbling Grenada Yacht Services facility in the lagoon. To get to the Venezuelan embassy take a taxi from the GYS dock, or tie your dinghy up at the St. George's Yacht Club catwalk on the eastern shore and walk to the embassy. Your visa photo can be had quickly and cheaply at a little shop below the fort in town (tel. #1722). In **San Juan, Puerto Rico**, you will have to pay for the visa. If you will be in Grenada anyway, it's better to get your visa there.

VENEZUELA

Here's how to get your visa in San Juan. ***First***, send a fax to the *Capitanía del Puerto* at your destination. If a voice answers, tell them to put on the fax tone or to give you the number of their fax (*tono de fax, por favor, or, cual es el número de fax?*)

Pampatar, Margarita:011 (58) 81-677454.
Puerto La Cruz: 011 (58) 81-677932, 011 (58) 81-677952.
All of Venezuela:011 (58) 2-509-2722 or 011 (58) 2-509-2881.

Include in the fax:

- Boat's name, registration number and nationality.
- Length of boat.
- Full Name of owner and/or captain.
- Estimated date of entry and estimated duration of stay.
- Radio frequency bands used.

Second, present yourself/selves at the Venezuelan Consulate on the 6th floor of the Mercantil Plaza Building, Ponce de Leon Avenue on the south side of bridge between Hato Rey and Santurce in San Juan (809-766-4250). Bring with you:

- A copy of the fax with proof it was sent.
- Ship's papers.
- A copy of your credit card.

For each visa bring a 2"x2" passport photo, your passport and $30 cash.

If all is in order you shall be instructed to deposit the cash in their bank account across the street. When you return they will stamp your passport with an entry visa valid for one or more entries sometime in the future. It is best to get an entry visa valid as long as possible. It can often be valid for a year. The actual duration of your stay shall be established at the border when they stamp it in your passport. Stay beyond the specified duration, and you shall be asked to pay fees to extend your stay in country regardless of how long your entry visa may be valid. The boat's permitted time in country, probably for six months, also shall be established at the border.

Clearing in and out in Venezuela can be complex with many places to go and everyone, including the taxi drivers, with their hands out for servicing yachts. Agent services are often available for yachts. For a few dollars they will take care of everything for you while you drink beer under a palm tree. I recommend using them for anything rather than facethe hassles. In **Puerto La Cruz**, call Marisol on VHF channel 16. In Pampatar inquire at the beach restaurant, or call Venezuela Marine Supply on VHF channel 16.

Venezuela has an economy in crisis which is government controlled. From time to time things happen like soldiers in combat boots boarding you and telling you that you have too much coffee, or beer aboard. Keep your cool and give them what they want: often just some coffee or beer. And a chance to see a yacht. The alternative is to learn all the export controls before shopping, and they change every month. See also the section on "Refitting".

Call ahead to the Trinidad and Tobago Yacht Club on VHF channel 16 for the latest scoop on how to enter. It changes. With no advice to the contrary, act like a big ship as follows:

After entering **Port of Spain** harbor, motor eastward close to the docks, past the seagoing tugs, until you see the ricketiest, tackiest little wooden wharf to be seen. It will front a small, wooden building where Immigration hides out. Follow their lead for the rest of the procedure in clearing in.

It can be hilarious if you've got your sense of humor. If not, don't go. Port of Spain has exponentially growing yacht traffic, and exponentially growing number of functionaries from many ministries, all looking to serve you (or at least fill their day). Each official knows some of his department's procedures but none of the others', nor will he know the overall procedure. Rather than ask, "Where do I go from here?" it's best to take your currently assigned factotum by the arm and say, "Can you show me to the next step, please?" He or she undoubtedly will use the opportunity to schedule a car from the government car pool, which will take another half-day. You get a free tour of the town with pleasant company. Don't knock it.

Nonetheless, the officials at Port of Spain are the nicest you will run across in the whole Caribbean, and the people all over the island are uniformly cheerful, friendly and outgoing. Don't be scared off by their high crime statistics—unless you are married to a Trinidadian. Most violence is domestic.

The most abused word among American yachties going south is "confiscation." When one yachtsman sues another for damages after anchor dragging and dock whomping in a storm, the sued boat is put under a lien to prevent it from leaving port, the easiest way to avoid paying the damages. This is a normal and, for fellow boaties, often entertaining practice at all U.S. marinas. When it occurs in **Puerto Plata** or **Cumaná**, the SSB channels buzz with talk of the locals "confiscating" yachts. While headed home to the D.R., I often meet disgruntled gun nuts headed north. Like Yosemite Sam, they wave their arms and stomp about and yell, "They CONfiscated mah WE'p'ns!"

All countries can hold onto your arms and even your bonded stores while you're in port, the U.S. included. They may decline to check your arms depending on their own criteria, such as the length of your stay, security of your bonded locker, the length of your hair and so on. The U.S., where military assault rifles are hawked on every street corner, doesn't bother. The **Dominican Republic** and **Trinidad** always bother. The D.R. will check in your weapons on arrival and return them on departure at each port of entry. In the D.R., weapons are not confiscated and are always returned promptly in good condition. Once I even had mine cleaned (because they'd fired it). The **British Virgin Islands** and **Turks and Caicos** often want to check in your firearms as well.

Some boats have had their fancy weapons turn up "missing" when they went back to clear out, but never in Trinidad or the D.R. The best insurance against such official piracy is to use the same procedure advised above to avoid hassles: Check in at yacht-only ports of entry wherever possible. Better yet, don't have any arms aboard your vessel.

Finally, make sure your clearance-in papers are correct with respect to serial numbers and ammunition counts. If it's all checked on the way out and mistakes have been made, you're in for a major bureaucratic nightmare. Bullet counts are often off by one and corroded serial numbers are easily misread. Get it right on the way in. Especially in the **Bahamas** if you are an American.

If you sit long at a dock where gun-checking goes on, you become aware how some yachts look like mercenaries out to do in the government.

(See also the section on Culture Shock.)

APPENDIX E: SPANGLISH FOR CRUISERS

The following method to achieve rapid pidgin Spanish, or *Span-glish* as it's sometimes called, is only a guide, not, God forbid, instruction in Spanish. The objective here is to permit the totally uninitiated to get things done ashore by employing a pidgin Spanish which can be learned in minutes.

Below is a list of names of things with which the reader joins necessary modifiers and a verb to form a sentence which then can be phonetically read aloud in American English to a listener who will understand it as Spanish. Got that?

Cruisers should worry more about pronunciation than spelling or grammar, since many of the people they talk to ashore can barely read or write anyway. Showing written statements may get you a donation faster than comprehension.

You can successfully talk in nouns only, using your hands for verbs, and pointing around to find descriptors of size, location, color and so on.

All the correct grammar in the world doesn't help the perennial yachtie who goes all over town looking for the hardware store (*ferreteria*) by asking for the furry-TARRY-uh instead of the FAIR-ray-tah-REE-ah. After a few days this type usually goes and sulks on his boat, sails out of the country, and tells stories on the SSB how you can't get anything there and the people are evil.

To accurately name the thing you want, you must string together several items from the list of names of things. For instance: "motor head bolt." I know it's not called that, but keep it simple. Nothing transliterates.

Talk like an Indian in an old movie: "Ugh! Me need'em motor head bolt." In Latin lingoes you put nouns that modify each other in backward sequence with a *de* (day) between them. A head bolt is bolt of a head. A motor head is a head of a motor. Thus, your movie Indian might say "Ugh! Me need'em bolt of head of motor." So this becomes: "*Oye! Mi necessita tornillo de cabeza de motor,*" (me nay-say-SEE-tah tore-KNEE-yo day kah-BAY-tsah day moh-TOR). Look it up in the following pages.

In this example the pronoun is wrong and the verb is third person, but no matter, you will be clearly understood when quickly reading the phonetics aloud.

Verbs and modifiers are given later for the intermediate student. Those aspiring to black belts can dabble in pronouns and prepositions after that, ensuring massive miscommunication. For now, let's go in search of a bolt for your motor's head. Read on . . .

NAMES OF THINGS

The words given below are often not the most "correct" Spanish but will be useful throughout Latin America because I show common American usage as opposed to European usage. That's no surprise. American English is, after all, significantly different from British English. For example, the word *maní* (mah-KNEE) is used for "peanuts" instead of the Castillano *cacahuete* (kah-kah-WAY-taye). Both have Indian origins but American Latins never heard *cacahuete* in their lives.

Other words, like *suiche* (SWEET-chaye) for "switch," are chosen because, all other parameters being equal, the English-speaking boater can remember it easier than other names for switches. After all, *suiche* is real Spanglish. It is also the most commonly used form.

The words below are spelled with "phony phonetics" rather than have the reader learn the Spanish pronunciation or the international semanticist symbology. I chose to mimic the Spanish with written American English as it is commonly spoken.

A speaker of general American will give a good imitation of American Spanish when simply reading aloud the phonetic words below with good emphasis on the capitalized syllables. English words are used when their American pronunciation best simulates the Spanish (e.g., ace and day). Roll your R's if you can, but don't sweat it: some Latins don't either.

I spell the American "A" sound "aye," and "I" is spelled "eye." Just read what you see. The Spanish vowels are usually aspirated, that is, using lots of breath. In Spanish, "O" is pronounced "Oh!," "A" is pronounced "Ah!" (as in "father"), "I" is "Eeee...," "E" is "Aye" (as in "say"), "U" is "Oooo..." Thus you will read below -oh, -ah, -ee, -aye and -oo. Just say them in English.

When listening to Spanish, be careful of "V" and "B." Both sound the same and they are pronounced somewhere between the two. This is true of American Spanish versus the Spanish spoken in Europe. The American hispanics will also drop their "S" sounds. The fewer "S" sounds, the less educated the speaker, normally. It's kind of like "dese" and "dose" in American dialects, but it can really buffalo a foreigner when words whose principal sounds are *esses* are spoken entirely free of the *esses*.

Therefore, when the street urchins ask you if you "peek a panich?" they're not asking you to peek at a dirty postcard, but they are asking you if you "speak Spanish."

Almost all Spanish speakers add a vowel in front of initial "S" sounds when speaking English, because that's what Spanish does. And when the waiter adds an "E" and drops the "S," "spaghetti" can come out "up a Ghetty!" Don't be offended if that's your name.

You'll also notice "Y" is often a "J" sound and double "LL" is a "Y" sound. If you're Judy Yeltsin, they'll spell it Yudy Lleltsin.

Now! Having said all that, here's the list:

acetone	*acetona*	ah-say-TONE-ah
adapter	*adaptador*	ah-DOPT-ah-DOOR
air filter	*filtro de aire*	FEEL-tro day EYE-ray
air vent	*ventil de aire*	vent-EEL day EYE-ray
alternator	*alternador*	all-tern-ah-DOOR
aluminium	*aluminio*	ah-loo-ME-knee-um
amperes	*amperes*	am-PAY-rees
anchor	*ancla*	AN-klah
anchorage	*anclaje*	an-KLAH-hey
avocado	*aguacate*	ah-gwah-KAH-taye
awning	*toldo*	TOLD-oh
back	*posterior*	post-tier-ee-OR
bananas	*guineo*	ee-NAY-oh
band-aid	*curita*	koo-REE-tah
batten	*iston de day vela*	lee-STONE VAYE-lah
battery	*bateria*	bah-taye-REE-ah
beam, boat's	*manga*	MAHN-gah
bearing	*bearing*	BEAR-ring
bilge	*sentina*	sen-TEEN-ah
block	*bloque*	BLOW-kay
block (pulley)	*polea, motón*	poe-LAY-ah, moh-TONE
block & tackle	*tecle*	TAYE-clay
boat	*bote*	BOAT-aye
boathook	*botavara*	BOAT-ah-VAH-rah
bollard	*hierro*	E-AIR-roe
bolt	*tornillo*	tore-KNEE-yoh
boom	*botalón*	BOAT-ah-LONE
bottom paint	*pintura de fondo*	peen-TOO-rah day FONE-dough
bow, boat's	*proa*	PRO-ah

brass	*latón*	lah-TONE
bread	*pan*	PAHN
breakwater	*rompeolas*	rome-pay-OH-las
bronze	*bronce*	BRONE-tsay
bulb	*bombilla*	bom-BEE-yah
buoy	*boya*	BOH-jah
bushing	-	BOO-shing
butter	*mantequilla*	mahn-taye-KEY-ya
can	*lata*	LAH-tah
case	*caja*	KAH-hah
catalyst	*activador*	act-tee-vah-DOOR
caulking	*calafate*	cal-ah-FAH-taye
caulking putty	*masilla*	mass-SEE-yah
celery	*apio*	AH-pee-oh
certificate	*certificado*	sair-tee-fee-KAH-dough
chain	*cadena*	kah-DAY-nah
chain plate	*cadenote*	kah-day-NOH-taye
charger	*cargador*	car-gah-DOOR
chart	*carta*	CAR-tah
cheese	*queso*	KAYE-so
circuit	*circuito*	seer-QUEE-toh
clamp	*abrazadera*	ah-bra-sah-DAY-rah
clearance	*despacho*	day-SPAH-cho
cleat	*tojino*	toe-HEE-noh
also	*cornamusa*	core-nah-MOO-sah
come-along	*gato*	GAH-toh
compass	*brujula*	BRU-hu-lah
conch (D.R.)	*lambi*	lahm-BEE
conch (P.R.)	*carrucho*	car-ROO-choo
conch (Venezuela)	*concha*	CONE-cha
connector	*conector*	coh-neck-TOR
copper	*cobre*	KOH-bray
cotter pin	*passador abierto*	pass-ah-DOOR ah-bee-AIR-toh
coupling	*junta*	HOON-tah
cove	*enseñada*	ain-sane-NAH-dah
crab (D.R.,Venezuela)	*cangrejo*	Kahn-GREY-ho
crab (P.R.)	*jueyes*	HWAY-jace
crew	*tripulante*	tree-pew-LAHN-tay
cushions	*cojines*	co-HEE-nays
customs	*aduana*	ah-DWAH-nah
damage	*daño*	DAHN-yos
depth	*hondura*	own-DOOR-ah
diesel	*gasoil*	gas-OIL
dinghy	*lanchita*	lan-CHEE-tah
dinghy dock	*muellecito*	mwaye-yea-SEE-toh
dock	*muelle*	MWAYE-yea
documentation	*documentación*	dock-oo-main-tah-see-OWN
dolphin fish	*dorado*	doh-RAH-dough
draft	*calado*	kah-LAH-dough
eggs	*huevos*	WAY-vos
electric	*electrico*	aye-LAKE-tree-ko
electrician	*electricista*	aye-lake-tree-SEE-stah

engine	*motor*	mo-TORE
exhaust	*escape*	ace-KAH-pay
eye	*ojo*	OH-ho
eyebolt	*tornillo de ojo*	tor-KNEE-yo day OH-ho
fathometer	*sonda*	SOHN-dah
fees	*derechos*	day-ray-chose
fender	*defensa*	day-FAIN-sah
fiberglass	*fibra de vidrio*	FEE-bra day VEE-dree-oh
fins, swim	*chapuletas*	chap-oo-LATE-ahs
flag	*bandera*	bahn-DAY-rah
flashlight	*linterna*	leen-TAIR-nah
floor	*suelo*	SWAY-low
fresh water	*agua dulce*	AH-gwah DOOL-say
front	*frente*	FRAIN-taye
funnel	*embudo*	aim-BOO-dough
fuse	*fusible*	foo-SEE-blaye
garbage	*basura*	bah-SOO-rah
gas, natural	*butano*	boo-TAH-no
gasket	*junta*	HOON-tah
gasoline	*gasolina*	gas-oh-LEE-nah
gauge	*medidor*	may-dee-DOOR
generator	*generador*	hey-nay-rah-DOOR
glue	*pegamento*	pay-gah-MAIN-toh
grapefruit	*toronjas*	tore-OWN-hahs
grease	*grasa*	GRAH-sah
grouper	*mero*	MAY-roh
guns	*armas*	ARM-ahs
hammer	*matillo*	mah-TEE-yo
harbor	*puerto*	PWAIR-to
harbormaster	*capitán de puerto*	kah-pee-TAHN day PWAIR-to
hardware store	*ferreteria*	fair-ray-tah-REE-ah
head (motor)	*cabeza*	kah-BAY-tsah
head (toilet)	*inodoro*	een-oh-DOOR-oh
heat	*calor*	kah-LORE
heat exchanger	*enfriadór*	ain-free-ah-DOOR
hill	*loma*	LOH-mah
hose	*mangera*	mahn-GAIR-ah
hull	*casco*	kah-skoh
hurricane	*ciclón,*	see-CLONE,
also....	*hurracán*	oor-roo-KAHN
ice	*hielo*	ee-AYE-loh
impeller	*impeledór*	eem-PAY-lay-DOOR
injectors	*inyectores*	een-jake-TORE-ace
insurance	*seguros*	say-GOO-ros
iron	*hierro*	ee-AIR-roh
jack	*gato*	GAH-toh
juice	*jugo*	HOO-goh
kerosene	*kerosena*	kay-roh-SEE-nah,
also....	*gaz*	GAZ
knot	*nudo*	NOO-dough
l.o.a.	*eslora*	ace-LORE-ah
laundry-place	*lavandaria*	la-VAHN-dah-REE-ah

laundry-clothes	*ropas sucias*	ROPE-ahs SOOj-see-ahs
left	*izquierda*	ees-key-AIR-dah
license	*licensia*	lee-SANE-see-ah
liferaft/vest	*salvavida*	sal-vah-VEE-dah
lighthouse	*faro*	FAH-roh
lights	*luces*	LOOSE-ace
limes	*limónes*	lee-MOAN-ace
line	*linea*	LEE-nay-ah
list	*lista*	LEASE-tah
lockwasher	*arandela de muelle*	ah-rahn-DAY-lah day WAYE-yea
margarine	*margerina*	mar-hair-EE-nah
marmelade	*mermelada*	MAIR-may-LAH-dah
mask, swim	*alcafondra*	ahl-kah-FOND-rah
mast	*palo, mastil*	PAH-loh, mah-STEEL
mayonaise	*mayonesa*	my-oh-NAY-sah
meal	*comida*	comb-EE-dah
mechanic	*mecánico*	may-KAHN-ee-Koh
metric	*metrico*	MAY-tree-koh
miles	*millas*	ME-yahs
milk	*leche*	LAYE-chaye
mountain	*montaña*	moan-TAHN-yah
mountain range	*cordillera*	core-dee-YAIR-ah
nail	*clavo*	CLAH-voh
nut (hex)	*tuerca*	TWER-kah
oars	*remos*	RAY-mos
oil	*aceite*	ah-say-EE-taye
oranges	*naranjas*	nar-AHN-hahs
outboard	*fuera borda*	FWAYE-rah BOOR-dah
packing	*empaque*	aim-PAH-kaye
paint	*pintura*	peen-TOO-rah
paintbrush	*brocha*	BROH-chah
parts (spare)	*repuestas*	ray-PWAYE-stahs
peanuts	*maní*	mah-KNEE
pear	*pera*	PAY-rah
pineapple	*piña*	PEE-nyah
pipe	*tubo*	TOO-boh
pistons	*pistones*	pee-STONE-ace
plantains	*plátanos*	PLAH-tah-nos
pliers	*alicates*	ah-lee-KAH-tace
porpoise	*delfín*	dale-FEEN
pressure	*presión*	pray-see-OWN
propane	*propano*	pro-PAH-no
propeller	*hélice*	AYE-lee-say
pump	*bomba*	BOHM-bah
registration	*matriculación*	mah-TREE-koo-lah-see-OWN
repair	*reparación*	RAYE-pah-RAH-see-OWN
replacement	*repuesta*	raye-PWAYE-stah
resin	*resina*	raye-SEE-nah
regulator	*reguladór*	raye-goo-lah-DOOR
rigging	*járcia*	HAR-see-ah
right	*derecha*	day-RAY-chah
rings	*aníllos*	ah-KNEE-yos

rope	*soga*	SO-gah
rubber	*goma*	GO-mah
rudder	*oja de timón*	OH-ha day tee-MOAN
rust	*óxido*	OAK-see-dough
sail	*vela*	VAYE-lah
sailboat	*velero*	vaye-LAIR-oh
sailcloth	*tela de vela*	TAYE-lah day VAYE-lah
sandpaper	*papél lija*	pah-PAIL LEE-hah
sauce	*salsa*	SAHL-sah
saw	*serrucho*	say-ROO-cho
screw (bolt)	*tornillo para maquina*	tore-NEE-yo pah-rah MAH-key-nah
screw (wood)	*tornillo para madera*	tore-NEE-yo pah-rah mah-DAY-rah
screwdriver	*destorneador*	day-STORE-nay- ah-DOOR
scrubbrush	*cepillo*	say-PEE-yo
seacock	*llave de toma*	YAH-vaye day TOH-mah
seal	*sello*	SAY-yoh
seas	*oleaje*	oh-lay-AH-hey
seasick	*mareado*	mah-ray-AH-dough
seawater	*agua salada*	AH-gwah sah-LAH-dah
shackle	*grillete*	gree-YAYE-taye
shaft	*je*	AYE-hey
shell	*caracól*	car-ah-COAL
ship	*barco*	BAR-coh
shower	*ducha*	DOO-chah
showers	*aquaceros*	AH-gwah-SAY-ros
shrimp	*camarones*	kah-mah-ROAN-ace
side	*lado*	LAH-dough
smoke	*humo*	OO-moh
snapper	*chillo*	CHEE-yo
soup	*sopa*	SO-pah
sparkplug	*bujía*	boo-HEE-ah
spring	=	ace-SPRING
stainless	*inoxidable*	een-ox-ee-DAH-blaye
stainless (P.R.)	=	ace-STAIN-less
starboard	*estribor*	ace-tree-BOOR
starter motor	*motór de arranque*	mo-TORE day ah-RAHN-kaye
stay	*soporte de mastil*	so-PORE-taye day mah-STEEL
steel	*acero*	ah-SAY-roh
stern	*popa*	POPE-ah
storm	*tormenta*	tore-MAIN-tah
straight	*derecho*	day-RAY-choh
strainer	*coladór*	coal-ah-DOOR
street	*calle*	KAH-yaye
stuffing box	*prense*	PRAIN-say
swells	*oleadas*	oh-lay-AH-dahs
switch	*suiche*	SWEET-chaye
tank	*tanque*	TANG-kaye
tape	=	TAYE-pee
tax	*impuesto*	eem-PWAYE-stow
telephone call	*llamada*	yah-MAH-dah
temperature	*temperatura*	taim-pair-ah-TOOR-ah
thermostat	*termostato*	tair-moh-STAH-toh

thinner	*tinner*	TEEN-air
thread (string)	*hilo*	EEL-oh
threads (screw)	*roscas*	ROH-skahs
through-hull	*toma*	TOE-mah
tiller	*timón*	tee-MOAN
time	*tiempo*	tee-AIM-poh
tip	*propina*	pro-PEE-nah
tomato	*tomate*	toh-MAH-taye
tools	*herramientas*	air-rah-mee-AIN-tos
top parte	*arriba*	PART-taye ah-REE-bah
transducer	*cebolla*	say-BOY-yah
transmission	*transmisión*	trahns-me-see-OWN
tropical	*tropical*	troh-pay-KAHL
tropical storm	*tormenta*	tore-MAIN-tah
tropical wave	*onda tropical*	OWN-dah troh-pay-KAHL
turnbuckle	*torniquete*	tore-knee-KAY-taye
two-stroke oil	*aceite de dos tiempo*	ah-say-EE-tay day dose tee-AIM-po
valve	*valvula*	VALVE-you-lah
vanilla	vanilla	vah-KNEE-yah
varnish	*barníz*	bar-KNEES
Vee-belt	*banda*	BAHN-dah
vegetables	*vegetales*	vaye-hay-TAHL-ace
volts	*vóltios*	VOLT-ee-os
washer	*arandela*	ah-rahn-DAY-lah
water	*agua*	AH-gwah
watts	*vátios*	VAHT-ee-os
waves	*olas*	OH-las
welding	*soldadura*	sold-ah-DOOR-ah
wheel	*rueda*	roo-AYE-dah
wing nut	*tuerca mariposa*	TWER-kah mar-ee-POSE-ah
wire	*alambre*	ahl-AHM-braye
wood	*madera*	mah-DAY-rah
work	*trabajo*	trah-BAH-ho
wrench	*llave*	YAH-vaye
yacht	*yate*	YAH-taye
zinc	*zinc*	TSINK

VERBS

To talk movie-Indian Spanish, forget the finer distinctions. For instance, use "need" for both "need" and "want." Use "go" for all of the go's, like come, walk, ride, fly and so forth. The only pronoun you really need is the English "Me," the most important, after all. Everyone else can be identified by pointing a finger.

Just about all of the operable verbs for a gringo (GREEN-goh) needing help are below. To use a verb, piece together the words above, in backwards order with lots of de's (da'sy) thrown in, and stick a verb on the front. Thus: "BOO-kah tore-KNEE-yo day kah-BAY-tsah day moh-TOR" means, "me look-um for motor head bolt." Don't laugh. It works. If you want to talk better Spanish then learn their 26 (mostly irregular) verb forms. The guy behind the counter is so used to the dumb tricks of gringos that he won't blink an eye, but he will hand you the bolt. Here are some verbs for the intermediate student:

buy	*compra*	COMB-prah
do, make	*hace*	AH-say
eat	*come*	COMB-aye
find	*consigue*	cone-SEE-gay
go	*va*	VAH
have	*tiene*	tee-AYE-nay
leave	*sale*	SAHL-aye
liste	*noye*	OH-jay
look	*mira*	MEE-rah
look	*forbusca*	BOO-kah
need	*necessita*	nay-say-SEE-tah
rent	*renta*	RAIN-tah
repair	*repara*	ray-PAR-ah
sell	*vende*	VAIN-day
sleep	*duerme*	DWAIR-may
talk	*habla*	AH-blah
work	*trabaja*	tra-BAH-hah

You may have noticed the "being" verbs are not included. To use the complex "being" verbs in Spanish can be an art. Better just to not use them. Or just say es (ACE), anywhere you want to have "is," "was," "will be" or "might could have been." ACE is great.

NUMBERS

Unlike adjectives, Spanish puts numbers in front of the word they modify to make it easy for gringos. One gringo: uno gringo. Two gringos: dos gringos. And so it goes. Now count to a zillion gringos.

zero	*cero*	SAIR-oh
one	*uno*	OO-noh
two	*dos*	DOSE
three	*tres*	TRACE
four	*cuatro*	QUAH-troh
five	*cinco*	SINK-oh
six	*seís*	SAY-ees
seven	*siete*	see-AYE-taye
eight	*ocho*	OH-cho
nine	*nueve*	NWAYE-vaye
ten	*diéz*	dee-ACE

eleven	*once*	OWN-say
twelve	*doce*	DOSE-say
thirteen	*trece*	TRAY-say
fourteen	*catorce*	kah-TORE-say
fifteen	*quince*	KEEN-say
sixteen	*diéz y seís*	dee-ACE ee SAY-ees
seventeen	*diéz y siete*	dee-ACE ee see-AYE-taye
eighteen	*diéz y ocho*	dee-ACE ee OH-cho
nineteen	*diéz y nueve*	dee-ACE ee NWAYE-vaye
twenty	*veinte*	VAIN-taye
twenty-one	*veinte uno*	VAIN-taye OO-noh etc.
thirty	*treinta*	TRAIN-tah
forty	*cuarenta*	quar-AIN-tah
fifty	*cincuenta*	seen-QUAINT-ah
sixty	*sesenta*	say-SANE-tah
seventy	*setenta*	say-TAIN-tah
eighty	*ochenta*	oh-CHAIN-tah
ninety	*noventa*	no-VAIN-tah
one hundred	*ciento*	see-AIN-toh
two hundred	*dos cientos*	DOSE see-AIN-tos
thousand	*mil*	MEAL
million	*millón*	me-YONE

For example, 1989: *mil novecientos ochenta nueve.*

You can now say you're looking for two motor headbolts: BOO-kah DOSE tore-KNEE-yo day kah-BAY-tsah day moh-TOR" — and you don't have to go shopping twice to get them!

MODIFIERS

If you must modify a name, do so by putting the modifiers in backwards order but without all the de (DAY) stuff you put between the names when you strung them together.

Thus "two big black motor head bolts" becomes "two bolts of head of motor black big," or,

BOO-kah DOSE tore-KNEE-yo day kah-BAY-tsah day moh-TOR GRAHN-day NAYE-grow.

And just like in English, let everyone guess if it's the motor or the bolts which is big and black or is it a combination of both.

COLORS

black	*negro*	NAYE-grow
blue	*azúl*	ah-TSOOL
brown	*marrón*	mar-ROAN
green	*verde*	VAIR-day
grey	*gris*	GREASE
orange	*naranja*	nah-RAHN-hah
pink	*rosado*	rosa-AH-dough
red	*rojo*	ROH-hoh
white	*blanco*	BLANK-oh
yellow	*amarillo*	ah-mah-REE-yo

big	*grande*	GRAHN-day
broken	*roto*	ROH-toh
cheap (thing)	*barato*	bah-RAH-toh
clean	*limpio*	LEEM-pee-oh
closed	*cerrado*	say-RAH-dough
cold	*frio*	FREE-oh
deep	*hondo*	OWN-dough
different	*diferente*	dee-faye-RAIN-taye
dirty	*sucio*	SOO-see-oh
down	*abajo*	ah-BAH-ho
dry	*seco*	SAY-koh
electrical	*electrico*	aye-LAKE-tree-ko
expensive	*caro*	CAR-roh
fast	*rapido*	RAH-pee-dough
fine	*fino*	FEE-noh
fixed-repaired	*reparado*	ray-pah-RAH-dough
fixed-unmoving	*fijado*	fee-HAH-dough
galvanized	*galvanizado*	gal-van-ee-SAH-dough
heated	*calientado*	kah-lee-ain-TAH-dough
heavy	*pesado*	pay-SAH-dough
high	*alto*	AHL-toh
hot	*caliente*	kah-lee-AIN-taye
less	*menos*	MAY-nose
light	*ligero*	lee-HAIR-oh
little	*no mucho*	NO MOO-cho
long	*largo*	LAHR-go
loose	*flojo*	FLOW-ho
low	*bajo*	BAH-ho
more	*mas*	MAS
open	*abierto*	ah-bee-AIR-toh
portside	*babor*	bah-BOOR
same	*mismo*	MEESE-moh
self-tapping	*autorroscante*	ow-toe-ros-KAHN-taye
shallow	*bajita*	bah-HEE-tah
slow	*despacio*	day-SPAH-see-oh
small	*pequeño*	pay-CAIN-yo
thick	*grueso*	grew-ACE-oh
thin	*delgado*	dell-GAH-dough
tight	*apretado*	ah-pray-TAH-dough
up	*arriba*	ah-REE-bah
wet	*mojado*	moh-HAH-dough
wide	*hancho*	AHN-cho

PAST AND FUTURE

Movie Indians conjugate their verbs by modifying them with a word like "yesterday." Thus "Me need'um head bolt yesterday. Today need'um band-aid." So, say anything you want in present tense and add from the following list:

today	*hoy*	OY
tomorrow	*mañana*	mah-NYAH-nah
yesterday	*ayer*	ah-JAIR
last night	*anoche*	ah-NO-chaye
day before yesterday	*ante ayer*	auntie ah-JAIR
...days ago	*hace.....dias*	AH-say.....DEE-ahs
...weeks ago	*...semanas*	...say-MAH-nahs
...months ago	*...meses*	...MACE-ace
...years ago	*...anos*	...AHN-yos
next week	*proxima semana*	PROHKS-ee-mah say-MAH-nah
next month	*proximo mes*	PROHKS-ee-moh MACE
next year	*proximo año*	PROHKS-ee-moh AHN-yo

PREPOSITIONS

These are the condiments the advanced students will sprinkle onto their crude sentences in order to throw the hearer off the track. Proper use requires years of practice.

after	*despus de*	days-PWACE day
before	*antes de*	AHNT-ace day
between	*entre*	AIN-tray
by	*por*	PORE
to	á	AH
for	*para*	PAH-rah
from	*de*	DAY
in	*en*	AIN
inside	*dentro de*	DAIN-troh day
of	*de*	DAY
on	*en*	AIN
under	*abajo de*	ah-BAH-ho day
with	*con*	CONE
without	*sin*	SEEN

PRONOUNS

Finally, for the black belters, peppering a fancy construction with pronouns will ensure confusion but impress the dickens out of fellow yachties. These are the advanced student's tools with which to make clear that which was better off left vague. When instead of a big, black head bolt for your motor, the guy behind the counter hands you two tickets to the cock fights, if you are a real black belt student you say, gracias, and thread your way through the throng of thunderstruck fellow boaters with a satisfied grin and just the hint of a swagger. You can get the headbolts tomorrow.

Once again, this short list of pronouns is only to enable you to rapidly employ a pidgin Spanish which works, not to speak properly.

Now you're able to say "ME look'um for 2 big black motor head bolts FROM HE TOMORROW." Or,

ME BOO-kah DOSE tore-KNEE-yo day kah-BAY-tsah day moh-TOR GRAHN-day NAYE-grow DAY AYEL mah-NYAH-nah.

I	*yo*	JOE
you	*tu*	TOO
he	*él*	AYEL
she	*ella*	AYE-ya
it	*lo*	LOW
we	*nosotros*	no-SO-tros
you (plural)	*ustedes*	oo-STAID-ace
they	*ellos*	AYE-yos
this	*esto*	ACE-tos
that	*eso*	ACE-oh
each	*cada*	KAH-dah
which	*cual*	QUAL
something	*algo*	AHL-go
nothing	*nada*	NAH-dah
other, another	*otro*	OH-troh
any, -thing, -body	*cualquir*	qual-key-AIR
all, everybody, everything, everyone	*todo*	TOE-dough
none, nobody, no one	*ninguno*	neen-GOO-noh
some, -body, -one	*alguin*	ahl-gee-AIN

QUESTIONS

Questions are best asked as statements with lots of body language, helpless expressions and the voice turned up in pitch toward the end, even panicky, as in

DOAN-day me BOAT-aye?!

for "Where's my boat?!" A very important question if it's gone.

You can also make up a declarative sentence as shown above and slap any one of the following words on the front to have a neat sentence to go to town with:

how	como	KO-moh
how much	cuanto	QUAN-toh
when	cuando	QUAN-dough
where	donde	DOAN-day
who	quin	key-AIN
why	porqué	pore-KAY

But beware of asking why or how. You may get a torrent of rapid Spanish. Also, beware to phrase your questions bluntly in movie-indian talk. For instance, "I wonder if you could tell me where I might find oil pressure transducers for sale?" becomes "Where sell oil pressure transducers?" or:

DOAN-day VAIN-day say-BOY-yah day pray-see-OWN day ah-say-EE-taye?

— accompanied by a lot of shrugs and wiggling of the eyebrows. Other questions are:

What is it?	*Que es eso?*	KAY ACE ACE-oh
What's it/he/she called?	*Como se llama?*	KO-moh say YAH-mah?
What time is it?	*Que hora es?*	KAY OR-ah ACE?
At what time?	*A que hora?*	AH KAY OR-ah?
How far?	*Que lejos?*	KAY LAY-hos?
Where is it/he/she?	*A donde está?*	AH DOAN-day ace-TAH?
What's it cost?	*Cuanto cuesta?*	QUAN-toh KWAYE-stah?
How do I get there?	*Como llegar?*	KO-moh yaye-gar-RAY?
Can you help me?	*Puede ayudarme?*	PWAY-day ah-you-DAHR-may?
How do you say...?	*Como se dice..?*	KO-moh say DEE-say...?
What do you mean?	*Que quiere decir?*	KAY key-AIR-aye day-SEER?

Almacén (alma-SANE) a warehouse or wholesaler's

Arawak Antillean Indians; of the 3 groups, Caribe, Ciboney and Arawak, the Arawak were the post stone-age, agricultural people with a large production of ceramics; also father to the Tainos (see Taino).

Backing Wind counter-clockwise shifting of the wind

BASRA Bahamas Air Sea Rescue Association; volunteers, many retired foreigners who man a chain of VHF stations up and down the Bahamas and who can access means of rescue.

Baja Filter a California invention for use in cruising the Baja, this is a funnel, usually stainless, which has nested in it removable filters of successively finer mesh through which fuel is pumped into the boat's tank. The best will have a teflon coated filter to separate water as well.

Baruga (bar-OO-gah) Dominican yogurt with a slight lemony taste.

Beaufort Wind Scale Admiral Beaufort's Scale of Wind Speed, made to enable ships of the line to classify conditions from observations. Wind speed is assumed to be 10 meters above sea level and sea effects are for open sea far from land.

Blue Northers Colloquial expression for the arctic winds which scourge the plains states in the United States.

Bola (BOWL-ah) Dominican slang for a ride; *Pon* (PONE) in Puerto Rico.

Buccaneer Mean guys who jumped ship and collected on the north coast of Haiti. They survived by hunting wild cows, and selling smoked beef, called *boucain* in French, to ships. Thus they were *boucainiers*, or, as most pirates came to be called, buccaneers. They made the most blood thirsty pirates, and were therefore praised as recruits.

Burgoo a pressure cooker full of everything and anything to make a nourishing meal in a passage (ref. Tristan Jones, *Ice*) try a large container of yogurt, fruits and cereals thoroughly mixed; or plain old lasagna, cold or hot.

Caribbean Sea the sea bounded by all the Antilles, Greater as well as Lesser, and south and Central America; definitely not north of the Dominican Republic.

Coastal Front cumulus and cumulus nimbus clouds marking a zone of change at the margin of sea and land. In the islands these are usually pushed over the heated land by the stable sea Airstream. Depending on the colors and textures of the land below these clouds can show the mariner an outline of the coast before the coast is visible. This is particularly true in the Bahamas where an island's colors and textures can be very uniform. The island and the water behind it are often reflected in the lower surface of these clouds. On the larger islands, look for strong gusts and showers coming from Storm Cells (see below) spawned by the Coastal Fronts in the late afternoons and never make the mistake of forecasting sea conditions based on conditions in harbor beneath a Coastal Front over an irregular coastline (e.g., Puerto Rico).

Cold Front zone of division between Tropical and Polar Maritime air masses which generally moves eastward with the clear, colder air being at the rear of a depression. May be led by squalls.

Corsaires French seamen sailing under letters of marque from the king. The letters gave them shares in any booty they could wrest from Spanish vessels. When France and England reached accommodation with Spain the letters were withdrawn. Most crews persisted, however, making them pirates. The worst of them all was neither Bluebeard nor Morgan, but a mean little dandy named L'Olenois.

Deathtrap Any area which appears safe in most conditions but can be surprisingly unsurvivable when attacked by wind or wave from its not always obvious weak points. Examples: Calabash Bay, Long Island, Bahamas; Attwood Harbor, Acklins Islands, Bahamas; almost all Virgin Islands anchorages; and the anchorage at Phillipsburg, St.Martins. Also, Exuma Sound in a strong easterly blow: there is nowhere to run but through life threatening passes.

DMA Defense Mapping Agency, an agency of the US Government which performs the functions of the old Hydrographic Office cartographic department.

D.R. Dominican Republic

Dangerous Semicircle The half of a developed depression with cyclonic winds which contains the quadrant of highest winds, i.e., those which lie along the direction of travel of the depression.

Equatorial Current north Equatorial Current: the west going part of the clockwise circulation around the Sargasso Sea. south Equatorial Current: the current from the equator which runs counter to the earth's rotation along the coast of south America and into the Caribbean Sea. north of the Antilles the northern current blends elements of the southern current but the southern current off south America is nonetheless much stronger.

Far Out Islands islands to the east and south of the Exumas. "Out Islands" refers generally to all the islands out from New Providence where the capital is. Thus a weekend sailor from Miami can truthfully say he cruises the Out Islands when he goes to Bimini.

Force Beaufort Refer to the section entitled "Think Beaufort" and see the Figure of the Beaufort Wind Scale.

GPS Global Positioning System, capable of providing 3-dimensional position data every few seconds with great accuracy (20-300 meters), but statistically reliable to only 100 meters. This is a nearly indispensable device for confirming a navigator's dead reckoning which is maintained hourly in the usual old way.

Front line of separation between cold and warm air masses.

HO Hydrographic Office. Cartographer's department of government.

Hidalgo (ee-DAHL-go) corruption of "Hijos de Algo," literally "Sons of Somebody," implying children of rich and influential families. In the New World this usually meant the non-inheriting sons of Spanish nobility who came to seek their fortunes. Often they were spoiled and cruel to the point of sadism, corrupted by the opportunities for unlimited personal power in the New World. Only the more serious stayed and took root.

Hurricane from the Indian god of who wreaked distruction by wind, Oricn (or-ee-KHAN). This is the name given to the tropical cyclonic storm east of the Americas (Typhoon is west). It is also applied to Force 12 on the Beaufort scale regardless of cause.

Hurricane Warning there is a hurricane within 24 hours of the location for which the warning is issued.

Hurricane Games my name for the very serious business of posing all the "what if" questions when selecting an anchorage in the hurricane season. A good trick is to draw a hurricane spiral to scale on a piece of transparent plastic and move it around on the chart.

Hurricane Hole an anchorage protected from the seas, if not also the winds, of a hurricane.

Joy the only detergent I know which works as well in sea water as it does in fresh.

Katabatic a wind that flows down slope, usually at night, due to the cooling of the upper level air which then becomes heavier and flows down hill.

Leeward Islands the part of the Lesser Antilles which stretches from St. Martin through Dominica.

Leewards the Leeward Islands.

Leisure Sailor the reader of this guide. The Leisure Sailor is characterized by an old-fashioned leisure class lifestyle: thus the name *The Gentleman's Guide to Passages South.* He or she needn't be wealthy, only have the mindset and the minimum wherewithal to leisurely enjoy cruising without the deadlines and hustle of the working classes. The Leisure Sailor may work upon occasion, usually doing maintenance chores on his or her yacht. Working for a wage is allowed only if it goes toward maintaining the leisure lifestyle (recouping the cruising kitty). The Leisure Sailor may be athletic, but never a jock. He or she is first a seaman, and need be a real sailor only if the yacht bears sails.

Loran a spare dinghy anchor in the Caribbean.

Motoconcho (moh-toh-CONE-cho) a motorbike with or without a rickshaw-like conveyance in tow driven by an independent operator who offers rides to anywhere for almost nothing.

Muelle de Yates (MWAY-yay day YAH-tace) Spanish for Yacht Dock.

N.O.A.A. National Oceanic and Atmospheric Administration, a branch of the U.S. Government which regularly loses its weather satellites over the Atlantic.

Niño (KNEE-nyo) boy child. Also the name of a world-wide weather disturbance brought about periodically by a reversal in parts of the Humboldt Current (See *National Geographic,* Vol. 165, No. 2, February 1984). A new period of *El Nino* is forecast for 1998/99.

Nocturnal Wind night wind, a combination of land breeze which feeds the up-drafts over the warmer water, and the katabatic wind (see above).

Norther Colloquial expression for fierce and durable winter winds from the north. Used in New England, Holland, Iceland, Alaska, Lower Slobovia, but NOT between the Tropic of Cancer and the Tropic of Capricorn!

NWS National Weather Service

P.R. Puerto Rico.

Passage Making the actual doing of a voyage, as opposed to a sail or a crossing. Passage Making implies prudent navigation, sea-readiness and competent seamanship.

Pilot Charts charts for each of the twelve months which give the statistics compiled of the weather, wind, current and storm tracks over a period of nearly 150 years (thanks to Lt. Mathew Fontaine Maury, USN). The British know these as routing charts.

Privateers The English equivalent of the French Corsaires, Henry Morgan being the most famous. See Corsaires.

Rage The condition of the seas, especially the cuts in Exuma Sound, when the wind has been blowing hard onshore for some time.

Res (race) normal parlance for beef of any old kind in the Dominican Republic; normally chuck of old milch cow; delicious if stewed well.

Rule of Twelfths a rough rule for estimating the variable rise or fall of the tide, and therefore the tidal current if peak flow is known. The rule states that the first, second and third hour of tide rise or fall accounts for one twelfth, 2 twelfths and 3 twelfths, respectively, of the tidal range, whereas the fourth, fifth and sixth hours account for 3-, 2-, and one-twelfth(s), respectively. Thus, if the range is 3 feet, as in the Bahamas, 3 inches will fall (or rise) in the first hour, 6 in the second, 9 in the third and fourth hours, and finally, 6 and 3 inches in the fifth and sixth hours, for a total of 36 inches, or 3 feet. Similarly, the current, as a ratio of peak flow, will be an average of one sixth, one half, 5 sixths, 5 sixths, one half and one sixth, for hours one through 6, respectively. For example, if the peak flow on flood is 1.2 knots, as on Caicos Banks, then hours one through 6 of tide rise will average rates of 0.2, 0.6, 1.0, 1.0, 0.6, and 0.2 knots respectively.

SG&T Sundowner Gin and Tonic. A mneumonic for any inflexible custom which makes the Leisure Sailor perform all passage planning so that late afternoons are spent AT LEISURE in a safe anchorage with the yacht completely put away and ready for sea. This gives captain and crew a full evening of rest and relaxation with which to face the next day, or with which to face an anchor drill which invariably is called at 2 a.m. in the winter time Bahamas. Any other custom at sundown is NOT Leisure Sailing and is a mark of the anxiety-driven working class.

Storm Cells a cell of rising or sinking air currents with a lifetime of 20 minutes to a half an hour, scattered, or occurring in lines (frontal thunderstorms). Late summer afternoon Coastal Front (see above) thunderstorms can be vicious, especially on the larger or the higher islands. Winds can rotate around the cell either way.

Sundowner G&T See SG&T.

Taino descendents of the Arawaks found by Columbus on Hispaniola, Cuba and Puerto Rico, characterized by advanced political (tribal chiefs, chiefs of chiefs, etc.) and social (specialized labor) structures. Especially noted for extreme pacifism: suicide was preferred to fighting to such an extent it became an industry after the Spaniards invaded them with the Inquisition. See the Museo del Hombre in Santo Domingo, and the museum at Altos de Chaval in La Romana, Dominican Republic.

Thornless Path a way of PASSAGE MAKING (see definition above) to windward which creates a delightful, relaxed experience.

Thorny Path a way of PASSAGE MAKING (see definition above) to windward which tries the soul as well as the boat.

Trade Wind winds which blow from the high pressure areas of the Tropics to the relatively low pressure of the equatorial regions. In the Caribbean, the Northeast Trades of the Atlantic are bent with the Coriolus effect and the Equatorial Currents, becoming easterly by the time they pour over the Lesser Antilles into the Caribbean. These winds continuously switch like a cat's tail between northeast and east southeast in the winter, and between east northeast and southeast in the summer.

Trades short for the Trade Winds.

Tropical Depression a bad weather system characterized by closed isobars of barometric pressure, precipitation and mainly ascending air in which the gradient winds can be quite strong and will flow counter clockwise and toward the central low.

Tropical Disturbances any large area of disturbed weather in the tropics not yet and perhaps never to be classified a Tropical Depression (see above).

Tropical Storm a Tropical Depression which has developed into a full cyclonic Storm on the Beaufort Scale (see Figure 10 on page 25) with winds from 48 to 63 knots.

Tropical Systems the collection of summertime weather systems in the tropics: see Tropical Waves, Tropical Depressions, Tropical Storms, Hurricanes.

Tropical Waves atmospheric pressure waves forming off Africa in the tropics in the Summer. These can be up to a thousand miles long and move between 10 and 20 knots to the west. They usually have associated precipitation and spawn Storm Cells (see above) although some regions of the wave can be relatively clear. Troughs any elongated "valley" of low pressure with or without closed isobars. If the isobars are closed, the length of the trough renders circulation questionable. If the trough shrinks in length it can become a rotating low center and eventually a Tropical Depression.

Veering Wind clockwise shifting of the wind (e.g., north to east)

Wait for Weather Read the section on "Wait for Weather." This, and the SG&T, quite seriously, form the nucleus of the Thornless Path concept. If you can afford to wait for the appropriate Weather Window and you can always be in a snug harbor with a ready boat and getting lots of rest by late afternoon, you are absolutely a Leisure Sailor of the first order.

Weather Window the period during which wind and wave are favorable for completing a leg of a passage safely and easily.

Windward Islands the islands from Martinique through Grenada.

Xenophobia suspicion, fear or hatred of foreigners or things strange. Usually an infirmity of the French, but can reach virulent degrees in homo Americanus when found between the tropics.

CRUISING GUIDE PUBLICATIONS

ORDER FORM

To order, please fill out coupon on back and send check or money order to:
Cruising Guide Publications, P.O. Box 1017, Dunedin, Florida 34697-1017.
For credit card orders only, call 1-800-330-9542.

- ❑ $22.50 AT ANY COST: LOVE, LIFE & DEATH AT SEA (Hardcover) By Peter Tangvald; thrilling autobiography of a cruising sailor whose primary home for 50 years was a 49' handcrafted wooden sailboat.
- ❑ $13.50 AT ANY COST: LOVE, LIFE & DEATH AT SEA (Paperback).
- ❑ $16.95 CRUISING GUIDE TO THE VIRGIN ISLANDS (6th Edition) by Nancy and Simon Scott.
- ❑ $19.95 CRUISING GUIDE TO THE LEEWARD ISLANDS (3rd Edition) by Chris Doyle.
- ❑ $16.50 SAILOR'S GUIDE TO THE WINDWARD ISLANDS (6th Edition) by Chris Doyle.
- ❑ $24.95 VIRGIN ANCHORAGES (Aerial photos of the Virgin Islands with sailing directions) Edited by Nancy & Simon Scott.
- ❑ $12.95 CRUISING GUIDE TO THE SEA OF CORTEZ (From Mulege to La Paz) Edited by Nancy & Simon Scott.
- ❑ $16.50 SAILOR'S GUIDE TO A VENEZUELA CRUISE by Chris Doyle.
- NEW ❑ CALL CRUISING GUIDE TO THE NORTHERN COAST OF VENEZUELA, TRINIDAD AND TOBAGO by Chris Doyle (Available January 1994).
- ❑ $16.95 CRUISING GUIDE TO THE FLORIDA KEYS with Florida West Coast Supplement by Capt. Frank Papy.
- ❑ $29.95 CRUISING GUIDE TO TAHITI AND THE FRENCH SOCIETY ISLANDS by Marcia Davock.
- ❑ $12.00 CRUISING MANUAL TO THE KINGDOM OF TONGA IN THE VAVA'U GROUP (Chart included) The Moorings.
- ❑ $24.95 GENTLEMAN'S GUIDE TO PASSAGES SOUTH (4th Edition) The "Thornless Path to Windward," by Bruce Van Sant.
- ❑ $14.95 THE NATURE OF THE ISLANDS: PLANTS & ANIMALS OF THE EASTERN CARIBBEAN by Chris Doyle and Virginia Barlow.
- NEW ❑ $37.95 CARIBBEAN by Margaret Zellers with breathtaking photos by Bob Krist; oversized coffee-table book—perfect tropical souvenir or gift.
- ❑ $25.00 CARIBBEAN: THE OUTDOOR TRAVELER'S GUIDE by Kay Showker; lots of color photos illustrate flora, fauna & island geology.
- ❑ $18.95 DECK WITH A VIEW: VACATION SAILING IN THE CARIBBEAN by Dale Ward & Dustine Davidson — adventure sailing for the novice.
- ❑ $18.95 DECK WITH A VIEW: ON-THE-WATER VACATIONS IN GREECE & TURKEY by Dale Ward & Dustine Davidson—Sailing the waters of the gods.
- ❑ $13.95 UNDERSTANDING THE EASTERN CARIBBEAN AND THE ANTILLES by Prof. Nelson Marshall (oceanography/marine affairs).

☞

- ❑ $ 7.95 THE CONCH BOOK: ALL YOU EVER WANTED TO KNOW ABOUT THE QUEEN CONCH by Dee Carstarphen.
- NEW ❑ $19.95 JOHNNYCAKE & BULLFOOT SOUP: BEST RECIPES OF THE CARIBBEAN (Over 200 dishes from professional chefs).
- ❑ $14.95 SHIP TO SHORE I (A collection of 680 recipes & cooking tips from Caribbean charter yacht chefs) compiled by Capt. Jan Robinson.
- ❑ $14.95 SHIP TO SHORE II (440 more recipes from Capt. Jan Robinson).
- ❑ $14.95 SEA TO SHORE (280 seafood recipes and cooking hints—Robinson).
- ❑ $14.95 SWEET TO SHORE (Robinson's ultimate dessert collection).
- ❑ $10.95 SIP TO SHORE (Robinson's cocktails and hors d'oeuvres collection).
- ❑ $ 7.95 MAVERICK SEA FARE: A CARIBBEAN COOK BOOK by Dee Carstarphen (Simple shipboard recipes you can prepare at home).
- ❑ $29.95 **VIDEO** (VHS): ISLAND PORTRAITS: ST. VINCENT AND THE GRENADINES by Chris Doyle & Jeff Fischer.
- ❑ $29.95 **VIDEO** (VHS): SAILING THE WINDWARD ISLANDS by Chris Doyle & Jeff Fisher (The Windwards in full color splendor).
- NEW ❑ $ 4.50 CLEAR, WATERPROOF, HEAVY-DUTY PLASTIC ZIPLOCK CRUISING GUIDE COVER holds Cruising Guide open and dry, leaving hands free for sailing. Grease pencil included, 10⅞" x 14½".

WATERPROOF CHARTS

- ❑ $16.95 U.S. & BRITISH VIRGIN ISLANDS
- ❑ $16.95 BRITISH VIRGIN ISLANDS
- ❑ $16.95 UPPER FLORIDA KEYS
- ❑ $16.95 LOWER FLORIDA KEYS
- ❑ $ 8.50 CLEAR, WATERPROOF, REUSABLE PLASTIC STORAGE TUBE
- ❑ $10.00 LEEWARD ISLAND INTINERARY PLANNER CHART

ORDER FORM *(For orders only, call 1-800-330-9542).*

To order, check the appropriate box(es), fill out coupon and send check or money order to: Cruising Guide Publications, P.O. Box 1017, Dunedin, FL 34697-1017. Florida residents add 7% sales tax. See schedule for shipping charges. All books are shipped within 10 days of receipt of order.

SHIPPING & HANDLING:

U.S.A.		OVERSEAS	
Up to $10:	$2.50	Up to $25:	$9.00
$10.01-$25:	$3.75	$25.01-$40:	$10.50
$25.01-$40:	$4.75	$40.01-$75:	$12.00
$40.01-$75:	$6.25	$75.01 & up:	$13.50
$75.01 & up:	$7.25		

CANADA
Add $2 to U.S. prices.

$ ______________ Total Merchandise

$ ______________ Sales Tax 7% (Florida residents only)

$ ______________ Shipping & Handling

$ ______________ Total Enclosed

Name ____

Address ____

City ______________________ State __________ Zip ____________

Daytime telephone (_____) ________________________________

(Prices subject to change without notice)

NOTES

F

G

H

I

N

O

P